China's Economic Growth And Transition

Macroeconomic, Environmental And Social/Regional Dimensions

CHINA'S ECONOMIC GROWTH AND TRANSITION

MACROECONOMIC, ENVIRONMENTAL AND SOCIAL/REGIONAL DIMENSIONS

EDITED BY

CLEMENT A. TISDELL
JOSEPH C.H. CHAI

NOVA SCIENCE PUBLISHERS, INC.
COMMACK, NY

Editorial Production: Susan Boriotti
Assistant Vice President/Art Director: Maria Ester Hawrys
Office Manager: Annette Hellinger
Graphics: Frank Grucci
Acquisitions Editor: Tatiana Shohov
Book Production: Ludmila Kwartiroff, Christine Mathosian,
    Joanne Metal and Tammy Sauter
Circulation: Iyatunde Abdullah, Cathy DeGregory, and Maryanne Schmidt

Library of Congress Cataloging-in-Publication Data
available upon request

ISBN 1-56072-530-3

Copyright © 1997 by Nova Science Publishers, Inc.
        6080 Jericho Turnpike, Suite 207
        Commack, New York 11725
        Tele. 516-499-3103   Fax 516-499-3146
        E-Mail: Novascience@earthlink.net
        Web Site: http://www.nexusworld.com/nova

Printed in the United States of America

CONTENTS

REFORMS AND ECONOMIC GROWTH

ENVIRONMENTAL ISSUES

SOCIAL AND REGIONAL DIMENSIONS AND MORE ON
EFFICIENCY: GROWING DISPARITIES

LIST OF FIGURES

LIST OF TABLES

PREFACE

China's Economic Growth on Transition draws together a number of papers specifically prepared for an international conference on China and the Asian Pacific Economy which was jointly organised by the Economic Department of the University of Queensland, the Chinese Economic Studies Association (Australia) and the Centre for Asian Pacific Studies at Lingnan College, Hong Kong and held in Brisbane, Australia. All papers were revised and updated in the light of comments made at the conference and by the referees.

China's economic growth in the last few decades has been very rapid and China is well on the way to achieving its goal of becoming a middle-income country in the 21st century. *China's Economic Growth and Transition* covers the many dimensions of China's economic and transition to a market influenced economy. Areas given particular attention are:

- China's economic reforms, its economic growth and macroeconomics
- Economic inequality, regional issues and property rights in China
- Environmental issues and land-use
- Science and technology policies and issues

Several of the contributions involve comparative analysis, for example with the former Soviet Union, and with Vietnam.

We would like to thank the various sponsors who gave valuable financial and organisational support to the original conference:

AusAID
Australia-China Council
Centre for Pacific Law and Business, Victoria University of Wellington,
    New Zealand
Lingnan College, Hong Kong
Commonwealth Bank of Australia

Embassy of the People's Republic of China (Australia)
Hong Kong Society of Asia Pacific 21
Queensland Chamber of Commerce and Industry
TEMTAC Pty. Ltd. (Economic Consultants, PO Box 79, Corinda, Qld 4075, Australia)
The National Centre for Development Studies, Australian National University
The Economic Society of Australia (Queensland) Inc.

We would like to extend our deepest appreciation to Miss Margaret Cowan for her valuable assistance throughout the entire project, to Mrs. Robyn McDonald and Mrs. Barbara Dempsey for typesetting the manuscript and to all the conference participants, without whose sharp insights and diligent efforts this volume would not have been possible.

Clem Tisdell and Joseph C.H. Chai

CHAPTER 1

AN INTRODUCTION TO CHINA'S ECONOMIC GROWTH AND TRANSITION

CLEM TISDELL AND JOSEPH C.H. CHAI[1]

1.BACKGROUND

China's economic growth since commencing its economic reforms in 1978 has been impressive and its high growth rate has been sustained with relatively minor fluctuations. Furthermore, its high economic growth rate is expected to continue to the end of this century and beyond (Cf. Yeh, 1996; Zhang in this volume, Ng and Ng in this volume). *China will soon have the largest economy in the world* in terms of its real purchasing power (Cf. Ng and Ng in this volume). China's average growth rate of GNP in the period 1978 to 2000 is likely to be close to 10 percent. In this book, the sources and reasons for such growth, including China's economic reforms, are considered.

However, rapid economic growth is rarely an unmixed blessing and it often raises difficulties that have to be addressed by economic and social policies. Difficulties arising from China's economic growth considered by contributors to this book include environmental impacts and consequences for

---

1   Department of Economics, The University of Queensland, Brisbane 4072, Australia

inequality of income in China especially regionally, by locality and according to ethnic groups. The roles of township-village enterprises and of institutional structures, including systems of property rights, in influencing China's recent economic performance are given particular attention. It becomes quite clear that China's economic performance cannot be explained purely in narrow technical economic terms but only by considering the whole evolving socio-economic and political framework of China.

It should also be observed that China had a high economic growth rate by world standards even prior to 1978. This was attributable in part to its high level of savings and rate of capital accumulation (Tisdell, 1993). However, in no period since the establishment of the People's Republic has China sustained for so long the high growth rates which it has experienced since commencing its market-oriented reforms and open-door policy since 1979. Furthermore, it is unlikely that China's economic growth rates prior to 1979 would have been sustained without its economic reforms. China's previous socio-economic system had probably run its course in its ability to deliver improving economic outputs without increasing individual and social hardship. Without its economic reforms, China would have in all probability experienced substantial political instability not unlike that which led to the demise of the former Soviet Union. The ability of China to follow an evolutionary path in its economic reforms has given China economic and political strength.

Deng Xiaoping has rightly been given great credit for placing China on its path of economic reform (Ash and Kueh, 1996) and, partly through his charismatic influence, keeping it on this path. Nevertheless, China's reforms were not a 'one-man show' and the success of Deng's policies and their continuation were dependent upon wide and fundamental support within China. They continued even when Deng Xiaoping no longer held the central political stage. Furthermore, they have been continued and reaffirmed since his death. It is now highly improbably that the Chinese economic system will revert to that of the past and probable that it will continue to evolve as a mixed economic system, even though the pattern of this evolution cannot be predicted with certainty (Chai, 1997).

The contributions in this book touch upon and relate to all the basic issues involved in China's economic growth and transition as mentioned above. They have been grouped into three sets: (1) those dealing with the political economy of China's economic reforms and with macroeconomic aspects of China's economic growth, including its sources and the prospects for China's future growth, (2) environmental issues raised by China's economic growth, and (3) social and regional (spatial) consequences of China's economic performance and its efficiency as influenced partly by the location of enterprises and by institutional arrangements such as those applying to township and village enterprises and involving a relatively unique set of property rights.

Consider now an overview of the particular contributions to *China's Economic Growth and Transition*. This is organised in accordance with the grouping outlined above. It is of necessity a broad review and cannot do full justice to the individual contributions.

2. ECONOMIC REFORMS AND MACROECONOMIC GROWTH

In Chapter 2. Weiying Zhang and Gang Yi analyse the historical processes which were involved in gradual economic reform in China. Such reforms have provided the foundation for China's economic growth in recent decades. They see these reforms as resulting from an evolutionary process fostered by the interacting self-interest of agents who are guided by an "invisible hand", groping to a large extent in the dark. Nevertheless, they have more confidence in this process than a 'big-bang' alternative which could lack any real societal anchor.

Charles Harvie compares and contrasts economic transition in Vietnam with that in China and argues that Vietnam can learn from China's experience. However, Vietnam's industrial structure is different to that of China in that Vietnam lacks village and township enterprises and these have been responsible for a major share of China's economic growth (Cf. Mao and He in this volume, and also Kwong). In the circumstances, Harvie suggests that Vietnam could use "small and medium scale private sector enterprises, mainly in manufacturing and particularly in the south of the country" as a source of economic dynamism. Instead "the Vietnamese government has imposed rules and regulations on trade, investment and finance which make the development of private enterprise and dynamism very difficult".

Chapter 4 by Yiping Huang and Ronald Duncan argues that China's economy was structurally in better shape than that of the former Soviet Union to sustain economic growth when China's economic reforms got under way. China had a more favourable technological profile before 1978 than the former Soviet Union and this facilitated the success of its gradual economic reforms. Indirectly the suggestion is that the former Soviet Union had less capacity to implement gradual economic reforms successfully.

Yushi Mao and Ju-huang He attribute China's rapid economic growth since 1980 to flexibility and pragmatism in its economic policy, to China's high rate of savings and investment and to the dynamic and vigorous contribution made by non-state-owned enterprises. They also point out that China has since 1978 had one of the greatest mass internal migrations ever recorded by any country with about 8 million persons a year migrating from rural to urban areas and millions of persons moving between urban centres. Rural-urban migration (as might be expected from the theories of Lewis, 1954, 1965, 1979) has contributed greatly to China's economic growth and its lasting nature. They also mention that due to the importance of the underground economy in China, China's GNP is underestimated probably by around 10 percent or so. This means that the size of the Chinese economy is actually significantly larger than officially reported.

In Chapter 6, Xiaowen Tian examines the source of China's economic growth since 1978 using total factor productivity analysis. He finds that the main source of the increase is *not* from increased use of labour and physical capital (that is, from a rise in the quantity of inputs) but from positive qualitative changes in inputs e.g. greater human capital and economic improvements due to increased efficiency brought about by rising market orientation. In fact, he suggests that none of the increase in China's GDP since

1978 can be attributed to increased labour input, 25 percent can be attributed to increased physical capital input, 33 percent to the rise in human capital input, 29 percent to the increased efficiency arising from domestic market orientation and 13 percent from that due to international market orientation.

Attention turns in Chapter 7 to forecasting future economic growth and structural changes in the Chinese economy. Xiaoguang Zhang uses a general equilibrium approach for this purpose and among other things predicts a growth rate for China's GDP of 8-9 percent for the remainder of this century.

Siang Ng and Yew Kwang Ng analyse both China's recent economic growth performance and China's prospects for further growth. They claim that the political stability which China has enjoyed since 1978 has possibly been the prime contributor to its positive economic performance. They consider also that the development of a flexible and spatially decentralised political system has encouraged market reform and stimulated economic growth. Overseas Chinese in addition are regarded as valuable contributors to China's economic growth.

The Ngs believe secure property rights to be important for economic growth. Early reforms to property rights in agricultural land stimulated growth of agricultural output for just over a decade from 1979 onwards but since then growth in agricultural output has been sluggish. They suggest that this sluggishness could be because outright ownership of land is not yet possible.

They are also of the view that when China began to institute its economic reforms, it had a very favourable macroeconomic climate. For example, it had no external debts.

Various economic disparities and trends in these are discussed by the Ngs such as coastal-inland economic disparities, differences in rural and urban incomes and consumption levels, and in the economic performance of state-owned enterprises compared to that of other types of enterprises in China. For example, the ratio of urban to rural per capita consumption fell between 1978 and 1986 but has risen significantly since then. Therefore on the whole rural dwellers have become worse off relative to urban dwellers since 1986.

Contributions in the last part of this book also address economic disparities in China, some of which have widened with its economic growth.

The Ngs anticipate that China will avoid "chaotic disturbance" at least for the next decade or so, and consequently are optimistic about China's prospects for continuing economic growth. They predict on a plausible basis that the size of China's mainland economy estimated using purchasing power parity will exceed that of the US before 2010. Consequently, China's economy will soon become the largest economy in the world, even if Hong Kong's economy is excluded from the reckoning. With the reversion of Hong Kong to China in 1997 it is, however, reasonable to include Hong Kong in the reckoning.

Joseph Schumpeter (1942) hypothesised that the economic performance and growth of capitalist market economies may rely more on their ability to foster new inventions and technological progress than on their ability to achieve allocative economic efficiency. It is therefore important to consider what effects China's reforms have had on its technological and scientific effort and the economic application of research results.

The institutional structure for R&D (research and development) in China before 1978 was similar to that of the former Soviet Union in that R&D was carried out by research bodies largely divorced from productive enterprises. Therefore, in-house R&D by enterprises was virtually non-existent in China before its reforms in contrast to the situation in capitalist countries. China's R&D effort was driven more by political forces than by economic considerations and not integrated closely with the demands of economic enterprises. In Chapter 9, Charles Harvie and Tim Turpin outline how China's institutional structures for the generation and application of new science and technology have begun to change. For example, new forms of scientific and business alliances are being forged as a result of greater opportunities and changing incentives generated by China's economic reforms.

3. ENVIRONMENTAL ISSUES

Although China's economic growth is commendable, there are also environmental and social costs associated with it. Furthermore, as is now well known, economic growth need not result in sustainable development. Chinese authorities have become increasingly aware of such issues since 1978 and for example in 1994 drew up *China's Agenda 21* (State Council, 1994) to provide a framework for China's sustainable development taking into account its demographic and environmental situation.

In his contribution in Chapter 10, Clem Tisdell points out that some writers have questioned whether China's rate of economic growth is environmentally sustainable, particularly because China has a shortage of a number of important natural resources, for example water.

China's market reforms have had several consequences for its environmental policy. Its reforms have

1. made it *politically* easier to exert social controls on enterprises by financial levers e.g. pollution charges, and other means and
2. increased the willingness of Chinese authorities to consider market-related measures to control pollution. Furthermore, China's market reforms may well have had a positive impact in reducing China's pollution intensity, that is its level of pollution emissions relative to its GDP.

It is believed that pollution levels in relation to GDP (pollution intensity) may assume a form similar to that which Kuznets (1973) associated with changes in the distribution of income. Thus, pollution intensities may increase at first with rise in GDP (or GDP per capita) but eventually decline. In a market economy a Kuznets pollution intensity curve such as that shown by curve EFGH in Figure 1.1 might apply.

Empirical evidence suggests that pollution intensities in relation to GDP for a centrally planned economy (CPE) tend to be higher than for a market-based economy (Sterner, 1994). Thus in a CPE the Kuznets pollution curve indicated by curve ABCD may apply to a CPE rather than curve EFGH. This means that if by some magical means a CPE could be instantaneously transformed into a market economy with the same level of GDP its pollution levels and pollution intensity would fall. In Figure 1.1 if this transformation occurred at a GDP of Y_1, there would be a jump from point B to R and the country's pollution intensity would fall from r_1 to r_0. In practice, however, no such instantaneous transformation and sharp decline in pollution levels can be expected for several reasons.

First, market reforms are not instantaneous and old institutional structures and habits persist for some time. Secondly, much pollution in a function of the type and vintage of capital equipment used. Replacement of capital equipment takes time. Thirdly, during a reform period the level of a country's GDP is unlikely to remain stationary. Consequently, in Figure 1.1, the economy might move along the path indicated by the arrow marked BF as transition occurs. In such a case as market reforms occur, economic growth takes place and the country's pollution intensity rises but not by nearly as much as would be the case if same growth were to occur in a CPE. As China undertook its market reforms, it also experienced considerable economic growth, and it moved along the type of path indicated by BF.

The Kuznets-type pollution relationship indicates that if a country can achieve enough economic growth, its pollution intensity will eventually fall and ultimately its total level of pollution emissions could decline. This leads to the optimistic view that economic growth can provide a solution to environmental problems. For example, China may now have reached or have almost reached the summit of its Kuznets pollution curve. With further growth, therefore, a reduction in its pollution-intensity could be expected. Yet we can only draw limited comfort from this for a number of reasons.

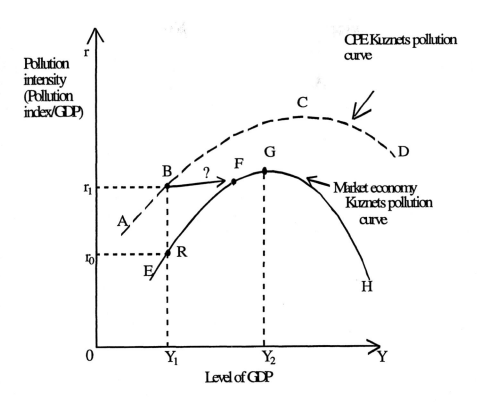

Figure 1.1: Kuznet-Type Pollution Curves for a Centrally Planned Economy (CPE) and a Market Economy

First, even if the *intensity* of pollution emissions falls in relation to GDP, the level of *total* annual emissions can continue to rise. Secondly, the damages caused by some pollutants is not just a function of their annual emissions (flows) but also of their accumulation or stocks. Some pollutants have long lives. Hence, if total annual emissions of pollutants fall, stocks of some pollutants may continue to rise. This is so for some greenhouse gases, for example, capable of global environmental impacts. There are now concerns about China's contribution to such gases. In the near future, China will overtake the United States as the world's major emitter of greenhouse gases.

As pointed out by Tisdell in Chapter 10, China's environmental impacts are not solely its own concern. Many have transnational and global consequences. For example, China is an important source of acid rains in Japan and Korea. Furthermore, China shares a number of important rivers and waterways with neighbouring countries. Conservation of China's biodiversity and its cultural heritage is of concern to all mankind, and so on.

It might be observed that China in developing its environmental management in the period since 1979 has followed a gradualistic and pragmatic approach. For example, environmental regulations are trialed in a limited regional area at first and then are extended in their regional application depending upon their degree of success. This evolutionary trial-and-error approach accords with the general philosophy of Deng Xiaoping of "crossing the river by touching stones".

Following Tisdell's general review of environmental issues in China, Zhai, Harrison and Xu consider sustainable land-use and management in the Three Gorges area of China. They point out that the Three Gorges area, the site for the massive Three Gorges Dam on the Yangzte (Chang) River, "has been attracting worldwide attention with controversies on the resettlement [of persons displaced by the dam] and [its] ecological and environmental impacts. Sustainable use and management of the scarce land resources will play an important role in the resettlement of the enormous population and the development of the whole economy as well as protection of the environment in that remote and underdeveloped area".

Zhuge Ren and Clem Tisdell introduce in Chapter 12 an environmental and socio-economic study relating to the mountainous area of Yunnan. Much of Yunnan is mountainous. Its upland areas are suffering severe environmental degradation due to economic and demographic pressures and unsustainable forms of land-use. Poverty is widespread in such areas which are chiefly inhabited by ethnic minorities. Zhuge and Tisdell believe that the development of community-based (social) forestry and related forms of land-use can contribute to sustainable economic development in these mountainous areas and alleviate poverty.

4. Social And Regional Dimensions And More On Efficiency: Growing Disparities

The socio-economic impacts of economic growth are often lopsided. Economic benefits do not always trickle-down evenly throughout society and socio-economic disparities can widen as economic growth occurs. Without doubt the benefits of economic growth in China have not been evenly shared or distributed. According to some measures, the gap between incomes in China's inland provinces and its coastal ones has widened since 1978 (although the Ngs in Chapter 8 express scepticism about some claims concerning the extent of China's growing regional inequality), the difference between rural and urban incomes has grown in recent years and so on. Growing disparities of income between villages are also observed and the socio-economic position of China's minorities may be declining relative to that of the dominant Han group. In addition, not all enterprises and locations contribute equally to economic growth. In China's case, township and village enterprises have been a prime contributor to its economic growth (Cf. Mao and He in Chapter 5). Their economic performances have been much more favourable in this regard than that of state-owned enterprises. The contributions in the last part of this book give attention to issues of this type.

In Chapter 13, Colin Mackerass discusses the likely impact of China's economic growth and modernisation on the integration of its minorities. Most of China's fifty-five state-recognised minority nationalities live near China's borders in areas potentially subject to political disruption. It has therefore been said that the importance of China's minorities for its long-term development is disproportionate to the size of their population.

Not only are China's minorities on the whole in a poorer economic position than the Han but income levels vary considerably between minority groups. There is some evidence that those disparities are growing as are other socio-economic disparities both between groups of minorities and in relation to the Han. Mackerass considers China's prospects for reversing these trends and for its control of any successionist tendencies which may emerge.

In Chapter 14, Jie Wen examines the role of tourism in the regional development of China and considers the experience of Yunnan province as a case study. The inland provinces of China lag behind its coastal provinces in terms of their economic development, and so far tourism development has been concentrated more on coastal areas than on China's inland. However, given the rich tourism resources of inland provinces including the special cultures of their minority groups, tourism development can contribute positively to economic growth in several inland areas. Some regions are especially well placed for the development of ecotourism and Yunnan is fortunate in this regard. So its experiences in tourism development are well worth considering. Therefore Jie Wen gives special attention to Yunnan as a case study. Tourism development in inland China could help reduce economic disparities between China's inland and its coastal areas.

Economic inequality has several spatial dimensions. Cheng Yuk-shing and Tsang Shu-ki consider trends in and sources of inter-village income inequality in Chapter 15 using a sample of 280 villages or towns from Fujian, Hubei, Jiangsu and Sichuan. They find that income inequality between villages fell initially between 1978 and 1984 but after reaching its trough in 1984 this inequality rose sharply. While much of the growing inequality after 1984 is explained by differences in the development of non-agricultural activities by villages, this does not entirely explain growing inter-village disparities in recent years, according to the findings of these authors.

After 1978, China reversed its policy of favouring the development of its inland region to one of preferring its coastal region for development so as to provide a window onto the outside world. As a result, the gap between incomes in China's inland and those in its coastal region widened as its economic growth continued.

Pak K. Lee points out in Chapter 16 that there has been growing central concern in China that such regional inequalities could become a source of socio-political instability, starting with the Ninth Five-Year Plan period (1996-2000) measures are being implemented to moderate the economic imbalance in favour of the development of coastal regions. Lee however, is not sure whether the proposed measures for giving the inland a better economic deal will be sufficient to satisfy inland leaders. China's problems with its unequal economic development are far from solved.

In Chapter 17, F. Kwan examines the pattern of capital use and labour absorption by township-village industries. From 1978 to 1985, he finds that township and village industries were quite effective in absorbing labour but since 1985 have been much less effective in this regard. Since then they have started to adopt capital-intensive rather than the labour-intensive methods for various reasons which are outlined by the author. Given that China still has a large surplus agricultural workforce, a slow down in labour absorption by town and village enterprises is not a welcome trend. In the longer term it could add to disguised or even overt labour unemployment.

The spread of a market economy always brings increasing risks for those who rely on markets for the employment of their labour. As China moves further towards a market economy, employment of its labour becomes more vulnerable to market forces and their fluctuations. Given China's booming economy, this problem has not yet emerged seriously but it would be rather optimistic to believe that China will avoid forever problems of mass unemployment of the type experienced by market economies at least periodically but now almost chronically.

Township and village enterprises (TVEs) have been a major contributor to China's economic success since it began its reforms in 1979. However, they existed prior to 1978 and are *communal* rather than private enterprises. Advocates of private property rights as a key to economic success might therefore be at a loss to explain the performance of such enterprises. However, Charles C.L. Kwong explains it in Chapter 18 using the theory of property rights and by paying particular attention to principal and agent relationships. He feels that China's experience with TVEs justifies the gradualism of its socio-economic reforms and its rejection of 'shock-therapy'. Supporters of the latter method advocate a rapid transition to a system of private property rights in centrally planned economies. Certainly Russia did not fare well in its attempts to apply such shock therapy with the aid of American economic experts.

5. FURTHER COMMENT

Different countries have different cultures and historical backgrounds. Contributions to this volume suggest that such differences should not be lightly considered in designing policies for socio-economic changes such as those for transition from a centrally planned economy to a more market-oriented one. While there were similarities between the economies and societies of the former Soviet Union and of China prior to 1978, there were also important cultural and economic differences. While many 'off-the-shelf' policies for economic transition for both countries were recommended, including 'big-bang' approaches, they were not grounded in the essence of these societies and were not evolutionary in character. Therefore, the likelihood of their success was slim. Fortunately for China, it kept its own council. While China is not completely out of the woods as far as the transition of its economy is concerned, there can be no doubt that it has made remarkable economic progress and achieved major but gradual institutional changes, most of which now appear to be irreversible. Furthermore, its institutional change is continuing. While no one can be sure what the future socio-economic pattern of China will be, there is reason to be cautiously optimistic about its nature, as is apparent from the contributions in this volume.

References

Ash, R.F. and Kueh, Y.Y. (1996) *The Chinese Economy under Deng Xiaoping*, Oxford University Press, Oxford.

Chai, J.C.H. (1997) *China: Transition to a Market Economy*, Clarendon Press, Oxford.

Kuznets, S. (1973) "Modern Economic Growth: Findings and Reflections", *American Economic Review*, Vol. 63, pp.139-191.

Lewis, W.A. (1954) "Economic Development with Unlimited Supplies of Labour", *The Manchester School of Economic and Social Studies*, Vol. 22, pp.139-191.

Lewis, W.A. (1965) *The Theory of Economic Growth*, George Allen and Unwin, London.

Lewis, W.A. (1979) The Dual Economy Revisited", *The Manchester School of Economic and Social Studies*, Vol. 47, No. 3, pp.211-229.

Schumpeter, J.A. (1942) *Capitalism, Socialism and Democracy*, 2nd ed., Harper Brothers, New York.

State Council (1994) *China's Agenda 21 - White Paper on China's Population, Environment and Development in the 21st Century*, China Environmental Science Press, Beijing.

Sterner, T. (1994) *Economic Policies for Sustainable Development*, Kluwer, Dordrecht.

Tisdell, C.A. (1993) *Economic Development in the Context of China*, Macmillan, London.

Yeh, K.C. (1996) "Macroeconomic Issues in China in the 1990's". Pp.11-54 in R.F. Ash and Y.Y. Kueh, *The Chinese Economy under Deng Xiaoping*, Oxford University Press, Oxford.
Australia 1

REFORMS AND ECONOMIC GROWTH

CHAPTER 2

CHINA'S GRADUAL REFORM: A HISTORICAL PERSPECTIVE

WEIYING ZHANG AND GANG YI[1,2]

ABSTRACT

This chapter provides an historical perspective on China's economic reform. It first summarizes nine stylized facts of China's gradual reform, and then explains what forces have driven China into gradualism and how China's gradual reform has become a success. The chapter shows that the transition from a centrally-planned system to a market economy is an evolutionary process with interactions among all self-interested agents under the guidance of the "invisible hand", which has been extremely powerful in creating new institutions.

---

1   The authors thank Shaoja Guy Liu, Dingding Wang and Robert Sandy for their helpful comments. Thanks also go to the audience at an 1995 AEA meeting, and at serial seminars held at Oxford University, London School of Economics and City University of Hong Kong.

2   China Centre for Economic Research, Peking University, Beijing 100871, China

1. INTRODUCTION

Almost all former socialist countries are marching towards a market economy. "Big bang" and "gradualism" have been identified as the two polar-case approaches of the transition. Roughly speaking, the East European countries and the former Soviet Union have taken more or less the "big bang" approach, while China has taken the gradual one.[3] In 1990 when the architects of the big bang drafted their blueprint of massive privatisation and price liberalisation, China's 12-year-old gradual reform was under a heavy attack both from Chinese economists and their western counterparts.[4] Surprisingly, just two years later, fashions reversed, even though the reform in China was almost stagnate during this period (until early 1992). Today China's gradual reform is widely described as successful.

There have been many papers discussing comparative advantages or disadvantages of the gradualism versus the big bang in transforming a socialist economy into a market economy. While the research is inconclusive, most economists attribute performance differences between China and the East European Countries and former Soviet Union to their different reform approaches.[5] The key point of the proponents of gradualism is that gradual reform can split and spread transitional costs over a long period and is thus more feasible, both politically and economically.

---

3   Hungary and Poland had practised gradualism before their "big bang" approach. Even the former Soviet Union practised gradualism before its collapse.

4   For example, Kornai (1990) wrote: "the reform process has a forty-year history in Yugoslavia, twenty in Hungary, and almost a whole decade in China. All three countries represent specific mixtures of amazing results and disastrous failures". (p. 210)

5   See, among others, Sachs and Woo (1993), Gelb, Jefferson and Singh (1993), Jefferson and Singh (1993), McMillan and Naughton (1992), Perkins (1992), Yi (1994), Zou (1993).

The existing studies of transition have been almost exclusively conducted either from an economic perspective, or from a social-choice theoretical approach.[6] There has been few studies from a historical perspective. Much of the debate has been focused on how the reform should proceed, ignoring how it has already proceeded.

The present chapter provides a historical perspective of China's gradual reform. Our purpose is not to argue which reform approach is "good" or "bad", but instead is to show how economic reforms have proceeded in China so far. The chapter is organised as follows. Section 2 describes some stylised facts of Chinese reform. Section 3 analyses the underlying reasons which have led China to gradualism. Section 4 discusses how China's gradual reform became a success. Our analysis shows that much of the success of Chinese economic reform can be attributed to those policies and factors which have been heavily criticised by many economists and some of which were actually implemented by the "conservatives". Section 5 concludes the chapter.

2. CHINA'S GRADUAL REFORM: STYLISED FACTS

China's economic reform has been identified by many economists as "gradualism" in comparison with Russia's "big bang". But there is no theoretical definition which captures even the major features of the Chinese economic reform process.[7] This fact reflects complexity of the reform. In this

---

6   See, for example, Murrell (1991), Murrell and Olson (1991), Dewatripoint and Roland (1992a, b), Kang Chen (1992), Murrell and Wang (1993), Fan (1993a), Liu (1993), Z. Wang (1993).

7   Wei (1992) defined gradualism versus big bang as follows: Gradualism refers to a sequential implementation of minimum bangs, and a minimum bang is a simultaneous implementation of a minimum set of reforms that exhibit "strong interdependence"; big bang refers to a simultaneous implementation of all small bangs. Wei's definition has several defects, as

section, instead of considering theoretical definitions of gradualism and big bang, we summarise the major stylised facts of China's gradual reforms as follows.

(i) Chinese economic reforms have not been conducted according to a well-defined and time-consistent objective model

This does not necessarily mean that Chinese reform has lacked objectives. Rather, the objective model of the reform has been under continuously re-adjusting during the reform process, from "planning economy with some market adjustment", to "socialist planned commodity economy", to "socialist market economy".[8] Furthermore, even the market-oriented direction has not

pointed out by Z. Wang (1993). First, his definition is actually a gradualist's definition and irrelevant for big bang economists since the definition per se excludes the underlying assumption of big bang approach that all components of a reform program exhibit strong contemporaneous interdependence. Second, Wei's definition ignores the intertemporal interdependence among different components of reforms which is crucial for understanding reform processes. Third, Wei does not consider the evolutionary process of even a minimum bang. As Z. Wang argued, the gradualism means not only a sequential but also a evolutionary process. According to Z. Wang, big bang refers to that a comprehensive reform program is implemented with on stroke; gradualism refers to that a comprehensive reform program is implemented in a sequential, evolutionary fashion. Although Wang's definition captures two important elements of gradualism (i.e., sequential implementation and evolutionary process) and might be sufficient for setting up a theoretical model of gradualism versus big bang (as he did), although it is far from explaining major dimensions of the China's gradual reform.

8   In the early period of reforms (until 1984), the objective of reforms was to "perfect and improve socialist planned economy by introducing some market elements". Some observers may like to argue that in the early stage, there was no objective at all. For example, Perkins (1992) wrote: "Most Chinese leaders did not have a clear reform objective in mind". (p. 4); also see Fan (1993b) for a similar argument. The September 1984 Third Plenum of the 12th Party Committee adopted "socialist planned commodity economy" as the objective model of reform. Although for many Chinese economists, this represented a revolutionary change in the reform objectives, interpretation of the "planned commodity economy" was controversial. Some emphasised its "planning nature", while the others emphasised its "commodity nature". "Socialist market economy" was officially adopted as the objective model by the 14th Part

proceeded uniformly. There have been frequent reversals. In addition, different people had different understandings of the same objective model, which made the objective model more ambiguous.

(ii)   *Chinese economic reforms have not been following a well-designed blueprint*

This does not mean that China has not drawn up any blueprint. On the contrary, up to 1988, there had been 14 blueprints drawn by the State Commission for Restructuring the Economic Systems (SCRES).[9] The first blueprint was drawn as early as in December 1979.[10] An overall plan of reforms was also drawn in 1981, on request of Premier Zhao Ziyang (Wu and Zhao, 1988; Shi and Liu, 1989). Two big bang-type blueprints were drawn respectively in 1986 and 1988. However, none of 14 blueprints has been implemented either because they were not politically and economically feasible or technically unimplementable. Gradualism does not mean that there is no need for a blueprint. If a well-designed reform program is implemented step by step, we still have gradualism. But China's gradualism is not such a case. For this reason, it might be more appropriate to call it "piece-meal" reform rather than "gradualistic".

Congress in 1992. Note that the official changes in the objective model do not necessarily represent the timetable of changes in reality. Normally they lagged.

9   In fact, SCRES was established in 1982 initially for drawing the reform blueprint. The then State Economic Commission was assumed to be in charge of implementing annual economic reform programs. The predecessor of SCRES was "The State Council's Reform Office", which was established in 1980, May 8 also for drawing the reform blueprint. See Appendix of Gao (1991).

10   This was drawn by the then "Economic System Reform Office under the State Council's Financial Commission" and submitted to the State Council on December 3, 1979. The office was set up in June 1979. See Appendix of Gao (1991).

(iii)   *Chinese economic reforms have been conducted with an easy-to-hard sequence*

Most economists agree that there is some intertemporal interdependence between different components of reforms, and in particular, implementation of some components may be preconditioned by implementing others. For example, Wu and Liu (1991) argue that price liberalisation should go before enterprises reform; whereas Newbery (1991) argues that the breakup of monopolies should precede price liberalisation. A wrong sequence may be worse than no reform since implementing some programs may block other more fundamental reforms. While it might be too early to determine if China has followed an optimal sequence, it is clear that China has followed an easy-to-hard sequence.[11] The easy-to-hard sequence may not be necessarily different from an optimal sequence, since the easiest reform might be just the precondition for the hardest. Nonetheless, China did not choose the easy-to-hard sequence because it is optimal. If it proves optimal, that is a fortune. In fact, there are many leading Chinese reform economists who have been critical of this easy-to-hard sequence for being short-sighted (Wu and Zhao, 1988).

(iv)   *Chinese economic reforms have been progressing through a dual-track system*

The dual-track system was first introduced in undertaking price reform. Under this system, most products have two prices: the planned quotas are allocated at the plan prices and the above-plan products are transacted at market prices; most (state-owned) enterprises acquire inputs and sell outputs through both

---

11   Tian Jiyun (1985), a then vice-premier, argued that the price reform should be conducted "from easy to hard and step by step". He wrote: "what is easy and what is hard must be judged according to its effects on people's direct interest".

the planning and market channels.[12] The dual-track system is also used in most of other reform areas, including foreign exchanges, labour reform, housing reform, social security reform, and ownership reform. As a result, the whole Chinese economy is evolved into a dual-track economy (Diao, 1989). The dual-track is the most important characteristic of China's gradual reform, and it encompasses most of the other features of the reform. The key point of the dual-track system is not the co-existence of the plan track and the market track, but that the market track was introduced at the margin in parallel to the plan track. For example, the market transactions was created not by cutting but by delimiting the planned allocations; the non-state sector was created not by denationalising or privatising the state-sector but by freeing the entry of new enterprises.[13] This is crucial for understanding the dual-track system.

(v) *Chinese economic reforms have not stripped any major interest groups of their vested interests but just changed the ways with which these vested interests are materialised*

One of the major features of the dual-track system is respecting the *status quo* of all agents formulated under the old planning system. This is the reason why it emerged spontaneously from the very beginning of reform without

12 Although some mutations of the dual-track prices existed even at the pre-reform period, it was until the early 1980s that the dual-track system became important, - although it was not legitimised in industrial sectors until 1985. The pre-1985 government's reform plans did not envisage this. Zhang (1984) was the first to propose the dual-track system as a transitional approach to a market price system. His ideas were "collectivised" in a young economists conference held in September 1984 in Zhejiang Province (nicknamed "Moganshang Conference"), which greatly influenced the government's 1985 policy. For some analyses of evolution of the dual-track system, see Wu and Zhao (1988), Byrd (1988), and McMillan and Naughton (1993), among others.

13 Cutting the planned allocations came much later than the introduction of the dual-track system; privatisation of the state-owned enterprises is yet to come.

much resistance. For many economists, the economic reform cannot be a Pareto improvement since there must be some people worse-off (Fan, 1993a). In particular, the government bureaucrats have been assumed to be the major losers since most of their privileges and rent-seeking opportunities will be reduced or eliminated by the reform (Shi, 1993). If this is true, success of the reform depends heavily on how to mitigate the resistance from the powerful bureaucrats. The dual-track system seems to have served this purpose very well. Moreover, the dual-track system actually makes the bureaucrats better off rather than worse off, since they now have better opportunities and more efficient ways to enjoy economic rents. This explains why more and more government bureaucrats have switched to supporting reform as it has proceeded,[14] - although they try to steer the reforms according to their interests.[15]

(vi)   Chinese economic reforms have been dominated by local government

Although it might be more appropriate to say that the whole reform has been a combination of top-to-bottom and bottom-to-top process (Chen et al., 1992).

---

14 At the beginning of rural reform, many town and village cadres opposed the reform because of loss of superiority. But they soon realised that they could do much better than ordinary peasants by using their accumulated personal connections and knowledge of the outside world. They then became "reformers". Today the richest people in the countryside are these former cadres. A similar phenomena can be observed during the urban reform.

15 It seems that they will continue to support the reform until they themselves become capitalists either by taking bribes or by going into business (xiahai). The Chinese experience shows that it is possible to compensate the bureaucrats during the reform period. The intuition is simple: if the reform implies transfer of economic power from bureaucrats to entrepreneurs, let the bureaucrats become entrepreneurs, - for those who are not qualified to become entrepreneurs, let them become "shareholders" (don't worry about where they get money). Because of improvement of efficiency of resources allocation, the entrepreneur in the market economy can enjoy higher return than the bureaucrat in the planning economy. Then, why should a bureaucrat oppose the reform? (Zhang, 1994).

The local government dominance is an important feature of the reform. Many reform programs have been initiated by local governments and even by the grass-roots, and then recognised and adopted as national policies by the central government.[16] Much of the planning system was dismantled by local governments. Many local governments have been far ahead their national leaders in reforming economy. This does not necessarily mean that local governments' movement is against the central leaders' will. In fact, it was Premier Zhao Ziyang's reform strategy to use local governments to fight against more conservative central ministerial bureaucrats.[17] As pointed out by Shi (1993), decentralisation of governance was a feature of the central leaders' style of governing the reform.

(vii)   *Chinese economic reform have exhibited great regional variations*

This is related to the last point and also is a mirror of the evolutionary process in spatial dimension. Some regions have been running far ahead of other regions. In the later 1980s, some coastal areas such as Guangdong Province became quasi-market economies, while most of the inland areas were still

---

16   Agriculture reform is a good example. The family farming system was first secretly adopted by some peasants in Anhui Province in 1978 and was nationally implemented by the central government much later. The industrial reform was pioneered by Sichuan Province in 1978 under the then governor Zhao Ziyang. More recent examples of bottom-up initiatives that only later became accepted by the central authority include stock exchanges in Shanghai and Shenzhen (Chen et al., 1992).

17   The leadership promotion system also reflects the local government dominance of reform. From the very beginning of reform, reform performance became a very important mark for local government leaders to be promoted up to the central level. Zhao Ziyang and Wang Li (former governor of Anhui Province) are two examples. This incentive system further strengthened the local government dominance of reform.

planning-dominant. The spatial picture of reform is similar to the spatial picture of economic development.

(viii)   China's economic reform has been an experimental process

It seems hard to find a single reform program which has been implemented without experiment first. Reform experiments have been either regional-based (typically city-based), or sectoral-based, or even firm-based. Typically a particular reform program is first tried in selected regions, sectors or enterprises. If a success, it is implemented in other regions, sectors or enterprises; if a failure, it is stopped. Experiment is used not only for single reform programs, but also for "comprehensive reform program".[18] From time to time, the SCRES select some experimental cities for a comprehensive reform.

(ix)   Chinese economic reforms have been an evolutionary process, which has proceeded with "stop-go cycle"

The evolutionary process means that many small and half-hearted reform measures accumulate into a radical change over time (Shi, 1993; Z. Wang, 1993). This feature applies not only to the whole reform program, but also to almost all single reform packages, including agricultural reform, price reform, enterprise reform, ownership reform, macro-control system reform, and even housing reform. The "dual-track system" exists everywhere as evolutionary approach. There has been no single area in which the reform was implemented at one stroke. For example, the price reform began in 1979 and is still under way. The reforms of state-owned enterprises have been on top of

---

18   A comprehensive reform program contains all aspects of the reform such as price, enterprise, financial, taxation, housing, and so on.

the agenda for a long time, but it is far from being completed. The "stop-go" cycle refers to the phenomenon that a reform push is usually followed by a setback which will in turn be followed by another push. In a push period, some important and even radical reform measures are implemented, while in the setback period, part of such measures are withdrawn. Since in most cycles, the pullbacks are less than the forward measures,[19] changes have accumulated gradually. As a result, the whole economic system has been moving towards a market system. Reform cycles have been related to political cycles. In the push period, "reformists" are active and "conservatives" keep silent, while in the setback period, the situation goes the other way. The correlation is obvious, but causality between reform cycles and political cycles is not unambiguous.[20]

3. RANDOM WALK: HOW HAS CHINA ADOPTED GRADUALISM

The Chinese economic reform process looks more or less like a random walk. Mr Deng Xiaoping's strategy was: "go a step and look for the next" and "groping for stones to cross the river". This random walk had really worried both the leaders in charge of reforms as well as reform-minded economists, as both economic and political problems had been accumulating rapidly. As early as in 1981, the then premier Zhao Ziyang pointed out, in his report to the People's Congress, "these reforms (implemented so far) are still partial

---

19   The largest and also the longest setback was after 1989. But this setback was followed by an unprecedented and the most radical push in 1992 and 1993.

20   Most outside observers would like to argue that setbacks are brought in by "conservatives". However, this argument might be too simple. If a push is always followed by a setback, there must be some reason beyond the political. The observation is that "conservatives" blame reformists for problems following the push, while "reformists" blame "conservatives" for problems following the setback.

and exploratory in nature and our work has suffered from certain
incongruities and from lack of coordination. The task before us is to sum up
our experience in these reforms and, after careful investigation and study and
repeated scientific confirmation, to draw up as soon as possible an overall
plan for reforming the economy and carry it out step by step".[21] Criticism of
"groping for stones to cross the river" among academics accelerated in 1985,[22]
which led to two aborted big bang type blueprints, respectively in 1986 and
1988. As Nolan (1992) observed, "(what) most economists of China have put
forward is that its industrial performance in the 1980s would have been much
better if it had followed the path of a rapid transition to a market economy. A
larger body of informed opinion both inside and outside the country
considered that in the early 1980s China's policy makers should have
liberalised industrial prices, eliminated the industrial material balance
planning system, opened the industrial market to international competitions
(the surest guardian against monopoly), and rapidly privatised state industry".
All these show that China's gradualism has not been a rigorously designed
strategy of reform. In other words, China did not "adopt" a gradualist strategy
purposely (Chen, 1992), although it has "become" a gradualist. Nevertheless,
the observed stylised facts of China's gradual reforms are not accidental. They
are consequences of underlying reasons. In this section, we shall analyse these
underlying reasons and show how China has embraced gradualism.

(i) No time to wait

China's economic reform began after the Cultural Revolution, which was
ended with economic chaos. Agriculture had stagnated for a decade with more
than 25 per cent of 800 million rural population living under poverty line by

---

21   Quoted from Wu and Zhao (1988) (p. 311). It might be safe to say that Zhao Ziyang was an
     advocate for the idea of a complete blueprint of economic system reform until 1986.

22   The most influential paper was Guo, Qiu and Liu (1985).

the Chinese standard. Discontent was mounting in the countryside and peasant uprisings were everywhere. In the urban areas, the planning system was out of order, many industrial production units did not produce at all, and many factory workers did not work. Shortages were everywhere and most necessities such as foodstuffs, matches and toilet paper were rationed. Millions of "young intellectuals" returned from the countryside and were waiting for jobs. The widespread dissatisfaction periodically erupted into major strikes and street protects in many industrial cities. Under this background, survival was the first priority for leadership and the reform became the only way to survive, although there was no consensus on how to reform. This gave the leaders no time to design a reform blueprint based on rigorous cost-benefit consideration before implementing any effective measures. The urgent issues of the moment were to restore production, to let peasants have incentives to produce and workers have incentives to work. Pragmatism was the only acceptable philosophy. Any measures which could move the economy were welcome, no matter what long-term effects they might have. Not surprisingly, the family responsibility system in agriculture which was initiated by some local peasants was recognised and adopted nationally by the central government, although it was taken as a matter of expediency by the leaders. The industrial reform began with "*fangquan rangli*" (downshifting decision rights and leaving profit to the firm) and performance-based bonuses even before problems of measuring performances were solved.[23] Another example is that non-state owned enterprises and private businesses in urban areas in the early 1980s were encouraged initially not for reforming urban economy but for creating jobs for millions of job-seekers who could not be absorbed by state-owned enterprises. There was no

---

23   Critics say that "right prices" are a precondition for enlivening enterprises, and therefore price reform should be done before enterprise reform. But China did not go this way.

time to wait for a well-designed blueprint and then to implement it step by step.

(ii) Nobody knows where to go

The frequent changing objective model is not only one major feature, but also one of major reasons for China's gradualism. China has been "groping for stones to cross the river" partly because there was no idea about where the opposite bank was (X. Wang, 1993). As Fan (1993b) correctly pointed out, the Chinese, either the leadership or the majority of people (including economists), had no clear idea about where to go at the beginning of economic reform in the late 1970s. What they knew was merely that the conventional centrally-planned system did not work well and some changes were needed. Most of the households and individuals did not totally lose faith in the old system. The "elites" still believed at that time if they got the chance to run the economy, they could solve the problems better than other socialist countries. The failure of the economy was mainly attributed to the ceaseless political movements, not to the defects of the basic structure of the system itself. The dominant objective of reform at the early stage was "to perfect the socialist planning economy" by improving planning methods with "input-output analysis" and computers, and by introducing some market elements at margin, rather than to change the whole system. In fact, until early 1984, the Soviet Union's planning system was still a model for the Chinese.[24] All these

---

24 Of course, this does not mean that there were no radical proposals for reform. For example, as early as in 1979, Yu Zhuyao, an economist, proposed "socialist market" as an objective model of reforms; Doug Furen (1979) argued for changing the state-ownership. Nevertheless, it is safe to say that in the early 1980s the majority of leaders and economists had not lost their trust in the planning economy and public ownership. Their major consideration was how to make public ownership-based planning economy more efficient. Even today, many economists still believe "advantages of public ownership".

ruled out the possibility of China to set up a radical reform program at the beginning of reform.

(iii) *Nobody knows how to reform*

Even if China knew where to go, it still faced a problem of how to reform. Designing a blueprint of transforming a planned economy into a market economy is not easy. Neither Chinese leaders nor Chinese economists had clear ideas about how a market mechanism works. Economists learnt some principles of the market economy from textbooks, but they had no experiences. Old generation economists were preoccupied with Marxism economics. They were incapable of answering the question of how the reform should be done. Consequently, young economists were mobilised in the middle of 1980s (see Shanren, 1987). Young economists were less ideological and more pragmatic, and therefore could concentrate on studies of how economic systems work rather than on whether a particular institution belongs to capitalism or socialism. They made great contributions to designing a series of post-1984 reform programs and even directly drawing the blueprints.[25] However, many of them were idealists. They were incapable of dealing with bureaucrats who were in charge of implementation of reforms. Modern economics is a necessary but not sufficient condition for one to draw a blueprint of reforms. Nobody knows how to reform partly because the reform by its nature is a learning-by-doing process, as pointed out by many economists, and because the interdependence between different reform

---

25 Many influential young economists worked in the following four research institutes: Economic System Reform Institute of China, Rural Development Institute of China, the Institute of Economics of Chinese academy of Social Science, and the State Council's Development Center. The World Bank economists also played active roles in the middle of the 1980s.

components are to be revealed (Zhang, 1984). Given that nobody knows how to reform, "groping for stones to cross the river" is the only choice China could take. The experimental feature of China's reforms partly reflects this problem. Reform cycles are also related to this problem. When not all consequences of a particular reform program are known *ex ante*, some *ex post* reversals are inevitable. Local governments are granted autonomy to reform partly because the central government does not know how to proceed.

(iv)   Nobody has authority to implement a well-designed reform program

Even if economists are able to design a reform blueprint, implementation of such a blueprint requires a strong reform-minded authority. Advocates of the idea of a complete blueprint of reforms assume (implicitly) that such an authority exists, but this assumption is not realistic. Lack of reform-minded authority was one of major reasons that several comprehensive reform blueprints failed in the 1980s. The Chinese structure of authority is a fragmented one. Authority is split not just between top leaders, but also between different level bureaucrats. Under such a structure, major policy initiatives requires not only the consensus among the top leaders, but also the active cooperation of many bureaucratic units who have nested power to block or manipulate any policies which are not in their interests. In modern economics terminology, a reform blueprint is implementable only if it satisfies concerned bureaucrats' participation constraints and incentive compatibility constraints. Since bureaucrats' interests are diversified, it is impossible to design such a blueprint. The bureaucrats always make best use of their position to steer the reform course following their own interests, which often transform bold initiatives into modest programs. As a result, as pointed out by Chen (1992), "the types of reform proposed, the attempted reforms that failed, and the elements of reforms that implemented were all a result of the complex of political forces within the centrally-planned system, rather than simply a matter of choice between abstract economic models".[26] For instance, in 1981, Zhao Ziyang, the then premier and China's reform-minded leader until 1989, intended to take advantage of the favourable macroeconomic environment after the rectification policy to implement an "overall" reform package with the price reform as its major component. However, this reform plan was never put in effect because of the opposition from various sources (Wu and Zhao, 1988; Shi and Liu, 1989). Instead, a marginal reform, which allowed enterprises to sell their above-quota products at "floating prices" within the range up to 20% higher or lower than the fixed prices, was carried out (World Bank, 1990). Those who were involved in the 1980s reform programs recall clearly that Zhao Ziyang's authority over central ministerial bureaucrats was very limited.[27] After a few failures to mobilise the central government ministries to follow his will,[28] he was forced to turn to local governments for support. By delegating part of autonomy of reforms to local governments through various ways such as "experimental cities" and "opening cities", he indirectly undermined the central ministries' economic power, which otherwise could not be done.[29] This partially explains why Chinese economic reform has been so local government-dominant. However, the local government-dominance did not only undermine the ministries'

---

26 Chen (1992), by applying Murrell and Olson's (1991) devolution theory to China, gives an excellent analysis, both theoretically and empirically, of how bureaucrats can use their power of collective actions to manipulate the reform process.

27 One reason is that some more powerful leaders were behind the ministers.

28 There was a vivid analogy with cooking to show the reform decision making process as follows. Mr Zhao Ziyang asked the minister to cook a light food for him, but the ministry delivered a salty one. Then Zhao sent it back and asked the minister to recook it. After a while, the minister delivered a food with the same salt but said that "I put little salt in it". After a few rounds, Zhao had to eat a salty food rather than his preferred light one.

29 For example, in 1984, after the proposed foreign trade system reform was blocked by the ministerial bureaucrats supported by Chen Yun, Deng Xiaoping's rival, Zhao Ziyang turned to "open 14 coastal cities to the world". By doing so, Zhao partially implemented his plan of trade reforms.

power, but also further undermined Zhao's own authority in implementing his economic policies. In the later 1980s, Zhao's authority became so weak that some reform-minded economists argued that China needed "new authoritarianism".[30]

(v) Nobody is willing to take a big risk

Under the Chinese political-social-economic structure, reform is a big venture which involves both economic and political risks. In applying Karl Marx's words mechanically, failure would destroy not only the reform but also reformers themselves.[31] This makes all the leaders very cautious in making their reforms decisions. Many proposed reform projects have been delayed or even cancelled simply because their perceived risks were too great. This was particularly true in the case of price reform. Under the old system, the pricing was a major tool for the government to collect revenues and to redistribute national income between different sectors, between regions as well as between different classes of people (particularly between rural and urban citizens). In some sense, the price reform is the reform of the whole economic system, including wages, subsidies, and taxation. Price reform involves two major risks. The first is inflation which directly affects people's living standard as well as income distribution.[32] A strong resistance against the price

---

30 Wu Jiaxing, a philosophical economist, was the most famous advocate of the new authoritarianism. It should be pointed out that although we argue that a strong reform-minded authority is necessary for implementing a reform blueprint, we do not believe that such an authority is necessarily good for the reform. The reason is that a strong reform-minded authority may implement a very bad blueprint. In this sense, lack of a strong reform-minded reform might be fortunate for China.

31 Karl Marx regarded the market mechanism as a "thrilling jump", failure of which would destroy not just the product but also its producer himself.

32 As Yi (1990) pointed out: It would be naive to argue that "the price reform is to change relative prices rather than to raise all prices; and it does not necessarily bring about inflation if the monetary policy is held tightly".

reform has come from ordinary people. The second is the government budget problem. The two are interrelated. In order to mitigate ordinary people's resistance to price reform, compensation must be made through various subsidies, which implies a great budget deficit which in turn further increases inflationary pressure. Theoretically, the price reform can also bring revenues to the government through improvements of efficiency. However, the increase in expenditure is certain and immediate but the increase in revenues is uncertain and takes time. Simple computation has always showed that the government revenue would decrease in the price reform. Even at the very beginning of reform both the leader and economists realised that the price reform was crucial and agreed that it must be done, fears of inflation and the budget deficit continuously delayed price reform (Zhang, 1984). The risk-averse attitudes of reformers have contributed to many other features of Chinese economic reforms, including "the easy-to-hard sequence", its experimental nature, and the local government-dominance. The easy-to-hard sequence is simply a consequence of aversion to risks.[33] Reform experiments can greatly reduce the risks of any particular reform program. By letting the local government try, the central government can not only diversify the risks of national-level reforms but also disassociate itself from a particular failure - at least in the short run.

(vi)   *It takes time for people to get used to a market economy*

Economic reforms do not only change the system but also change people, their habits, value judgment, and behaviour. The socialist planned economy was a quiet life under which everything seemed "fixed". Decision rights were

---

33   Tian Jiyun (1985), a then vice-premier, argued that the price reform should be conducted "from easy to hard and step by step". He wrote: "That what is easy and what is hard must be judged according to its effects on people's direct interest".

concentrated in the hands of a small group of people, the majority of people did not need to make many choices for themselves, and even for those who were decision-makers, most of their work was routine since the environment was stable. There was little need for initiative, creativity, and innovation. For people who have lived for decades under such a system, it is not easy for them to adjust to a market economy where everyone needs to make his own choice in the face of an uncertain environment. It takes time for them to learn how to deal with price fluctuation, uncertainty, multiple-choices, and competition. An entrepreneurial class is crucial for efficiency of a market economy. It takes time for entrepreneurial class to emerge. Much of the reform delays have been due to ordinary people's reluctance to be in an uncertain environment and from managers' incapability to manoeuvre in a market. Although two digit inflation is not a big problem today and government dared to free all foodstuff's prices in 1993, ten years ago raising the price of a box of matches from two cents to three cents was a political problem.[34] Enlarging autonomy of enterprises has been one major objective of state-owned enterprise reform. But at the early stage, many managers didn't like autonomy since they were used to obeying decisions made by their superiors rather than making decisions by themselves.

---

34   This example is worth an elaboration since it shows a story of how the one-track planned price system evolved first into a dual-track system and eventually into a one-track market price system. At the price of two cents per box of matches, all match factories made a loss. In the early 1980s, the government attempted several times to raise the price from two cents to three cents but failed to do so because of fear of citizens' opposition. Given that raising the official price proved impossible, the match factories began to seek alternatives. They either put fewer matches into a box but sold them at the same price or designed a new box and sold it at a much higher price (since it was a "new" product, it was legal to sell it at a new price). There were two match prices. The official price of the old box was not changed, but it was hard to find in the market, and it eventually disappeared. As a result, all matches are sold at the market price.

4. How China's Gradual Reform Has Become A Success

Murphy, Shleifer and Vishny (1992) have convincingly argued that partial reform is fraught with pitfalls. They showed that when some resources, but not all, are allowed to move into the private sector, and state prices remain distorted, the result may be a significant disruption of the state sector. Why has "the significant disruption" not happened in China? The following analysis shows that much of the success of the Chinese economic reform can be attributed to those policies or factors which had been heavily criticised by many economists and some of which were actually implemented by "conservatives". In some sense, China's economic reform has been a process of "hitting the mark by a fluke".

(i) The 1981 Rectification Policy and the 1989-90 Austerity Policy

In the late 1970s and the early 1980s, China faced two tasks: reforming an irrational economic system as well as rectifying a distorted economic structure. From the policy agenda point of view, these two tasks were assumed to be conflicting in the short run. So the problem was that in the first stage of reform which should be given a higher priority, reform or rectification?[35] In 1980, the government decided to delay reform during two

---

35 At the beginning, economists were divided into two groups. One group argued that the irrational structure was caused by the irrational system, reform was the only effective way to solve the structural problems and therefore priority should be given to reform. The other group argued that although introducing market elements was in line with the reform, a precondition for markets to function is a "buyer market"; reform may make worse when the serious structural problems were not solved first; and therefore in the first stage, the policy should "concentrate on rectification and delay reform" (*zhong tiaozheng huan gaige*). After a year's debate, the consensus emerged among economists. That is, in the first stage of reform, priority should be given to the rectification and the reform should serve the rectification; the overall reform should begin only after major structural problems were solved. See Liu (1982) and Wu (1985).

years of rectification. However, from the point of view of consequences, the reform was not actually delayed by the rectification. On the contrary, the first big market expansion of industrial production in the 1980s was a consequence of the rectification policy. When the government shifted priority of planned resource allocation from heavy industry to light industry, excess supplies were created in both heavy and light industries. In heavy industry, even such materials as steel products became over-supplied, and the machinery sector was particularly hurt because many planned orders were cancelled; in light industry, traditional consumer goods such as watches and sewing machines were also overproduced after being in chronic shortage. The excess supplies generated the strong pressure for price reductions and competition. At the beginning the government tried to control the situation by using planning mechanisms including price adjustments and limiting production. But the problem was so serious that the government eventually gave up: for many enterprises, finding markets for their products became the only way to survive. Thus the rectification policy created the first industrial products markets. The watch industry is a good example. As Byrd and Tidrick (1984) recorded, from 1980 to 1983, the government reduced official watch prices three times; the total reduction was more than 20% of the original prices. Nevertheless, the producers still produced far more than the production limitation issued by the planning authority. Commercial agencies accepted only those watches which were easy to sell at planned prices. The producers had to mobilise their workers to sell the rest on the street at, of course, market prices. The planning prices for watches gradually disappeared. It is worth noting that the rectification created not only consumer good markets but also producer goods markets. Most people might be surprised by that as early as in 1980 direct sales outside the state plan accounted for 46% of total sale by enterprises under the First Ministry of Machinery Industry and 33% of sale by all machinery producers (Byrd, 1987). Although the planning prices were not officially abolished, most machinery products were in fact sold at market prices by 1983.

The 1989-1991 austerity policy is another example to show how the consequences of a policy might be so different from its original purpose. Economists had no consensus in the 1989-90 austerity policy - partly because the policy was initiated and implemented by "conservatives". For many economists, the policy was the biggest reversal of the reform process. One of major purposes of the policy was to crack down township and village enterprises (TVEs) and to increase the dominance of state-enterprises in the economy. At the beginning, the policy seems to have followed its makers' will. Many TVEs went bankrupt. From 1988 to 1990, the total number of township enterprises fell by 377,600, and employment fell by 2.8 million (*Statistical Yearbook of China*, 1991, p. 395 and p. 377). However, the situation soon showed that the policy hurt the state-owned enterprises much harder than TVEs, although few state enterprises went bankrupt. From 1988 to 1990, the total after-tax profit of the state industrial sector decreased by 56.5%; the total loss increased 3.3 times; the proportion of loss-makers in all state-owned enterprises increased from 10.9% to 27.6% (*People's Daily*, November 25, 1991). In the first half of 1990, the total industrial output grew by 0.9%, while the state industrial sector's growth rate was negative. By the end of 1991, the total output value of TVEs accounted for 30.83% of total industrial output value (Fan, 1993a) in comparison with 24% in 1988. More importantly, after three years of the austerity policy, TVEs for the first time obtained its real legitimacy ("birth certificate") in mind of the central government.

(ii) Budgetary contracting system between adjacent levels of government

The budgetary contracting system was first introduced in 1980, renewed in 1984 with some modifications, and fully institutionalised in 1988 (Tang, 1990). Under such a system, lower level governments have an obligation to hand over a fixed amount or fixed proportions of their revenues to high level governments and keep all the remaining for themselves, and it is no longer possible to make arbitrary transfer of the residual between different levels and different governments at the same level. The system has been heavily attacked by many leading reform-minded Chinese economists because "it promoted regional protectionism, segmented the integrated market, and increased local governments' administrative interventions into enterprises".[36] In fact, the system was first introduced partly to stabilise the central government's budget revenue rather than to reform the economy (in the sense of marketisation) (Shi, 1993). However, analysis shows that this policy might have been the most important single contributor to marketisation of the Chinese economy in the 1980s.

First, this system actually splits up the whole Chinese economy into many small or mini-public economies. It is equivalent to delimiting the property rights between different levels of government such that each local community becomes a "conglomerate" and each level of government becomes the real residual claimant of its own public economy (Shi, 1993). As Zhang (1993) argued, such a splitting-up improves both monitoring incentives and work incentives of local bureaucrats and the firms in their localities. Because local governments are much closer to their "agents", firms face more pressure to deliver the residual to the local governments. Furthermore, local governments

---

36 See Wu and Liu (1991). Professor Wu was a leading critic of the budgetary contracting system; for him, the system was anti-reform.

cannot finance their spending by printing money, their budget constraint is much harder than the central government's constraint. It is the budgetary contracting system that has boosted the fast development of TVEs, which now are the major engines of economic growth in China.

Second, the system has forced local governments to compete with each other in markets and helped to marketise the whole economy. Although a local government may still use planning mechanism to control its own enterprises, it can only do businesses with other local governments by bargaining. The bargaining process between different local governments made the central planning system more and more difficult to operate, and eventually forced the planning system to evolve into a dual-track system which is now converging to a single market system.[37] The critics seem to have underestimated the force of the principles of the market mechanism: competition and the survival of the fittest. As the size of each community becomes small and the number of the communities becomes large, competition becomes more intense. Because the competitiveness of each public economy depends on its efficiency compared to its counterparts, this eventually forces the local government to grant more autonomy to its firms (if we believe that assigning the decision rights to the firms is more efficient).[38]

---

37 When the official prices were not at equilibrium level but could not be violated, local governments created a "bundling system" to bypass them. The operation of the bundling system can be explained as follows. Suppose the official price of one tonne of steel is 600 Yuans and its market price is 1000 Yuans; the official and market prices of a bicycle are 100 Yuans and 200 Yuans respectively. Liaoning Province supplies steel and demand bicycles, while Shanghai supplies bicycles and demand steel. Then when Shanghai buys 100 tonnes of steel, it must sell 400 bicycles to Liaoning. Both steel and bicycles are paid the official prices. By doing so, they both obey the official prices, but the transaction is dealt with at market prices. Note this system is different from barter system. How many bicycles are needed for one tonne of steel depends on the ratio of the market-official price gap of steel to that of bicycles, rather than the ratio of their market prices. For example, if the official price of a bicycle is raised to 150 Yuans, Shanghai must sell 800 bicycles to buy 100 tons of steel.

38 This can be formally modelled as a Nash-Cournot game. See footnote 60 of Zhang (1993).

The competition mechanism also works *vertically*. For example, when the
provincial government-controlled firms are challenged by the more efficient
TVEs, the provincial government has to make constructive responses, if it still
wants to get some revenue from its firms. Truly, all government bureaucrats
are greedy for rent and they resist giving up their power if possible. But
without monopoly, their rent can only be guaranteed by improving the
efficiency of the firms (to a great extent depending on overall competition).
Protection may work for a short time. but anti-protection forces are also
powerful. The more efficient firms and more efficient regions are always
trying to knock at the door and to break the barriers of their neighbours. Local
protection also have direct contributions to the marketisation of the whole
economy in the sense that they forced those firms and regions who had been
protected for a long time by the central government with under-priced raw
material supplies to go to the market.[39] Having 30 planned economies is of
course not the goal of the reform. But, we are sure that if the Chinese
economy were split into 2,181 or 55,800 mini-planned economies,[40] each of
them would soon either evolve into a private economy or die, and the whole
Chinese economy would be an integrated market economy based on private
property rights.

---

39   A commonly cited example against the fiscal revenue contracting system is that when this
     system was introduced, the less efficient provinces (like Inner Mongolia) discontinued
     supplying raw materials to the more efficient provinces (like Shanghai) and instead built their
     own manufacturers to process raw materials. This argument seems anti-economic. If Shanghai
     is more efficient in processing than Inner Mongolia, it should be able to pay higher prices. It
     would be foolish for Inner Mongolia to refuse a price offer which can bring a residual more
     than that by self-processing. If Shanghai cannot offer a higher price because its residual is
     claimed by the central government, this calls for the central government to make a revenue
     contract with Shanghai rather than to abolish the contract with Inner Mongolia. (Note:
     Shanghai was one of three municipalities to whom the revenue contracting systems were not
     applied in 1980).
40   China has 30 provinces, 2,181 counties and 55,800 towns (xian).

(iii)   *The lag of the state-owned enterprise reform*

The state-owned enterprise reform has been the focus of China's economic reforms. It has exhausted most of reformers' energy and intelligence. Although the overall performance of the state enterprises has been greatly improved through various reform measures (including expansion of autonomy, profit retention and contracting responsibility system),[41] the achievements are far away from desired. In comparing the achievements with the effort made by the government, many economists would like to argue that the state-owned enterprise reform has been a failure. After 15 years of reform, the government has not yet found an effective system for the state-owned enterprises.[42] However, if one views the state-owned enterprise reform in the context of the whole economic reform process, one may find that the lag of the state-owned enterprise reform might not be a bad thing as many assumed. Wei and Lian (1993) find that the development of the non-state sector is negatively dependent on the reform of the state sector in the initial stage of reform. We argue that the state sector's main contribution to the reform is that it has provided a "social security service" for the reform program. First, under the traditional planning system, the enterprise is not only a job-provider but also an insurer for workers. Doing business in the market is risky since business may be a failure. To induce an individual worker to leave a state enterprise to find a job in the market or setting up his own business, some premium must be paid. The Chinese experience shows that "unpaid leave" with the state enterprise can greatly reduce an individual worker's risk in moving into the market since his *status quo* is not affected. Second, the existence of the unreformed state sector can also reduce labour costs for the

41   For empirical studies on performance of the state enterprises, see Jefferson and Xu (1991) and Hay et al. (1994), among others; for a theoretical analysis, see Zhang (1994).
42   More recently the government has chosen to "corporatise" the state-owned enterprises.

non-state sector, which surely promotes the latter's development. The full labour cost of an employee must include daily life expenses as well as housing, medical insurance and so on. When an individual working with a non-state enterprise (e.g. a joint venture) can stay in a flat provided by his previous state employer or his family member's employer, the non-state employer needs only pay his daily life cost which is much lower than the full labour cost. This is exactly the situation in China where, because the joint-ventures do not need to provide housing as the state sector does, they can afford to pay higher nominal wages to attract high-quality employees. This is a kind of "implicit privatisation" in the sense that the state sector subsidises the private sector. If one thinks that privatisation is a right direction of the reform, he should be happy with this "implicit privatisation". Third, at macro-level, a mass privatisation or allowing the state sector to fire redundant workers would create massive unemployment. Although this might be justified by economic efficiency, it incurs too much political and social cost. Keeping unemployment within the state sector can provide much more favourable political and social conditions for the non-state sector to expand and for the whole economic reform to go smoothly.[43] In comparison to a market economy where the social insurance accounts for a significant proportion of the GNP, China's state-owned enterprises' losses may be not so high as many assumed. This does not mean that the state-owned enterprise reform should be postponed indefinitely. Rather, we argue that privatisation of the state sector is always necessary but would be more feasible and smooth after a large non-state sector has emerged.

---

43 In addition, domestic private enterprises and TVEs are disadvantaged in financing, technology, and labour skill when they start their businesses, partly because of the government's discriminatory policies. Their only advantage is freedom. Lag of the state sector reform may strengthen their competitiveness in markets.

(iv)   The development of township and village enterprises (TVEs)

The contributions of TVEs to both economic growth and marketisation have been widely appreciated today (Qian and Xu, 1993; Chen et al., 1992). What we like to emphasise is that TVEs' far reaching impacts on the reform process were hardly recognised until the late 1980s. Development of TVEs were initially promoted by local governments partly for absorbing the surplus labour force released from the rural sector. At the beginning, the central government accommodated this development only as a complement to the state sector and never encouraged it. Even many reform-minded economists were very critical of TVEs because of "their small scale, high consumption of energy and materials and pollution of environment".[44] As TVEs sector became a threat to the state sector, the central government tried to crack down on it. But it was too late to do so. As we have pointed out, it is until very recently that TVEs obtained real legitimacy with the central government. The failure of crack-down of TVEs by the 1989-90 austerity policy was mainly attributed to the local governments' resistance as well as to TVEs' efficiency.

(v) High growth of economy

The relationship between economic growth and economic reform during the reform period has been a hot topic among Chinese economists. The dominant argument in the 1980s was that during the reform period, the growth rate

---

44   Wu and Zhao (1988) wrote: "Undeniable, the development of a large number of township enterprises serves some purposes: increasing production, creating jobs for the rural population, and supplementing the output of state-run enterprises. But it is also evident that they are competing with the big enterprises for raw materials and energy. Therefore, one should not be surprised to see that occasionally the most well-equipped rolling mills or steel mills stand idle, while energy-consuming small township mills continue to produce, at much higher cost, simply because they have succeeded in obtaining raw materials and energy supplies". (p. 315-6)

should be set lower so as to create a "good environment" for reforms, since the high growth would inevitably generate inflationary pressure, which would make it impossible to implement reform policies (Wu, 1985). This argument shares the same spirit with the big bang advocators' argument for stabilisation. It was also occasionally supported by practice. However, Chinese experiences show that fast economic growth *per se* might facilitate rather than obstruct reforms. The reason is that marketising a growing economy is much easier than marketising a stagnant economy, given rigidity of economic relationships. As Wang (1993) argued, China's dual track system has been converging to a market track mainly because of expansion of the market track resulted in economic growth rather than because of shrinking of the planning track in absolute volume. For example, although the total volume of centrally allocated steel increased by 14.9% from 1979 to 1988, because the total steel supply increased by 89.25%, the ratio of centrally allocated steel to total steel dropped from 77% in 1979 to 46.8% in 1988. (Theoretically, as long as the market track grows faster than the plan track, the dual-track system will eventually converge to a market economy.) Similarly, fast expansion of the non-state sector has also resulted from high economic growth rather than the decrease of the state sector. From 1978 to 1990, the gross industrial output increased by 195%, while that of the state sector by 142% and the collective sector by 617%; as a result, the share of the state sector was reduced from 77.63% to 54.60%. In some sense, the Chinese economy has "grown" out of plan and "grown" out of public ownership. Growth itself is a vehicle for reform.

(vi)   *Corruption*

One of the major consequences of economic reform is that it has made corruption easier, and led to pervasive agency discretion, since as the industrial bureaucrats and management possess more autonomy and the economy is more commercialised, it is more difficult to have judicial and administrative checks on their behaviour. Corruption is widely regarded as a malignant tumour of the reform. Many people criticised the dual-track system partly because of its contribution to corruption. However, the following arguments show that corruption might have helped the economy in various ways,[45] apart from mitigating bureaucrats' resistance to the reform, although it has obvious negative effects.

a) Corruption has directly improved incentive systems for both bureaucrats and managers by giving them more freedom to enjoy rents "illegally". To a great extent how much perks or more generally how much personal benefit one can enjoy depends on how much profits one can make. As a result, the correlation between the performance and personal payoff is much stronger than official statistics shows. Not surprising, even bureaucrats have become quite profit-oriented in making their decisions.

b) Corruption does not only improve the incentives for bureaucrats and managers to monitor or to work, but also improves the efficiency of resource allocation. There are two reasons for this. First, now it is less necessary for them to combine personal enjoyment of rents with resource allocation as it was in the old system: they can first make a pie and then eat the pie. Secondly, when a bureaucrat in charge of resource allocation cannot take any bribes, he cares little about where the resources go; however, when he can take bribes, he cares about who can offer the highest bribe. On average those who can offer the highest bribe must be the most efficient. It is through bribing that so-called township and village enterprises got most of their resources (physical and

---

45   For a complete analysis, see Zhang (1993).

financial) out of the planned sectors (this is true specially in the
early stage of the reform).

c) Corruption has helped in hardening the budget constraint of the
   state-owned enterprises. The soft budget constraint has been
   argued as a major reason for inefficiency of the public economy.
   But the budget can be soft only if the central agent can make
   arbitrary transfer of profit between profit-makers and loss-
   makers. After deregulation, the central agent's ability to
   redistribute profits has been greatly reduced by the profit-maker's
   ability to manipulate accounting. Although the loss-makers may
   not need to go bankrupt, they find it more and more difficult to
   get subsidies from the government. This puts pressure on all firms
   to improve efficiency.

5. SUMMARY

The Chinese evolutionary reform itself demonstrates how powerful the
"invisible hand" is in creating institutions. We expect that the process will
continue with its own logic. There is a clear lesson economists can draw from
the Chinese experience. Marketisation of a planning economy is an
evolutionary process with interactions between all self-interested agents.
Although Social elites might be able to design a planning economy, nobody
can design a market economy. The reason is that, by its nature, the market
economy is created by all involved people (including politicians) through
their self-interested activities under governance of an invisible hand. The
Chinese leaders did not intend to bring a market economy to China when they
launched their reform program. Instead, their purpose was just to "perfect" the
existing public ownership-based planned economy by improving people's
incentives. However, the reform creates its own path to a market economy.

Policies encourage and tolerate people's self-interested actions also encourage and tolerate people to make institutional innovations. When peasants, workers and bureaucrats are allowed to pursue their self-interests, the defects of the old system are revealed, demands for further changes are created, and new institutions will emerge sooner or later. The distinction between a good economic system and a bad economic system is not that in a good system there are no thefts and in a bad system there are thefts, rather, that in a good system people have freedom and incentives to protect their assets from being stolen but in a bad system they do not have such freedom and incentives.

REFERENCES

Byrd, William A. (1988) "Impact of the two-tier plan/market system in Chinese industry", *Journal of Comparative Economics*, 11(3): 295-308.

Byrd, William A. and Tidrick, Gene (1984) "Adjustment and Reform in the Chongqing Clock and Watch Industry", *World Bank Staffing Working Paper*, No. 652.

Chen, Kang (1992) "Crossing the River while Groping for Planned Stones: A Public-Choice Analysis of China's Economic Reform", mimeo.

Chen, Kang, G. Jefferson and I. Singh (1992) "Lessons from China's Economic Reform", *Journal of Comparative Economics*, 6(2): 201-225.

Chen, Yizi (1990) "Origins of Economic Reforms, Outcomes of the Democracy Movement, and Prospects of China's Politics", in Jia Hao (ed) *The Democracy Movement of 1989 and China's Future*, The Washington Centre for China Studies, Washington, D.C.

Dewatripoint, M. and G. Roland (1992a) "The Virtues of Gradualism and Legitimacy in the Transition to a Market Economy", *The Economic Journal*, 102: 291-300.

Dewatripoint, M. and G. Roland (1992b) "Economic Reform and Dynamic Political Constraints", *Review of Economic Studies*.

Diao, Xinshen (1989) "An Analysis on China's Dual-Track Economy, in Chinese, *China: Development and Reform*, (2): 12-20.

Dong, Furen (1979) "On Forms of China's Socialist Ownership", *Journal of Economic Research*, (1).

Fan, Gang (1993a) "Two Reform Costs and Two Reform Approaches", in Chinese, *Journal of Economic Research*, (1): 3-15.

Fan, Gang (1993b) "Dual-Track Transition: China's Incremental Approach to Market-Oriented Reform", mimeo.

Gao, Shangquan (1991) *China's Economic Reform*, in Chinese, People's Press, Beijing.

Gelb, Alan, Gary Jefferson and Inderjit Singh (1993) "Can Communist Economies Transform Incrementally? The Experience of China", *NBER Macroeconomics Annual*, 87-133.

Guo, Shuqing, Jinrui Liu and Shufan Qiu (1985) "Comprehensive Economic Reform and Integrated Design", *People's Daily*, September 9, 1985.

Hay, Donald, D. Morris, G.S. Liu, and S. Yao (1993) *Economic Reform and State-Owned Enterprises in China: 1979-1987*, Oxford University Press, Oxford.

Jefferson, Gary and Inderjit Singh (1993) "China's State-Owned Industrial Enterprises: How Effective Have the Reforms Been?", Brandeise University and World Bank.

Jefferson, Gary and Wenyi Xu (1991) "The Impact of Reform on Socialist Enterprises in Transition: Structure, Conduct and Performance in Chinese Industry", *Journal of Comparative Economics*, 15(1): 22-44.

Kornai, Janos (1990) *Vision and Reality, Market and State - Contradictions and Dilemmas Revisited*, Corvina Books, Budapest.

Liu, Guoguang (1982) *On Economic Reform and Economic Adjustment*, in Chinese, Jiansu People's Press.

Liu Shijin (1993) "Transition to Market Economy in China: the Course of Actions and the Public Choice", Institute of Industrial Economics, CASS, Beijing, mimeo.

McMillan, John and Barry Naughton (1992) "How to Reform Planned Economy: Lessons from China", *Oxford Review of Economic Policy*.

McMillan, John and Barry Naughton (1993) "Evaluating the Dual-Track System", mimeo.

Murphy, Kevin M., Andrei Shleifer and Robert Vishny (1992) "The Transition to a Market Economy: Pitfalls of Partial Reform", *The Quarterly Journal of Economics*, August, pp. 889-906.

Murrell, Peter (1991) "Public Choice and the Transformation of Socialism", *Journal of Comparative Economics*, 15: 203-210.

Murrell, Peter and Mancure Olson (1991) "The Devolution of Centrally Planned Economies", *Journal of Comparative Economics*, 15: 239-265.

Murrell, Peter and Y. Wang (1993) "When Privatization Should be Delayed: The Effect of Communism Legacies on Organizational and Institutional Reforms", *Journal of Comparative Economics*, Vol. 17.

Newbery, David (1991) "Sequencing the transition", CEPR Discussion Paper, No. 575.

Nolan, Peter "Reforming Stalinist System: Chinese Experience", Faculty of Politics and Economics, University of Cambridge, unpublished paper.

Perkins, Dwight (1988) "Reforming China's Economic Reform", *Journal of Economic Literature*, 26: 601-645.

Perkins, Dwight (1992) "China's 'Gradual' Approach to Market Reforms", paper presented at the Conference "Comparative Experiences of Economic Reform and Post-Socialist Transformation", El Escorial, Spain.

Qian, Yingyi and Chenggang Xu (1992) "Why China's Economic Reforms Differ: The M-Form Hierarchy and Entry/Expansion of the Non-State Sector", *The Economics of Transition*, 1(2): 135-170.

Sachs, Jeffrey and Wing Thye Woo (1993) "Structural Factors in the Economic Reforms of China, Eastern Europe and the Former Soviet Union", mimeo.

Shanren (1987) "China's Economic Reform and Chinese Economists", *Intellectuals*, Winter Volume, USA.

Shi, Xiaomin and Liu Jirui (1989) "Economists Must Primarily Esteem History and Facts", in Chinese, *Journal of Economic Research*, (3): 11-33.

Shi, Z. Jeffrey (1993) "Reform for Decentralisation and Decentralisation for Reform: a Political Economy of China's Reform", mimeo.

Tang, Minfeng (1990) *Ten Years' Reform*, in Chinese, Beijing Press, Beijing.

Tian, Jiyun (1985) "Actively Doing a Good Job in the Price System Reform", *People's Daily*, 28 January 1985.

Wang, Xiaoqiang (1993) "Groping for Stones to Cross the River: Chinese Price Reform Against 'Big Bang'", Discussion Papers No. DPET 9305, Department of Applied Economics, University of Cambridge.

Wang, Zhigang (1993) "Gradualism versus Big Bang: An Economic Perspective", mimeo, presented at the ASSA-CES Joint Session of ASSA Meetings, 3-5 January 1994, Boston.

Wei, Shangjin (1992) "Gradualism versus Speed and Sustainability of Reforms", mimeo.

Wei, Shangjin and Peng Lian (1993) "Love and Hate: State and Non-State Firms in Transition Economy", mimeo.

Wu, Jinglian (1985) "On Development Strategy and Macro-control during the Initial Stage of Reforms", *People's Daily*, 12 February 1985, p. 3.

Wu, Jinglian and Liu, Jirui (1992) *On Competitive Market System*, in Chinese, Financial and Economic Press, Beijing.

Wu, Jinglian and Zhao, Renwei (1987) "The Dual pricing system in China", *Journal of Political Economy*, 11(3): 209-318.

Wu, Jinglian and Zhou Xiaochuan (1988) *The Integrated Design of China's Economic Reform*, in Chinese, Zhanwang Press, Beijing.

Yi, Gang (1990) "The Price Reform and Inflation in China, 1979-1988", *Comparative Economic Studies*, Winter, pp. 28-61.

Yi, Gang (1994) *Money, Banking and Financial Markets in China*, Westview Press.

Zhang, Weiying (1984) "The Way out of the Price Reform is Liberalising Price Control", *China: Development and Reform: 1984-1985*, Qiushi Press, Beijing, pp. 500-508.

Zhang, Weiying (1994) "Decision Rights, Residual Claim and Performance: A Theory of How Chinese Economy Works", Nuffield College, Oxford, mimeo.

Zou, Gang (1993) "Modelling the Enterprises Behaviour under the Two-Tier Plan/Market System in the PRC", University of Southern California.

| CHAPTER 3 |

CHINA AND VIETNAM IN TRANSITION: A COMPARATIVE ANALYSIS OF ECONOMIC REFORMS AND THEIR OUTCOMES

CHARLES HARVIE[1]

ABSTRACT

The economies of China and Vietnam have undergone major economic reforms and developments during the period of the 1980s to the present, with each striving towards the attainment of a market economy while maintaining the "socialist" nature of their economies. Unlike developments in Europe where a number of formerly centrally planned countries adopted a "big bang" transition approach to a market economy from the outset, in China, and initially in Vietnam, the transition process has been a much more gradual one with overriding political power still residing with their respective Communist Parties.

The process of economic reform in Vietnam and China contains a number of parallels. Starting in 1978 China's economic reforms proceeded through

---

1   Department of Economics, University of Wollongong, Wollongong, NSW 2522

four phases (1978-84 (initial phase), 1984-88 (expansionary phase), 1988-91 (retrenchment phase), and 1992 to the present (socialist market economy phase)) with each characterised by a gradual pragmatic approach to economic reform, culminating in October 1992 with the acceptance that the market system was not incompatible with the ideals of socialism and the advocacy thereafter of the need to establish a socialist market economy.

In Vietnam a similar gradual and pragmatic approach to economic reform was initially adopted. Early piecemeal reforms over the period 1979-85 led to more extensive but still gradual economic reforms during the period of "doi moi" (economic renovation) 1986-89. The early success of doi moi, but more importantly the country's pressing external difficulties in the late 1980s, resulted in more comprehensive reforms being implemented over the period 1989-92 which were more akin to a big bang approach, with the objective of moving as quickly as possible towards a market economy. Since 1992 the country has attained many benefits, but a number of weaknesses still remain. The primary objectives of this chapter are, firstly, to conduct a comparative analysis of the transition process to more market oriented economies for China and Vietnam, identifying and contrasting the major reform measures adopted in both.

Secondly, to conduct a comparative analysis, and appraisal, of the performance of these economies with regard to developments in key macroeconomic variables during their respective transition periods. Thirdly to identify key differences and similarities in their respective reforms and outcomes, which could provide valuable policy lessons for each other.

1. INTRODUCTION

The economies of China and Vietnam have undergone major economic reforms and developments during the period of the 1980s to the present as each strives towards the attainment of a market economy, while maintaining the "socialist" character of their respective economies. Unlike developments in Europe where a number of formerly centrally planned countries adopted a "big bang" transition approach to a market economy, in China and, at least initially, Vietnam the transition process has been a much more gradual one with overriding political power still residing with their respective Communist Parties. However both countries have experienced considerable decentralisation of economic power, which has resulted in substantial difficulties for the centre in regard to macroeconomic management.

The process of economic reform in Vietnam and China contains a number of similarities. Starting in 1978 China's economic reforms proceeded through four phases (1978-84 (initial phase), 1984-88 (expansionary phase), 1988-91 (retrenchment phase), and 1992 to the present (socialist market economy phase)) with each characterised by a pragmatic approach to economic reform, culminating in October 1992 with the acceptance that the market system was not incompatible with the ideals of socialism and the advocacy thereafter of the need to establish a socialist market economy.

In Vietnam initially a similar gradual and pragmatic approach to economic reform was adopted. Early piecemeal reforms over the period 1979-85 led to more extensive economic reforms during the period of "doi moi" (economic renovation) from 1986-89. The early success of these reforms but more importantly pressure in the form of external factors, spurring the pace of economic reform in the late 1980s, was intense, with the demise of the Council for Mutual Economic Assistance (CMEA) trading arrangements[2] and the substantial reduction in foreign assistance from an increasingly constrained benefactor in the form of the former Soviet Union. Such difficulties led to the implementation of much more comprehensive reforms being implemented over the period 1989-92 with the objective of moving rapidly towards a market economy, and was more akin to a big bang approach. The extent of the evolution toward a market economy in Vietnam was encapsulated in the constitution of the country being amended in 1992, to

---

2   The CMEA was formally wound up on 1 January 1991.

give explicit rights to the private sector including rights against nationalisation.

Economic developments in China and Vietnam have been quite contrasting during their respective reform periods. While China has experienced, with the exception of 1989 and 1990, very rapid rates of growth of real GDP, Vietnam experienced low and sometimes negative rates of growth of GDP until the middle of the 1980s. More recently, however, Vietnam has seen a significant improvement in its growth rates although they are still noticeably below that for China. In terms of inflation a similar picture emerges, with China achieving much lower, and in some years considerably lower, rates of inflation.

The primary objectives of this chapter are, firstly, to conduct a comparative analysis of the transition process to more market oriented economies for China and Vietnam, identifying and contrasting the major reform measures adopted in both. Secondly, to conduct a comparative analysis, and appraisal, of the performance of these economies with regard to developments in key macroeconomic variables during their respective transition periods. Finally to identify issues of commonality and divergence in each country's respective transition process, and the lessons which can be learned from the experiences of the other.

2. A COMPARISON OF THE RESPECTIVE REFORM PROGRAMS OF VIETNAM AND CHINA

Vietnam's Economic Reforms

In April 1975 communist controlled North Vietnam took control of Saigon, leading to the fall of the government of South Vietnam. The nation was officially reunified in January 1976, and in July of the same year the Socialist Republic of Vietnam was established. The reunification of the North with the South brought together two very different economic systems. The North with a state socialist centralised economic system, and that of the South with its decentralised market economic system. Initially, during the Second Five Year Plan (1976-80), the communist government attempted to impose the northern model on the South (the so called "transition to socialism") - collectivisation of agriculture, nationalisation of industries, state monopoly over trade etc., however as early as 1977 it was becoming apparent that such a strategy was not working. Declining agriculture production in 1977 and 1978, indicative of a general deterioration of the economy, prompted the first steps towards reform which were initiated by the Sixth Plenum of the Central Committee in September 1979. This resulted in a number of piecemeal reform measures thereafter and over the course of the Third Five Year Plan (1981-85). The reform measures included giving private enterprise, predominantly based in the South, greater autonomy from the state, collectivisation of agriculture, subject to resistance in the South, was suspended, the introduction of a contract system giving households more freedom to sell their excess production in the open market, and finally individual households were allowed to cultivate land not in use by the cooperatives.

Economic Reform Under "Doi moi" or Renovation (1986-89)

At the Sixth National Congress in December 1986 the government introduced, against a background of hyper-inflation, food shortages and structural imbalances in the economy, a comprehensive reform program, with the objective of liberalising and deregulating the economy. The reform measures explicitly recognised the failure of central planning and marked a major turning point in the economic development of the economy. The objectives of the reforms were:

1. to develop the private sector
2. to increase and stabilise agricultural output
3. to shift the focus of investment from heavy to light industry
4. to reduce the role of the state enterprises

5. to focus upon export led growth, based upon the experience of Vietnam's dynamic regional neighbours
6. to attract foreign direct investment, seen as essential for economic development.

After 1987 a number of the far reaching reforms were implemented, and this process was accelerated from 1989 onwards and into the 1990s, and included the following:

a. *Rural reforms* - the collective agricultural system was largely dismantled, with the focus on family farming on the basis of long term leases.

b. *Price liberalisation* - virtually all price controls were removed with the exception of fuel, electricity, transport and postal services.

c. *Devaluation* - the exchange rate was unified and sharply devalued. Foreign exchange trading floors were created which enabled the exchange rate to be largely determined by the market.

d. *Interest rate reforms* - interest rates were raised to very high levels, with the objective of achieving real rates positive, as part of the fight against inflation. After some initial success in reducing inflation in 1989, real rates of interest were allowed to become negative again and in 1990 and 1991 inflation returned. Since 1992 real interest rates have primarily remained positive, contributing to the sizeable decline in inflation thereafter.

e. *Fiscal reforms* - the government implemented measures to reduce the growth of public expenditure, including the demobilisation of the military (500,000 soldiers in total have been released) and the elimination of direct subsidies to state owned enterprises. Tax reform, in addition to the fortuitous revenue from petroleum operations, enabled the government to increase its revenues.

f. *State enterprise reforms* - included the elimination of direct budgetary subsidies from the government, and a further hardening of the budget due to the higher real interest rates which had to be paid for credit as previously identified. State enterprise managers by 1989 were no longer subject to the need to achieve centrally determined production targets, the influence of which had declined significantly since 1986, but had greater autonomy in determining where their output was sold and where input could be obtained from on the basis of market prices.

g. *Promotion of the private sector* - after many years of discrimination the government now actively promoted the development of the private sector, although its contribution to GDP is still small. Laws introduced for companies and private enterprises gave the once informal sector official sanction. This was identified further in the country's new Constitution (in 1992) which clarified the rights of the private sector.

h. *Financial sector reform* - this involved the restructuring of the banks, which dominate the financial system, into a two tier system with the State Bank of Vietnam performing the function of a modern central bank, and the four major state owned commercial banks providing banking facilities. The financial system is being further expanded to include shareholding banks, credit cooperatives and joint venture banks. Foreign banks have been allowed to operate since 1991 and the government is developing a securities market which is planned to be operative in 1996/97.

i. *Legal system reform* - arising from the creation of a market system is the need to develop the institutional structures necessary for its functioning. Of particular importance is the reform, or creation, of a legal framework to provide the framework for the operation of the market system, given the reduced direct involvement of the government. For example the introduction of a foreign investment law (1987), bankruptcy law (1993), environmental law (1993), land law (1993), and most importantly the 1992 Constitution which proclaimed individual rights and guaranteed against the nationalisation of foreign investments.

j. *Openness to direct foreign investment* - the government recognised the importance of direct foreign investment in the process of economic development, and a new investment law, with subsequent revisions, indicated the government's desire to attract such investment.

k. *Foreign trade reform* - this had been the monopoly of the state, but now firms both state and private were to have easier access to imports and more incentives to export. The latter aspect was clearly seen as being important, being based upon the export led growth of its dynamic regional neighbours in East Asia.

l. *Social reform* - the reform program was seen as likely to contribute to a transitional rise in unemployment, and in response to this likelihood the government initiated programs including retraining schemes and soft loans for the small scale private sector.

In essence doi moi has been characterised primarily by its focus upon four key areas in particular - agricultural reform, price liberalisation, state enterprise reform, trade liberalisation, and foreign direct investment liberalisation.

Agricultural reform was regarded as a key constituent due to problems with inconsistent and unpredictable yields. In April 1988 under the guidelines of resolution number 10, farming cooperatives were no longer considered to be the centre of production. Instead, farm households became the essential production unit, with the cooperatives providing farm supplies, storage facilities and marketing arrangements, and compulsory deliveries ceased. Membership of a cooperative became optional, and rights of full land use, inheritance, and transfer were recognised by the state. Long term leases were also extended, from 15-20 years for annual crops and 50 years for longer term crops such as trees. These measures led to an immediate jump in farm output such that after facing near famine conditions in some parts of the country in 1988, Vietnam emerged as the world's third largest rice exporter one year later. These measures were later supplemented by further agricultural reforms.

A second key area for reform was that of trade. Under the centrally planned system, external trade was tightly controlled by the government and it was focused towards that with the Soviet Union and Eastern Europe. All foreign trade transactions had to be channelled through central state trading corporations. Prices were administered by the government and targets were fixed for both imports and exports. Adding to the difficulty of trading was the maintenance of a complex system of multiple exchange rates. To improve the country's trade performance the Dong was devalued in early 1988, narrowing the spread between the official and parallel market rates. In 1989 a new tariff schedule was introduced, while quotas on imports and exports were lowered. The monopoly held by the central state trading corporations was eliminated when provincial and local authorities were allowed to establish competing foreign trade companies.

Complementing the deregulation of trade was the liberalisation of foreign direct investment, another key component of doi moi. New regulations governing foreign investment became effective in January 1988, and are considered to be some of the most liberal in Asia. All sectors of the economy, in principal, are open to foreign investors, although special incentives were attached to investments that promoted exports and generated hard currency earnings. Since the new foreign investment regulations came into effect, Vietnam has approved nearly $9 billion in foreign investment projects. However the number of projects actually carried forward has been considerably less.

The program of renovation began at a time when the economy was in a very weak position. Not only had the country's economic infrastructure been ravaged by 30 years of war, or been allowed to run into a dilapidated state, but agricultural production was stagnant leading in some parts of the country to malnutrition, the economy was facing hyper inflation and people were fleeing the country. While the need to resolve this situation was extremely pressing, such difficulties were further compounded by external developments toward the end of the 1980s and 1990s. With the initial success of the gradual reform measures implemented during the 1986-89 period, the authorities engaged in a much more extensive and full sped ahead stabilisation and reform program from 1989. It is often suggested that the pace of reform in Vietnam was a gradual one and certainly this appears to have been so during the 1986-89 period, however the pace of reform from 1989 to 1991 was anything but gradual. The implementation of further comprehensive reform measures, as well as a stabilisation program, was certainly as ambitious as anything described as "shock therapy" in other countries. The privatising of agriculture, the dominant sector of the economy, decontrolling prices and opening up the economy in a matter of a few years represented a radical reform program While the initial success of the reform measures during 1986-89 were important in this process, this pales into insignificance in comparison to the external difficulties which were emerging in 1989. The fall of numerous Communist governments in Eastern Europe resulted in the loss of both markets and cheap imports, the Soviet indication of its withdrawal of financial assistance (which at its peak amounted to US$1 billion a year), led to the need for Vietnam to radically reorientate its trade towards the convertible currency area in Asia and to seek alternative sources of foreign savings. The success of its dynamic market oriented regional neighbours, including that of China, could also not have gone unnoticed.

China's Economic Reforms

China initiated its reform process in 1978 when the reformist views, led by Deng Xiaoping, became dominant within the party, resulting in the leadership at the Third Plenum of the Central Committee of the Communist Party resolving to focus the party's work on economic development. The economic reforms implemented were not obtained from a comprehensive blueprint, but rather have been firstly introduced on an experimental basis in some localities and if successful then introduced at the national level. Such a pragmatic approach to economic reforms was designed to avoid major disruptions, and to gradually transform the economy from a predominantly centrally planned one to one in which the market mechanism played an important role.

An important ideological issue arising from the reform process was the consistency of a market system with that of socialism. During the initial stages of the reform process, this issue was resolved by the argument that the adoption of markets served a useful supplementary role in the context of a predominantly planned economy. By the mid 1980s the objective of the economic reforms was stated as being the establishment of a "socialist planned commodity economy", that combined both planning with the use of the market mechanism. In October 1992, at the Fourteenth Party Congress, the party adopted the argument advanced by Deng Xiaoping that the market mechanism was merely an instrument of economic development and not a defining characteristic of an economic system. The predominant ownership over the means of production by the public sector (the state and the collectives) would maintain the socialist character of the economy. Hence the market mechanism was viewed as being perfectly compatible with either a capitalist or socialist economic system. The aim of reform was to establish an economic structure in which the market mechanism, under the influence of the state, would determine relative prices and the allocation of resources.

Key Features Of The Chinese Approach To Economic Reform

Some of the key features of the approach of the Chinese to economic reform are as follows:

- the reform process in China can be characterised as being both gradual and incremental.

- the reforms were undertaken first on an experimental basis in chosen localities before being applied, if successful, to the whole country. This gradual approach to reform had several advantages - (a) it avoided major disruptions to the economy, and if the policies turned out to be unsuccessful they could be modified to accommodate national and local conditions (b) by implementing only those policies that were likely to be successful, the leadership was able to build support for the process of further economic reform (c) certain reforms required new institutions, new legal and regulatory frameworks and the training of personnel conversant with the new practices, all of which required time (d) the administrative apparatus of the planning system would continue to be available until a new system could become effective.

- the reform process utilised intermediate mechanisms to enable the transition from one economic system to another to be a smooth as possible, thereby avoiding major disruptions that could arise from an abrupt shift. Specific example of this process include: the dual-track pricing system to improve the allocation of resources at the margin; establishing a swap market in foreign exchange retention rights to improve the use of foreign exchange; establishing open economic zones to introduce foreign capital and technology to the country; using the contract responsibility system to encourage economic agents to behave in a market oriented fashion; and authorising some local governments to enact and experiment with market oriented legislation. Using such intermediate mechanisms was a means of encouraging economic agents to behave in such a way as to be compatible with a market system, prior to the phasing out of central planning.

- the Chinese leadership has attempted to maintain the socialist character of the economy, focusing upon the public ownership of key sectors of the economy. However the authorities have

attempted to sever the close links between the SOE's and the state particularly in the areas of finance and management, with the objective of making them autonomous units responsible for their own profits and losses.
- the reforms have been characterised by a progressive decentralisation of economic decision making both in terms of depth and extensiveness.
- China's partial approach to economic reform has contributed to the economy experiencing "stop-go" periods of macroeconomic instability, arising from the authorities having given up direct control over the economy while indirect instruments have remained ineffective because of the incompleteness of the reforms. Achieving and maintaining macroeconomic stability will remain a major challenge to the authorities, and in the latest phase of reform major initiatives will be taken to establish a more effective system of macroeconomic management.

Phases of Economic Reform (1978-Present)

The process of economic reform in China can be broken down into a number of phases, and covering key areas such as - agriculture, price liberalisation, SOEs, employment, social benefits and housing, the financial sector and foreign trade and investment. The first phase from 1978-84, the second phase from 1984-88, the third phase from 1988-91, the fourth phase from 1992-93 and, as argued here, the most recent phase from 1994 to the present.

First Phase (1978-84)

During this first phase emphasis was placed upon bringing about a recovery of the economy, by overcoming the major obstacles to economic development in the pre-reform era which were: a deep mistrust of the market system; reliance on collective efforts and lack of individual work incentives; emphasis on self reliance bordering on autarky at all levels from the national to the provincial and commune. The reform policies placed emphasis on material incentives and an expanded role for the market. Specifically procurement prices for agricultural products were increased, diversification and specialisation of crops were encouraged, restrictions on rural markets (trade fairs) were relaxed, and with the introduction of the household responsibility system the organisation of farming was decentralised from the collective to the household level. In the industrial sector the bonus system was reintroduced, the retention of depreciation allowance was permitted and the retention of profits by state owned enterprises on an experimental basis began. To encourage exports and the attraction of foreign investment and technology special economic zones were established, and were to be used as laboratories for more radical market orientated reforms.

Second Phase (1984-88)

The success of the rural reforms during the first phase of the reform process encouraged the authorities to expand such reforms to include the urban-industrial sectors in 1984. The major measures adopted included: the establishment of a dual-track pricing system; the introduction of enterprise taxation; the reform of the wage system linking in a closer way remuneration with productivity; and breaking up the monobank system with the objective of creating a central bank.

Enterprises were encouraged to borrow from the banking system for their investment requirements rather than depending upon the state for such funds as in the past. Revenue sharing arrangements between the central and local governments was revised in favour of the latter. Fourteen major cities were "opened up" to encourage foreign trade and investment, including the accumulation of technical know how. Many of these measures were further expanded and revised in 1986 to include: the establishment of swap centres for trading in retained foreign exchange earnings; decentralising trade through the establishment of local foreign trade corporations; and the adoption of a contract responsibility system for state owned enterprises similar to that adopted for the agricultural sector.

Third Phase (1988-91)

The success of the earlier reforms contributed to rising demand and production but also contributed to a sharp increase in inflation. Plans for a new round of price reforms were postponed and in fact some of the previous price reform was reversed with increased re-centralisation of price controls under a "rectification program", in conjunction with other strong measures designed to reduce the inflationary pressures within the economy. The country entered a period from mid 1988 to 1991 of retrenchment, in which further reform measures were delayed. While the retrenchment measures were successful in reducing the inflationary pressures, they contributed to a major reduction in the growth of the economy. This was felt particularly strongly in the industrial sector where SOEs experienced increased losses, a substantial increase in inter-enterprise debt and a sharp increase in stock levels. Such developments were contributing to a major economic crisis, resulting in late 1990 with the authorities deciding to stimulate the economy using monetary and investment policies. This contributed to a recovery of the economy in 1991. Generally stable prices during this period encouraged the authorities to make substantial realignments in relative prices and liberalise certain other prices.

Fourth Phase (1992-1993)

By early 1992 the authorities had declared an end to the rectification program, announcing their intention to further accelerate the reform process and the opening up of the economy. This message became clear during Deng Xiaoping's tour of the prosperous coastal cities at this time, when he called upon the whole country to accelerate growth and accelerate the policy of reforming and opening up the whole economy. He prepared the ideological groundwork for the adoption of a more comprehensive reform strategy aimed at transforming the Chinese economy to a fully market based system, by announcing that the market mechanism was a tool for economic development and was consistent with socialism. At the Fourteenth National Congress of the Chinese Communist Party in October 1992 his views were formally endorsed setting the establishment of a "socialist market economy" as the national goal. This goal was later included in the country's constitution during the first session of the Eighth National People's Congress in March 1993. A new reform strategy was later adopted during the Third Plenum of the Fourteenth Central Committee in November 1993.

Fifth Phase (1994-2000)

By 1994 China had entered a new phase of economic reforms aimed at overcoming the legacies remaining from the period of partial reform. The objective was to achieve by the year 2000 a "socialist market economy", where the market mechanism would play the primary role in the allocation of resources while public ownership (including in the form of corporatised enterprises and collectives) would remain at the core of the economy. The reform strategy would require fundamental changes in a broad range of important areas consistent with the development of a market economic system, and the mechanisms for indirect macroeconomic management of it. The latter would require reforms in the areas of the exchange rate and trade system, central banking and the financial system, the tax system and inter-governmental fiscal relations and the investment system. A further crucial area of reform relates to that of the SOEs, and the need to transform these into autonomous, competitive and legal entities with full accountability for profits and losses. In addition there would be a need to fully develop the legal and regulatory system.

The reform measures were therefore to be comprehensive, far reaching and ambitious, with the objective of creating a competitive market environment in all sectors and throughout the country, and providing the basis for sustained growth of the economy.

3. COMPARATIVE MACROECONOMIC PERFORMANCE IN CHINA AND VIETNAM

This section attempts to identify recent macroeconomic developments in China and Vietnam arising from the reform program outlined in the previous section. In doing so emphasis is given to developments in GDP, savings and investment, consumer price inflation, public finance, foreign trade (exports, imports and the current account), foreign direct investment and foreign debt primarily over the period 1989-94.[3]

GDP and Sectoral Growth

The reforms have had a major impact upon both economies. Over the extended period 1980-97 the GDP growth of the Chinese economy has been generally superior to that of Vietnam's, however since 1995 the reverse has been the case (see Table 3.1). Projections by the Asian Development Bank for 1996 and 1997 suggest that China will achieve a real GDP growth rate of 8 and 9% respectively, while Vietnam is projected to achieve growth rates of 9.8 and 9.9% respectively.

In the case of Vietnam there has been a significant improvement in the growth of real GDP from 1989 (see Table 3.1), occurring in conjunction with the comprehensive reform measures adopted at this time. Initially this was primarily due to a substantial increase in output in the agriculture and services sectors (see Table 3.2). These offset a sharp decline in industrial production

---

3   Data availability and reliability for Vietnam prior to 1989 present a number of difficulties for comparison purposes.

arising from: the loss of markets and cheap imported inputs from the CMEA; the elimination of budgetary subsidies to the state owned enterprises; the additional hardening of the budget for them with the imposition of positive real interest rates; and loss of financial assistance from the former Soviet

Table 3.1:Real GDP Growth Rate (%) 1980-97*

Year	China	Vietnam	Year	China	Vietnam
1980	8.6	-3.7	1989	4.2	7.6
1981	4.1	5.1	1990	3.9	5.1
1982	8.1	8.2	1991	8.4	6.0
1983	10.2	7.1	1992	14.3	8.7
1984	14.4	8.4	1993	14.0	8.1
1985	12.9	5.6	1994	12.6	8.8
1986	8.4	3.4	1995	10.2	9.5
1987	11.1	4.0	1996	8.0	9.8
1988	11.3	5.2	1997	9.0	9.9

*   The figures for 1996 and 1997 are projections by the Asian Development Bank.
Sources: World Bank, World Tables, Nguyen and Bandara (1993).

Union. During 1990-91 these external developments, in particular, contri-buted to a downturn in the economy, which was very mild in comparison to the recessions being experienced in Eastern Europe at the time.[4] The growth of industrial production now overtook that of the agriculture and services sectors (see Table 3.2). The period 1992-95 has since seen a rapid pick up in the growth of the economy, with industrial production (manufacturing in particular) leading the way. The growth of services production has also been

---

4   The structure of the Vietnamese economy, the relative importance of agriculture in
      comparison to that of the economies of Eastern Europe, can account for such a difference.

strong, whilst that of agriculture has declined as the impetus from the reforms of the late 1980s has declined.

Table 3.2: Gross Domestic Product: Real Growth by Sector (%)

	1989	1990	1991	1992	1993	1994	Average * 1989-94
CHINA							
Agriculture	3.0	7.3	2.4	4.7	4.0	na	4.3
Industry of	3.8	3.2	13.3	21.8	20.4	na	12.5
which:	4.9	2.1	13.2	21.0	19.1	na	12.1
	6.0	2.1	5.8	9.4	9.8	na	6.6
Manufacturing	4.2	3.9	8.4	14.3	14.0	12.6	9.6
Services							
GDP							
VIETNAM							
Agriculture	7.9	4.9	7.0	7.2	3.8	3.9	5.0
Industry of	-2.8	6.0	9.1	14.0	13.1	14.1	8.7
which:	-4.0	10.7	9.9	14.6	12.1	13.9	9.3
	15.4	5.3	3.3	7.0	9.2	10.1	8.3
Manufacturing	7.5	5.1	6.0	8.7	8.1	8.8	7.4
Services							
GDP							

*   For China, average growth rate from 1989-93.
Sources: World Bank, World Tables, Central Institute for Economic Management, Hanoi.

For China the period from mid 1988 to late 1990 represented a period of retrenchment. The success of the reform phase from 1984-88 increased demand and led to double digit inflation in 1988. The authorities took strong measures to control the overheating economy and this led to a sharp downturn in the economy in 1989-90, as exemplified by declining industrial and services sector output growth. The agriculture sector, however, remained buoyant in 1990. The downturn exacerbated the losses of state owned enterprises, inter-enterprise debt, and accumulated inventories, and threatened macroeconomic stability. In late 1990, to avoid a possible crisis, the authorities used monetary and investment policies to stimulate the economy, resulting in a rapid pick up of the economy in 1992 and 1993 with the industrial sector leading the way.

Over the period 1989-94, in both economies, the major engine for economic growth has been provided by the industrial sector, most obviously so in the case of China, and more specifically manufacturing. The services sector, which had been severely neglected in both economies during the period of central planning, also emerged as an important source of economic growth, and both economies have experienced continually lower growth in the agricultural sector. Such differences in sectoral growth rates account for the changing structure of these respective economies (see Table 3.3). Both countries have experienced a relative decline in the contribution of the agriculture sector, and a relative increase in the contribution of the services sector to GDP. The industrial sector is much more important in China than in Vietnam (where its relative share has actually declined from that of the mid 1980s) contributing about 50% of GDP, while in Vietnam its contribution is only 30%. This is also indicative of the more advanced stage of economic development which the Chinese economy has achieved in comparison to that of the Vietnamese economy.

Table 3.3: Share of GDP and Employment (%)

	CHINA			VIETNAM		
	1985	1990	1994	1985	1990	1994
Share of GDP (%)						
Agriculture	29.8	27.0	17.8	47.2	37.5	27.7
Industry:	45.3	41.6	49.7	34.5	22.7	29.6
Manufacturing	37.2	33.6	39.8	na	18.8	22.0
Services	24.9	31.4	32.5	18.3	39.9	42.7
Share of Employment (%)						
Agriculture	62.4	60.2	56.4	72.3	71.6	72.5
Industry	16.7	17.1	17.4	10.8	11.2	10.7
Mining	0.2	0.2	0.2	-	-	-
Others	20.5	22.5	26.0	16.9	17.2	16.8

Sources: World Bank, Asian Development Bank.

In terms of employment (see Table 3.3), however, the agriculture sector dominates in both countries. In China 56% of the employed workforce is employed in the agriculture sector, in steady decline since the mid 1980s, while in Vietnam some 73% of the workforce is employed in the agriculture sector having barely changed since the mid 1980s. The latter is also indicative of the poor productivity performance in Vietnamese agriculture. The industrial sector accounts for 17% of employment in China compared to 11% in Vietnam, while the services sector accounts for a sizeable 26% of the workforce in China but only 17% in Vietnam. The latter figure again having barely changed from its level in the mid 1980s. Hence in the context of Vietnam the sizeable structural output developments in the economy are not

reflected in terms of employment share by sector, which has remained
remarkably static.

Overall the performance in terms of GDP growth over the period 1989-94
has been impressive for both of these transition countries, and particularly
that of China. China has been able to achieve high growth rates of GDP over a
long period and is clearly at a more advanced stage of economic development.
For Vietnam, the ability to achieve and sustain high growth rates is primarily
a phenomenon of the 1990s.

Saving and Investment

A major contributory factor behind the growth of output is domestic
investment. If both China and Vietnam are to fulfil their ambitious growth
targets of 8% annual growth of real GDP until the end of the century, they
will both require the maintenance of a substantial investment program. The
improving economic climate of recent years has seen large increases in both
domestic and foreign direct investment in Vietnam. In 1988 (see Table 3.4)
total domestic investment accounted for 8.1% of Vietnam's GDP, of which
half occurred through the state budget with foreign direct investment a paltry
0.5% of GDP. Thereafter total investment accrued steadily reaching 22.2% of
GDP in 1994, of which only 6.6% took place through the state budget and the
remainder coming increasingly from the domestic private sector and FDI. FDI
accounted for 6.4% of GDP, a twelve fold increase over the figure in 1988.
For China the primary factor contributing to the very high rates of growth
which the country has achieved has been "investment hunger". The various
phases of reform alluded to in an earlier section has contributed to sizeable
expansions in investment and overheating of the economy. As Table 3.4
indicates China has been investment driven, with gross domestic investment
as a per cent of GDP reaching some 44% in 1994.

Table 3.4: Saving and Investment, % of GDP, 1988-94

	CHINA		VIETNAM	
	GDI*	GDS**	GDI*	GDS**
1988	38.1	37.5	8.1	-2.4
1989	36.8	36.5	9.8	5.0
1990	33.2	37.3	11.4	6.8
1991	32.7	37.0	15.0	10.1
1992	34.4	37.0	17.6	13.8
1993	41.2	40.2	20.5	14.8
1994	43.6	44.2	22.2	16.6

* Gross Domestic Investment
** Gross Domestic Saving
Sources: World Bank, World Tables, Vietnam national sources.

To fund such investment, and hence growth, the need for domestic savings and access to foreign savings becomes imperative. In the case of Vietnam in 1988 domestic savings were negative (see Table 3.4) and domestic investment had to be funded from foreign savings, primarily financial assistance from the Soviet Union. Thereafter, as a result of the confidence engendered by the further reforms from 1989 in terms of recognition of private sector rights, reduced inflation, banking sector reforms and positive real interest rates, domestic savings displayed a remarkable transformation rising steadily from a figure of 5% of GDP in 1989 to 16.6% in 1994. The contribution of foreign savings declined during the period 1989-92, but increased again in 1993 and 1994. For China, as with many other East Asian economies, domestic saving as a percentage of GDP is very high, enabling the substantial amount of domestic investment to be funded primarily from domestic sources. China is clearly in a much stronger position to fund its domestic investment requirements without the need for access to substantial foreign savings. Vietnam, however, will remain for some period of time dependent upon foreign savings in the form of foreign direct investment and overseas development assistance, to fund its desperately needed investment.

Inflation

Consumer price inflation (see Table 3.5) abated considerably in 1989 to 34.7% for Vietnam from 394.0% in 1988 (World Bank), arising from measures to bring monetary growth under control and to stabilise the dong as well as from the increased availability of products. However monetisation of the budget deficit in 1990 further fuelled inflation. The authorities, determined to crack down on this, decided that from 1991 the budget deficit would no longer be monetised. Since then the economy has provided an excellent example of how to successfully reduce hyper inflation, which has declined noticeably and continuously since with the exception of 1994. The economy also achieved a reasonable inflationary outcome in 1995. Despite having achieved more favourable inflation outcomes to that of China since 1993, the economy remains vulnerable to inflationary shocks. As in 1994 when inflation increased mainly due to an increase in food prices arising from the summer floods in the Mekong Delta. But to its credit the government has continued with its policy of not borrowing from the State Bank, despite being faced with inadequate funds to finance its public investment program.

Table 3.5: Consumer Price Inflation (%), 1977-95

YEAR	CHINA	VIETNAM	YEAR	CHINA	VIETNAM
Av. 1977-86	3.4	62.8	1991	2.9	68.1
1987	7.3	316.7	1992	5.4	17.5
1988	18.5	394.0	1993	13.0	5.2
1989	17.8	35.0	1994	24.1	14.4
1990	2.1	67.0	1995	15.0	12.2

Source: IMF, World Economic Outlook, May 1995.

China experienced a rapid increase in inflation in the late 1980s as alluded to previously, although the country never experienced the hyper inflationary rates of Vietnam. The retrenchment program of the late 1980s was very successful at reducing inflation in 1990 and 1991. But with the recovery in the economy thereafter, inflation has again rapidly picked up. The poor recent performance of inflation must be of concern to the authorities, although with the further liberalisation of prices must be regarded as almost inevitable.

Public Finance

In the past in Vietnam, under the central planning system, budgets operated under a soft budgetary constraint, resulting in spending running ahead of projected expenditure levels so as to achieve plan requirements. Under this fiscal system around three quarters of revenue consisted of transfers from state enterprises, total revenue was generally not sufficient to cover expenditure, capital spending represented only a quarter of total expenditure and the financing of the deficit relied on loans and grants but even more heavily on borrowing from the State Bank. However since 1988 in Vietnam, much progress has been made in dismantling this system. Progress has been made in:

- broadening the tax base. For example in 1990 new tax laws were passed setting rates for turnover, profits and sales taxes,
- domestic revenue has tended to exceed current expenditure, enabling the state to generate public savings,
- capital spending now represents a higher proportion of total expenditure,
- the state has taken a firm line, as previously mentioned, against monetising its deficits.

New tax measures, and the legitimisation of the non state sector, has resulted in a major change in the structure of state revenue. In the 1993 budget, 75% of domestic revenue was projected to come from taxation (of which 37% was to be derived from the non state sector) and only 10% from transfers from state enterprises. However in this same year state enterprises were still receiving subsidies, often in disguised form. They contributed in 1993 around $1 billion to the budget in taxes and capital levies, that is about 30% of total government revenue, or 7% of GDP. At the same time, however, they received $300 million from the government in grants and $200 million in assistance for paying foreign debt.

Based upon targets agreed with the IMF in November 1994 for the 1994-97 period, the aim is to reduce the overall deficit (excluding grants) to 4% of GDP, to continue to avoid financing the deficit through borrowing from the State Bank, and to increase the surplus on current operations (excluding grants) from 3.75% of GDP in 1994 to 4.25% of GDP in 1997. As Table 3.6 indicates Vietnam has made considerable progress in regard to reducing the state budget, using either an accruals or cash basis, with the recent exception of 1993. The maintenance of this progress will be crucial in the fight against inflation.

Table 3.6: State Budgetary Balance, % of GDP, 1990-94

	China	Vietnam	
		Accruals Basis	Cash Basis
1990	-2.1	-8.1	-5.8
1991	-2.4	-3.7	-1.5
1992	-2.5	-3.7	-1.7
1993	-2.3	-6.2	-4.8
1994	-2.6	-3.5	-1.8

Sources: China Statistical Yearbook, Vietnam national sources.

Fiscal policy in China has operated in a difficult environment in recent years. The central government's influence on public finances has weakened and budget deficits have persisted. At the same time, ongoing reforms, as well as recurrent macroeconomic cycles, have increased the demands on fiscal policy to both support the reform process and help stabilise the economy. This contributed to the authorities' major program of fiscal reform in 1994, covering the tax system and tax administration, intergovernmental fiscal relations, budgetary procedures and the government administrative and personnel system. The objective being to build an infrastructure for fiscal policy compatible with a market economy.

Over the period 1983-93 the size of the state budget to GNP fell by more than 10 percentage points to 17.5%. Budget deficits have persisted, averaging about 2% of GNP over the past decade (see Table 3.6 for developments during the 1990s). Such deficits have largely been financed by the People's Bank of China and through the domestic sales of bonds to mainly captive sources. About one-fourth of the deficits were financed by foreign sources, which were used primarily for imports of capital equipment for key construction projects.

The reforms which have had the most important impact on the fiscal system relate to the greater autonomy given to the SOEs, the larger role of market forces in determining resource allocation, and the devolution of revenue and expenditure responsibilities to local governments. However the growing market orientation of the economy has highlighted important structural weaknesses in fiscal policy, most notably declining revenue buoyancy and a lack of uniformity and transparency in the tax system and tax administration. Since 1985 revenue from major taxes has declined relative to GNP, with the exception of VAT and the business turnover tax. The biggest decline was that for the income tax on SOEs. As a result the structure of tax revenue has shifted towards taxes on goods and services from taxes on income and profits. The reduction in revenue from SOEs was an expected outcome of the reform process. However the lack of revenue buoyancy and the erosion of the tax base stemmed from the continued weak financial performance of the SOEs, as well as from the failure of the tax system to expand into the booming nonstate sector.

A number of other weaknesses in the fiscal system exist including: unequal distribution of the tax burden (most of the burden is placed on the state sector with relatively little on the non state sector); widespread bargaining in the fiscal process; the erosion of the central government's control over fiscal policy; the expansionary bias of the system; the widening of regional disparities; and inefficiencies in budgetary procedures and government administration. Recognising that these weaknesses in the fiscal system undermine macroeconomic management and allocative efficiency, and hinder the transformation to a market based economy, the authorities launched a major program of fiscal reforms in early 1994. This covered the tax system and tax administration, intergovernmental fiscal relations, budgetary procedures, and the government administrative and personnel system.

Foreign Trade

Until the reforms of 1988-89, Vietnam's recorded exports covered only between one-third and one-half of imports. The country's chronic trade

Table 3.7: Foreign Trade and Balance of Payments, US$billion

CHINA	Total Exports (fob)	Total Imports (cif)	Trade Balance	Total Trade/GDP (%)	Current Account/GDP (%)
1985	27.35	42.25	-14.90	25.0	-4.1
1988	47.52	55.28	-7.76	36.0	-1.3
1989	52.54	59.14	-6.60	35.0	-1.3
1990	62.10	53.35	8.75	34.0	3.4
1991	71.84	63.79	8.05	36.0	3.5
1992	84.94	80.53	4.41	42.0	1.4
1993	91.76	103.95	-12.19	49.0	-2.8
1994	122.59	115.17	7.42	49.0	0.4

VIETNAM	Total Exports (fob)	Total Imports (cif)	Trade Balance	Total Trade/GDP (%)	Current Account/GDP (%)
1985	0.70	1.86	-1.16	na	-2.8
1988	1.04	2.76	-1.72	na	-2.8
1989	1.95	2.57	-0.62	na	-9.3
1990	2.40	2.75	-0.35	60.0	-5.4
1991	2.09	2.34	-0.25	60.0	-2.0
1992	2.58	2.54	0.04	62.0	-0.8
1993	2.99	3.92	-0.94	61.0	-8.3
1994	3.80	5.00	-1.20	na	-4.8

Source: World Bank.

deficits were largely covered by grant aid and highly concessional credits from the former Soviet Union. The collapse of the communist regimes of Eastern Europe from 1989 caused the gradual loss of those countries' markets and commodity assistance, resulting in their almost complete disappearance in 1991 when the CMEA was formally wound up and the Soviet Union disintegrated. However the reforms to the trade and foreign exchange regimes of 1988-89, and Vietnam's emergence as an exporter of rice and crude oil, generated a compensating increase in exports to the convertible area, primarily - Japan, Singapore, Hong Kong, Taiwan and South Korea, but also increasingly Western Europe. In dollar terms merchandise export earnings increased by 87% in 1989, and grew at an annual average rate of 23% in the six years to 1994. However, even after several years of rapid growth merchandise exports still represented only around 20% of GDP and in 1994 were worth less than $50(US) per head, well behind that of Thailand ($750(US) per head) and Indonesia ($199(US) per head). But the ratio of total trade to GDP at 61% in 1993 (see Table 3.7), indicates the importance of overall trade to the economy.

Vietnam experienced a dramatic change in the direction of its trade over the period 1985-93 (see Table 3.8), which saw a sizeable switch of merchandise exports and imports away from the CMEA countries towards Asia in particular.

In terms of Vietnam's overall current account performance (see Table 3.7), the traditional deficit is likely to increase in the future on the basis of the trade pattern which is already beginning to emerge. Strong export growth is usually outpaced by an even stronger and largely investment related import increase. The key issue will be to ensure that such current import growth enhances the export capacity of the economy.

Table 3.8: Direction of Trade

	Merchandise Exports (% of total)				Merchandise Imports (% of total)			
	CHINA		VIETNAM		CHINA		VIETNAM	
	1985	1993	1985	1993	1985	1993	1985	1993
Asia	61.4	55.4	20.5	60.7	52.4	54.9	35.2	75.8
W.Europe	10.1	14.7	8.6	20.9	17.9	20.5	21.0	12.6
North/ Central America	9.6	21.6	0	0.7	15.2	14.3	0.2	0.4
Middle East	6.4	2.8	0.4	0	0.4	1.5	0	0
South America	1.7	1.1	0	1.4	4.1	2.0	0	0.1
Africa	1.7	1.4	0	0.9	0.7	1.0	0	0.1
Oceania	0.8	1.4	0.4	5.6	3.1	2.7	1.1	1.8
ROW*	8.4	1.6	70.2	9.8	6.3	3.0	42.6	9.2
Total	100.0	100.0	100.0	100.0	100.0	100.0	100.0	100.0

*   Rest of the World. For Vietnam this consisted primarily of the former CMEA economies.

Sources: Asian Development Bank.

During the 1970s China's exports grew by some 3.4% on an annual average basis in real terms, but this rose dramatically to 14.1% over the extended reform period from 1978-88. Some 70% of these exports were manufactures. Imports also rose dramatically with the reduction in trade barriers. In 1985 China had a sizeable trade deficit arising primarily from the rapid growth of the economy, induced by the process of economic reform. Total exports were worth US$27.4 billion, of which almost half (US$13.5 billion) were in the form of manufactured goods, 26% in fuel exports and

14.8% in food exports. These three export items alone contributed over 90% of total exports. Total imports amounted to US$42.3 billion, with the largest single item being that of capital goods (44% of the total). Hence even by the mid 1980s the reform process and the opening up of the economy was having a major impact. The country had experienced a dramatic increase in manufactured goods exports, and the importation of capital goods would assist in a further rapid expansion of the economy through improved productivity and efficiency of Chinese industry. By 1994 total exports increased to US$122.59 billion, consisting of 80% in the form of manufactured goods, 3.5% in the form of fuel and 10.8% in the form of food. Total imports also increased substantially to US$115.17 billion, with capital goods, the largest single item, making up 54.6% of the total.

The opening up of the economy to trade and its increased significance to the economy, as reflected in the doubling of the total trade to GDP ratio from 25 to 49% (see Table 3.7), alone does not explain the country's success in foreign markets for manufactured goods. Other countries which opened their economies have not experienced the same level of success as China's in the area of manufactured exports. A very important explanatory component relates to connections with Hong Kong. In 1979 22.6% of Chinese exports went to Hong Kong and 79% of those exports stayed in Hong Kong. By 1987 Hong Kong's share of all exports rose to 31.1% and 62% of these exports to Hong Kong were re-exported. By 1992 Hong Kong's share of total Chinese exports amounted to 44%. In the 1990s a similar process appears to be happening through Taiwan. The formidable marketing talents of Hong Kong and Taiwan are being grafted on to the manufacturing capacity of the mainland.

The direction of China's trade is identified in Table 3.8. Three major markets have become increasingly important for China's merchandise exports over the period 1985-93 - Asia, Western Europe and North and Central America. In 1993 around 55% of China's merchandise imports came from other Asian countries, up slightly from its share in 1985, 21% from Western

Europe, up again from its share in 1985, and 14% from North and Central America down slightly from its share in 1985.

Foreign Direct Investment

In Vietnam a new foreign investment law was promulgated on 1 January 1988, which offered terms as generous as anywhere else in the region. The priority areas specified in the code for investment were production for export and import substitution. The duration of a venture with foreign capital generally could not exceed 20 years, but could be extended in special cases. In September 1988 the State Committee for Cooperation and Investment was created to manage and administer all foreign direct investment. The major foreign investors in Vietnam are the four Asian Tigers (Taiwan, Hong Kong, Singapore and South Korea in that order). Japan, Vietnam's largest bilateral aid donor and its largest trading partner, was fifth on the list of leading investors in January 1995 while Australia was sixth. The lifting of the US embargo in February 1994 led to a rapid increase in US investment, which, by the end of 1994, made it stand fourteenth on the list of approved investments by country.

Total realised capital since 1988 amounts to US$3.86 billion, a substantial proportion of which was in the oil and gas sector which accounted for US$1.43 billion or 37% of the total. This implied an implementation rate of 35% which is high by regional standards, but is misleading because of the predominance until recently of oil and gas. Recently there has been a shift away from oil and gas and hotels and tourism, which accounted for 32% and 21% respectively of approvals in the years 1988-90. By January 1995 industry had taken a clear lead over these two sectors with 36% of total approved investment compared to 11% for oil and gas and 19% for tourism and hotels (see Fforde and Goldstone, 1995).

By 1994 foreign invested companies for the first time were having a real impact upon the economy. The turnover of foreign invested projects in 1994 was US$851 million, more than their cumulative turnover of US$780 million in the previous six years. In 1994 they generated US$390 million in export earnings (compared with US$260 million in 1993). Tax receipts from foreign invested companies in 1994 was US$133 million (not including receipts from oil and gas, and import-export duties). They have also become an increasingly important employer. According to the SCCI 65,000 people were employed by them at the end of 1994. This compared with 25,000 for these same enterprises a year earlier. Having reached an estimated 26.6% of total investment in 1994, FDI's share is expected to rise to an average of around 30% of the total in the remaining years of the century. It will play a crucial role in the future economic development of the economy.

China has achieved remarkable success in comparison to other developing economies, such as Vietnam, in attracting FDI (see Table 3.9). From virtually zero in 1981 the figure has risen to US$30 billion by 1994, with the latter figure representing virtually half of all FDI to developing countries. This success in attracting FDI may initially seem puzzling, since traditionally foreign investors have had little security in China as the country does not have a strong legal tradition. The lure of a billion customers goes some way towards an explanation. However the rapid growth of export oriented foreign investment, in the face of insecure property rights, is perhaps best understood by recognising that most of this foreign investment came from Hong Kong, and to a lesser degree other overseas Chinese, and was going into Guangdong province next door to Hong Kong. In 1990, for example, 55% of all realised foreign investment came from Hong Kong and Macao, and 46% of all investment whose regional destination could be identified went to Guangdong Province. Fujian Province, with the closest ties historically and culturally to Taiwan, came next with 9%. The FDI of Japan and the US in 1990, in contrast, was 14 and 13% of the total respectively and no other country had over 2%.

Table 3.9:   Foreign Direct Investment (US$ billion)

YEAR	CHINA	VIETNAM
1985	1.03	0
1989	2.61	0.10
1990	2.66	0.12
1991	3.45	0.22
1992	7.16	0.26
1993	23.11	0.30
1994	30.00	na

Source: Asian Development Bank.

The willingness of Hong Kong and Taiwanese investors to move into China in a big way had two primary components. First, most Hong Kong investments were small in scale and payback periods were short, often three years or less. The security of property rights are not so important if a high rate of return on investment is possible in a short period. Secondly there were family ties and connections with friends in the mainland. The Hong Kong - Guangdong connections really mattered in day to day operations. Such foreign investment, as well as foreign trade, has played, and will continue to play, a central role in moving China towards a market economy.

External Debt

The extent of Vietnam's external debt has been the subject of some disagreement.[5] The World Bank put the total debt stock at the end of 1993 at US$24.2 billion. This suggested that Vietnam's debt/GDP ratio and its

---

5   Arising from the appropriate exchange rate to use in converting the country's transferable rouble debt to US dollars.

external debt per head were worryingly high at 189% and US$342. However at the end of 1993 Vietnam's bilateral hard currency donors agreed to reschedule and write-off US$791 million of debt, about half of the total on enhanced Toronto terms (which the Paris Club has offered the poorest, most indebted countries since 1991). The World Bank still categorises Vietnam as being severely indebted, and could potentially constrain the room for manoeuver which the authorities have in regard to the rate of economic development and growth of the economy.

The Chinese situation is quite different to that of Vietnam. While the country's total external debt increased to US$97 billion in 1994 from US$84 billion at the end of 1993 (see Table 10), its creditworthiness indicators improved. By the end of 1994, total external debt was equivalent to 83% of exports of goods and services (92% in 1993), or 19% of GDP, which was comfortably below the averages for East Asia and the Pacific. Short term debt amounted to US$15.4 billion at end 1994, or 16% of the total, less than in 1993. The share of external debt at variable rates has been declining steadily from 44% in 1990 to 39% in 1994, thereby reducing China's vulnerability to interest rate fluctuations in international financial markets. The debt service ratio, which stood at a low 11.1% in 1993, declined further to 9.7% in 1994.

Overall, China's external debt and debt service position remains sound. It is expected, however, that repatriation of profits and dividends by foreign direct investors will make a rising claim on export earnings as more foreign invested projects come on stream. In addition, as SOEs become more autonomous, the Chinese authorities will need to be concerned with too rapid a build up of their external debt obligations.

Table 3.10: External Debt

	CHINA		VIETNAM	
	Total External Debt (US$ billion)	External Debt/GDP (%)	Total External Debt (US$ billion)	External Debt/GDP (%)
1985	16.70	5.8	10.34	0.7
1989	44.86	13.9	19.37	329.5
1990	52.63	14.8	22.11	341.6
1991	59.64	15.8	22.28	231.8
1992	69.19	16.5	23.69	240.1
1993	83.80	19.7	24.22	188.7
1994	97.00	19.2	na	146.4

Source: World Bank, World Tables.

4. LESSONS FROM THE REFORM PROCESS

There are many similarities between the two countries in terms of their process of economic reform. The initial focus was placed upon agricultural reform in China in 1978 with the introduction of the household responsibility system, with the equivalent introduced in 1988 in Vietnam. In China, after the initial success of these reforms, focus was then placed upon the industrial sector by the mid 1980s, allowing greater autonomy at the enterprise level. However SOE reform has been slow and even by the mid 1990s the reform of SOEs is incomplete and increasingly pressing. Vietnam likewise has also had to focus upon reform of the SOEs and the need to subject them to a hard budget constraint. This need has been even more pressing for them than for China. The rapidly deteriorating economic conditions facing the country in the mid 1980s was quite unlike that of China in the late 1970s. Vietnam had little choice but to reform its economy, or else face the imminent prospect of its collapse. The economy was financially dependent on the Soviet Union and the markets of the CMEA. Facing the imminent demise of both in the late 1980s and early 1990s a more radical and urgent response was required. However like China the problems with the state enterprises remain, but as in China they are facing increasingly hard budgets constraints and this will be assisted by the process of financial reform and the establishment of commercially based banks in each country. Both countries have committed themselves to the development of socialist market economies. The early successes of the program of renovation in Vietnam, in addition to intense external pressures, resulted in the country in 1989 implementing more comprehensive reform measures with the clear objective of moving towards a market economy. By October 1992 China too had made the clear decision to move towards a market economy, and by 1994 more ambitious and comprehensive reforms of the economy were to be implemented in order to make this objective possible. Their respective objectives of attaining a socialist market economy will provide interesting case studies of the viability of this system, and the competing and overlapping measures available to achieve such an outcome.

Economic reform in China has been both gradual and incremental, with the economy's better initial economic situation enabling it to pursue such an approach, and characterised by decentralisation of decision making. While such decentralisation can be seen to be essential in the context of a market economy, the partial nature of China's reforms has made macroeconomic control of the economy increasingly difficult without the use of direct administrative measures. Indirect instruments of macroeconomic control need to be developed rapidly. This difficulty is compounded by the Chinese leadership's intention to maintain public ownership of the SOEs and to reject wholesale privatisation. The issue of separating governance from ownership, through the corporatisation of such enterprises, therefore becomes increasingly important.

For Vietnam, because of its more precarious economic situation, the pressure for economic reform was much more intense and pressing. Initially the reform measures progressed gradually, but by the late 1980s the pace became more rapid due to both internal, but more importantly, external developments. As with China only the privatisation of agriculture was acceptable, and the authorities have been demonstrably against the wholesale privatisation of state owned industrial enterprises. Vietnam will also have to face up to the issue of ownership and governance of such enterprises in the context of a market economy. There is also a pressing need to develop the financial sector to enable the use of macroeconomic policy instruments, to enable indirect control over macroeconomic developments in the economy. Vietnam, like China, still lacks the necessary infrastructure, in terms of both institutions and instruments, appropriate for the functioning of an efficient market economy.

Areas of Commonality

There are a number of areas of commonality which exist between the two countries. Both have maintained centralised political control in the hands of their respective Communist Parties, unlike other transition economies in Europe which have seen the demise of their Communist governments. There is still a lack of democratic institutions in both countries, and political pluralism is certainly not on the agenda, although political stability and continuity are seen as being essential. There is a common belief in the need to achieve a socialist market economy in which: there is considerable decentralisation of economic decision making; the agriculture and services sectors are effectively privatised; public ownership of industry remains substantial and wholesale privatisation is rejected; each economy is characterised by openness to both foreign trade and investment, where export led growth and the attraction of FDI is seen as important for economic development.

Both countries have experienced a major expansion in their exports and imports. China has experienced a major increase particularly in its exports of manufactured goods and importation of capital goods. Vietnam too has seen an expansion in its exports, with that of oil and rice leading the way. Its exports of manufactured goods, such as textiles and clothing as well as shoes, is increasing, and this diversification of exports will be essential for its future growth. Both countries are strategically placed to export and import from the most rapidly developing region of the world economy, the Asia-Pacific region, which also contains capital exporting countries. While neither country is currently a member of GATT, both will strive to become members of the new WTO. Trade for both will continue to be crucial for their further economic development, and particularly so for Vietnam. In this context Vietnam's recent membership of ASEAN should be seen as being very important. Membership of organisations which will stabilise and expand both country's trading relationships will be a key factor in their sustained development. In addition FDI will continue to play a key role in the process of economic development. China with its cultural, family and historical connections to Hong Kong and Taiwan is in a particularly advantageous position. For Vietnam such connections are much more limited in nature, but can still play an important role in developing the domestic private sector. With a cheap, literate and adaptable workforce, China and Vietnam are obvious rivals in attracting FDI from labour intensive industries in other countries.

Despite numerous common successes achieved during their respective periods of economic reform, a number of common problems remain. Reform of the SOEs still remains and is hindering the development of other sectors of their economies, such as that of the financial sector. Many still remain loss making, inefficient, and producing low quality output which is difficult to sell, and are still subject to soft budget constraints. Despite the existence in both countries of bankruptcy laws, these have only been used in the cases of small to medium size SOEs and not for large SOEs. In China moves have been made to overcome the problem of ownership and governance as discussed previously, with the objective of corporatising such enterprises and separating their ownership from management. Similar moves will be required in the context of Vietnamese SOEs.

Both countries still lack the necessary infrastructure, institutional and instruments, necessary for the efficient functioning and control of a market economy. In the context of the financial sector, the banks, which dominate, lack the necessary autonomy, and expertise to make commercial lending decisions. Policy directed lending needs to be reduced and moves are underway in both countries to bring this about. Both countries also lack the necessary legal and regulatory framework for the proper functioning of a market economy. For example there are still ambiguities relating to property rights and access to land. Both countries still do not have properly functioning factor markets. In addition the partial nature of the reform process in both countries, makes it difficult for the authorities to exercise macroeconomic control over their economies without resort to administrative or direct means. Indirect instruments for macroeconomic management require to be developed and this will relate closely to reform of the financial sector.

Other joint areas of concern relate to increasing regional income and development disparities. In China this is most apparent between the open coastal provinces, which have benefitted from the open trade and investment policies during the 1980s, and the poorer inland provinces, who are also demanding the same privileges. Should this not occur, with the development of factor markets specifically for labour, there will be increased migration to these areas, creating possible social tension which the authorities would wish to avoid. Similarly in Vietnam regional disparities are increasingly emerging between the north and south of the country, which is of particular concern, and between the cities and countryside. This will cause migration to the towns with social tension unless sufficient jobs are generated.

Environmental issues are also of common concern. In Vietnam there has been considerable environmental degradation arising from 30 years of war and population pressures. The ability to achieve the rapid economic growth laid down for it by the government, will require substantial attention to be paid to environmental consequences. Similarly in China, which has been a recipient of investment from other countries because of its less stringent environmental controls, such a situation could cause major problems in the future. However there is increasing awareness by the Chinese authorities that this is an important issue, and recently there have been cases where TVEs have been closed down because they did not achieve pollution standards. Sustainable development will be the key for both countries.

Major Disparities between the Economies

It is apparent that a number of differences exist between the pressures for reform, the progress of reform, developments during the reform process and the general economic circumstances of the two economies under study. China started its reform process in 1978 in a much more advantageous position compared to that of Vietnam. The country was already experiencing economic growth, it had low inflation, low budget deficits, high savings and low external debt. The reform process could proceed gradually and incrementally. There was no need for the economy to start off the transition process with a stabilisation program. Industry played an already significant role within the economy. It already existed in rural communities, a legacy arising from developments in earlier years. Vietnam on the other hand began its program of renovation in 1986 in a very weak economic position. Declining economic growth, hyper inflation, large budget deficits, reliance on foreign savings and food shortages. Deteriorating external circumstances in the late 1980s required urgent attention, in the form of a tough stabilisation program and comprehensive economic reforms.

There are important structural differences between the two economies. The industrial sector, a legacy from earlier periods, contributed half of China's GDP in 1994, compared to only 30% in Vietnam. Agriculture is relatively more important in Vietnam as both a source of employment as well as a contributor to output. The service sector contribution to output is also much lower in Vietnam. While both countries can be classified as poor, it is apparent that China began the reform process at a higher stage of economic development and this difference is still apparent today.

In the industrial sector the declining significance of the SOEs in China has occurred through the expansion of the non state sector, although public ownership still contributes around 90% of total output. In this sector China has a dynamic ingredient which is missing in Vietnam - the Township and Village Enterprises (TVEs). There is no equivalent in the non state sector in Vietnam except for the private sector, which is still under heavy influence by the authorities. In a recent paper by Reidel and Comer (1995), they argue that this missing dynamic component in Vietnam's industrial sector does not bode well for the long term growth of this sector nor for the economy as a whole. The existence of the TVEs in China act as competition for the SOEs, provide a major source of exports, assist in the increased marketisation process of the economy as well as enhance rural industrial development. For Vietnam this missing ingredient could considerably assist in the process of moving to a dynamic market economy, and, if rurally oriented as in China, assist in the development of the rural economy.

China has attained a vastly superior performance in terms of the generation of domestic saving and in investment levels. Although China has an ICOR in the range of between 3-3.5 (see Tables 1 and 4), its substantial investment enables it to maintain high growth rates. Not so for Vietnam, whose domestic saving and investment levels are considerably lower. For the country to sustain a real GDP growth rate of 8% until the end of the century, and with an ICOR of around 2-2.5, it will require an increase in investment to around 25% of GDP. The further domestic saving is from this figure the greater the dependence which the country will have to place upon FDI and ODA.

While both countries have adopted an export oriented strategy for long term development and growth, and both have been successful, it is apparent that the composition of China's exports suggest a higher level of development. While the Vietnamese economy is relatively more open to trade, as indicated by the total trade to GDP ratio, it is apparent that its exports are heavily biased toward the export of commodities (rice and fuel), which together accounted for some 35.9% of total exports in 1994. This makes the economy more open to adverse developments in commodity prices. Vietnam needs to diversify its exports into manufactured goods, and this process is gradually occurring. China's exports, on the other hand, are primarily in the form of manufactured goods (some 80% of total exports in 1994), providing a stronger foundation for sustained economic growth. On the import side some 55% of China's imports are in the form of capital goods, essential for the acquisition of new technology and improvements in productivity, while the comparable figure for Vietnam is only 36%.

China has been very successful during the 1990s in attracting FDI, contrasting starkly with that of Vietnam whose approved level of investment is quite high but realised investment considerably lower. China's cultural, family and historical links with capital exporting countries such as Hong Kong and Taiwan puts the country in a particularly favourable position. Vietnam does not have such close links with these or other Asian economies. The country has only relatively recently, since 1988, allowed FDI in the country, and hence still has some way to go to catch up. Vietnam's bureaucracy and lack of infrastructure will continue to remain a major problem in this regard.

Finally, China is in a much stronger position in terms of its external debt. It represented only 19% of GDP as against 146% of GDP for Vietnam in 1994 (or US$80 per capita in China as against US$331 per capita in Vietnam). This has important implications for debt servicing and possible constraints on economic growth. The Chinese authorities are in a much better position to pursue their own independent economic policies rather than in the case of Vietnam, whose ODA assistance will be crucial but influenced by the attitudes and lending conditions of international lending institutions such as the World Bank.

Lessons to be Learned

The experience of the newly industrialising economies of East Asia suggests that the basis for rapid and sustained economic growth is an export oriented industrialisation strategy. Such experiences have been learned well by both Vietnam and China, forming the basis of their respective developments strategies. While there may be disagreement as to the relative significance of each, general agreement would suggest that there are three components to successful export oriented growth:

- macroeconomic stability
- relatively high rates of saving and investment
- if not free trade, at least free access for exporters to imported capital goods and intermediate inputs

Both China and Vietnam have made progress in regard to the attainment of macroeconomic stability. For the Vietnamese authorities it has been their greatest achievement. Fiscal deficits have been cut and, since 1991, have not been monetised, and inflation has been considerably reduced. China has experienced periods of macroeconomic instability due to the incompleteness of its reforms, and this will remain a top priority for the country.

China has achieved, and must maintain, very high rates of both saving and investment. The performance of Vietnam is much poorer and must be given priority in that country. This will require further and urgent reform of the financial sector.

Free access to imported capital goods by exporters can be achieved through the establishment of Special Economic Zones or Export Processing Zones. These have been proven to be highly successful in China's open coastal zones, and have also been tried in Vietnam. However in Vietnam bureaucratic procedures for importing are inhibiting this process, and in this regard important lessons can be drawn from the Chinese experience.

Finally, a major issue relates to the likely success of the market oriented economies both countries are attempting to create. Here a key component for success lies in the dynamism of the system. The reforms in China have triggered off dynamism in the industrial sector through the rapid growth of the non state sector, and particularly that of the township and village enterprises. While publicly owned they have proven to be a particularly robust form of enterprise ownership, competing with the SOEs, filling niches unfilled by the SOEs, exporting, providing employment, generating profits and revenue for the local township and village authorities. They have also been developing new forms of scientific and technological alliances, indicative of their adaptability and flexibility. They now account for around 38% of total industrial production. Their contribution to the marketisation of the economy has been significant. In the case of Vietnam the obvious source of dynamism should have been found in small and medium scale private sector enterprises, mainly in manufacturing and particularly in the south of the country. However the Vietnamese government has imposed rules and regulations on trade, investment and finance which make the development of private enterprise and dynamism very difficult. While the government has accepted the need for a market economy, its track record suggests a continued wish to exert substantial control and command over it.

5. SUMMARY AND CONCLUSIONS

Vietnam and China present fascinating examples of economies in transition which are very different from those of Eastern Europe and the countries of the former Soviet Union. They both wish to move towards market economies but in the process retain the socialist character of their economies through public ownership of key industries. While the pressure for reform has been very different for each of them, there was the unambiguous conclusion that the system of central planning had failed and that gradual, or rapid, economic reform was required if they were to attain the economic growth performances of their rapidly growing regional neighbours.

While both countries have achieved remarkable outcomes from their respective reform programs in terms of output growth, inflation, export growth and foreign direct investment, many weaknesses remain to be resolved. The need to separate ownership from governance of the SOEs needs to be resolved, otherwise other reforms such as that of the financial sector and the development of indirect instruments for control of the macroeconomic will be stalled. The incomplete nature of the reforms in both countries, has resulted in the necessary institutions and instruments essential for the proper functioning of a market economy to still be attained. A questions mark still remains over the commitment of the Vietnamese authorities in particular to the involvement of an unfettered private sector in its development. This sector, as in other East Asian economies, would provide the essential, but as yet missing, dynamic ingredient in Vietnam's fledgling market economy. In China such a dynamic non state sector exists in the form of the township and village enterprises. While many economists question their ability to survive during the 1990s, they have shown themselves to be a robust and adaptable form of public ownership unique amongst the economies in transition. They have played a key role in the marketisation of the economy and providing the necessary dynamism for the functioning of a successful market economy. In this regard Vietnam can learn much from the Chinese example.

While much has been done, much still remains undone. However the success or otherwise of these two countries in the future will provide an invaluable insight as to the long term viability of the socialist market economic system. Chance would have it that they are in a particularly advantageous geographical situation, strategically situated in the fastest growing region in the world with capital exporting economies searching for cheap labour. This, in conjunction with each country's proven adaptability and resilience, could bode well for the future.

REFERENCES

Asian Development Bank (1995) Key indicators of developing Asian and Pacific countries, Manila.

Bell, M.W., Hoe Ee Khor, and Kochhar, K. (1993) China at the threshold of a market economy, IMF Occasional Paper, No. 107, IMF, Washington, DC, September.

Fforde, A. and Goldstone, A. (1995) Vietnam to 2005: advancing on all fronts, Economist Intelligence Unit, Research report, April.

Harvie, C. and Tran Van Hoa (1996) A macroeconomic analysis of developments and future prospects of the Vietnamese economy to 2010, Report submitted to AusAid, July.

Nguyen, D.T. and Bandara, J.S. (1993) Recent developments in the Vietnamese economy with special reference to the macroeconomic conditions, unpublished manuscript, Griffith University.

Perkins, D. (1994) Completing China's move to the market, *Journal of Economic Perspectives*, Vol.8, No.2, Spring, pp23-46.

Riedel, J. and Comer, B. (1995) Transition to a market economy in Vietnam, in W.T. Woo, J. Sachs and S. Parker. (eds), *Economies in Transition: Comparing Asia and Eastern Europe*, MIT Press, forthcoming.

Tseng, W., Hoe Ee Khor, and Kochhar, K. (1994) Economic reform in China: a new phase, IMF Occasional Paper, No. 114, IMF, Washington, DC, November.

World Bank (1993) Vietnam: transition to the market, Washington, DC, September.

World Bank (1993) The East Asian Miracle, Oxford University Press, New York.

World Bank (1994) Vietnam: public sector management and private sector initiatives; an economic report, Report no. 13143-VN, September.

World Bank (1995) World Tables, Washington, DC.

Yusuf, S. (1994) China's macroeconomic performance and management during transition, *Journal of Economic Perspectives*, Vol.8, No.2, Spring, pp 71-92.

```
┌─────────────────────┐
│   CHAPTER 4         │
└─────────────────────┘
```

SUSTAINABILITY OF RAPID GROWTH: IS CHINA THE SAME AS THE FORMER SOVIET UNION?

YIPING HUANG AND RONALD DUNCAN[1,2]

ABSTRACT

This chapter examines China's growth potential in a comparison with the extensive growth profile of the former Soviet Union (FSU). The production function approach is applied using yearly data for 1952-92. It is found that the technological profile of the pre-reform Chinese economy resembled in many respects that of the FSU. But the situation in the former was not as bad as in the latter. The results suggest that economic reforms brought important changes to China's technological profile which are more

---

1   Department of Economics and National Centre for Development Studies, Research School of Pacific and Asian Studies, Australian National University, Canberra 0200

2   We wish to thank Justin Yifu Lin and Wing Thue Woo for valuable comments.

favourable for sustainable growth. The chapter also draws implications for different reform approaches in China and the former Soviet Union given their different development profiles.

1. INTRODUCTION

The Chinese economy achieved a reasonable rate of growth during its pre-reform period. Growth has accelerated in the post-reform period, however, recording an average rate of 9.3 per cent during 1978-94 (SSB). Although official income data still position China as one of the poorest countries in the world, recent studies re-evaluating per capita income level suggest that the Chinese economy has already ascended to the middle-income group (Perkins, 1992; Garnaut and Ma, 1993; Summers and Heston, 1993).[3]

China's rapid growth follows the remarkable expansion of Japan in the 1950s and 1960s and that of the newly industrialised economies (NIEs) in the late 1960s through the 1980s; a chain of events which leads many economists to believe that not only has the world growth centre already shifted to the western Pacific but also that China and East Asia will dominate the world economy in the twenty-first century (Garnaut, 1989). Given that Japan's growth rate has fallen back to near other OECD countries and that the growth of the NIEs is also likely to slow down as they mature, whether or not the East Asia region is able to maintain its strong growth momentum largely depends on the growth performance of China and other rapidly growing East Asian developing economies including Indonesia, Malaysia, Philippines, Thailand and Vietnam.

---

3   World Bank statistics report China's per capita GNP at US$370 in 1990. This is widely regarded as a significant underestimate. Perkins (1992) estimates China's per capita GNP having passed US$1,000 by 1990. Based on evidence from the food economy, Garnaut and Ma (1993) propose an income level of $1,200 in the early 1990s. Using purchasing power parity measurement, Summers and Heston (1993) suggest China's per capita GNP was US$2,472 in 1988. All these estimates put China at the lower end of the range of the middle-income countries.

But is China's rapid growth sustainable? Growth sustainability is a complex issue which depends on a range of factors including government policy, resource allocation mechanisms, resource availability, technological development and importantly political stability. As a formerly centrally planned economy, the successfulness of policy transition is of crucial importance. Most economists agree that the remarkable economic expansion has come mainly from reforms at the micro level and that the biggest challenge now arises from the conflicts between the reformed micro system and the old macro economic regime. If so, high growth will continue only if the transition of the macro economic system is managed smoothly.[4]

Recent studies on development in the former Soviet Union (FSU) and in other East Asian economies raise further questions about China's growth potential. The FSU experienced good economic performance in the 1930s, 1950s and 1960s which, as research as since shown, relied on extensive growth (see Powell, 1968; Bergson, 1987; Desai, 1987; Easterly and Fischer, 1994). One explanation advanced is that, because of the low elasticity of substitution between capital and labour, the high growth could not be sustained. As the capital stock accumulated, the marginal return to capital in real terms fell - from about 0.5 in the early 1950s to a level very close to zero

---

4   Lau (1994) believes that the most critical challenge facing China in maintaining its strong growth is controlling inflation. He projects that the Chinese economy will grow at an average annual rate of 8 percent between 1995 and 2020. Lin, Cai and Li (1994) point to the importance of compatible micro and macro economic systems. Assuming the Chinese government will push forward with its reform programs, they predict that China will overtake the United States and Japan and become the largest economy in the early 21st century. In a paper presented at the Distinguished Lecture Series in Stanford University, Garnaut (1994) suggests that China has some advantages and some disadvantages in sustaining its rapid growth as compared to other East Asian economies in their early phase of expansion. One disadvantage is that a very big country finds it harder to maintain social and political stability around the objective of rapid growth; another is the fear that export expansion will turn the terms of trade against itself. An advantage is that China could grow more rapidly because, starting later, it was further from its frontier when it began. The biggest danger to China's continued success, Garnaut argues, is that the Chinese leadership will make errors of a more prosaic kind, that interact with each other and magnify effects; until the accumulation of errors requires a response that is too big to manage.

in the mid-1980s. Economic decline, therefore, was inevitable even if the growth rate of the capital stock was maintained (Easterly and Fischer, 1994). Countries in East Asia, especially the NIEs, have also been found to exhibit the patterns of extensive growth, relying on mobilisation of resources and with little technological progress (Young, 1992, 1994; Kim and Lau, 1994). It has been predicted that high growth in East Asia cannot be sustained because "it is unlikely that a generation from now most Singaporeans will have PhDs" (Krugman, 1994).

One implication of these findings is that a country's technological profile plays an important role in the sustainability of rapid growth. Whether or not a country can sustain rapid growth depends on its ability to achieve strong productivity growth and to maintain stable flows of factor inputs and stable returns to capital (because in most cases the capital stock increases faster than the labour force). The technological profile itself is largely policy-determined.

The purpose of this study is to examine China's technological profile before and after reform, in comparison with that of the FSU. It addresses questions of whether the roots of development in pre-reform China were the same as those of the FSU and whether the economic reform has changed China's technological profile. Investigation of these issues has important implications for assessment of growth potential and the making of reform policies. A production function approach is applied using time series data for the period 1952-92.

The chapter is organised as follows. The next section reviews the development of China's economic system in the pre-reform period. Section 3 discusses the data set used in the analysis and presents results of the production relationships derived using the transcendental logarithmic (translog) function. The estimated coefficients are applied in Section 4 in an analysis of China's economic development. The elasticity of substitution between capital and labour, marginal returns to capital and labour, shares of capital and labour in total output (or the output elasticity of capital and labour) and total factor productivity (TFP) growth are calculated for both the pre- and post-reform period and compared with those of the FSU. Section 5 concludes by drawing out some implications for the debate over the different reform approaches adopted in China and the FSU.

2. THE HYPOTHESES

It is widely accepted among economists and international organisations that China copied its economic system from the FSU in the early 1950s (Xue, 1981; World Bank, 1983; Nolan, 1994). Lin et al. (1994) demonstrate that the pre-reform economic system in China was determined by its heavy-industry-oriented development strategy. The so-called 'Soviet model' is a comprehensive economic system which, in essence, contains three important elements - a heavy-industry-oriented development strategy, a central planning system and public ownership. All three elements were reflected in the pre-reform Chinese economy.

When the new Chinese government came to power in 1949, it inherited a war-torn agrarian economy. Developing the economy and raising living standards were major objectives set for both political and economic reasons. It seemed to the Chinese leadership that one common feature of the advanced economies in North America and Western Europe was the high proportion of industry, especially heavy industry. Development of heavy industry was, therefore, seen as the avenue to economic modernisation (see Xue, 1981; Lin et al., 1994). The FSU seemed to provide a good model to follow. Its economic growth in the 1930s impressed the world, especially in contrast with most of the western countries which were experiencing great depression at the time.[5] Economic growth continued at a high rate in the immediate post-

---

5   Official statistics report an average growth rate of 12.5 percent for FSU industrial
     production during 1928-39 (Ofer, 1987). Western sources adjust this growth rate
     downward to 5 percent which was still much higher than the world average in the 1930s
     (Easterly and Fischer, 1994).

war period, recording 2.4 percentage points higher than the world average in the 1950s.[6]

The development of heavy industry was, therefore, assigned top priority by the Chinese government. The share of state capital construction investment in heavy industry, for instance, rose from 36.2 per cent during the period of the first five-year plan (1952-57) to 54 per cent in the second five-year plan (1958-62) and remained around 50 per cent until economic reform (Lin et al., 1994). The proportion of workers in 'secondary' industry (mainly light and heavy industrial processing) also increased - from 7.4 per cent in 1952 and to a peak of 26.4 per cent in 1958 (SSB).[7]

To direct resource flows, a comprehensive central planning system was adopted. To facilitate industrialisation the government implemented a set of macro economic measures including a depressed interest rate, an over-valued foreign exchange rate, and below-market prices for raw materials and agricultural products. Administrative measures dominated almost all areas of resource allocation. The banking and financial system was restructured, with the People's Bank of China at its core, to facilitate the transfer of funds towards heavy industry. Foreign exchange allocation was also centralised. Foreign trade was monopolised by a handful of large trading companies which were arms of the central government. The relatively scarce foreign exchange was only allowed to be spent on importing modern equipment and advanced technology. Not only were prices of important raw materials and

---

6   The fact that the rapid development of its (defence-related) heavy industry also helped the FSU significantly in international politics perhaps made this development strategy more appealing to the Chinese leaders.

7   The Chinese economy is sometimes divided into three broad categories (industries): "primary" industry includes agriculture and mining; "secondary" industry is the industrial processing sector; and "tertiary" industry is the service sector. The proportion of workers in the secondary industry is used to illustrate labour force growth in heavy industry because light industry accounted for a declining share before the mid-1960s.

agricultural products depressed below market levels, the government also monopolised all important transactions.[8]

Public ownership was enforced to facilitate the smooth implementation of the development strategy. Factories in the urban areas were gradually nationalised through a process called 'socialist transformation'. The newly-established heavy industry factories were exclusively owned by the state, partly to ensure that the artificially high profits (created basically by the taxing of agriculture) were handed over to the state or re-invested in heavy industry. Farms were collectivised and the formation of the collectives was formalised as the People's Commune in 1957 and 1958 (Lin, 1990).

This institutional setting significantly changed the pre-reform Chinese economy, generating characteristics typical of the 'Soviet model'. First, heavy industry grew rapidly. In 1952, heavy industry accounted for about 15 per cent of China's total agricultural and industrial output. This share rose to 26 per cent in 1957 and peaked at 52 per cent in 1960 (Table 4.1). In most years from 1960 to 1978, the share of heavy industry fluctuated between 35 and 40 per cent (SSB). Heavy industry, indeed, became a dominant sector in the Chinese economy. Second, the state sector played an increasingly important role. The share of the state sector in Chinese industry rose quickly from below 30 per cent in the early 1950s to around 90 per cent in the late 1950s through both rapid development of the newly established firms and the 'socialist transformation' of previous privately-owned enterprises (Xue, 1981). Third, the rapid industrialisation was supported by high rates of domestic saving and investment. The aggregate investment ratio in total GNP was around 30 per

---

8   The holding down of prices of raw materials and agricultural products was said to reduce the costs of industrial production and to generate more profits for re-investment. From 1953 to 1957, the number of raw materials and industrial products covered by this material control system increased from about 110 to more than 300 and accounted for more than 60 percent of total industrial output in 1957 (Lin, Cai and Li, 1994).

Table 4.1: Composition of China's Agricultural and Industrial Output,
1952-92 (per cent)

Year	Agriculture	Light industry	Heavy industry
1952	56.9	27.8	15.3
1957	43.3	31.2	25.5
1960	21.8	26.1	52.1
1965	37.3	32.3	30.4
1970	32.5	31.1	36.4
1975	28.2	31.6	40.2
1980	27.2	34.3	38.5
1985	27.1	34.3	38.6
1990	24.3	37.4	38.3
1992	19.7	37.9	42.4

Source: SSB (State Statistics Bureau), *China Statistical Yearbook*, various editions, Beijing:
China Statistics Press.

cent in most years during both the pre- and post-reform periods (Figure 4.1).[9]
Fourth, capital stock accumulated quickly and the capital/output ratio rose
sharply over time, from 0.6 in 1952 to 2.2 in 1962.[10] It fell following the
economic collapse. For the whole period 1952 to 1992, we find a strongly
increasing trend from a regression of the capital/output ratio on time:

---

9   The investment ratio fell below 20 percent only in 1961-63 when the economy collapsed
     as a result of the 'Great Leap Forward' movement. It fell to around 21 percent in 1967-68
     at the height of the 'Cultural Revolution'.

10   Capital stock is not reported in the Chinese official statistics. Our derivation of the net
     value of capital stock at 1980 prices was based on estimates from other studies. Data
     sources and data processing are discussed in the section on the model, data and estimation
     results.

$$capital/output\ ratio\ =\ 1.024\ +\ 0.032time$$
$$(11.2)\quad(8.5)$$

$\bar{R}^2 = 0.64$ Log of likelihood function = -5.94

The regression result suggests that the ratio increased on average by 0.03 each year during this period. This is much the same as that observed in the FSU.

But were there any differences between the pre-reform Chinese and FSU economies which may be significant enough to lead to a different developmental pattern? Some economists suggest that the peculiar technological profile of the FSU, most importantly the low elasticity of substitution between capital and labour and the sharply declining marginal returns to capital, was associated with two factors. The first was the simple industrial structure, concentrating on heavy industry, and the dominance of the state within that sector. The second was the low stock of managerial skill and marketing knowledge (see Desai, 1987; Easterly and Fischer, 1994). A simple industrial structure dominated by the state sector with heavy administrative intervention reduces substantially the diversity and the flexibility of the capital stock and weakens its transformability. Managerial skill and marketing knowledge are important in the sense that physical capital can only substitute for labour in production when combined with them. These two characteristics were largely determined by the ideology of central planning and the strict controls over markets.

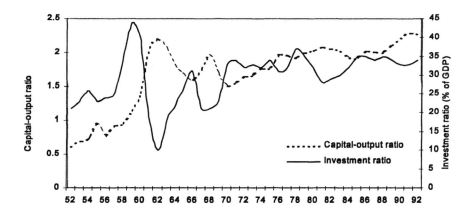

Figure 4.1: Capital/Output Ratio and Investment
Ratio in China, 1952-92

Sources: SSB (State Statistics Bureau), *China Statistical Yearbook*, various editions, Beijing:
China Statistics Press; Data set of this study.

We find that pre-reform China diverged from the experience of the Soviet economy in both of the above directions. In China the heavy industry strategy was enforced most enthusiastically in the 1950s and reached its height during the 'Great Leap Forward' at the end of the 1950s.[11] This irrational policy, coupled with crop failures, led to collapse of the Chinese economy in the early 1960s. National product fell by 42 per cent in 1961. At the same time,

---

11   Over-ambitious objectives were set to overtake the United States and the United Kingdom.
During the 'Great Leap Forward', all available labour was mobilised to make steel and
hundreds of thousands of small furnaces were built, both in villages and in urban
courtyards.

the ideological debate between the FSU and China came to the force.[12] The economic collapse forced the Chinese leadership to re-think its economic policies. Although the main features of the pre-1960 regime were continued, adjustments did occur. The government realised the importance of maintaining appropriate proportions between agriculture and industry, between light and heavy industry and between investment and consumption in achieving sustainable growth. Restrictions on development of the non-state sectors were relaxed. In the urban areas in particular, a number of industrial collectives were established. The proportion of the state sector in total industrial output gradually declined from around 90 per cent in the second five-year plan (1958-62) to 77 per cent in 1978 (SSB). By 1992, the state sector accounted for only 48 per cent of total industrial output. The industrial collectives established in the pre-reform period, though still operating within a distorted macroeconomic environment and under the central planning system, were able to give more scope to consideration of opportunity costs and marginal returns. Most were in light industry and adopted more labour-intensive technology. Light industry accounted for about 50 per cent of total industrial output in the 30 years after 1960 (SSB).

Compared to the FSU, pre-reform China probably had higher levels of managerial ability and marketing knowledge. Although the central planning system dominated the Chinese economy in the pre-reform period, small markets were permitted in urban and rural areas from time to time. Most urban and rural residents had frequent opportunities to refresh their knowledge about the operation of a market. In the countryside, private plots of land were maintained in most years, allowing farmers to practice their marketing and entrepreneurial skills. This may in part explain why the rural sector, especially the township, village and private enterprises, developed so rapidly after the governmental controls were loosened; many farmers became outstanding entrepreneurs within a very short period. Writers have stressed

---

12 The official Chinese explanation of the economic collapse blamed the bad weather conditions in agriculture and the cancellation of all technological transfers and cooperative projects by the FSU.

the role of Hong Kong and Taiwan in providing human capital as well as physical capital for China's economic development, especially in the post-reform period. While current generations in the FSU do not have any experience with markets, the fact that the central planning system existed in China for only about twenty-five years before 1979 meant that many Chinese still had memories about the operation of a market. Moreover, China has had a strong capitalist tradition stretching back at least a thousand years. The southern part, especially Zhejiang, Jiangsu and Guangdong provinces, were advanced areas of capitalist production for many centuries before the European Industrial Revolution (Rawski, 1989; Nolan, 1994).

If industrial structure and knowledge related to management and marketing are two of the most important factors influencing an economy's technological profile, we may hypothesise that China's development experience in its pre-reform period may be different from that of the FSU although both countries followed similar economic policies for a period.

Economic reforms in China have targeted granting more autonomy to enterprises and giving greater roles to the market mechanism. Market-oriented sectors have experienced dramatic growth. Within the industrial sector, the share of light industry rose quickly (Table 4.1). Non-state sectors, especially the rural township, village and private enterprises, gradually became one of the most important industrial sectors. At the same time, the knowledge stock related to management and marketing increased accordingly. We may further hypothesise therefore that, because of the important changes due to policy reform, China's technological profile may evolve in the post-reform period in favour of sustainable growth.

3. THE MODEL, DATA AND ESTIMATION RESULTS

There are several commonly applied functional forms for study of production relationships. The most popular - the Cobb-Douglas function - assumes a unity elasticity of substitution between capital and labour. The Constant Elasticity of Substitution (CES) function relaxes this restriction and assumes the elasticity to be an unknown number between 0 and 1 (Arrow et al., 1961). Easterly and Fischer (1995) apply the CES functional form in their study of the FSU mainly because it is superior to the Cobb-Douglas function when the elasticity of substitution is likely to be low.

Assuming a constant elasticity of substitution between capital and labour, however, may also be a restrictive assumption in studying an economy over several decades. In this study, we apply the more flexible translog production function which allows the elasticity of substitution to vary at each point of observation. The translog function has the form:

$$lnY_t = \alpha + \beta_k lnK_t + \beta_l lnL_t + \delta_{kk}\frac{(lnK_t)^2}{2} + \delta_{ll}\frac{(lnL_t)^2}{2} + \delta_{kl} lnK_t lnL_t + \epsilon_t \quad (1)$$

where is GNP, and are, respectively, capital and employment, and the disturbance term at the tth year. Constant returns to scale implies that and $\delta_{kk} + \delta_{kl} = \delta_{kl} + \delta_{ll} = 0$. Omitting the error term, equation (1) can be rewritten as:

$$lnY_t = \alpha + \beta_k lnK_t + (1-\beta_k)lnL_t - \delta_{kl}\frac{(lnK_t)^2}{2} - \delta_{kl}\frac{(lnL_t)^2}{2} + \delta_{kl} lnK_t lnL_t \quad (2)$$

From this equation, we can easily derive the elasticities of capital (v_t^k) and labour (v_t^l) with respect to output (or their shares in total value added, assuming marginal pricing):

$$v_t^k = \frac{dlnY_t}{dlnK_t} = \beta_k - \delta_{kl}(lnK_t - lnL_t) \quad (3)$$

$$v_t^l = \frac{d\ln Y_t}{d\ln L_t} = (1 - \beta_k) + \delta_{kl}(\ln K_t - \ln L_t) \tag{4}$$

Contribution by capital (c_t^k) and labour (c_t^l) to output growth can be calculated using the above two elasticities (shares) and their changing rates $(\dot{K}, \dot{L})$.

$$c_t^k = v_t^k \dot{K}_t \text{ and } c_t^l = v_t^l \dot{L}_t \tag{5}$$

The residual output growth after subtracting the contributions of capital and labour represents TFP growth:

$$TFP_t = \dot{Y}_t - c_t^k - c_t^l = \dot{Y}_t - v_t^k \dot{K}_t - v_t^l \dot{L}_t \tag{6}$$

Marginal products of capital (m_t^k) and labour (m_t^l) are:

$$m_t^k = \frac{dY_t}{dK_t} = (\frac{Y_t}{K_t})(\beta_k - \delta_{kl}(\ln K_t - \ln L_t)) \tag{7}$$

$$m_t^l = \frac{dY_t}{dL_t} = (\frac{Y_t}{L_t})((1 - \beta_k) + \delta_{kl}(\ln K_t - \ln L_t)) \tag{8}$$

The elasticity of substitution between capital and labour is defined as:

$$e_t^{kl} = \frac{\partial(\frac{K_t}{L_t})}{\partial(P_t^k/P_t^l)} \frac{(P_t^k/P_t^l)}{(\frac{K_t}{L_t})} \tag{9}$$

where and are prices of capital and labour, respectively, at the tth year. Assuming marginal pricing, we have:

$$P_t^k = P_t^y m_t^k \text{ and } P_t^l = P_t^y m_t^l \tag{10}$$

where is the output price. The elasticity of substitution can, therefore, be rewritten as a function of capital and labour inputs and the coefficient estimates of the production function,

$$e_t^{kl} = \frac{(1-\Omega)\Omega}{(1-\Omega)\Omega - \delta_{kl}} \tag{11}$$

where $\Omega = (1 - \beta_k) + \delta_{kl}(lnK_t - lnL_t)$. Clearly, here the elasticity is not a constant but varies when levels of inputs change.

Output and net value of capital stock are measured in million yuan at 1980 prices. Total national output is the total GNP from the SSB. Estimation of the net value of capital stock of the national economy was based on the indices provided in Li Jingwen et al. (1993) and assumes a starting value of 100 billion yuan (1980 prices) in 1952.[13] It was updated to 1992 using information on capital investment and changes in capital goods prices. Employment is measured by the year-end labour force which is also reported in the *Chinese Statistical Yearbook*. This is the only available labour force series for the national economy. The data set is described in detail in the Appendix.

A modified form of equation (2) (incorporating period intercepts and slope dummies for the pre-reform years) is estimated using this data set applying nonlinear least squares estimation and the results are reported in

13   The starting value assumed in the study by Li *et al.* (1993) is similar to the number
      estimated by Su (1993) in his PhD dissertation on China's economic growth. Problems for
      the current study arising from an error in the starting value are minimised because of the
      depreciation of the capital stock with time and the focus hence on changes over time.

Table 4.2. Estimates of β_k, and are highly significant. The coefficients for the time dummies represent each period's aggregate productivity. Taking the period 1970-78 as a reference point (the coefficient estimate of was not significantly different from 0), aggregate productivity in the period 1960-69 was lower, but productivity during 1952-59, 1979-83 and 1984-92 was higher.

4. CHINA'S TECHNOLOGICAL PROFILE

The estimated coefficients can be applied, using the definitions derived in the previous section, to analyse what might be called the technological profile of the Chinese economy. The important aspects that we look at include the elasticity of substitution between capital and labour, the marginal returns to capital and labour, the contributions of capital and labour to total output (or output elasticity of capital and labour) and growth of TFP. The estimated coefficients can also be applied in a growth accounting exercise to show the contributions of the different sources of growth. These results can be used to test the two hypotheses formulated earlier in the chapter by comparing the technological profiles between pre-reform China and the FSU and for the Chinese economy between the pre- and post-reform periods.

The elasticity of substitution between capital and labour was actually quite high in pre-reform China, averaging 0.9 in the period 1952-78. This is more than double the elasticity estimate, 0.37, for the FSU. Compared to the FSU, it appears to have been easier in pre-reform Chinese economy to substitute capital for labour (Easterly and Fischer, 1994).

Changes in marginal returns to capital and labour (measured at 1980 constant prices) in the pre-reform period were mixed. The marginal returns to labour exhibited an increasing trend in the pre-reform period, accompanied by two significant declines around 1962 (the period of economic collapse) and 1968 (at the height of the 'Cultural Revolution') (Figure 4.2).

Table 4.2: Regression Results for the Translog Production Function
(Assuming constant returns to scale)

Variable	Coefficients	National economy
Period intercepts		
D_{52-59}	γ_1	0.081** (2.61)
D_{60-69}	γ_2	-0.272*** (-4.28)
D_{70-78}	γ_3	0.022 (0.24)
D_{79-83}	γ_4	0.324*** (4.66)
D_{84-92}	γ_5	0.462*** (4.48)
$\ln K$	$\beta_k = 1 - \beta_l$	0.017
$\ln L$	β_l	0.983*** (17.54)
$(\ln K)^2/2$	$\delta_{kk} = -\delta_{kl}$	0.370
$(\ln L)^2/2$	$\delta_{ll} = -\delta_{kl}$	0.370
$\ln K \ln L$	δ_{kl}	-0.370** (-2.65)
$D_{52-78}*\ln K$	$\beta_k^d = -\beta_l^d$	0.408
$D_{52-78}*\ln L$	β_l^d	-0.408*** (4.56)
$D_{52-78}*(\ln K)^2/2$	$\delta_{kk}^d = -\delta_{kl}^d$	-0.355
$D_{52-78}*(\ln L)^2/2$	$\delta_{ll}^d = -\delta_{kl}^d$	-0.355
$D_{52-78}*\ln K \ln L$	δ_{kl}^d	0.355* (2.31)
Log likelihood function		50.24

Notes: Numbers in parentheses below coefficient estimates are associated t-ratios. Coefficient estimates with ***
are significant at the 0.01 significance level; with ** significant at the 0.02 significance level; and with *
significant at the 0.05 significance level.

Source: Authors' own estimation.

Figure 4.2: Marginal Returns to Capital and Labour: Chinese National Economy

1952-92

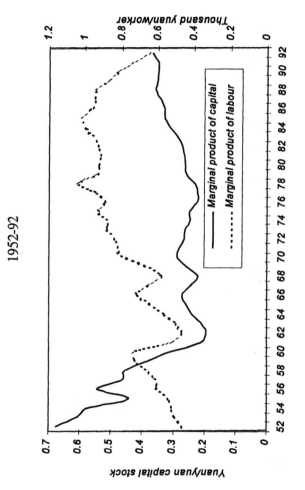

Source: Authors' calculations using estimation results.

The marginal product of capital experienced a dramatic decline between 1952 and 1962, from about 0.7 to around 0.2. It then rose gradually with the economic recovery during 1963-65 but fell again from 1966 to 1968. In the 1970s, the marginal return to capital declined steadily. Overall, two points are worthy of note. First, consistent with what was observed in the FSU, the marginal product of capital in pre-reform China exhibited a clear and strongly decreasing trend. Second, from the beginning of the 1960s, the marginal product of capital was no longer falling so dramatically, although fluctuations from year to year were significant.

The marginal return to capital in pre-reform China was roughly comparable to that in Hong Kong in the 1960-86 period and in Singapore in the 1974-89 period. This result is in striking contrast to the sharply decline in the returns to capital to near zero in the FSU (Table 4.3).

Table 4.3: Real Rates of Returns on Capital, China and Other
Countries, 1950-92

Year	China	Soviet Union	Hong Kong	Singapore
1955	0.44	0.43	--	--
1960	0.31	0.30	0.29	--
1965	0.26	0.20	0.14	0.37
1970	0.29	0.13	0.24	0.40[*]
1975	0.25	0.09	0.09	0.17
1980	0.26	0.06	0.24	0.17
1985	0.33	0.03	0.22	0.09
1990	0.35	--	--	0.13[**]
1992	0.37	--	--	--

Notes: The rates for the Soviet Union are drawn from Figure 7 of Easterly and Fischer, thus there might be some errors in measuring numbers from the diagram. The rates for Hong Kong and Singapore are for fiscal years, i.e., the rate for 1960 was actually for 1960-61. [*] For 1970 we use the rate for 1969-70 and [**] for 1990 we use the rate for 1988-89.

Sources: The authors' own estimation; Easterly and Fischer (1995); Alwyn Young (1992).

Figure 4.3: Contribution of Capital: China and the Former Soviet Union, 1952-92

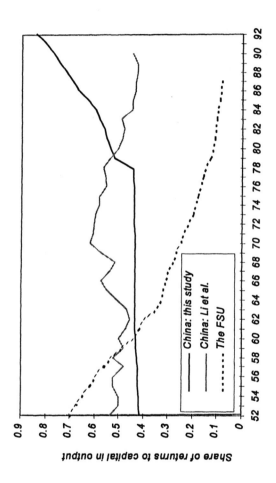

Note: While this study on China covers the period 1952-92, the period covered by Li et al. on the Chinese economy ends at 1987 and that by Easterly and Fischer on the FSU ends at 1990.

Sources: For China, authors' calculations using estimation results and Li et al. (1993); For the FSU, Easterly and Fischer (1995).

The shares of capital and labour in total output (assuming that marginal pricing is observed) or the output elasticity of capital and labour provide a piece of complementary information. Easterly and Fischer (1995) find that the share of capital decreased dramatically in the case of the FSU (Figure 4.3).[14] However, for China we find that the share of returns to capital in total output was relatively stable in the pre-reform period, around 0.4. One way to interpret this elasticity is that a 1 per cent increase in capital stock would, on average, result in a 0.4 per cent increases in output.[15]

As a comparison, Figure 4.3 also plots the share of capital in total output computed by Li Jingwen et al. (1993). Although there was an increase before 1970 and a decrease after that, their estimated share is relatively stable. The difference between the two series of estimates for China may arise from the fact that while estimates by Li Jingwen et al. were based on the costs actually incurred, our estimates of shares assume marginal pricing. It is safe to conclude, however, that the drastic decline seen in the FSU's capital share in total output did not happen in China.

The final analysis undertaken of the development of the pre-reform Chinese economy is a growth accounting exercise (Table 4.4). The result shows that, first, increases in capital stock dominated economic growth in the pre-reform periods. Second, the contribution of labour to growth was only about 24.4 per cent. Third, there was negative TFP growth of -0.1 per cent per annum. Therefore, growth in pre-reform China was extensive as in the FSU.

Thus, we conclude that the technological profile in pre-reform China was similar to that in the FSU generating declining returns to capital, especially in the 1950s, and negative productivity growth during 1952-78. But the situation in the pre-reform period was not as bad as that in the FSU because China's substitution elasticity between capital and labour was higher, the sharply falling trend in the marginal product of capital came to an end in the early

---

14   The numbers are also read from Figure 8 of Easterly and Fischer (1995) which may, again, have some measurement errors.

15   The estimates involved, 0.3 and 0.5, are, respectively, calculated average shares (or elasticities) for the period 1952-78 and 1978-92.

1960s, and the share of capital in GNP was relatively stable. We believe that these differences related, directly or indirectly, to (i) changes or adjustment in the policy position which was at least partly responsible for limited changes in economic structure; and (ii) knowledge stock related to management and marketing.

Table 4.4: Sources of Growth in the Chinese Economy, 1952-92

	The pre-reform period (1952-78)			The post-reform period (1978-92)		
	Growth rate (%)	Contribution		Growth rate (%)	Contribution	
		absolute (% points)	share (%)		absolute (% points)	share (%)
Output	6.0		100.0	8.8		100.0
Capital	10.8	4.6	77.8	10.1	6.5	73.9
Labour	2.6	1.5	24.4	2.8	1.0	11.5
TFP		-0.1	-2.2		1.3	14.6

Sources: Authors' estimates.

We repeated the above exercises for the post-reform period. The results can be summarised as follows: (i) the marginal product of capital increased from 0.25 in the mid-1970s to 0.37 in 1992 (Figure 4.2); (ii) the marginal return to labour, however, fluctuated throughout the 1980s and then decreased sharply from 1989; (iii) the share of capital in GNP has increased steadily in the reform period, 1978-92 (Figure 4.3); and (iv) the growth accounting exercise reveals that, during 1978-92, although the capital contribution still dominated in output growth, the TFP improved steadily at an annual rate of 1.3 per cent (Table 4.4).

These results suggest that the technological profile in post-reform China is different from that in the pre-reform period. The changes, mainly derived from the market-oriented policy reforms, are favourable for sustainable growth.

5. DISCUSSION

This study examines China's technological profile in its pre- and post-reform periods, in a comparison with the FSU. Because the data set used in this study was directly drawn from official Chinese statistics, the results are subject to known criticisms of the quality of China's economic data, especially concerning the robustness of GNP and its deflator.

It is found that the technological profile in pre-reform China, especially in the 1950s, resembled in many respects that of the FSU, such as decreasing marginal product of capital and negative productivity growth. Thus the growth of the pre-reform Chinese economy, at around 6 per cent per annum, was likely not sustainable given its extensive nature. Differences existed in the technological profiles of the two economies, however. China had a relatively high substitution elasticity between labour and capital and a relatively stable GNP elasticity of capital.

We speculate that these two factors probably determined the differences in economic development between pre-reform China and the FSU. Heavy industry and the state sector were not as dominant as in the FSU. Non-state sectors and light industries were permitted to grow (at limited speed) after the economic adjustment in 1963-65. The knowledge stock related to managerial and marketing skills was higher in China both because of its stronger capitalist tradition and because of the less strict controls over small-scale market operations.

Economic reform in China significantly changed its technological profile. Both the marginal product of capital and the GNP elasticity of capital have since increased. A positive rate of TFP growth has been achieved. These changes were directly associated with the market-oriented reform and are favourable for sustained growth.

An important implication of these findings is that policy reform can change an economy's technological profile. Granting autonomy to enterprises and giving importance to market mechanisms encourages accumulation of managerial skill and marketing knowledge which is critical for capital to be substitutable for labour, helps to maintain the marginal return to capital and facilitates the achievement of productivity growth. The growth pattern can be changed from extensive to intensive.

Whether or not China can sustain its rapid economic growth for a considerable period depends on factors additional to those analysed above. Economic policies can have important impacts on the sustainability of growth in two ways. First, even given a favourable technological profile, an inappropriate policy setting may reduce economic efficiency significantly. Slow economic growth in pre-reform China, with the two extreme periods of the 'Great Leap Forward' and the 'Cultural Revolution', illustrates this vividly. Second, institutional arrangements are an important factor shaping a country's technological profile. The economic structure in the FSU, including its institutional structure, was a result of its economic policies.

China's existing technological profile, therefore, only provides a necessary condition for sustained rapid growth. It becomes a part of the sufficient condition only when combined with good policies and available inputs. The sustainability of rapid growth in China will thus be dependent on further economic reforms and a smooth transition from central planing to markets. But the important point is that when the technological profile reaches an extreme such as was the case in the FSU in the mid-1980s, even good policies and rapidly increasing inputs cannot produce output growth.

Adjustment costs and time lags may be different when reform policies are introduced to economies with different technological profiles. In an economy with high returns to capital and labour and a large elasticity of substitution between factors, a small change in institutional arrangements may produce substantial benefits within a short period, while in an economy with very low or close to zero marginal returns to capital and labour and a small elasticity of substitution, a major change in economic policy may not be able to generate any significant result. This is best illustrated by comparing the experiences of agricultural reform in both China and the FSU. Reforms at the micro level in China between the end of the 1970s and the beginning of the 1980s led to a remarkable expansion of agricultural production, now regarded as an economic miracle (Lin, 1992). Similar reforms in the FSU, however, failed to deliver anything approaching comparable consequences.

The adjustment costs and time lags involved in policy change may have further implications for the political economy of reform and for the debate over different reform approaches, e.g., gradualism and 'shock therapy'. In the late 1980s, most economists favoured a rapid transition approach (IMF, World Bank, OECD and EBRD, 1990). It was even argued that "there is no theory supporting a gradual switch of system" (Aslund, 1990). In the early 1990s, however, most formerly centrally planned economies in transition adopting shock therapy experienced significant economic decline. By contrast, gradualism has had a very successful record in China and this experience is being regarded as providing possible "pointers for other economies in transition" (Lin et al., 1994).

The findings of this study, however, imply that the impacts of economic reforms following different approaches may also be determined, in part, by initial conditions, i.e., including the existing technological profile. Gradualism has been successful and is likely to continue to be superior to 'shock therapy' in China because China's technological profile has helped the gradualism approach to gather strong momentum in reform and growth without incurring the significant adjustment costs seemingly associated with rapid transition. But given the technological profile in the FSU, a gradual approach to reform would probably "lead to nowhere" (Prybyla, 1990).

APPENDIX

DATA SET USED IN EMPIRICAL STUDY

Y	The current value GNP in yuan [*Guomin Shourou*] is drawn from the *China Statistical Yearbook* (various years); it is then deflated by the national price index [*Quanguo Lingshe Wujia Zhong Zhishu*] which is also taken from the *China Statistical Yearbook* (various years); the series is set at 1 for the year 1980.
K	Net value of capital stock in yuan uses the estimated indices provided by Li et al. (1993) and assumes a starting value of 100 billion yuan (at 1980 prices) in 1952. The data series is updated to the year 1992 using information available on capital investment and changes in capital goods prices for the recent years from the State Statistics Bureau.
L	The year-end labour force (persons) is directly taken from the *China Statistical Yearbook*.
K/GNP	Capital/output ratio is calculated from the constant price GNP and capital stock data described above.
I/GNP	Investment ratio of GNP [*Jilai Lu*] us directly taken from the *China Statistical Yearbook*.

 The date set used in the empirical estimation is reported in the table on the next page.

GNP, Net Value of Capital Stock and Year-end Labour Force of the Chinese Economy 1952-92

	GNP	Capital stock	Labour force
1952	165.3	100.0	207.3
1953	188.4	129.9	213.6
1954	199.3	144.3	218.3
1955	212.1	202.0	223.3
1956	242.0	187.6	230.2
1957	252.9	230.9	237.7
1958	308.6	288.6	266.0
1959	333.9	375.2	261.7
1960	329.1	461.7	258.8
1961	231.4	476.2	255.9
1962	216.4	476.2	259.1
1963	239.5	490.6	266.4
1964	279.0	505.0	277.4
1965	326.3	548.3	286.7
1966	381.8	606.0	298.1
1967	354.2	620.4	308.1
1968	331.1	649.3	319.2
1969	395.0	663.7	332.3
1970	486.9	735.9	344.3
1971	521.2	808.0	356.2
1972	536.0	880.2	358.5
1973	580.5	966.7	366.5
1974	587.1	1038.9	373.7
1975	635.9	1125.5	381.7
1976	619.0	1212.0	388.3
1977	667.3	1312.5	393.8
1978	749.4	1442.9	401.5
1979	801.8	1601.6	410.2
1980	853.4	1731.5	423.6
1981	895.1	1861.3	437.3
1982	968.3	1991.2	453.0
1983	1064.8	2149.9	464.4
1984	1209.8	2337.5	482.0
1985	1372.9	2626.1	498.7
1986	1478.5	2972.4	512.8
1987	1629.3	3275.4	527.8
1988	1813.6	3621.7	543.3
1989	1879.7	3968.0	553.3
1990	1976.1	4328.7	567.4
1991	2128.6	4891.4	583.6
1992	2435.1	5527.3	594.3

REFERENCES

Arrow, K.J., Chenery, H.B., Minhas, B.S. and Solow, R.M. (1961) "Capital-Labour Substitution and Economic Efficiency", *Review of Economics and Statistics*, 3(43): 223-250.

Aslund, A. (1990) "Gorbachev, Perestroika, and Economic Crisis", *Problems of Communism*, January-April, pp. 13-41.

Bergson, Abram (1987) "Comparative Productivity: The USSR, Eastern Europe, and West", *American Economic Review*, 3(77): 342-257.

Desai, Padma (1987) *The Soviet Economy: Problems and Prospects*, Oxford: Basil Blackwell.

Easterly, William and Fischer, Stanley (1995) "The Soviet Economic Decline", *The World Bank Economic Review*, 9(3): 341-371.

Garnaut, Ross and Ma, Guonan (1993) "How Rich Is China: Evidence from the Food Economy", *Australian Journal of Chinese Affairs*, 30 (July), pp. 121-148.

Garnaut, Ross (1989) *Australia and Northeast Asia Ascendancy*, Canberra: Australian Government Publishing Service.

Garnaut, Ross (1994) "The World Economy with a Dynamic China", paper presented at the Distinguished Lecture Series, *China in the Twenty-First Century*, Stanford University, November 3, 1994.

IMF, World Bank, OECD and EBRD (1990) *The Economy of the USSR: Summary and Recommendations*, Washington, D.C.: The World Bank.

Kim, Jong-Il and Lau, Lawrence J. (1994) "The Sources of Growth of the East Asian Newly Industrialised Countries", *Journal of the Japanese and International Economics*, 3(8):235-271

Krugman, Paul (1994) "The Myth of Asia's Miracle", *Foreign Affairs*, 6(73): 62-78.

Lau, Lawrence (1994) "The Chinese Economy in the Twenty-First Century", Department of Economics, Stanford University, mimeographed.

Li, Jingwen, Jorgenson, Dale W., Zheng, Yiujing and Kuroda, Mashiro (1993) *Productivity and Economic Growth in China, the United States and Japan* [*Shengchanlu Yu Zhong Mei Re Jingji Zhengzhang Yanjiu*], Beijing: China Social Science Press.

Lin, Justin Yifu (1990) "Collectivisation and China's Agricultural Crisis in 1959-61", *Journal of Political Economy*, 6(98): 1228-1252.

Lin, Justin Yifu (1992) "Rural Reforms and Agricultural Growth in China", *American Economic Review*, 1(82): 34-51.

Lin, Justin Yifu, Cai, Fang and Li, Zhou (1994) "China's Economic Reforms: Pointers for Other Economies in Transition?", Policy Research Working Paper, No. 1310, Agricultural Policies Division, Agriculture and Natural Resources Department, The World Bank.

Nolan, Peter (1994) "Introduction: The Chinese Puzzle", in Qimiao Fan and Peter Nolan (eds) *China's Economic Reforms: The Costs and Benefits of Incrementalism*, New York: St Martin's Press.

Ofer, Gur (1987) "Soviet Economic Growth: 1928-85", *Journal of Economic Literature*, 4(25): 1767-1833.

Perkins, Dwight (1992) "China's Economic Boom and the Integration of the Economies of East Asia", paper prepared for the Korean Institute of Public Administration and the Economic Research Institute of the Daishin Group, Seoul, Korea.

Powell, Raymond (1968) "Economic Growth in the U.S.S.R.", *Scientific American*, December.

Prybyla, J. (1990) "A Broken System", in G. Hicks (ed.) *The Broken Mirror*, Harlow, Essex: Longman.

Rawski, T.G. (1989) *Economic Growth in Pre-War China*, Berkeley: University of California Press.

SSB (State Statistics Bureau), *China Statistical Yearbook*, various editions, Beijing: China Statistics Press.

Su, Yuan (1993) *An Analysis of China's Economic Growth* [*Zhongguo Jingji Zhengzhang Fenxi*], Shanghai: Fudan University Press.

Summers, R. and Heston, A. (1993) "The Penn World Tables [Mark 5]: An Expanded Set of International Comparison, 1950-88", *Quarterly Journal of Economics*, May, pp. 327-368.

World Bank (1983) *China: Socialist Economic Development*, Washington, D.C.: The World Bank.

Xue, Muqiao (1981) *China's Socialist Economy*, Beijing: Foreign Languages Press.

Young, Alwyn (1992) "A Tale of Two Cities: Factor Accumulation and Technical Change in Hong Kong and Singapore", in NBER, *Macroeconomics Annual 1992*, Cambridge, MA: The MIT Press, pp. 13-54.

Young, Alwyn (1994) "The Tyranny of Numbers: Confronting the Statistical Realities of the East Asian Growth Experience", NBER Working Paper, No. 4680, March.

CHAPTER 5

An Analysis Of China's Economic Growth

Yu-Shi Mao And Ju-Huang He[1]

Abstract

Attributes China's rapid growth since 1980 to flexibility and pragmatism in its economic policy and to China's high rate of savings and investment. Argues that changes in the ownership structure of China's industry have significantly stimulated economic growth in China. Non-state-owned enterprises are more dynamic and vigorous than state-owned enterprises and the growing relative importance of the former has stimulated China's economic growth. Deficiency of effective demand is not a dampener on economic growth in China unlike in some Western economies. It is also observed that China's GNP is under recorded by at least 10 per cent because of unreported income. China's underground economy is substantial in size. A major contributor to China's recent economic growth has been internal migration. Since 1978, about 8 million persons per year have migrated from

---

1   Unirule Institute of Economics, Beijing, China and Institute of Quantitative and Technical Economics, Chinese Academy of Social Sciences, Beijing, China

rural areas to urban areas. This is one of the greatest mass migrations ever recorded. In addition, it is believed that around 10 million persons per year move between urban areas. Between 1979 and 1994 it is estimated that about 128.2 million people moved from the countryside to urban areas in China. They have made a substantial contribution to production in urban areas and have played a major role in China's economic growth.

1. INTRODUCTION

China's rapid economic growth of the past seventeen years is unprecedented in the three thousand years of China's written history and also rare in the world history too. Since the beginning of the industrial revolution in Europe in the eighteenth century, only a few countries have embarked on institutional change a towards market system and have become affluent. Others became trapped by institutional rigidity and suffered poverty which they can hardly get rid of. The world has become divided into rich developed countries and poor developing countries.

After World War II, some Asian small countries began to change. They had been classified as developing countries but achieved remarkable economic growth by adopting flexible and pragmatic economic policies. The so called "four tigers" are examples. However, they are small countries; their total population is much less than 100 million, and the impact produced by their growth on the world economy is limited. So the question has arisen of whether their policies and experience can be applied to many other developing countries?

China's economic achievement has provided a positive answer. Flexibility and pragmatism may be essential for such economic growth. Moreover, China created a unique and fruitful path to change its centrally planned economy into a market economy. Such an experience with institutional change was badly needed in the world context, because there were dozens of countries following a centralized economic system which had already reached a dead end. China's economic accomplishments are particularly significant because they happened in a country with more than one fifth of the world's total population and with hundreds of years of economic stagnation.

Although China's economic growth has been continuous and its per capita income has quadrupled within the past seventeen years, people still doubt whether such growth rate can be maintained. China achieved such an economic miracle under conditions of political stability. There has been little deliberate political reform except that forced forward by economic forces, yet the system has allowed rapid economic change. In reality, every country in the world is facing some special economic difficulties, and all countries are facing uncertainty too. Nobody can predict accurately what will happen in the future. This chapter will analyse some fundamental features of China's economic growth and review the economic records which outsiders may ignore.

2. DOMESTIC SAVINGS AND INVESTMENT ARE IMPORTANT SOURCE OF GROWTH

Capital, labour, technology, and institutional change, interacting with each other are sources of economic growth. Institutional change in particular alters the incentive structure and the mechanisms of information transmission. Both are significant influences on economic performance. In China's case, planned or mandatory economic institutions have gradually been replaced by market institutions. Most price controls have been lifted. Correct price signals have been introduced to direct resource allocation. Non-state ownership has grown very fast, thus firms have become more aggressive in the market, and internal efficiency within firms has improved. These changes increased employment of all kinds of productive factors such as, capital, labour, natural resources, and also increase their marginal productivity.

China has been a country of high saving, but this did not help its economic growth much before the reforms began in 1978 owing to the low efficiency its investment. Ill conceived economic theory and a distorted price system caused such low efficiency. After the reform these offending elements have been gradually removed, and the high level of investment due to high saving rates has become an outstanding factor in helping China's development. Using the statistics published by the World Bank, the average investment rate for China in the period 1981-90 was 35% of GNP, and its average growth rate was 9.4%. These figures indicate that every yuan of investment added 0.27 yuan to China's GNP, or that an association of this type existed.

A similar relationship between savings rate and growth rate for other countries can be found in Table 5.1.

Table 5.1: Average Investment Rate and Growth Rate, 1980 - 1991

Country (1)	Investment rate % (2)	Standard deviation of (2) (3)	Growth rate % (4)
Bangladesh	12.9	0.16	4.3
India	23.7	0.06	5.4
China	35.3	0.12	9.4
Pakistan	17.6	0.05	6.1
Indonesia	21.5	0.18	5.6
Thailand	27.4	0.22	7.9
Philippines	19.6	0.25	1.1
Nigeria	15.1	0.27	1.9
Turkey	22.3	0.09	1.1
Brazil	20.0	0.11	2.5
Korea Rep.	31.1	0.13	9.6
Italy	20.9	0.09	2.4
UK	18.2	0.09	2.9
Japan	30.1	0.07	4.2
Germany	20.1	0.07	4.2
USA	16.6	0.09	2.6

Sources: World Bank, *World Bank Development Reports*, 1984-1994

We indicate in Table 5.1 the standard deviation of investment rate during the twelve years period, which reflects the stability of economic relationship. There appears to be a relationship between the growth rate of GNP and the investment rate. This is graphed in Figure 5.1. The boundary line AB has a slope of 0.28. Hence, every one per cent rise in the investment rate could potentially add 0.28 units to the growth rate of GNP. Thus China's growth rate appears to be only 0.01 below the potential one. However, some countries are well below the potential. Philippines, Nigeria, and Turkey, for example, have a low efficiency in their investment. This is associated with a higher variable rate of investment than for most other countries. The standard deviation of the rate of investment is 0.25, 0.27 for Philippines and for Nigeria respectively, but that for Turkey it is somewhat lower at 0.09. Turkey has its own special conditions. Developed countries have a much lower "efficiency" of investment though the standard deviation of the rate of investment is small, varying from 0.04 to 0.09, or the rate of investment is rather stable. This explains why capital flows from developed countries to developing countries where the efficiency of investment (return on investment) is higher. Seven countries have GNP growth rates which cluster along the line AB. All of these countries have a relatively small standard deviation in their investment rate. Thailand is an exception. In fact, Thailand's investment rate did not fluctuate but steadily rose from 21% in early eighties to 37% in 1990.

Foreign direct investment has accounted for only about 15% of the total investment in China in the recent years (*Statistical Yearbook of China*, 1992, 93, 94, 95). State appropriations for investment are even smaller, about a quarter of foreign investment. So the major portion of China's investment comes from domestic loans and fund raising, which are drafted from deposits in the bank, or from the people's savings. Therefore, we can conclude that China's high investment rate is mainly due to the high savings rate of Chinese people. This high propensity to save is a result of China's culture, tradition, habit, and social structure, and is beyond the direct control of government policy. Consequently, the high growth rate of China's GNP seems to continue.

Figure 5.1: The Growth Rate and Investment Rate (of GNP)
of 16 Countries, 1980-91

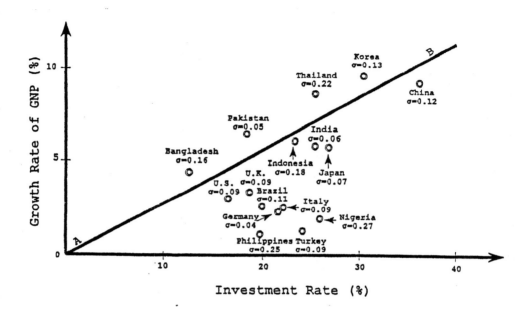

3. OWNERSHIP STRUCTURE AFFECTS THE GROWTH RATE

As stated before, China's investment efficiency was low before its economic
reforms. This low efficiency can be attributed to political factors and to
economic ones. One example of political causes was the billions of yuan
wasted to build the so called "Third Line Construction" for defence purpose,
which took the lion's share of the national investment during the ten years of
the Cultural Revolution. Many of the factories constructed under this scheme
were built in high mountains and even in tunnels. They produced products at a
cost much higher than the market price because of their poor location and
strange factory layout. Most of these factories have thousands of staff have
formed a small city around their workshops. So it is very difficult to move

them. Third Line factories have become a burden on the national economy, and we do not see any effective measures to change the situation.

Economic factors which caused low efficiency in investment were distorted prices and the absence of ownership responsibility. Price distortions have been gradually rectified since 1978.

Although some distortions still remain, such as in interest rates, tariffs for energy and transportation, most price controls have been lifted. However, the ownership problem is still a severe barrier to improving efficiency. In public investment, no one assumes the responsibility of the owner who should take care of the profit generated by a project through careful management. State-owned enterprises are owned by the whole people, but nobody acts on behalf of whole people. Low efficiency prevails in state owned enterprises not only in new projects but also in old existing ones.

Since 1984, multiple forms of ownership have emerged, and efficiency differences between state-owned and non-state-owned enterprises can be observed. Non-state-owned enterprises have been more dynamic and vigorous than state ones and this has resulted in their share of industrial output growing as shown in Table 5.2.

Both the shares of gross output and net output of collective and other non-state ownership have increased dramatically and at the same time the share of state owned enterprises has declined. The figures for 1995 were not available [at the time of writing of this contribution], but officials at the Statistics Bureau say that the share of value added by non-state-owned enterprises has reached more than 50%. These figures show that the ownership structure of enterprises in China has undergone some fundamental changes in recent times.

Table 5.2:   Gross Output, Value Added and Net Output of Industrial Sector by Ownership in China in billion yuan, current value

Year	State owned bn yuan	%	Collective bn yuan	%	Others bn yuan	%
Gross output						
1978	329	78	95	22	0	0
1985	630	65	321	32	30	3
1990	1306	55	852	36	234	10
1994	2620	34	3143	34	1927	25
Value added						
1994	790	54	412	28	267	18
Net output						
1981	132	79	34	21	0.9	0.6
1985	206	74	68	25	3.0	1.1
1990	357	70	132	26	20.1	4.0

The difference in the rate of growth of output between state-owned and non-state-owned sectors is a result of differences in efficiency of management and in investment. Our impression has been that the efficiency of state-owned enterprises is low, because of their rigid internal management, dull response to market changes, and more importantly, lack of monitoring of the behaviour of managers. Jefferson et al. (1995) reported that the efficiency of state-owned enterprises seems to be better (refer to Annex I). But they used total output or revenue to measure efficiency in their comparison and counted intermediate inputs as factors of production. We rearrange the calculation using only labour and capital as factors of production while keeping the proportion of the labour elasticity and capital elasticity unchanged assuming returns to scale to be constant. The elasticities for labour and capital thus calculated are 0.37 and 0.63 respectively for state-owned enterprises, and 0.46, 0.54 for collective enterprise respectively.

A better measure of efficiency is the ratio of real value added to total factor input (TI). We calculated this in the way shown in the table in Annex I. The result clearly illustrates that the efficiency of collective enterprises has been higher than that of state-owned since 1988, and the difference in efficiency has increased year by year.

To identify the efficiency difference caused by ownership, we study how the growth rate of output depends upon investment rate and ownership. A regression was made using provincial figures for 1993 and 1994. The explanatory factors are: investment (rate) in fixed assets FI (relative to provincial GDP), ownership structure NS (share of industrial output of non-stated-owned enterprises), and foreign investment rate FC (share of direct foreign investment in provincial GDP).

These provincial figures are listed in Annex II. Regression gives the following results:

$$G = 0.1033FI + 0.12925NS + 0.0366FC, \quad R^2 = 0.655 \quad (1)$$
$$(3.42) \quad\quad (10.1) \quad\quad (0.47)$$

where G denotes the growth rate of provincial GDP, and the figures in the bracket are t values.

Since the coefficient of FC is rather small, foreign investment did not play an important role. If this factor is ignored, the regression gives the following result:

$$G = 0.1081FI + 0.1937NS, \quad R^2 = 0.652 \quad (2)$$
$$(3.85) \quad\quad (10.42)$$

These results indicate that the share of non-state-owned enterprises has positive effects on the growth rate. This is because their efficiency of management is higher.

4. COULD DEMAND CREATE MORE INCOME?

In Western economies, economic structure is determined by the price mechanism, so microeconomic relationships are almost in equilibrium, or there are no enduring bottlenecks. But their macroeconomic situation is different, as savings can not be completely invested. Hence, aggregate demand is less than aggregate supply and recession results. In such a case, additional demand will create income, and the created income will in turn generate further additional demand, thus there will be a multiplier effect. Keynes theory describes such chain of events. And the Keynesian multiplier is the reciprocal of the savings rate.

However, in China's case, the demand for investment always exceeds savings, so there should not be any recession. However, there have been always bottlenecks in Chinese economy such as transportation and telecommunication. Therefore the economy is not in micro-economic equilibrium. Even when aggregate demand equals aggregate supply, still there will be many commodities in short supply and others in over-supply. Then the question arises: in such conditions would additional demand create more income?

Superficially, additional demand, regardless of consumption, investment, or export, will finally turn into income, and these incomes will turn into purchasing power creating more demand. Since in China's case all income will turn into purchasing power due to insufficient funds for investment, the Keynesian multiplier, should it exist, would be infinity, and the only constraint is enough time to let the whole process take place. But in fact, the process described above will not happen, because if investment equals savings, the aggregate demand will equal aggregate supply, or the precondition of Keynes theory does not apply, and the Keynesian multiplier does not apply.

China's economy is in disequilibrium. Then what will be the impact of additional demand? This question can be answered by tracing out how money changes hands. Suppose a portion of additional investment in a project becomes the wages of workers which are used for purchasing a bundle of goods. This purchasing represents extra demand. This bundle of goods can be divided into two categories: those under-supplied (including those for which supply and demand is in equilibrium), and those over-supplied. Let q and d denote the share of under-supplied and over-supplied goods respectively, and q + d = 1. In relation to under-supplied goods, the extra demand will not promote production, since the production is already limited by the production capacity, or the bottleneck. The only effect of such extra demand is an increase in price if the price is not under governmental control. However, extra effective demand for under-supplied goods will increase their production, since their production capacity has not been fully utilized because of insufficient demand. Therefore, one unit of extra demand will create d units of output on the first round of money changing hands.

This process will proceed continuously as the money changes hands further, so the total increased output G will be:

$$G = 1 + d + d^2 + d^3 + \ldots\ldots$$
$$= 1/(1-d) = 1/q \ (3)$$

This equation states that extra demand will create a chain of increases in demand and expand output. One unit of extra demand will create 1/q units of output, where q is the portion of goods which is under-supplied. The lower is q the more the output created. But when q approaches zero, G will not become infinity, because when fewer and fewer goods are under-supplied, or more and more goods are over-supplied, the aggregate supply will exceed aggregate demand, and the Keynes multiplier will come to play. In this condition the increased output will be controlled by savings rate.

The value of q has not been specifically studied for Chinese economy, but it is important for understanding the operation of the Chinese economy. We made a rough estimation according to a urban household survey which classifies the consumption into sixteen categories (Mao, 1995). Per capita consumption was 2111 yuan in 1993. Among goods and services in oversupply were clothing, recreational articles and services, plus one third of household appliances and services, medicines, medical service, and

miscellaneous items. The sum of oversupplied goods and service amounts to
623 yuan, or 0.3 of the total consumption. Therefore, this estimation gives a
value for q of 0.7, and G would therefore be 1.43. That means in addition to
the initial extra demand, there is an additional income of 0.43 times the
original extra demand This is generated due to a chain effect. However, this
estimation applies only to urban households and does not include capital
goods.

The multiple creation of income implies multiple creation of employment
because unemployment exists if the consumption structure is insufficient to
support the production structure. It takes time to accomplish the process of
multiple creation of employment. The speed of employment creation equals
the speed of the circulation of money. In a one year period the number of
times that money changes hands, the velocity of circulation of money, v, for
Chinese economy is 3.75 (*Statistical Yearbook*, 1995). Within one year, one
unit of extra demand will create G additional income where G is:

$$G \; = \; 1 + d + d^2 + d^3 + ... + d^v$$
$$= \; (1 - d^{1+v})/q \quad (4)$$

In our case G =1.42. The calculation shows that the G converges to G
(equals 1.43) rather quickly.

5. AN ESTIMATION OF CHINESE UNDERGROUND ECONOMY

The extent of the underground economy is measured by the output not included in official statistical estimates of GNP. Every country has an underground economy, but China's is particularly big. This is because its statistics are incomplete, especially its tax system is at a primitive stage of development so tax evasion and corruption are rather common. Furthermore, Chinese are very active in finding new ways to earn income which often are not under the state supervision. The omissions in measurement of China's GNP could result in serious errors in all aspects of policy formulation and academic research. However, to correct such a mistake is extremely difficult because this part of the economy is underground and no statistics are available. Literature regarding this area is hardly available.

The existence of an underground economy implies that there are incomes which have been hidden by households. In China there is a good system of household surveys providing information on household income and consumption. But the figures reported by households may be less than the real ones because households tend to disguise their real income. Fortunately, there are some figures which households can not hide. These include the bank deposit and treasury bond purchased by households. From the difference between the estimates from the household survey and the value of bank deposits and treasury bonds on issue, we can estimate the extent of hidden household income, a good approximation for the size of the underground economy.

We first estimate household savings using bank statistics then figure out the hidden income using the data from the household surveys. In theory, the increase of household saving should equal the sum of the following items:

(1. increase in bank deposits) + (2. increase in cash held) + (3. increase in stock shares and securities) + (4. increase in insurance deposits) + (5. increase in household fixed assets) + (6. increase in stock of commodities) + (7. increase in liability to bank) + (8. depreciation of household fixed assets).

Of these items, (1), (2), (5) and part of (3) can be found in the *China Statistics Yearbook*, and others can not be identified. So we have to simplify the estimation using the following relationship:

Increase of household savings = (increase in bank deposit) + (increase in cash held) + (newly issued treasury bonds - matured treasury bonds) + (increase in fixed assets not paid for by bank loans)   (5)

Here we ignore (4) and (6), and securities other than treasury bonds, but we drop (7) to compensate for this ignorance. Such an estimation should be practically correct since these items in the Chinese cases are rather small. Using the simplified equation (5), figures from the *Statistical Yearbook of China* can be employed to estimate the increase of household savings as shown in Table 5.3.

According to Table 5.3 by applying relationship (5), we can estimate the household savings shown in Table 5.4. The unreported savings can be estimated as the difference in savings calculated from the figures in Table 5.3 and the reported savings obtained in household survey, i.e.:

Unreported savings = estimated savings - (reported income - reported consumption)   (6)

where estimated savings are deduced from (5) as per Table 5.3, reported figures are obtained from household survey etc. listed in the *China Statistical Yearbook*, and which are quoted in Annex III. We use expression (6) to estimate the size of China's underground economy. This is a rough approximation, since unreported savings do not coincide with the underground economy. Just because of the difficulty in obtaining underground figures, it is used as an approximation for estimation purposes.

The calculated annual figures for the size of China's underground economy based on unreported incomes are shown in Table 5.4.

Table 5.3: Figures Used to Estimate China's Household Savings in bn
Current Yuan

Year	Total bank deposits	Cash held	Bonds issued	Bond matured	Increased fixed assets
1979	28.1	21.6	--	--	--
1980	40.0	28.1	--	--	11.9
1981	52.4	33.3	--	--	17.8
1982	67.5	37.3	--	--	21.1
1983	89.3	45.8	4.2	--	32.2
1984	121.5	65.9	4.3		40.9
1985	162.3	82.0	6.1		53.5
1986	223.8	97.2	6.3	0.8	71.0
1987	307.3	116.1	6.3	2.3	72.7
1988	380.2	169.3	13.2	2.8	102.0
1989	514.7	185.0	13.9	1.9	99.7
1990	703.4	208.9	19.7	11.4	96.5
1991	911.0	251.1	28.1	15.7	113.0
1992	1154.5	340.8	46.1	34.2	117.1
1993	1520.4	460.4	38.1	22.4	142.2
1994	2151.9	571.5	102.9	36.5	190.5

The figures in the last column of Table 5.4 show that the underground economy accounts for about ten per cent of China's GDP. For 1982, the estimates of the unreported income or the size of the underground economy turned out to be negative, probably because there are also unreported levels of consumption. Therefore, we think that the real underground economy may be somewhat larger than the figures indicate in Table 5.4.

Table 5.4: Household Savings, Reported Income and Reported Consumption and Size of Unreported Income bn Current Yuan

Year (1)	Estimated savings (2)	Reported income (3)	Reported consumption (4)	Unreport-ed income (5)	GDP (6)	(6)/ (5)% (7)
1980	30.3				451.8	
1981	35.4	244.7	279.6	0.6		
1982	40.3	276.6	330.3	-13.4		
1983	66.5	316.5	380.9	2.2		
1984	97.5	354.3	444.0	7.8		
1985	116.4	425.3	509.0	32.7	896.4	3.6
1986	153.2	500.3	583.7	69.7	1020.2	6.8
1987	179.2	569.0	657.7	157.1	1196.3	7.6
1988	238.6	790.0	709.5	157.1	1492.8	10.5
1989	261.9	803.0	910.2	154.6	1690.9	9.1
1990	317.5	878.1	1037.3	158.3	1853.1	8.5
1991	375.2	972.6	1127.5	220.3	2161.8	10.2
1992	462.1	1100.0	1322.5	239.7	2663.5	9.0
1993	643.3	1359.5	1646.4	356.4	3451.5	10.3
1994	999.5	1847.91	2245.9	601.5	4500.6	13.4

Using China's estimated level of household savings we can estimate the importance of household savings for its investment. Table 5.5 indicates the situation.

Table 5.5: Chinese Household Savings and Total Investment in Current Yuan bn

Year	Household savings S	Investment I	Savings rate	Ratio of S/I
1980	30.3	159	.115	--
1981	35.4	158		.224
1982	40.3	176		.229
1983	66.5	201		.332
1984	97.5	247		.395
1985	116.4	339	.201	.344
1986	153.2	385	.227	.398
1987	179.2	432	.230	.415
1988	238.6	550	.237	.434
1989	261.9	610	.234	.430
1990	317.5	644	.257	.493
1991	375.2	752	.266	.499
1992	462.1	964	.269	.480
1993	643.3	1500	.290	.429
1994	999.5	1894	.324	.528

The figures in Table 5.5 show that China's savings rate has increased rapidly in the past decade. This is because of the high growth rate of the economy. The ratio of savings to investment has more than doubled in the same period. This reflects some fundamental changes in the sources for funding investment. Previously, the government provided the main source of funding, and government collected all the profit of enterprises and retained their depreciation allowances and even retained a part of their employees' pension and social insurance. But after the economy changed into a market

The figures in Table 5.6 show that household savings account for the lion's share of domestic investment. The inflow of foreign capital comprises 16.2% of the total investment, and is a significant source of capital for China.

Table 5.6:   Sources of Funds for China's Investment 1994 Current Yuan bn[1]

Source	Yuan bn	%
Household savings	999.5	52.8
Government	79.8	4.2
Foreign capital	307.5	16.2
Depreciation	577.0	30.5
Savings by firms	-69.4	-3.7
TOTAL	1894.4	100

[1] Note: Foreign capital is calculated according to the exchange rate $1.00 = RMB 8.6; depreciation is calculated according to the share of depreciation in total investment for 1990 which was 30.5% (refer to "Input output table for Chinese economy 1990"); savings by firms is the difference between the sum of other items and the total investment, and its negative sign can be explained by the poor management of many state-owned enterprises.

6. THE MOVEMENT OF CHINA'S POPULATION

China has a huge surplus of labour in rural areas. This provides an almost unlimited supply of labour for urban areas resulting in a stable, even declining wage rate for unskilled labour. However, the demand for highly skilled and senior professionals is increasing with China's rapid economic growth. Yet, their supply increases slowly and thus the wage level of skilled and professional work force is escalating.

Labour movements from rural to urban areas keeps China's wage level competitive in the international context, relieves the pressure on rural unemployment, and augments China's GDP to a remarkable extent. The government has gradually lifted restrictions on population movement. The food coupons which were required to buy food and to which only urban citizens were entitled, have been phased out; the household registration system has been relaxed; the labour market in urban areas has become less regulated. All these changes help rural labour to move into cities. To understand the scale of China's population movement is the key to understanding China's economic growth, its structural change, its regional economic differences, and many emerging social problems.

We have the annual statistics of the level of population in urban and rural areas and their natural growth rates. Using these figures the movement of population can be estimated by the following formula:

Migration from or to an area = Its current population - Its population of last period
(1+ natural growth rate)   (7)

Estimates of China's population movements from rural areas and to urban areas are set out in Table 5.7.

Only statistics of annual national population growth rates are available. There are no statistics of natural population growth rate separately for urban and rural areas in the period 1982-88, so we split the growth rate assuming the ratio of growth rate for urban to rural is the same as the average in latter periods which is 0.69. The numbers of people moving into cities and out of rural areas are broadly consistent. The average annual migration from rural to urban areas has been about 8 million. This is an unprecedented event. China's rural to urban migration is occurring on a truly massive scale. In addition to this movement, there are believed to be more than ten million urban migrants moving annually to other urban areas. It can be expected that most of the population migrating to urban areas will finally settle down in cities. The importance of these migrations for Chinese economic growth and changing social structure can hardly be overestimated.

Table 5.7: Urban and Rural Population Levels, Growth and
Migration in China

Year	Urban population level mn	Rate of natural growth (a)	Migrat-ion to urban areas mn	Rural population level mn	Rate of natural growth (a)	Migrat-ion from rural areas mn
1978	172.5	8.4		790.1	12.5	
1979	185.0	8.6	11.0	790.5	12.0	-9.2
1980	191.4	8.7	4.8	795.7	12.4	-4.6
1981	201.7	11.3	8.2	799.0	15.0	-8.6
1982	214.8	11.6	10.7	801.7	16.9	-10.7
1983	222.7	9.8	5.8	807.3	14.3	-5.8
1984	240.2	9.7	15.3	803.4	14.0	-15.3
1985	250.9	10.6	8.2	807.6	15.4	-8.2
1986	263.7	11.7	9.8	811.4	16.9	-9.8
1987	276.7	12.5	9.8	816.3	18.1	-9.8
1988	286.6	11.8	6.6	823.7	17.1	-6.6
1989	295.4	11.9	5.7	831.6	16.5	-5.6
1990	301.9	10.4	3.4	841.4	15.8	-3.4
1991	305.4	10.0	0.5	852.8	14.0	-0.4
1992	323.7	9.7	15.3	848.0	12.2	-15.2
1993	333.5	9.4	6.8	851.7	12.2	-6.6
1994	343.0	9.6	6.3	855.5	12.0	-6.4
TOTAL			128.2			-126.3

Note: (a) Number per thousand.

REFERENCES

(IN CHINESE UNLESS OTHERWISE INDICATED)

Chow, Gregory C. (1995) "The Formation of Capital in China and China's Economic Growth", *Techno-quantitative Economics Study*, Vol 13.

Jefferson, Gary., Rawksi A. and Zheng, Yuj-zin (1995) "An Estimation of the Changing Trend in Industrial Productivity in China and Analysis of its Reliability", *Economic Research*, Dec. 1997.

Mao, Yu-shi and Li, Qun-ren (1995) *The Social Impact of San-mao Railway*, A Report to the Asian Development Bank (in English).

Minzhe, Li and Hongbo, Cao (1990) "How Price Distortion Swells China's Industrial Growth Rate", *Theory and Practice of Price*, Vol. 5.

National Bureau of Statistics:(1949-1985) *Collection of Statistics of National Income*, Beijing.

ANNEX I. A COMPARISON OF PRODUCTION EFFICIENCY OF STATE-OWNED AND COLLECTIVE ENTERPRISES

Table I.1 is obtained from Jefferson et al. (1995). The elasticities which are relative to total output are the results obtained from regression. The figures are only for state-owned and collective enterprises owned by counties and villages and for the period 1980-92.

Table 5AI. 1: Production Characteristics of State-owned and Collective
Enterprises According to Jefferson et al. (1995)

	Stated-owned	Collective
growth rate of total output, %	6.9	12.4
growth rate of capital, %	6.7	10.2
growth rate of labour, %	2.7	3.2
growth rate of intermediate input, %	4.0	9.6
elasticity of capital	0.205	0.134
elasticity of labour	0.120	0.116
elasticity of intermediate input	0.675	0.75
Contribution to total output and their share in %		
capital	1.38 (20.0)	1.36 (11.0)
labour	0.33 (4.8)	0.37 (3.0)
intermediate input	2.69 (39.0)	7.19 (58.2)
total factor of production	2.50 (36.2)	3.43 (27.8)

We change their figures for elasticities relative to total output into
elasticities relative to value added assuming that their proportion does not
change and returns to scale are constant. Then the elasticities of capital and
labour are respectively 0.63 and 0.37 for state-owned enterprises and those for
collectively owned enterprises are 0.54 and 0.46 respectively. This is so
because 0.2505: 0.120 = 0.63:0.37; and 0.134:0.116 = 0.54:0.46.

In addition, we use the figures for capital, labour, intermediate inputs and
total output given by Jefferson et al. (1995) as shown in Table I.1 to calculate
the comparative efficiency of state and collective enterprises. (Figures are in
abstract units only for comparison).

Table 5AI.2: Input and Output Attributes by Different Types of Ownership

Year	Labour	Capital	Intrmdt input	Total output	Value added
State owned					
1980	2701	4935	5729	6586	857
1984	3037	5684	7153	8736	1583
1988	3596	7870	8411	12573	4161
1990	3736	9300	8249	13020	4771
1992	3884	11071	9242	15605	6363
Collectively owned					
1980	1961	566	1513	1621	108
1984	2352	797	2455	2789	332
1988	2888	1415	3897	5295	1398
1990	2862	1711	3702	5418	1716
1992	2984	1926	4788	7410	2630

The efficiencies obtained by our calculation can be seen from Table I.3.

Table 5AI. 3: Productivity by Ownership of Enterprises in China

Year	Y/L	Y/K	Y/TI
State owned			
1980	3171	1736	2169
1984	5213	2785	3513
1988	11527	5288	7065
1990	12771	5130	7189
1992	16383	5747	8468
Collectively owned			
1980	549	1902	1069
1984	1410	4163	2519
1988	1841	9883	7097
1990	5996	10028	7899
1992	8815	13657	11147

In Table I.3, TI means total factor input calculated from $TI = L^a K^B$ using the elasticities obtained above.

ANNEX II

Table 5AII. 1: Factors Affecting the Growth Rate by Province of China of 1993-94 (Average)

Province	FI	NS	FC	G
bj	0.545	0.556	0.095	0.128
tj	0.429	0.647	0.111	0.132
heb	0.288	0.672	0.021	0.163
sx	0.325	0.563	0.008	0.106
im	0.360	0.346	0.010	0.103
ln	0.344	0.572	0.055	0.130
jl	0.322	0.376	0.027	0.135
hlj	0.262	0.307	0.018	0.081
sh	0.503	0.576	0.150	0.146
js	0.350	0.801	0.081	0.186
zj	0.402	0.839	0.042	0.210
ah	0.258	0.812	0.022	0.208
fj	0.323	0.680	0.205	0.235
jx	0.251	0.628	0.026	0.158
sd	0.302	0.755	0.58	0.173
hen	0.280	0.652	0.017	0.148
hub	0.291	0.556	0.032	0.148
hun	0.252	0.556	0.029	0.120
dg	0.511	0.783	0.242	0.206
gx	0.300	0.571	0.073	0.186
hn	0.646	0.500	0.246	0.163
sc	0.273	0.629	0.027	0.126
gz	0.248	0.302	0.010	0.091
yn	0.331	0.266	0.008	0.111
tb	0.420	0.214	0.000	0.118
sax	0.306	0.421	0.028	0.109
gs	0.273	0.300	0.010	0.110
gh	0.379	0.16	0.002	0.089
nx	0.406	0.293	0.008	0.091
xj	0.463	0.247	0.017	0.106

ANNEX III

Table 5AIII. 1: Per Capita Figures from Household Surveys of Household
Consumption and Current Income in Current Yuan

Year	Consumption		Income	
	urban	rural	urban	rural
1978		116		134
1979		135		160
1980		162		191
1981	457	191	500	223
1982	471	220	535	270
1983	506	248	573	310
1984	559	274	660	355
1985	673	317	749	398
1986	799	357	910	424
1987	884	398	1012	463
1988	1104	477	1192	545
1989	1211	535	1388	602
1990	1279	585	1523	686
1991	1454	620	1713	709
1992	1672	659	2032	784
1993	2111	770	2583	922
1994	2851	1017	3502	1221

CHAPTER 6

AN ENDOGENOUS MODEL FOR CHINA'S GROWTH SINCE 1978

XIAOWEN TIAN[*][**]

National Centre for Development Studies, Research School of Pacific and Asian Studies,
Australian National University, Canberra ACT 0200 Australia

ABSTRACT

China's growth since 1978 challenges the dominant neoclassical growth paradigm characterised by an exogenous growth theory and numerous TFP accounting exercises. A 'two-way net-increase effect' model of economic growth is presented here in the chapter to capture the key mechanics of China's growth in the period: the interaction between the net increase in various inputs on the one hand and the net increase in efficiency in input allocation on the other. In contrast to the neoclassical TFP accounting,

* The paper is based upon one of the Chapters of my Ph.D thesis. My thanks go to Professor Ron Duncan and Dr Peter Larmour who made, as my supervisors, valuable comments on the draft of the Chapter. My thanks also go to Dr Yiping Huang and Mr. Xinpeng Xu, who provided technical help. All errors are mine.

** National Centre for Development Studies, Research School of Pacific and Asian Studies, Australian National University, Canberra ACT 0200 Australia

the model shows that increased market efficiency and increased human capital input have contributed to 75 percent of China's GDP increase and they have been, therefore, the main dynamics of China's rapid growth in the period.

INTRODUCTION

China's growth performance in recent years has shocked the world. From 1978 to 1993, China's average annual growth rate was 8.98 percent, ranking third in the world. No matter what ideological preference you might have, there is no denying that the growth 'miracle' should be attributed, first of all, to the reform and open-door policies adopted by the CPC since 1978. These policies signify that China has moved away from a de-linking towards a re-linking development strategy: re-linking China's version of socialism with market mechanisms **both domestically and internationally** so as to speed up economic growth and modernisations (Tian, 1996, p.75). From 1978 onwards, therefore, accelerated marketization at both the domestic and the international levels ushered in a new era in the history of the PRC. Any effort to model China's growth performance in the period would be unconvincing if it ignores or 'exogenesis' the significant 'institutional' changes in the direction of marketization.

The 'institutional' changes can, however, hardly be captured satisfactorily by the dominant neoclassical growth paradigm, which is characterised by an exogenous growth theory and numerous TFP accounting exercises. An official Chinese newspaper the Economic Daily announced, for instance, a TFP accounting result on October 20,1995: of the observed growth in the period, physical capital and labour inputs account for 71.3 percent and TFP accounts for the remaining 28.7 percent. The accounting result cannot tell us where TFP comes from, what role the 'institutional' change plays, and what happens with human capital inputs. It only implies that China's growth in the period seems to be driven mainly by massive physical inputs, not much different from the previous period. Given both the theoretical as well as the methodological pitfalls in the paradigm, as we shall see below, the unconvincing accounting results could be expected. We will first give a critical survey of the current debate on growth between the dominant neoclassical growth paradigm and the rising 'new growth theories'. We will then present a new model for China's growth in the period and discuss the regression results.

CURRENT DEBATE ON GROWTH

Since the seminal work of Robert Solow (1956, 1957), the neoclassical growth paradigm began to take shape, and it has dominated empirical studies on growth for decades. The neoclassical growth paradigm is no doubt a great progress over the classical one in the Smithian and Malthusian tradition (see Griliches, 1994). Meanwhile, however, theoretical as well as methodological problems with the paradigm have been proven to be so serious that they are leading to confusing and wrong conclusions about the dynamics of growth (Chyi, 1995; Srinivasan, 1995).

There could be no denying that the neoclassical growth paradigm is based upon an aggregate production function which can be written as

$$Y=AF(K,L) \tag{1}$$

where Y represents output, K and L represent physical capital and labour inputs respectively, and A represent TFP (total factor productivity) progress or all that cannot be explained by the inputs . It is quite obvious that what distinguishes the model from the classical one is the special role ascribed to TFP. To depreciate the conventional inputs, the disembodied TFP was invented to capture 'any kind of shift in the production function' (Solow, 1957, pp.312-313). To this end, a number of top assumptions were made such as that of constant return to scale, that of neutrality of TFP progress, and that of a closed economy with competitive output and inputs markets (Solow, 1957; Chow, 1995).

By now, it has been well acknowledged in the profession that the most evident pitfall in the theoretical framework of the neoclassical growth paradigm lies in its exogenizing TFP and its inability to explain where it comes from. As a result, TFP has actually become, no matter it is measured as a residual or a coefficient on a time trend, 'a measurement of our ignorance', and it has little, if any, policy implications (Griliches, 1994; Chyi, 1995). It has also been well acknowledged that most of the assumptions underlying the model violate the most obvious facts about the real world, and they have inevitably led to serious problems with estimation in growth accounting exercises (Boskin and Lau, 1992; Srinivasan, 1995). From equation 1, we can easily see that the TFP progress is 'exogenized' as a Hicks neutral factor in the production function. As constant return to scale is assumed, the exogenous TFP actually becomes the most dynamic source of growth. Neutral TFP progress is, however, a serious distortion of reality. It is here that 'new growth theories' have given the strongest challenge to the paradigm and they have thereby made the greatest contribution to the profession. They proved that TFP progress is embodied in various inputs, and it is expressed in increased human capital accumulation or improved quality of physical inputs. Various new growth models developed so far have been trying to 'endogenize' TFP by means of including such factors as 'learning by doing', 'knowledge spillover', government fiscal policies on trade and R&D. They not only undermine the basic assumption of constant return to scale and neutral TFP progress (Romer,1986; Lucas, 1988), but also discredit the growth accounting results based on them (Szirmai, 1993; Srinivasan, 1995)).[1]

---

1   According to the estimation made by Solow (1957) without allowance for quality change
     in physical inputs, for instance, technical change accounted for 87.5 percent growth in the
     USA in the century while the remaining 12.5 percent was accounted for by capital and
     labour inputs. According to the estimation made by Jorgenson (1990) with allowance for
     the quality change, however, technical change accounted for only 22 percent of the growth
     while the remaining 78 percent was accounted for by capital and labour inputs. Although
     they did not examine exactly the same period, the strikingly variant estimations could not

A related pitfall in the theoretical framework of the neoclassical growth paradigm lies in its oversimplifying inputs and its inability to explain the mechanisms by which inputs are efficiently allocated. As has been repeatedly pointed out by 'new growth theories', inputs should not be understood in a narrow sense as if they only include 'capital and labour inputs in physical units'(Solow, 1957, p.312), but they should include human capital accumulation in a broad sense. However, the missing in the neoclassical growth paradigm of an analysis of the mechanisms by which various inputs are efficiently allocated has not been drawn sufficient attention to from 'new growth theories'. Given that the mainstream neoclassical economics is characterised, among other things, by a predominant role ascribed to market mechanisms in improving efficiency in resources (inputs) allocation, it is quite questionable whether a Solowian model failing to explain the role of market mechanisms in growth deserves the name of 'neoclassical' in the true sense.

It is true that Solow and his followers would justify this by adding such assumptions as that of a closed economy with competitive markets, but the arbitrary assumption is extremely harmful to the understanding of the dynamics of growth. It is extremely harmful in the sense that it has actually led researchers to focus only on the supply side to the effect that the demand side is basically ignored. As Adrian Pagan (1995, p.327) pointed out:

It is intriguing to see how demand management has been relegated to a back-seat in the discussion. Historically, economists treated demand in its various guises, e.g. trade, as a most important factor in generating growth, as evidenced by the staple theory of growth.

The missing of demand side might not be a problem if the Solowian model had remained a production function per se. It would be so, however, if

---

be explained away by the time difference, as noted by Srinivasan (1995, p.55). A similar controversy also occurred between Denison and Kendrick, as point by Szirmai (1993, pp.6-8). The sharp contradicting accounting results show that the exogenous neoclassical growth model has to be transcended before we can make any allowance for human capital accumulation and quality changes in physical inputs.

it becomes, as it had been, a framework of a growth model, especially a framework of a 'long-run macro-model' of growth as Solow (1957, p.312) called.

It is extremely harmful also in the sense that it makes the model especially inapplicable to the case of developing countries which are experiencing a process of transition towards a mature market economic system. Not only opening up to international markets is essential to rapid economic growth as shown by the experience of the NICs', but also developing domestic markets is indispensable for sustained long-run growth as suggested by the experiences of China's and the former Soviet Union's. The on-going debate on sources of economic 'miracles' in South East Asian countries after the Second World War, and the issuing debate on China's growth in recent years could not result in convincing conclusions if domestic as well as international market mechanisms are excluded from the discussion (see, for instance, Young; 1993, Kim and Lau, 1994; Ito and Krueger, 1995).

It is worthy noticing here that recent efforts in 'new growth theories' and empirics to relate trade to growth have either concentrated on the role of foreign trade in transferring knowledge, or isolated foreign trade from domestic trade (see, for instance, Lucas, 1988; Grossman and Helpman, 1990a, 1990b, 1991; Tybout, 1992; Wei, 1995). That is, the 'invisible hand' is only partly rediscovered in 'new growth theories'. It is here that perhaps lies the most outstanding theoretical problem with 'new growth theories' and empirics: while there is a consistent theoretical framework in the exogenous neoclassical paradigm, there is not one in endogenous new growth models to link contributive factors together logically and effectively, as admitted by Romer (1995).[2] Given the fact that at least 50 variables have been found to be significantly correlated to economic growth in regression analyses, the absence of a consensus theoretical framework to group key explanatory

---

2   Romer (1995, p.69) said: 'We have not yet reached consensus about how to write down a
     model that blends elements like learning by doing, knowledge spillovers, patents, explicit
     research and development, and government support for science. But we are once again
     making a serious effort toward reaching this goal'.

variables in a logical way in 'new growth theories' and empirics would inevitably lead researchers to focus on so vastly divergent elements that the resulting estimates are doomed to be very fragile. As Levine and Renelt (1992) pointed out:

There does not exist a consensus theoretical framework to guide empirical work on growth, and existing models do not completely specify the variables that should be held constant while conducting statistical inference on the relationship between growth and the variables of primary interest. This has produced a diverse and sometimes unwieldy literature, in which few studies control for the variables analysed by other researchers.

The theoretical confusion in new growth models help explain why the neoclassical growth paradigm can still, though with so many pitfalls, enjoy wide popularity in empirical works until recently (see, for instance, Dowrick and Nguyen, 1989; World Bank, 1991,1993; Benhabib and Jovanovic, 1991; Boskin and Lau, 1992a, 1992b; Kin and Lau, 1992, 1994; IMF, 1995).

In a sense, the epistemological problem with both the neoclassical growth paradigm and the 'new growth theories' and empirics is the same: overdue eagerness for exhaustiveness in explanation. While neoclassical growth theorists exercisers try to find 'a way of exhaustively accounting for the ingredients that lead to the observed growth trend' by a single TFP without any concrete meaning (Samuelson, Nordhaus, Richardson, Scott and Wallace, 1992, p.496), 'new growth theorists and exercisers' tend to find ways of exhaustively explaining the observed growth by as many variables as possible without a systemic link between them. The realistic and yet promising goal of a growth model should lie in between, that is, to capture the key rather than all the mechanics of growth. As we all know, we can never explain completely such a complicated process as economic growth due to both the limited ability of our intellectuality and the limited availability of our data. A theoretical model or a well-established paradigm can, no matter how 'perfect' it appears, only be justified relatively, and this has been proved to be true by our intellectual history (Kuhn, 1970). In the next section, a 'two-ways effect' approach to modelling growth is presented to capture one of the most important mechanics of growth: the interaction between various inputs on the one hand and efficiency in inputs allocation introduced by market mechanisms on the other.

Table 6.1: Estimates of Average Annual TFP Growth Rate for Singapore

Source	Period covered	TFP growth (%)
Chen (1977)	1957-1970	3.62
Tsao (1986)	1966-1972	0.6
Elias (1990)	1950-1987	1.81
Bosworth, Collins and Chen (1995)	1960-1992	0.6
IMF (1995)	1961-1991	1.8
Kim and Lau (1994)	1964-1990	1.9
Young (1992)	1966-1985	-0.5
Young (1993)	1970-1985	0.10
Young (1994)	1966-1990	-0.3
Nehru and Dhareshwar (1994)	1960-1973	4.7
	1973-1987	1.5
	1960-1987	-0.8
Kawai (1994)	1970-1990	1.1
Toh and Low (1994)	1970-1992	1.37

Besides theoretical pitfalls, there are also methodological problems with neoclassical growth paradigm, which have, together with the theoretical problems analysed above, resulted in enormous imprecision in estimation in TFP accounting. Table 6.1 shows, for instance, vast variations in TFP growth rates of Singapore estimated by different researchers. To analysis possible causes of the striking variations, it is necessary for us to distinguish between different effects and to look into various effect estimation approaches. Two broad approaches to effect estimation could be identified in various growth accounting exercises. The first could be labelled as stock/rate effect approach, which estimates either the effect of input stocks on GDP (equation 1) or the effect of growth rates of the input stocks on GDP growth rate (equation 2).

$$\frac{\Delta Y}{Y} = AF\left(\frac{\Delta K}{K}, \frac{\Delta L}{L}\right)$$

(2)

where Δ = change over previous period. The stock/rate effect approach is 'typical' of the neoclassical growth accounting exercises initiated by Solow, and it is also 'ideal' according to the neoclassical growth theoretical framework if only data are available. It is here, however, that growth accounting exercisers have met almost insurmountable difficulties.

Being more or less an 'accumulative effect' estimation as shall be analysed in the next section, both the stock and the growth rate effect estimations demand, among other things, an **accurate** calculation of accumulated physical capital stock which is so difficult, or even actually impossible, that Solow himself (1957, p.314) had to admit that it 'will really drive a purist mad'. As a result, growth accounting exercisers have to face two choices in empirical studies. On the one hand, they could content themselves with one or another estimation of physical capital stock no matter how arbitrary it is. The unreliability of the existing three approaches to capital stock estimation (ie. gross capital stock at replacement cost new; the net capital stock; cumulative gross investment) have been, however, pointed out by Scott (1989, pp.xxix; 90-93). If the capital stock could not be estimated accurately, how could we expect the accounting results based on the estimation to be precise? On the other hand, they have to give up estimating capital stock and its growth rate, and then they try to find a proxy for them. This leads us to the second broad approach to effect estimation in the neoclassical growth paradigm: mixed effect estimation.

Mixed effect estimation occurs when the right-hand variables in a
regression are not in an unified form and thereby the estimated effect is
actually mixed up. The mixed effect approach is very popular in neoclassical
growth accounting exercises in recent years as capital stock growth rate is
increasingly proxied by the ratio of gross investment to GDP in the
accounting. In that case, the mixed effect estimation could be expressed
mathematically as

$$\frac{\Delta Y}{Y} = AF\left(\frac{I}{Y}, \frac{\Delta L}{L} \right)$$

(3)

where I = gross investment. The inconsistency in effect estimation could
be easily seen from the equation. Although there could be a justification for
the investment ratio to proxy for capital stock growth rate (see, for instance,
Feder, 1982, pp.62-63), their effects on GDP growth rate could not be the
same since investment and GDP might not increase proportionally at the same
pace as that capital stock grows.[3] The capital stock in the USA in the first half
of the century tended, for instance, to rise rather steadily from \$ 146,142
million in 1909 to \$ 289,360 million in 1949 (Solow, 1957). On the contrary,
however, the investment ratio in the USA in the same period displayed a
steadily declining pattern form 17.9 percent in the period between 1890 and
1909 to 12.7 percent in the period between 1930 and 1949 (Barro and Sala-I-
Martin, 1995). The mixed effect approach would inevitably produce
inaccurate estimates in growth accounting where the shares of the right-hand

---

3   In a year, for instance, investment remains the same as in last year while GDP grows due
     to increases in other contributive factors such as labour and human capital inputs or
     efficiency in inputs allocation. In that case, the growth rate of physical capital stock will be
     zero while the investment ratio might decline
     from, say, $\dfrac{4}{10}$ to $\dfrac{3}{10}$. The effect of a zero growth rate and that of a declined
     investment ratio are obviously not the same in a regression.

variables in the total effect need to be calculated and compared according to regression coefficients. In that situation, the effect of capital stock growth (proxied by the investment ratio) could be either overestimated or underestimated, and the decomposed contribution of TFP to growth could be very misleading.

Two reasons stand out for the popularity of the mixed effect approach. One is the insurmountable difficulties in calculating capital stock as noted above, and the other is the increasing interest in cross-country comparison. As Dowrick and Nguyen (1989, pp.1016-1017) admitted[4]:

> Lacking estimates of capital stock for all countries in our sample, we will initially follow the common practice of proxying capital growth by the average annual share of investment in output, (I/Q). Implicit in this practice is an assumption that capital-output ratio are constant across countries and over time.... This assumption is clearly open to criticism.

It is perhaps exactly due to the same two reasons that the mixed effect approach is also quite popular in existing endogenous new growth models, where not only the investment ratio but also the export ratio, schooling ratio, illiterate ratio, government expenditure ratio... are mixed up with growth rates such as labour input growth rate, population growth rate, inflation rate, domestic credit growth rate...(see Levine and Renelt, 1992; Barro and Sala-I-Martin, 1995). It is quite obvious that future growth models need to address, along with the theoretical problems analysed above, the effect estimation problems faced by both the exogenous neoclassical growth paradigm and the endogenous new growth theories and empirics. To this end, a new approach to

---

4   Their assumption that 'capital-output ratio are constant across countries and over time' is in violation of the reality. As shown by Barro and Sala-I-Martin (1995, p.8-9), for instance, the investment ratio declined steadily in the USA but rose steadily in Canada, France, Japan, Australia, and other countries in the first half of the century. The variant investment ratios apparently implies a variant capital-output ratios.

effect estimation is presented in the next section to capture 'net increase effect'.

TWO-WAY NET-INCREASE EFFECT MODEL

Before specifying and illustrating the model, I have to admit from the very outset that the model is intended to identify the main rather than exhaustive sources of growth, due to the epistemological reason analysed above. The theoretical framework of the model is quite simple, and it could be expressed mathematically as

$$\Delta Y = F(\Delta I, \Delta E) \tag{4}$$

where $Y = GDP$, I = various inputs such as labour, physical capital and human capital inputs, E = efficiency in inputs allocation introduced by domestic as well as international market mechanisms. Δ stands for net increase, so $\Delta Y = Y_t - Y_{t-1}$, $\Delta I = I_t - I_{t-1}$, $\Delta E = E_t - E_{t-1}$. As can be seen from equation 5, the model is better named 'two-way net-increase effect' model.

By 'two way' effect, I mean that economic growth is assumed to take place because people increase either various inputs or efficiency in inputs allocation, or both. The dynamics of growth comes, therefore, from the two main directions. A diagrammatic exposition of the theoretical framework of the model can be found in Figure 6.1,

Figure 6.1: Economic Growth Stemming from Increased Use
of Inputs or Increased Efficiency in Input Allocation

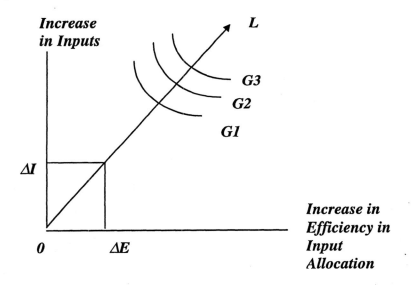

where the vertical axis expresses net increases in various inputs and the
horizontal axis expresses net increases in efficiency in inputs allocation
introduced by market mechanisms. Line *L* stands for growth locus whose slop
is determined by the ratio of inputs increase to efficiency increase in a
particular growth process. In this hypothesised case, the ratio is

$$\frac{O\Delta I}{O\Delta E}.$$ *G1, G2, G3* are growth isoquants, *G1<G2<G3*.

A growth isoquant shows all the possible combinations between an inputs
increase and an efficiency increase that are functionally capable of producing

a given amount of an increase in GDP. Economic growth is expressed here in the Figure as the movement along the growth locus upwards from *G1* to *G2*, *G3*...due to the effect of the interaction between increases in inputs and increases in efficiency in inputs allocation.

Obviously, underlying the 'two way effect' argument is an assumption that market mechanisms has been the most efficient in resources allocation so far. The rationales of the assumption are well known due to the predominant influence of the mainstream neoclassical economics in our profession, and it is not therefore necessary for us to review them. We should pointed out here, however, that in developing countries which are experiencing a transition towards a mature market economic system as China, development of domestic and foreign markets is not only a measurement of the increase in efficiency in resources allocation but also a measurement of success of government policy reforms. We should also be aware that the assumption should not be held against the positive role of government intervention in economy as has been shown by the experience of the NICs' (see, for instance, Krueger, 1995). The assumption does imply, however, that 'good' government policies and intervention measures should be directed to correcting 'market failures' and any other errors so as to ensure making full use of market mechanisms in long-run growth of the country concerned. Therefore, the increase in the real value of domestic and foreign trade is a more appropriate measurement of the increase in efficiency in resources allocation introduced by domestic and international market mechanisms than the decrease in government intervention, though the latter could also be a measurement especially when a country has survived the stage of 'infant industry'.

Another assumption underlying the 'two way effect' argument is that human capital input is a 'special' input different from physical capital and labour inputs, as it actually represents accumulation of human knowledge and improvement in the quality of physical capital and labour inputs. As such, its increase indicates, together with the increase in efficiency in inputs allocation, 'productivity' progress, and the conventional definition of productivity has to be modified thereby.[5] All these 'nonphysical' factors are, as 'endogenized' TFP in the 'exogenous' neoclassical growth model, the most active driving forces of long-run sustainable economic growth. Their aggregate share in the total effect on growth is, therefore, a very important indicator of the performance of an economy. In a socialist transitional economy like China, however, the share of the latter is more important than the share of the former, as increased human capital inputs might be simply misused without an accompanying improvement in efficiency in inputs allocation introduced by market mechanisms, such was the case in the period of the Cultural Revolution.

By 'net increase effect', I mean that economic growth boils down to net increases in GDP which are a function of net increases in all contributing factors. The argument distinguishes mine from almost all existing models, no matter whether it is a consistent stock effect model (equation 1), growth rate effect model (equation 2), or an inconsistent mixed effect model (such as that in equation 3). The distinction between a net increase effect model and consistent stock/rate effect models is not as easy to be recognised as that between a net increase effect model and inconsistent mixed effect models, and therefore it should be paid more attention to here. In a word, both the stock effect and the growth rate effect are more or less an 'accumulative effect' while the net increase effect not. The most obvious case is the stock effect which is characteristic of any aggregate production function in the form of equation 1. It tells us only how GDP increase from **zero** to a certain level due to the effect of factor accumulation (stocks), but it cannot tell us exactly how GDP increases from a previous level to another level due to the effect of factor net increase. That is, it cannot tell how **growth** happens! It is therefore

---

5   Productivity is conventionally defined as 'the ratio of aggregate output to aggregate input' or 'our economic ability to turn resources into output' (Sargent, 1986, p.3). As conventional inputs or resources include only 'capital and labour inputs in physical unit' (Solow, 1957, p.312), human capital increase should be taken as part of productivity progress. In that context, the above definition of productivity should be modified by limiting inputs and resources to 'physical' inputs or 'physical' resources.

basically a 'static' effect model as Sarel (1995) called, and it should not be used as a growth model in the true sense, although it could be used to measure the aggregate performance of an economy **if data available**.

The growth rate effect is more 'dynamic' than the stock effect, but it is still overshadowed by an 'accumulative effect' since a net increase has to be divided by a previously accumulated level $\left(\Delta x/ x\right)$. Only the net increase effect model is 'accumulation-effect free' (Δx), as is the case in equation 4. The difference between a growth rate effect and a net increase effect has long been neglected to the effect that only the former is taken as 'dynamic' (Saral, 1995) and is used in growth modelling. Their difference can, however, be shown in a simple test in any regression. As growth rate effect estimation is very sensitive to the previously accumulated level of the right-hand variables, net increase effect estimation is highly recommended in growth modelling. The recommendation is further justified by the insurmountable difficulties in calculating accumulated capital stock and its growth rate analysed in the last section, since all these difficulties could be avoided in a net increase effect model.

Underlying the 'net increase effect' argument is an assumption that what have an effect on net increases in GDP are **ultimately** net increases in, rather than previous accumulated levels of, all the interacting contributive factors. A related counter-factual hypothesis would be: if a country maintains the same previous accumulative level of all the interacting contributive factors **for years** (it is actually impossible), its GDP could not possibly increase or even might decrease in a competitive global market context.

To illustrate the 'two-way net-increase effect' model of growth, I collect a set of panel data which covers all the thirty provinces and metropolitan cities in China for a period of sixteen years from 1978 to 1993. The increase in inputs is divided into three divisions: the increase in labour input (ΔL), the increase in physical capital input(ΔPc) and the increase in human capital input (ΔHc), which are proxied respectively by the increase in the number of labourers employed, new investment in fixed assets, and new government expenditures on culture, education, science and health care (including the so-called 'three funds' for science and technology). The increase in efficiency in inputs allocation introduced by market mechanisms is divided into two divisions: the increase in efficiency in inputs allocation through domestic market mechanisms (ΔDm) and the increase in efficiency in inputs allocation through international market mechanisms (ΔIm), which are proxied by the increase in the total value of retail sale and the increase in the total value of imports and exports respectively[6]. To substitute these divisions for ΔI and ΔE in equation 4, we obtain

$$\Delta Y = F(\Delta L, \ \Delta Pc, \ \Delta Hc, \ \Delta Dm, \ \Delta Im) \tag{5}$$

where ΔY stands for the increase in GDP.

We then specify the exact relationship in equation 5 with the familiar statistical model known as the exponential regression model.

$$\Delta Y_{it} = A \Delta L_{it}^{\beta_1} \Delta Pc_{it}^{\beta_2} \Delta Hc_{it}^{\beta_3} \Delta Dm_{it}^{\beta_4} \Delta Im_{it}^{\beta_5} e^{u_{it}} \tag{6}$$

where u stands for stochastic disturbance term, e for base of natural logarithm, i for the ith province and t for the tth time period. In our model, $i = 30$ and $t = 16$, thus giving us a total of 480 observations. To log-transform equation 6, we obtain

$$Ln\Delta Y_{it} = LnA + \beta_1 Ln\Delta L_{it} + \beta_2 Ln\Delta Pc_{it} + \beta_3 Ln\Delta Hc_{it}$$

$$+ \beta_4 Ln\Delta Dm_{it} + \beta_5 Ln\Delta Im_{it} + u_{it}$$

$$= a + \beta_1 Ln\Delta L_{it} + \beta_2 Ln\Delta Pc_{it} + \beta_3 Ln\Delta Hc_{it}$$

---

6   All data come from various statistical yearbooks published by the state and local governments in China, including China Statistical Yearbook (1980-1995), Almanac of China's Foreign Economic Relations and Trade (1984-1995), Statistical Yearbooks of the thirty provinces and metropolitan cities. Occasional missing values are estimated on regressions with 'goodness of fit' (R^2) no less that 0.95.

$$+\beta_4 Ln\Delta Dm_{it} + \beta_5 Ln\Delta Im_{it} + u_{it} \tag{7}$$

where $a = LnA$.

Upon equation 7, we can now proceed to apply two broad categories of technics of pooled cross-sectional and time series data analysis to our case: classical pooling to obtain invariant parameters for China in the period as a whole and controlled pooling to obtain variant parameters for different regions and periods. In the chapter, however, we will confine our analysis only to the first so as to illustrate our model. Equation 7 is actually already a statistical model for classical pooling with its invariant parameters. To make clearer the distinction between the classical pooling we are doing now and the controlled pooling we shall do later, we rewrite equation 7 in a simple summation form.

$$Ln\Delta Y_{it} = a + \sum_{K=1}^{K} \beta_K Ln\Delta X_{Kit} + u_{it} \tag{8}$$

where X stands for explanatory variable, k for the kth explanatory variable and $k = 1,2,3,4,5$ in our case. a and β are the mean intercept and the mean slop respectively (Dielman, 1989).

Before running the regression, we have to deal with one more technical problem: there are negative and zero values in both dependent and explanatory variables which cannot be log-transformed and which are therefore treated as missing data. We could, of course, use $Ln(Y_{it}+w)$ or $Ln(X_{Kit}+w)$ to transform negative values into positive ones, as suggested by Gujarati (1995, p.387).[7] However, the treatment of data would, especially in a multiple regression, distort the real relationship between variables in the model, since the value given to w could be very arbitrary. In this way, a researcher could achieve almost any output he wants simply by changing the

---

7   Here w is a positive number chosen in such a way that all the values of Y and X_k become positive.

value of w. We would rather, therefore, leave the data as they are without any 'manipulation' so as to 'let data speak themselves'. The 'objectivism' in data treatment has actually a very significant advantage for the 'two-ways net-increase effect' model: it allows us to capture the 'net increase effect' in the true sense since all the decrease effect are excluded by in the regression procedure. As we all know, the effect on growth of an increase of 1 million labourers could be drastically different from that of a decrease of 1 million labourers. By excluding all the decrease effect, we can now safely say that what is being captured in the model is the 'net increase effect' per se. The cost of the 'objectivism' in the data treatment would be, first of all, a loss of a considerable amount of observations, and, therefore, a considerable amount of degrees of freedom. This would not do much harm to our estimation due to the large size of our sample. Another cost would be that we cannot apply the Kmenta model to our case due to the unequal length of time periods. Therefore, we will use OLS instead with the normal statistical assumption that the errors u_{it} are independent and normally distributed $N(0, \sigma_u^2)$ for all individuals and in all time periods. The regression is run on Shazam, and the regression results are reported in Table 6.2.

The slope coefficients of explanatory variables can be taken as elasticities of the change in net increases in GDP with respect to the change in net increases in explanatory variables. For example, the coefficient of the increase in physical capital input shows that a 1 percent change in the net increase in physical capital input will lead to a 0.27 percent change in the net increase in GDP.

With this in mind, we can now proceed, making use of the technics developed in growth accounting exercises, to decompose the contribution of the net increase in each of the factors to the net increase in GDP. We could take the elasticities as equal to the effective shares in GDP increases introduced by increases in the contributive factors, as the neoclassical growth accounting did (Solow, 1957; Jess, 1991). We then weight each of the shares by the average annual percentage change of the net increase in each of the factors. To divide the average annual percentage change of the net increase in

GDP by the weighted effective share of each of the factors, we obtain an estimation of the contribution of the net increase in each of the factors to the net increase in GDP. The formula for the calculation can be written as

$$\Delta X_k c = \frac{\Delta X_k s \Delta X_k r}{\Delta Yr} \tag{9}$$

where $\Delta X_k c$ stands for the contribution of the net increase in the kth factor, $\Delta X_k s$ for the effective share (β) of the net increase in the kth factor, $\Delta X_k r$ for the average annual percentage change of the net increase in the kth factor, and ΔYr for the average annual percentage change of the net increase in GDP. The decomposed contribution of each of the factors are reported in Table 6.3.[8]

Table 6.3 shows that conventional labour and capital inputs in 'physical units' have contributed only to 25 percent of the observed growth while the rest could be attributed to 'nonphysical' factors, or TFP if you are still to stick to the conventional growth accounting terminology. I would rather, however, leave aside the vague term of TFP, and decompose the contribution the way as shown in the Table. The overwhelming aggregate contribution of market efficiency and human capital input (75 percent) do not, however, indicate that China's market efficiency and human capital input have reached at a high level, and it only tell us that they have played an overwhelming role in

---

8   The effective share tells us how much percentage change in the net increase in GDP can be
     introduced by 1 percent change in the net increase in the contributive factor (other factors
     held constant), whereas the average annual percentage change tells us how much
     percentage change in the net increase in the contributive factor has actually occurred
     annually on average. Therefore, the sum of the weighted effective shares could be seen as
     the total contribution, and it is, as could be expected, very close to the average annual
     percentage change of the net increase in GDP. We should be aware, however, that, in
     statistics term, there is still 13 percent net increase in GDP unexplained by the model, as
     indicated by the R^{-2} value in Table 2.

Table 6.2: Regression Results on Equation 7 (Dependent Variable:
Ln Net Increase in GDP)

Variable	Coefficient
Constant	-0.02 (-0.09) [-0.08]
Increase in labour input	0.03 (0.09) [0.09]
Increase in physical capital input	0.27*** (3.06) [2.59]
Increase in human capital input	0.48*** (4.92) [3.91]
Increase in efficiency due to domestic market orientation	0.38*** (6.09) [6.03]
Increase in efficiency due to international market orientation	0.09*** (3.47) [2.30]
F statistic	527.94***
$\bar{R}^2$	0.87
Degrees of freedom	386

Notes: Numbers in parentheses under the coefficient estimates are associated t-ratios.
Coefficient estimates with *** are significant at the 0.03 significance level. White
heteroscedasticity consistent t-statistics are in square brackets [].

Table 6.3: Decomposed Contribution

Variable (ΔX_k)	Effective Share (β) ($\Delta X_k s$)	Annual Change (%) ($\Delta X_k r$)	Contribution (%) ($\Delta X_k c$)
Increase in Labor Input	0.03	0.45	0
Increase in Physical Capital Input	0.27	17.46	25
Increase in Human Capital Input	0.48	13.36	33
Increase in efficiency due to Domestic Market Orientation	0.38	14.71	29
Increase in Efficiency due to International Market Orientation	0.09	27.40	13

Notes: Average annual percentage change is calculated using the 'constant growth model' $Ln\Delta x_t = \beta_1 + \beta_2 t$, where x stands for the variable to be calculated.

promoting China's growth in the period concerned. This is because what is measured here is a 'dynamic' net-increase effect rather than a 'static' accumulative effect, as explained before.

In the case of China, special attention should be paid to the effective share (0.38) and the contribution (29 percent) of domestic market efficiency as well as the effective share (0.09) and the contribution (13 percent) of international market efficiency. They provide us with a framework to judge the role the 'institutional' change in the direction of marketization has played in China's rapid growth, thereby a framework to evaluate China's reform and open door policies. The regression results show that China's reform and open door policies have been quite effective and successful, as suggested by the aggregate effective share (0.47) and the aggregate contribution (42 percent) of the domestic and international market efficiency. It is quite obvious that China's domestic and international re-linking has been an extremely important driving force behind China's growth 'miracle' in the period. China's domestic re-linking is, however, much more effective than China' international re-linking, and its contribution to growth is much greater than the latter. An explanation might be found in the size of China's population, the administration errors in China's foreign trade and in China's other international interchanges (e.g. overdue foreign currency control, overdue tariff and non-tariff trade barriers, overdue government control over exports, and corruption in misusing imports for luxuries). A detailed analysis of the dynamics of China's growth in the period is, however, beyond the scope of the chapter, and it is therefore left for future scrutiny.

CONCLUSION

The key dynamics of economic growth is the interaction between various inputs on the one hand and efficiency in inputs allocation introduced by both domestic and international market mechanisms on the other. Economic growth boils downs to net increases in GDP which are a function of net increases in the interacting contributive factors. However, the integrated 'two-way' mechanics of growth and the 'net-increase' effect have been completely ignored by the neoclassical growth paradigm, and they are also basically missing in the current discussion on economic growth. The 'two-way net-increase effect' model presented in the chapter is to fill in the gap. Illustrated with China's experience, the model proves to be quite effective in decomposing sources of economic growth, and drawing policy conclusions. It shows that increased conventional physical inputs contribute to only 25 percent of China's growth in the period, and the remaining contribution could be largely ascribed to increased market efficiency and increased human capital input. The model has passed, however, only the test against China's growth performance since 1978, and further studies are called for to test it against economic performances in different counties and in different periods, and to address the issuing theoretical and technical problems.

REFERENCES

Editorial Board of the Almanac of China's Foreign Economic Relations and Trade. (1984-1995) *Almanac of China's Foreign Economic Relations and Trade,* China Resources Advertising Co, Hong Kong.

Barro, R. J. and Sala-I-Martin, X. (1995) *Economic Growth*, McGraw-Hill Inc, New York.

Benhabib, J. and Jovanovic, B. (1991) Externalities and Growth Accounting, *American Economic Review*, 81(1), 82-113.

Boskin, M.J and Lau, L.J. (1992a) Capital, Technology, and Economic Growth, Pp. 17-55 in: N. Rosenberg, R. Landau and D. Mowery. (eds.), *Technology and Wealth of Nations*. Stanford University Press, Stanford.

Boskin, M.J. and Lau, L.J. (1992b) Post-war Economic Growth in the Group-of-Five Countries: A New Analysis. Department of Economics, Stanford University. Processed

Bosworth, B., Collins, S.M. and Chen, Y.C. (1995) Accounting for Differences in Economic Growth, paper presented to the Conference on Structural Adjustment Policies in the 1990s: Experience and Prospect, Institute of Developing Economies, Tokyo, November 5-6, 1995.

Chen, E.K.Y. (1977) Factor Inputs, Total Factor Productivity, and Economic Growth: the Asian Case, *Developing Economies*, 15(1), 121-143.

Chow, J. (1995) Old and New Development Models: The Taiwanese Experience, Pp.105-128 in: T. Ito and A.O. Krueger, (eds.), *Growth Theories in Light of the East Asian Experience*, the University of Chicago Press, Chicago.

Chyi, W.F. (1995) A Comment, Pp.272-278 in: P. Anderson, J. Dwyer and D. Gruen, (eds.), *Productivity and Growth: Proceedings of a Conference*, Ambassador Press Pty Ltd, Australia.

Dielman, T.E. (1989) *Pooled Cross-Sectional and Time Series Data Analysis*, Marcel Dekker Inc., New York.

Dowrick, S. and Nguyen, D.T. (1989) OECD Comparative Economic Growth 1950-1985: Catch-up and Convergence, *American Economic Review*, 79(6), 1010-30.

Elias, V.J. (1990) The Role of Total Factor Productivity on Economic Growth, paper prepared for the 1991 World Development Report, World Bank.

Feder, G. (1982) On Exports and Economic Growth, *Journal of Development Economics*, 12, 59-73.

Griliches, Z. (1994) Productivity, R&D, and the Data Constraint, *American Economic Review*, 84 (1), 1-23.

Grossman, G.M. and Helpman, E. (1990a) The 'New' Growth Theory: Trade, Innovation, and Growth, *American Economic Review*, 80(2), 87-91.

Grossman, G.M. and Helpman, E. (1990b) Comparative Advantage and Long-run Growth, *American Economic Review*, 80(4), 796-815.

Grossman, G.M. and Helpman, E. (1991) *Innovation and Growth in the Global Economy*, MIT Press, Cambridge.

Gujarati, D.N. (1995) *Basic Econometrics: International Edition*, McGraw-Hill Inc., New York.

Huang, Y.P. (1995) Can Institutional Transition Stimulate Long-run Growth?, National Centre for Development Studies, Australian National University. Processed.

International Monetary Fund (1995) Singapore: A Case Study in Rapid Development, IMF Occasional Paper No.119, IMF, Washington, DC.

Ito, T. and Krueger, A.O. (1995) *Growth Theories in Light of the East Asian Experience,* the University of Chicago Press, Chicago.

Jorgenson, D.W. (1990) Productivity and Economic Growth, chap 3 in: E.R. Berndt and J.E. Triplett, (eds.), *Fifty Years of Economic Measurement:*

the Jubilee of the Conference on Research in Income and Wealth, University of Chicago Press, Chicago.

Kawai, H. (1994) International Comparative Analysis of Economic Growth: Trade Liberalization and Productivity. *Developing Economies*, XXX II-4, 373-397.

Kim, J.I. and Lau, L.J. (1992) Sources of Economic Growth of the Newly Industrialised Countries on the Pacific Rim, Department of Economics, Stanford University. Processed.

Kim, J.I. and Lau, L.J. (1994) The Sources of Economic Growth of the East Asian Newly Industrialised Countries, *Journal of the Japanese and International Economics*, 8, 235-271.

Krueger, A.O. (1995) East Asian Experience and Endogenous Growth Theory, Pp.9-36 in: T. Ito and A.O. Krueger, (eds.), *Growth Theories in Light of the East Asian Experience*, the University of Chicago Press, Chicago.

Kuhn, Th.S. (1970) *The Structure of Scientific Revolutions*, Second Edition, University of Chicago Press, Chicago.

Levine, R. and Renelt, D. (1992) A Sensitivity Analysis of Cross-country Growth Regression, *American Economic Review*, 82(4), 942-63.

Lucas, R.E. (1988) On the Mechanics of Economic Development, *Journal of Monetary Economics*, 22, 3-42.

Nehru, V. and Dhareshwar, D. (1944) New Estimates of Total Factor Productivity Growth for Developing and Industrial Countries", World Bank Policy Research Paper No.1313.

Pagan, A. (1995) Final Discussion, Pp.326-329 in: P. Anderson, J. Dwyer and D. Gruen, (eds.), *Productivity and Growth: Proceedings of a Conference*, Ambassador Press Pty Ltd, Australia.

Romer, P.M. (1986) Increasing Returns and Long-run Growth, *Journal of Political Economy*, 94 (5), 1002-37.

Romer, P.M. (1985) A Comment, Pp.66-70 in: T. Ito and A.O. Krueger, (eds.), *Growth Theories in Light of the East Asian Experience*, the University of Chicago Press, Chicago.

Samuelson, P.A., Nordhaus, W.D., Richardson, S., Scott, G. and Wallace, R. (1992) E*conomics: Third Australian Edition*, Australia.

Sargent, J. (1986) *Economic Growth: Prospects and Determinants*, University of Toronto Press, Toronto.

Sarel, M. (1995) Growth in East Asia: What We Can Learn and What We Cannot Infer From It, Pp.237-259 in: T. Ito and A.O. Krueger, (eds.), *Growth Theories in Light of the East Asian Experience*, the University of Chicago Press, 1995.

Scott, M.F.G. (1989) *A New View of Economic Growth*, Clarendon Press, Oxford.

Solow, R.M. (1956) A Contribution to the Theory of Economic Growth, *Quarterly Journal of Economics,* 70, 65-94.

Solow, R.M. (1957) Technical Change and the Aggregate Production Function, *Review of Economics and Statistics,* 39, 312-20.

Srinivasan, T.N. (1995) Long-run Growth Theories and Empirics: Anything New? Pp.37-66 in: T. Ito and A.O. Krueger, (eds.), *Growth Theories in Light of the East Asian Experience*, the University of Chicago Press, Chicago.

State Statistical Bureau of the People's Republic of China. (1978-1995) *China Statistical Yearbook*, China Statistical Publishing House, Beijing

Szirmai, A. (1993) Introduction, Pp.1-36 in A. Szirmai, B. Van Ark and D. Pilat, (eds.), *Explaining Economic Growth: Essays in Honour of Angus Maddison*, Elsevier Science Publishers. B.V., Netherlands.

Tian, X.W. (1996) China's Open Door Policy in Development Perspective, *the Canadian Journal of Development Studies,* XVII(1), 75-95.

Toh, M.H. and Low, L. (1994) Capital Stock, Latent Resource and Total Factor Productivity in Singapore, paper presented at the Workshop on Measuring Productivity and Technological Progress, National University of Singapore, August 3, 1994, Singapore.

Tsao, Y. (1986) Sources of Growth: Accounting for the Singapore Economy, Pp.17-44 in: Lim Chong-Yah and P.J. Lloyd, (eds.), *Singapore: Resources and Growth*, Oxford University Press, Oxford.

Tybout, J.R. (1992) Linking Trade and Productivity: New Research Direction, *The World Bank Economic Review*, 6(2), 189-211.

Wei, Sh.J. (1995) The Open-door Policy and China's Rapid Growth: Evidence from City-level Data, Pp.73-102 in: T. Ito and A.O. Krueger, (eds), *Growth Theories in Light of the East Asian Experience*, the University of Chicago Press, Chicago.

World Bank (1991) *World Development Report 1991*, World Bank. Washington.

World Bank (1993) *The East Asian Miracle: Economic Growth and Public Policy*, Oxford University Press, Oxford.

Young, A. (1992) *A Tale of Two Cities: Factor Accumulation and Technical Change in Hong Kong and Singapore*, NBER Macroeconomics Annual 1992, 13-54, The MIT Press, Cambridge.

Young, A. (1993) Lessons from the East Asian NIC's: A Constrain View, NBER Working Paper no.4482, National Bureau of Economic Research, Cambridge.

Young, A. (1994) The Tyranny of Numbers: Confronting the Statistical Realities of the East Asian Growth Experience, NBER Working Paper No.4680, National Bureau of Economic Research, Cambridge.

CHAPTER 7

FORECASTING THE GROWTH AND STRUCTURAL CHANGES IN THE CHINESE ECONOMY: 1996-2000: A GENERAL EQUILIBRIUM APPROACH[*]

XIAOGUANG ZHANG[**]

ABSTRACT

The chapter reports the forecast results for growth and structural changes in the Chinese economy over the period 1996-2000 from a dynamic computable general equilibrium (CGE) model. Based on macroeconomic forecasts made by conventional and less formal methods and the proposed future policy reforms, the model is capable of tracking, at micro-level, the

---

[*]   The author thanks Peter Lloyd and Malcolm Dowling for helpful comments on an early draft of this paper. Financial support from the Faculty of Economics and Commerce and from the University of Melbourne is gratefully acknowledged.

[**] Department of Economics, University of Melbourne, Parkville, 3052

sectoral responses over the forecasting period. In addition to the conventional features of CGE models, the crucial dynamic part of the model is its specification of investment and capital accumulation. The strength of the model is that it produces forecasts which can be interpreted fully in terms of the models theory, data and the assumption underlying the exogenous inputs.

1.Introduction

The Chinese economy has grown at an average annual rate of over 9 per cent since 1978 when the economic reform and open door policies were first introduced. At this rate, China's real GDP will double every eight years, thanks to the power of compound interest. In fact, the target of quadrupling industrial and agricultural gross output before the turn of the century, set by the government in 1980, has been successfully reached recently, five years ahead of the schedule. The Chinese government has just completed new medium- and long-term development plans which set the new agenda for economic growth and development in the early next century.

How the Chinese economy will evolve in the remaining years of this century and the early decades of the next century has been of great interest to not only scholars but also policy-makers and business societies in many countries in the world. Ten years ago, the Chinese government organised a research project to forecast the Chinese society and economy toward the year 2000.[1] The rapid growth and marketisation occurred thereafter have exceeded the expectation of most observers and made many aspects of the projected results out of date. As China's importance in the world rises in recent years, there is a renewed effort to forecast the future of the Chinese economy. Chinese and overseas scholars and organisations have made numerous attempts to foresee the growth trend of the Chinese economy and its

---

[1] The report for this research project has recently been made available for public, see Sun, 1996.

implications for the rest of the world (Li, 1995; Lau, 1995). With a few exceptions, however, most of these forecasts are based on informal and less consistent methods and confined narrowly to the issues on short-term growth and stability of the economy.

This study provides an alternative way of forecasting China's economic growth and structural changes which is oriented to not only short-term but also medium and longer terms. The forecasts are based on a dynamic computable general equilibrium (CGE) model of the Chinese economy (Zhang, 1996).

The CGE approach to economic policy analysis, pioneered by Johansen (1960), has been developed rapidly in recent years from its early static form to various dynamic forms. A recent example is the development of the ORANI-F and the MONASH models for the Australian economy (Horridge, et al., 1993, and Adams, et al., 1994).

The dynamic model used in this study is a further development of its comparative static version (Zhang, 1994). The static model, calibrated to the 1987 data, originally designed to catch the transitional features of the Chinese economy, namely the two-tier price system or the interactions between plan and market. Since 1987, the Chinese economy has gone through tremendous changes toward marketisation. The two-tier price system has been largely phased out and the prices of almost all goods are now determined by markets. In most industries, direct plans no longer play any significant role in allocating resources. To build a dynamic model for forecasting, the database of the static model needs to be completely updated to incorporate all the major changes. In addition, the model itself needs to be modified to reflect the changes in economic structure and government policies.

Most importantly, the dynamic features have to be built into the model. The conversion of the static model to its dynamic form benefits from the experiences of the ORANI-F and the MONASH models. In addition to the conventional features of CGE models, the crucial dynamic part of the model is its specification of investment and capital accumulation. In the annual simulation, aggregate investment growth is assumed to be constrained by that of total domestic savings plus trade surplus. The allocation of total investment funds and fixed capital across sectors is driven by expected rate of return on capital.

The built-in capital accumulation mechanism allows the model to automatically update its entire database after each simulation to the next period (year). This dynamic feature is crucial for forecasting purpose. A series of simulations can be conducted on subsequently updated databases to generate a set of annual growth rates for all endogenous variables. The process can proceed until all the years within the forecasting period are covered. Therefore, the model is dynamic in the sense that it projects annual time paths of growth rates of sectoral variables, such as outputs, prices, factor employment, and external trade.

CGE models are based on micro-behaviour of economic agents: producers, consumers and government. They are therefore microeconomic by nature. Macroeconomic environment has to be determined from outside. Based on macroeconomic forecasts made by conventional and less formal methods and the proposed future policy reforms, the dynamic model is capable of tracking, at micro-level, the sectoral responses over the forecasting period. The advantage of CGE model forecasting is that it produces forecasts which can be interpreted fully in terms of the model's theory, data and the assumptions underlying the exogenous inputs.

This chapter presents the preliminary results of forecasting the growth and structural changes in the Chinese economy from 1996 to 2000. The chapter first outlines the basic structure of the model, especially its dynamic features, and the data compilation. It is then followed by a set of simulations forecasting the annual growth rates and structural changes in the 22 sectors of the Chinese economy from 1996 to 2000.

2.MODEL STRUCTURE

The model structure can be viewed in two parts. The static part includes the equations specifying the behaviours of economic agents and the government within one period (a calender year). The dynamic part includes the equations usually needed for intertemporal decision making. In this model, dynamic equations normally involve decisions based on previous year's information. In the following, only those key behavioural equations are described. A full set of model equations (in percentage change form), variables and coefficients are referred to Zhang (1996).

2.1 Static Equations

Static equations constitute all those equations affecting economic activities with the current year.

Domestic production structure

The model allows each industry to produce one type of goods or services, using as inputs domestic and imported goods, labour, capital and 'other costs'. The multi-input, multi-output production specification is kept manageable by a series of separability assumptions, illustrated by the nesting in Figure 7.1.

At the top level, domestically produced and imported goods form composite goods through a CES (constant elasticities of substitution) function. This is the result of Armington assumption (1969, 1970) that imports are imperfect substitutes for domestic supplies. The composite goods are then used either by industries as intermediate inputs or by household or government for final consumption and investment. For each industry, the required composite intermediate inputs are combined using a Leontief production function. They are all demand in direct proportion to the total output of the industry.

Figure 7.1: Current Production Structure

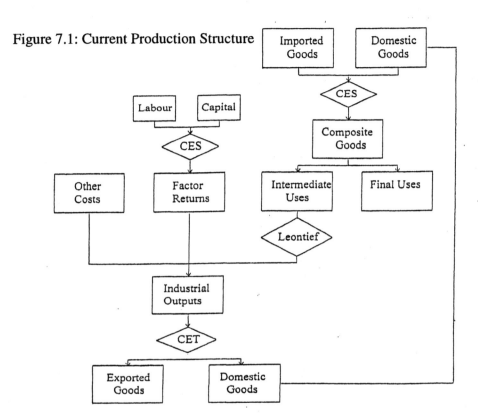

The primary factor composite is a CES aggregate of capital and labour. Capital supply is endogenously determined by investment decisions which will be discussed in the next section. The sectoral wage rates are indexed to consumption price index which guarantees a positive real wage for all industries. The inclusion of shift variables in the equation allows for flexible treatment for aggregate or sectoral labour supplies. For instance, sectoral labour supply can be determined in such a way that wage income is eventually equalised across industries. This is particularly important for long-term simulations. It is also important for a developing country like China to model its rapid changes in employment structure because sectoral wage differentials have always been a principle reason for labour to move from one sector to another. At the equilibrium, the demand for each factor must equate its supply in every industry.

At the bottom level, the industrial outputs supplied are the CET (constant elasticities of transformation) composite of domestically produced and exported goods and services.

To complete the production structure, the supply of and demand for domestically produced goods and services must be equal in order to clear the markets. Although all industries share the common production structure, they may be differentiated by input coefficients and behavioural parameters. The prices of total outputs from industries are determined by zero profit conditions, in which the total revenue is equal to the total cost in each industry.

External links

The above system is linked with the rest of the world through two channels: import and export. The supply of imported goods is defined as a function of the world price of imports. The demand for China's exports is specified as a CES function under the assumption that Chinese exports are somehow differentiated from that of other countries. The prices of imported and exported goods are determined by imposing the zero profit conditions in importing and exporting activities. The markets for exports and imports are both cleared.

Since the domestic currency RMB is still not internationally convertible, China's imports will remain subject to foreign exchange constraint. Although , in recent years, this constraint eases considerably due to a rapid expansion of exports and a large inflow of foreign investment, maintaining a balanced trade has remained to be a key component in China's current economic policy. The model reflects this policy priority by introducing flexible treatment for trade balance so that trade balance can be treated either as a policy variable or as an endogenous variable. The latter implies a full currency convertibility. It is also assumed that, if imports are constrained by limited foreign exchange earnings from exports, then the domestic price of imports will be pushed up. This impact is captured by a shift variable in the equation for import prices.

Final demands for composite goods

Four types of final demands for composite goods are distinguished in the model: household consumption, government expenditure, investment and inventory. Investment demand is related to intertemporal decision making and therefore deferred to the next section. Household demands, government demands and inventory demands are discussed in the following.

The household consumption demands for composite goods are derived from conventional utility maximisation problem subject to household's expenditure constraint. The household nominal expenditure is determined by household nominal income and the average propensity to spend. The household demand for good *i* is therefore a function of household expenditure and the prices of all goods including *i* itself. The expenditure elasticity and the own- and cross-price elasticities are used in the equation as parameters.

The government demand for composite good *i* is treated flexibly either as an exogenous variable or as an endogenous variable determined by the total expenditure of household. In a forecasting simulation, for instance, if information is available for likely changes in government expenditure on individual commodities, these demands can be treated exogenously. Otherwise, they are assumed to be directly linked to household consumption level.

Similarly, the inventory demand for composite good *i* is also flexibly specified which can either be linked to the aggregate demand for that good or be exogenously determined.

Household and government incomes

Household nominal income is composed of wages, capital returns (depreciation and profits) and other costs of production. A portion of household income is spent on consumption goods and services while the remainder is private savings. The split of household income between consumption and saving is determined by the average propensity to spend. According to empirical studies, the household average propensity to spend in China over the current decade is quite stable (Zang, 1994) and thus can be treated as an exogenous variable.

The government collects its revenues from various taxes on domestic or traded goods. After the 1994 taxation reform, the value-added tax became the single most important source of revenue for the government. This tax is based on the value-added of industries, which includes wages, profits, depreciation funds and other costs. Import tariffs is another source of government revenues though they account only for a small portion of total revenues. For those goods exported, the government returns value-added tax revenue to the producers. Such tax rebates are an outlay for the government. The balance of government budget is public savings.

The above sectoral variables for quantities and prices of goods and factors can be readily aggregated to form various macroeconomic indicators for output, income and price indices.

2.2 Dynamic Equations

The central part of the dynamic equations is the specification of investment behaviour and the links between annual investment and total savings, on the one hand, and between annual investment and net capital stock, on the other. The basic structure of savings-investment-capital stock relationship is shown in Figure 7.2.

At the top level, total investment funds are constrained by total savings which is the sum of private, public savings plus trade surplus. Investment over

Figure 7.2: Investment and Capital Accumulation

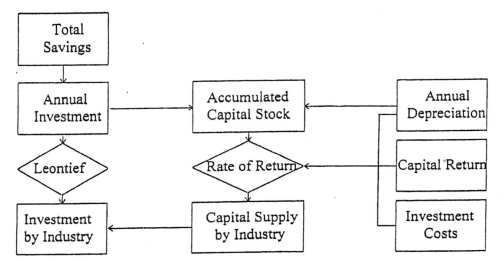

a given period (year) is added to the stock of accumulated capital in that industry. The fixed capital stock in each sector is depreciated each year according to a given depreciation rate.

Capital return, rate of depreciation and the unit cost of producing investment goods constitute the expected rate of return on capital in a given industry. The supply of accumulated fixed capital to individual industries is determined by the relative level of the expected rate of returns. Once capital supply is determined, investment funds can then be allocated to each industry. The demands for investment goods are also determined by sectoral investment allocation through a Leontief function. The total sectoral capital stock is then linked to the demand for capital to determine the current production. Some key intertemporal behavioural equations will be discussed in detail on the next page.

The rate of return on capital investment

Investment funds and fixed capital are allocated to individual industries according to the expected rate of return on capital. The net rate of return on a unit of capital goods invested in industry j in year t is

$$R_{j(t)}^{N}$$

$$= \frac{(P_{j(t)}^{K(2)} + P_{j(t)}^{K} D_{j(t)})(1 + i)^{-1} - [P_{j(t-1)}^{K} - P_{j(t)}^{K}(1 - D_{j(t)})(1 + i)^{-1}]}{P_{j(t-1)}^{K}} \qquad (1)$$

$$= \frac{P_{j(t)}^{F(2)} + P_{j(t)}^{K}}{(1 + i)P_{j(t-1)}^{K}} - 1$$

where

i is the rate of interest;

$D_{j(t)}$ is the rate of depreciation on a unit of industry j's capital stock;

$P_{j(t)}^{F(2)}$ is the nominal rental rate on a unit of capital in industry j over year t; and

$P_{j(t-1)}^{K}$ is the cost of a unit of capital goods in industry j at the beginning of year t.

In growth rates, this can be written as

$$\frac{R_{j(t)}^{N}-R_{j(t-1)}^{N}}{R_{j(t-1)}^{N}} = \frac{P_{j(t-1)}^{F(2)}}{(1+i)P_{j(t-1)}^{K}R_{j(t-1)}^{N}}\left(\frac{P_{j(t)}^{F(2)}-P_{j(t-1)}^{F(2)}}{P_{j(t-1)}^{F(2)}}+1\right)+$$

$$\frac{1}{(1+i)R_{j(t-1)}^{N}}\left(\frac{P_{j(t)}^{K}-P_{j(t-1)}^{K}}{P_{j(t-1)}^{K}}+1\right)-\frac{1}{R_{j(t-1)}^{N}}-1$$

(2)

Or in the percentage growth rate form,

$$r_j^N = \frac{P_{j(t-1)}^{F(2)}(P_{j(t)}^{F(2)}+100)}{(1+i)P_{j(t-1)}^{K}R_{j(t-1)}^{N}}+\frac{P_{j(t)}^{K}+100}{(1+i)R_{j(t-1)}^{N}}-\frac{100}{R_{j(t-1)}^{N}}-100 \qquad (3)$$

The rates of capital return used in the model is in the form of 'power of rate', that is, one plus the rate of return, to avoid possible negative rates.

Allocation of investment funds and fixed capital supply

The growth of accumulated fixed capital over year t is assumed to be motivated by the expected rates of return on capital from individual industries in year t, more precisely, by the ratio of the expected return in year t to the realised return in the previous year $t - 1$:

$$\frac{K_{j(t)}-K_{j(t-1)}}{K_{j(t-1)}} = \beta_j\frac{R_{j(t)}^{N}}{R_{j(t-1)}^{N}}+f_j^K+f^K. \qquad (4)$$

where

$K_{j(t)}$ is the stock of fixed capital accumulated in industry j by year t,

β_j is a positive parameter, and f_j^K, f^K

are shift variables allowing (4) to be compatible with a forecast of aggregate investment from outside the model.

We can rewrite (4) as:

$$\frac{K_{j(t)} - K_{j(t-1)}}{K_{j(t-1)}} = \frac{\beta_j}{P_{j(t-1)}^{F(2)} + 1} (R_{j(t-1)}^N + \Delta R_{j(t)}^N) + f_j^K + f^K \qquad (5)$$

Using

$\Delta R_{j(t)}^N = \dfrac{R_{j(t-1)}^N}{100} r_{j(t)}^N$, the percentage growth form of Equation (5) can be written

as

$$k_{j(t)} = \frac{\beta_j R_{j(t-1)}^N}{P_{j(t-1)}^{F(2)} + 1} (100 + r_{j(t)}^N) + f_j^K + f^K \qquad (6)$$

Investment and capital accumulation

We assume that the capital stock available for use in production in industry j in year t equals the capital stock in the previous year net of depreciation plus investment over year t. The underlying accumulation relation is therefore

$$K_{j(t)} = K_{j(t-1)}(1 - D_{j(t)}) + \alpha_j^K Q_{j(t)}^K \qquad (7)$$

where $Q_{j(t)}^K$ is the quantity of capital goods invested in industry j over year t,

a_j^K is the parameter of investment efficiency in industry j.

Notice that fixed capital assets sometimes take more than one period to install. Furthermore, capital investment has its losses. In a given year, the value of investment usually is less than the value of newly established capital assets. In China, for instance, the rate of investment completion in 1994 was about 60 per cent. This low completion rate reflects partly the fact that many projects invested in that year might take more than one year to install. It also reflects some inefficiency or losses involved in capital investment. Therefore, a capital investment efficiency parameter a_j^K is introduced to take these into account.

Investment in year t determines capital growth over year t, ie.

$$\frac{K_{j(t)}-K_{j(t-1)}}{K_{j(t-1)}} = \frac{\alpha_j^K Q_{j(t-1)}^K}{K_{j(t-1)}}\left(\frac{Q_{j(t)}^K-Q_{j(t-1)}^K}{Q_{j(t-1)}^K}+1\right)-D_{j(t)} \tag{8}$$

or, in percentage growth rates,

$$k_{j(t)} = \frac{\alpha_j^K Q_{j(t-1)}^K}{K_{j(t-1)}}(q_{j(t)}^K + 100) - D_{j(t-1)}(d_{j(t)} + 100) \tag{9}$$

This is the underlying investment-capital relationship.

From equations (6) and (9), we see that initial conditions play a crucial role in the investment specification. In equation (6), the rate of return in year t-1 is an important determinant of $k_{j(t)}$ while, in equation (9), the investment capital ratio for year t-1 and the investment efficiency parameter are critical in translating capital growth for year t into an investment growth for year t.

In recent years, foreign capital, including foreign direct investment and foreign borrowing, has been making increasingly important contribution to the growth of the Chinese economy, though it still accounts for a small proportion of total annual investment in China. The flow of foreign capital is introduced into the model as a proportion of total sectoral capital investment, eg., one plus the ratio of foreign capital to domestic investment. An increase in foreign capital inflow will enlarge total investment in a given industry. Sectoral foreign capital inflows are treated as an exogenous variable.

1.3 MACRO-CLOSURE

The model's closure involves a split of exogenous and endogenous variables. The model contains 3,714 equations and 2,137 variables. The number of variables is larger than that of equations. It implies that 1,577 variables must be specified exogenously in order to resolve the system. The exogenous variables in the model mainly include those for policy instruments, foreign markets, technical and taste changes, shifters and certain variables which are deemed to be constrained by external factors. A model can have many different closures depending on the nature of simulation and the objectives of policy analysis.

The following variables can be switched flexibly between endogenous and exogenous. For lack of reliable forecasts for the future changes in these variables, their growth rates are thus endogenised for the following simulations:

- Government expenditure is linked to the total consumption of households;
- The inventory demands are determined by the aggregate (private and public) demands for composite goods;

- Sectoral wage rates are indexed to the consumer price index and sectoral labour supplies are driven by sectoral wage differentials;
- Trade is balanced in US dollar terms by government policy. As the domestic currency RMB is unlikely to be made fully convertible very soon, imports will remain to be constrained by the size of foreign exchange earnings from export.

The model's numerair is money supply which is defined in the model on the basis of the classical quantity theory of money expressed by Fisher in the equation of exchange.

3. DATABASE CONSTRUCTION

The basic structure of the database is shown in Figure 7.3. The Chinese economy is divided into 22 sectors each of which produces a distinctive category of goods or services. The database itself is an extended input-output table which includes not only the current flow table (the area AA in the figure) but, more importantly, a capital formation table (the area AB).[2] The capital formation table shows the commodity composition of investment in each industry which is required by any dynamic model to simulate the impact of investment on current production and capital accumulation. China has not officially published any capital formation table. Considering the limited available information, to construct a new capital formation table is a formidable task.

3.1 Current Production

The current production table is updated from the 1987 input-output table (State Statistical Bureau, 1992) to 1994. The changes in the basic structure of

---

2   This table is also called the B matrix compared with the A matrix of the current flow table.

the Chinese economy between 1987 and 1994 is revealed in Table 7.1. The GDP of the Chinese economy had nearly doubled (1.9 times) in real terms during this period while, in nominal terms, it had nearly quadrupled (3.8 times). The ratio of investment and inventory to GDP had increased slightly. In 1987, 38.2 per cent of GDP was invested while 63.7 per cent was consumed. In 1994, 38.5 per cent of GDP was invested while 60.4 was consumed. In regard to production, in 1987, 56 per cent of gross output was used as intermediate inputs while, in 1994, the similar figure rose to about 60 per cent.

Many significant reform measures have been introduced and implemented since 1987 which requires the database to be altered to reflect these changes. A major policy change in 1994 was in the taxation regime: the implementation of value-added tax in all productive industries. This tax has replaced the turn-over tax to become the single most important revenue source for the government. In addition, the corporate tax rates were uniformed to allow all types of enterprises, public or private, domestic or foreign owned, to compete on equal footing.

Another significant reform was in the external sector (Liu, 1994). Nominal import tariff rates have been reduced significantly for a number of times since 1987 and many implicit non-tariff restrictions have also been removed. On the export front, direct fiscal subsidies were abolished in 1992. An export tax rebate system was gradually introduced thereafter. This system eventually, in 1994, extended to cover almost all exported goods (crude oil exports are excluded due to the remaining control over domestic oil prices).

The foreign exchange regime has also undergone tremendous transformations. In 1987, as an export promotion measure, export revenues could be partially retained by foreign trade companies and export producers. These retained foreign exchange were allowed to be traded in the local foreign exchange swap markets. As a result, in 1987, China virtually had two exchange rates: an official rate and much higher swap market rates. This dual exchange rate system finally phased out in 1994 when a new round of financial reform was introduced. The two exchange rates were unified and a

Figure 7.3: Database Structure

		Industries (current production) A	Industries (capital formation) B	Household consumption C	Government expenditure D	Inventory demands E	Exports F	Imports G	Sum of rows
Commodities	A	AA 22*22	AB 22*22	AC 22*1	AD 22*1	AE 22*1	AF 22*1	AG 22*1	Total absorption
Depreciation	B	BA 1*22							Deprec-iation
Value-added tax	D	DA 1*22							Value-added tax revenue
Other costs		EA 1*22							Other costs
Sum of Columns		Gross output	Capital investment	Total household consumption	Total government expenditure	Total inventory demands	Total exports	Total imports	
Factor returns (capital, labour)	C	CA 2*22							Factor returns

Table 7.1: Major Aggregate Economic Indicators of China: 1987 and 1994
(100 million yuan)

	1987	1994
Final Demand		
- Private Consumption	5,943	21,656
- Public Consumption	1,330	4,803
- Investment	3,803	13,993
- Inventory	566	2,866
- Trade Balance	-217	481
GDP (Expenditure)	11,424	43,799
Value-Added		
- Depreciation Funds	1,202	4,753
- Labour Income	5,681	21,674
- Capital Income	1,812	6,566
- Indirect Tax	1,550	5,614
- Other Costs	1,179	5,191
GDP (Factor Returns)	11,424	43,799
Gross Output	25,663	111,814

Note: Figures are in current prices.

Source: State Statistical Bureau of China, *Input-Output Table of China 1987*, China Statistical Publishing House, 1992, Beijing ; State Statistical Bureau of China, *Statistical Yearbook of China 1995* (*Zhongguo tongji nianjian 1995*), China Statistical Publishing House, 1995, Beijing.

national inter-bank foreign exchange market was established. The uniform foreign exchange rate is now determined on the inter-bank exchange market. The government can no longer set foreign exchange rate through

Table 7.2: Gross Output and Gross Domestic Product (GDP) in China: 1994
(100 million yuan)

Sectors	Gross Output	GDP (value-added)	GDP (final demands)
1. Crops	10,766	6,185	4,294
2. Other Farm Products	4,984	2,046	2,883
3. Metallurgy	9,130	2,721	191
4. Coal	1,243	740	320
5. Crude Petroleum	1,363	797	-97
6. Refined Petroleum	2,036	488	-95
7. Chemicals	6,590	1,963	159
8. Machinery	13,488	3,884	2,695
9. Building Materials	3,784	1,534	210
10. Wood	822	324	240
11. Processed Food	5,900	2,001	3,913
12. Textile and Clothing	7,160	2,013	4,316
13. Paper	2,211	658	564
14. Misc. Manufactures	818	274	69
15. Electricity and Water	2,196	962	126
16. Construction	11,224	2,900	11,224
17. Transport	4,921	2,686	719
18. Commerce	9,959	4,049	4,715
19. Services	2,615	1,579	1,941
20. Education and Sports	3,395	1,835	1,946
21. Finance	4,030	2,665	286
22. Public Administration	3,179	1,496	3,179
TOTAL	111,814	43,799	43,799

administrative means. Instead, it can only influence it through foreign exchange market. Additional adjustments are needed to incorporate these changes into the model database.

The sectoral demands for intermediate inputs are estimated using the RAS approach (Stone, 1961). An underlying assumption of the RAS approach to updating input-output tables is that the technical relationships between sectors remain largely unchanged. To minimise the possible errors resulted from this unrealistic assumption, additional information on input coefficients is sought from a more aggregated 1990 input-output table (State Statistical Bureau, 1993). The resultant sectoral gross outputs and GDPs are shown in Table 7.2.

3.2 Fixed Capital Formation

The fixed capital formation table is constructed using available Chinese statistics. The procedure of compiling the table and data sources are described in detail by Zhang (1996) and not to be repeated here. Table 7.3 reports only the estimated results for capital foods demand and sectoral distribution of investment funds in 1987 and 1994.

3.3 Coefficients and parameter settings

The settings for model's coefficients and parameters such as various elasticities were mainly drawn from the static version of the model (Zhang, 1994). However, the parameters in that model were based on the 1987 Chinese economy. Since then, great changes have taken place in many aspects of the economy. Some of the trade elasticities were readjusted to be consistent with China's current status as a major trading nation in the world.

Table 7.3: Fixed Capital Investment in China: 1987 and 1994 (100 million yuan)

Sectors	Capital Goods Demand		Investment by Industry	
	1987	1994	1987	1994
1. Crops	82	126	362	310
2. Other Farm Products	14	30	365	193
3. Metallurgy	13	41	242	786
4. Coal	-	-	128	248
5. Crude Petroleum	-	-	174	304
6. Refined Petroleum	-	-	28	197
7. Chemicals	-	-	240	899
8. Machinery	1,175	2,460	253	1,155
9. Building Materials	-	-	136	702
10. Wood	10	23	30	96
11. Processed Food	-	-	137	683
12. Textile and Clothing	-	-	187	623
13. Paper	-	-	60	326
14. Misc. Manufactures	-	-	8	120
15. Electricity and Water	-	-	279	1,359
16. Construction	2,431	11,066	73	254
17. Transport	24	41	326	2,283
18. Commerce	54	206	170	588
19. Services	-	-	219	1,191
20. Education and Sports	-	-	262	804
21. Finance	-	-	18	224
22. Public Administration	-	-	104	650
TOTAL	3,803	13,993	3,803	13,993

Note: Figures are in current prices.
Source: State Statistical Bureau of China, *Input-Output Table of China 1987*, China Statistical Publishing House, 1992, Beijing ; State Statistical Bureau of China, *Statistical Yearbook of China 1995* (*Zhongguo tongji nianjian 1995*), China Statistical Publishing House, 1995, Beijing.

4. MACRO FORECASTS FOR 1996-2000

In this section, the external conditions in which the Chinese economy is supposed to grow over the period from 1996 and 2000 are to be specified.

4.1 Exogenous Assumptions 1996 to 2000

Due to lack of long-term reliable macroeconomic forecasts, most macro settings of the model for the forecasting period are drawn from the 'Ninth Five-Year National Economic and Social Development Plan of the PRC' passed in the annual meeting of the National People's Congress in March 1996 (March 20, *People's Daily*). The ninth five-year plan covers the period from 1996 to 2000. Some of the major targets, forecasts and proposed policy reforms of the plan are summarised in the following:

- Gross Domestic Product

  The targeted real GDP in 2000 is 8.5 trillion yuan (1995 constant price), an increase from the 1995 level of 5.76 trillion at an annual growth rate of 8 per cent.

- Consumption

  The real per capita income of urban households is expected to increase at 5 per cent a year while that of rural households to grow at 4 per cent a year.

- Employment

  China currently has a workforce of over 630 million. The annual growth rate of workforce has been around 3.3 per cent since 1980. In recent years, this growth rate has been slowed down slightly. Even at a rate of 2.5 per cent, however, it means that total workforce will increase by more than 80 million in the next five years.

The current agricultural workforce is 350 million while non-agricultural workforce is 280 million. If agricultural workforce grow at 2.5 per cent per year, the increase in agricultural workforce in the next five years will be 46 million. It has been stated in the plan that, between 1996 and 2000, 40 million of agricultural workers will be transferred to non-agricultural sectors. It means that agricultural labour will actually increase only by 6 million, or at an annual rate of 0.3 per cent. Actually, according to latest statistics, the number of agricultural labour declined by 4 per cent from 1993 to 1994.

It is also estimated that non-agricultural labour will increase at an annual rate of 2.7 per cent or a total of 40 million in the next five years. Plus the transfer of agricultural labour 40 million, the total increase in non-agricultural workforce will be 80 million, averaging a growth rate of 5 per cent every year. Agriculture is most likely to be a net labour-outflow sector for the next five years.

- Capital investment

China invested 19.4 trillion yuan in 1995, which was 33.7 per cent of GDP. The expected total investment in the next five years is 13 trillion yuan. The value of total investment each year is said to be maintained at around 30 per cent of GDP. It implies that the growth rate of fixed capital investment will be similar to that of GDP in the coming years.

- External sectors

  The value of exports is targeted at US$ 200 billion in 2000, representing an increase of 34.3 per cent from the 1995 level of $149 billion. The value of imports is also expected to increase to US$ 200 billion, a rise of 51.2 per cent from the 1995 level of US$ 132 billion.

- Proposed policy reforms

  Trade policies: China has already once again substantially lowered the nominal rates of import tariffs for a wide range of products in April this year. The final target of import tariff reduction is to reach an average level of protection by the year 2000 which is compatible with other developing countries within the World Trade Organisation (WTO). It should be pointed out, however, that although the nominal rates of protection remain high in China, the aggregate ratio of tariff revenues in the value of total imports has been extremely low in recent years. This is largely due to the widespread practice of import tariff exemptions for various forms. One of the major challenges of trade reform in the near future will be to reconsolidate protection measures and unify the trade policies in various regions. A 30 per cent reduction of nominal import tariff is planned for the period from 1995-2000. However, it should be clear that, if many imported goods are exempted from paying tariffs, even a 30 per cent reduction in nominal tariff rates is unlikely to generate a significant impact on the domestic market.

  Financial policies: Money supply will remain to be relatively tight to ensure a stable domestic currency and general price level. The supply of narrow money (M1) will be controlled at an annual growth rate of 18 per cent while the supply of broad money (M2) will be at 23 per cent a year in the next five years.

Exchange rate policy: Exchange rate is now determined by the inter-bank foreign exchange market and can no longer be fixed by the government. However, exchange rate can be influenced by other policy instruments. Among them is monetary policy. Money supply can be adjusted to stabilise the value of the domestic currency. China has announced that its currency, the RMB, will be made internationally convertible by the year 2000. It is understood that, as the first step, this convertibility will apply only to the current account and then, at a late stage, extended to capital account. Due to lack of detailed information on the plan for currency convertibility, it is assumed here that the authority intends to maintain the value of RMB at the current level.

Fiscal policies: It is unlikely that fiscal policies will substantially change in the next five years, following a major overhaul of the taxation system in 1994. The main task for fiscal reform in the near future will be to consolidate the 1994 taxation reform measures and reinforce the implementation of the newly established tax system at both central and local levels.

• Technical and taste changes

The annual growth rate of labour productivity is expected to be 6.5 per cent. The incremental capital-output ratio is estimated to decline from 3.6 in 1996 to 3 in 2000.

Energy-saving technologies will be introduced to reduce the consumption of non-renewable energy products, such as coal and crude oil. The average energy costs of per 10,000 yuan of national income is estimated to be reduced from 2.2 tonne of standard coal in 1995 to 1.7 tonne of standard coal in 2000, or annual improvement rate of 5.2 per cent.

4.2 Forecasts for structural variables

According to the above targets and forecasts for the period 1996-2000, the macro-conditions and external technical changes are set in Table 7.4. As no year-by-year forecasts are available, these settings are assumed to persist for the whole period.

Most of the indicators in the table have been discussed above, except the last one, average propensity of consume. Since the beginning of economic reform in 1978, there has been a steady decline in household's average propensity to consume in China. The trend has been confirmed by a number of recent studies (for instance, see Zang, 1994). This phenomenon provides some explanation for rapid increase in saving rates in recent years. In the

Table 7.4: Forecasts of Growth Rates of Major Aggregate Indicators: 1996-2000

Indicators	Per cent
Agreement employment	2.7
Transfer of agricultural labour	3.0
Money supply	18.0
Labour productivity	6.5
Capital-saving technical change	3.6
Energy-saving technical change	5.0
Intermediate input saving	1.0
Export and import price	5.0
Import tariff rates	-10.0
Average propensity to consume	-2.0

early 1980s, a conventional view among Chinese economists was that a ratio of investment to national income over 30 per cent was unsustainable. However, in recent years, the investment and income ratio has increased dramatically and is now approaching 40 per cent level. This high ratio is not unprecedented among East Asian newly industrialising countries. In the foreseeable future, therefore, as income continues to rise strongly, saving rate is likely to increase even further in China. The household average propensity to consume is most likely to continue declining.

5. PRELIMINARY RESULTS

This section reports preliminary results from forecast simulations. Before proceeding to more detailed discussion of the forecast simulation, it should be noticed that dynamic models have some features distinctive from static ones. This dynamic model has its own momentum of growth due to the specification of investment and capital accumulation. Even if all exogenous variables are constant, the economy will still grow. This is because a zero growth rate for investment does not mean no investment at all. Actually, it means that the level of investment in the current period is maintained at the same level as in the pervious period. Even without any increase in the use of other inputs, the existing investment will be enough to move the economy ahead.

The following results are derived from the simulations in which all the macro and technical changes are simultaneously imposed on the model. The simulations are conducted in the following way. The model was first used to update the entire database to 1995 which was made consistent with the observed growth performance of the Chinese economy between 1994 and 1995 (State Statistical Bureau, 1996). It was then followed by five sequential simulations based on the same macro-closure. Each of these simulations updated the database to the next year so that the next simulation would be based on a renewed database. The underlying assumption is that the macro-environment, policy measures, technical and taste shifts will remain unchanged over the forecasting period.

5.1 Aggregate indicators

The projected percentage growth rates of major aggregate indicators are reported in Table 7.5. They are discussed in turn in the following.

- Exports and Imports

  The projected growth rate for imports and exports is about 18 per cent in the next five years. This forecast is slightly different from the observed export and import growth rates in 1995. In 1995, exports and imports actually grew by 23 and 14 per cent, respectively. This is mainly the result of restricting the growth of imports in the model. Under the current macro environment, the growth of trade is expected to accelerate slightly overtime implying a relaxation of foreign exchange constraint. It should also be noticed that the forecasted performance of trade is influenced, to some extent, by the assumptions on the changes in world export and import markets. Should these assumptions be altered, the performance of exports and imports could be quite different.

- Private and Public Consumptions

  Private and public consumptions are expected to grow at the same rate between 8.98 and 10.11 per cent per year which is largely within the range set by the five-year plan if the growth of households is also considered. Both private and public consumptions are expected to slightly accelerate their growth over the forecasting period as labour supply grows at a constant rate.

Table 7.5: Projected Growth Rates of Major Aggregate Indicators: 1996-2000

	1996	1997	1998	1999	2000
Exports	18.03	18.36	18.58	18.74	18.88
Imports	18.03	18.36	18.58	18.74	18.88
Real GDP	9.35	9.16	9.16	9.01	8.81
Private Consumption	9.98	9.39	9.71	9.94	10.11
Public Consumption	8.98	9.39	9.71	9.94	10.11
Fixed Capital Investment	17.57	16.30	15.22	14.25	13.37
Exchange Rate	-4.28	-4.41	-4.52	-4.61	-4.67
Consumer Price Index	9.80	9.48	9.48	9.42	9.42
GDP Deflator	11.93	11.88	11.88	11.98	11.95
Cumulated Fixed Capital Stock	14.97	16.28	17.16	17.67	17.89
Real Gross Output	6.65	6.67	6.64	6.57	6.46

- Fixed Capital Investment

  Annual fixed capital investment will increase at a rate of 17.57 per cent in 1996 and then gradually slow down to 13.37 per cent by 2000. It seems to suggest that an annual increase of 2 per cent in average household propensity to save is not enough to keep investment growth rate constant. As we will see, the accelerating of consumption growth and the slowing down of investment growth have an impact on real GDP growth and sectoral output growth.

- Real GDP and Gross Output

  The annual growth rate for real GDP is likely to be maintained at about 8-9 per cent. At this rate, the economy will be able to exceed the growth target set by the five-year plan to reach 8.5 trillion yuan by the year 2000. The annual time path of real GDP growth shows that it begins with 9.35 per cent in 1996, then gradually slows down and finally reaches a level of 8.81 per cent. This largely resulted from the diminishing rate of investment growth.

The annual growth rate of real gross output follows a similar pattern to that of real GDP, but at a lightly lower level. This result is influenced by the assumption that there is a one-per cent saving of intermediate inputs across all industries. In fact, for some years, the growth of gross outputs in many industries was much higher than that of net outputs which implies an increase in the use of intermediate inputs.

• Exchange Rate

In 1995, yuan appreciated by about 4 per cent. This trend is likely to continue in the coming years. Given a constant money supply, exchange rate is likely to be kept reasonably stable over the forecasting period. However, as the economy grow strongly, a fixed money supply is likely to lead to appreciate the domestic currency. This can be seen in the time path of exchange rate: in the last year of the forecasting period, it will appreciate slightly by about 0.4 per cent.

• Inflation

Inflation pressure seems to be high during the forecasting period which is suggested by two indicators: consumer price index (CPI) and GDP deflator. At the beginning of the period, CPI is expected to stay high at the level of 9.8 per cent and by the end of the period it declines only marginally by less than 0.4 per cent. GDP deflator shows a slightly different pattern of changes: it first falls marginally and then bounces back again. The assumption of increase in the prices of exports and imports certainly contributes to this result. This also suggests that high inflation pressure is likely to persist at least in the near future and how to control inflation should remain to be high on policy agenda.

- Accumulated Capital Stock

The growth rate of accumulated fixed capital stock is expected to increase over time during the forecasting period. High saving and investment ratios and relatively low depreciation rates can be seen as major factors contributing to such a rapid expansion. However, it is also clear that as investment grows at a diminishing rate, such rapid expansion of capital stock is unlikely to last long. This has already been indicated by the forecasts that the pace of annual growth rates for fixed capital stock is dampened rapidly.

5.2 Sectoral indicators

The projected sectoral aggregate output growth rates are reported in Table 7.6.

The patterns of projected sectoral output growth show that the two agricultural sectors have slightly below average rates of growth. The construction sector apparently has the highest growth rates. This leads to high growth rates for the construction related industries, such as building material and wood.

Within the industrial sector, the growth of coal and crude petroleum industries is expected to slow down over the forecasting period. Given the current level of resource deposits and production capacities, these resource based industries are unlikely to grow continuously at a high rate. Especially, by the year 2000, the crude oil and natural gas industry will have a negative growth rate if no major new oil or gas fields are to be discovered and put in productive operation in the near future. An alternative experiment can be carried out with any increase in productive capacity to modify the current forecasting results.

Table 7.6: Projected Sectoral Aggregate
Output Growth: 1996-2000

Sectors	1996	1997	1998	1999	2000
1. Crops	3.49	3.87	4.11	4.24	4.29
2. Other Farm Products	3.76	4.21	4.48	4.64	4.72
3. Metallurgy	6.41	5.97	5.62	5.32	5.03
4. Coal	4.10	3.88	3.73	3.61	3.50
5. Crude Petroleum	2.63	1.27	-0.40	-2.47	-5.07
6. Refined Petroleum	5.96	5.77	5.49	5.07	4.52
7. Chemicals	6.25	5.90	5.60	5.32	5.03
8. Machinery	6.90	6.66	6.38	6.18	6.05
9. Building Materials	10.78	9.91	9.27	8.73	8.23
10. Wood	10.53	11.24	11.96	12.64	13.26
11. Processed Food	4.75	5.07	5.26	5.37	5.39
12. Textile and Clothing	4.14	4.55	4.81	4.98	5.11
13. Paper	4.89	5.52	5.96	6.28	6.51
14. Misc. Manufactures	4.74	4.85	4.92	4.93	4.89
15. Electricity and Water	6.27	6.14	5.92	5.51	4.87
16. Construction	14.65	13.06	11.90	10.93	10.06
17. Transport	5.69	5.80	5.85	5.84	5.78
18. Commerce	5.97	6.08	6.12	6.12	6.07
19. Services	6.22	7.45	8.34	8.98	9.41
20. Education and Sports	6.40	6.80	7.09	7.29	7.41
21. Finance	2.19	2.92	3.50	3.96	4.29
22. Public Administration	7.38	8.40	9.10	9.57	9.88
TOTAL	6.65	6.67	6.64	6.57	6.46

The growth of heavy industries such as chemicals (7), machinery (8) and electricity and water (15) is expected to be moderate. The growth rates are likely to fall slowly in the coming years. This can be largely attributed to the slowdown in fixed capital investment as these industries are the major supplier of capital goods. The building material industry (9) will enjoy a very high growth rate initially due to the current construction boom. As new capital investment slows, however, the demand for building materials will be gradually diminishing.

Unlike heavy industries, the light industries,[3] such as wood (10), processed food (11), textiles and clothing (12), paper (13) and other manufactures (14), are to be benefited from the steady rise in consumption. The forecasted growth rates for these industries are expected to increase over the five year period. The wood industry has had a quite high rate of growth in recent years. Given continuous consumption growth, this trend is apparently to remain in the near future.

Among the remaining sectors, the current boom of construction is set to continue over the five-year period. However, as capital investment cools down, the rate of growth in the construction sector will be severely affected.

All service sectors, on average, are expected to grow strongly. The financial and banking sector (21) is expected to grow particularly strong: its growth rate will be almost doubled from its current low level in five years. The underlying driving force for service sectors to perform well is again the forecasted consumption expansion. It should also be noted that the growth of the public administration sector is forecasted to be relatively high. This result is, to a large extent, influenced by the model's configuration of public sector: a direct link of government expenditure with household consumption demand.

---

3   The distinction between heavy and light industries is relatively loose here, as some of the light industries include heavy industrial activities. However, the classification is based on the nature of major activities within a given industry.

6. CONCLUDING REMARKS

A dynamic CGE model is applied in this chapter to forecast the growth and structural changes in the Chinese economy toward 2000. The built-in dynamic features of the model enable the entire database to be updated continuously and produce a set of forecasts which are internally consistent and can be fully interpreted by the model's theoretical structure.

The simulation results show that the targeted GDP growth rate is achievable under the macro conditions and technical improvements specified in the model. However, inflation will remain to be high for the period which may require some response from monetary authority. The results also show that trade will continue to grow strongly even under foreign exchange constraint. Another problem revealed in the simulation is the decline in investment growth and the rise in consumption growth. From a long term point of view, maintaining a high saving and investment growth rate is the key for sustained rapid economic growth and development. If consumption growth outpaces saving or investment growth, some measures will have to be taken to ensure a balanced growth of consumption and investment.

One of the major advantages of CGE model forecasting is that it can produce forecasts at the detailed industrial level. The simulation results show that the sectoral time paths follow closely with the indicators at the national level.

It should also be reminded that, all these results are subject to changes in external shocks and in the model's macro settings. With this model, however, some controlled experiments can be easily carried out to identify, separately, the sources of growth or the responsiveness of the economy to individual conditions, technical changes and external shocks.

The model may be improved on many aspects. A special feature of the model is the link of aggregate savings with investment. Savings in the model is merely an accounting concept: the difference between GDP and aggregate consumption plus trade balance. Alternatively, a saving behavioural function can be specified which may require a multi-period framework.

Another area which may be improved on is the role of natural resource. In the model, all industries are treated equally in terms of flexibility in the utilisation of capital and labour. This specification may overestimate the responsiveness of some resource-dependent industries. For example, it is impossible for the crude oil industry to suddenly expand at a rate higher than what the current deposits and extracting capacity allow. Certain constraints must be imposed on such resource-dependent industries. One option is to use land as an additional factor of production, representing the role of natural resources in production. Unfortunately, the information about rent on land is impossible to find in China simply because there is no market for land. Alternatively, the outputs of resource industries can be made as exogenous variables and therefore, a ceiling level can be imposed on them. This option, though less desirable, will certainly confine the output growth of these industries in a more realistic range.

The model's database is calibrated to the 1994 data. Ideally, as the first step, the model should be used to generate 1995 input-output data *via* a multistep simulation as suggested by Adams et al (1994). However, this approach can not be adopted in this chapter since the detailed 1995 statistics have not yet been made available. The advantage of this approach is that it can not only update the entire database but also, in the process, generate a set of internally consistent technical and tastes change variables which can be used late in forecasting simulations.

Probably the most serious challenge for modelling a rapidly growing developing economy is how to establish links between capital investment and technical changes. At the moment, technical changes are all set exogenously. This conventional practice is borrowed directly from the modelling work for industrialised market economies. These economies have very low rate of growth driven largely by marginal increase in consumption demand. However, a rapidly growing economy like China has entirely different sources of growth. In such an economy, shifts in supply side conditions dominate the process of growth and structural changes. In particular, technical shifts and efficiency improvements in the utilisation of intermediate inputs and primary factors usually contribute more to economic growth than changes in demand conditions do. These technical changes and improvements in the use of resources are closely related to capital investment, especially foreign investment, and technology transfer. Further studies are needed to establish such links between technical changes and investment. If technical improvements can be endogenised, the capacity of the dynamic CGE model for forecasting will be significantly enhanced.

REFERENCES

Adams, P. D., Dixon, P. B., McDonald, D., Meagher, G. A., and Parmenter, B. R. (1994) "Forecasts for the Australian economy using the MONASH model", *International Journal of Forecasting*, 10: 181-89.

Armington, P.S. (1969) "The geographic pattern of trade and the effects of price changes", IMF Staff Papers, XVI, July, pp. 176-99.

Armington, P.S. (1970) "Adjustment of trade balances: some experiments with a model of trade among many countries", IMF Staff Papers, XVI, July, pp. 176-99.

Horridge, J. M., Parmenter, B. R. and Pearson, K. R. (1993) "ORANI-F: a general equilibrium model of the Australian economy", *Economic and Financial Computing*, 3(2): 71-144.

Johnansen, L. (1960) *A Multi-Sectoral Study of Economic Growth*, North-Holland, Amsterdam.

Lau, L., (1995) "Long-term economic growth in the PRC and its sectoral implications", Ferris, Andrew, ed. *The Economy of the PRC: Analysis and Forecasts*, Salomon Brothers, pp. 71-96.

Li, Jingwen, ed. (1995) *The Chinese Economy toward the Twentieth Centaury (Zouxiang Ershiyi Shiji De Zhongguo Jing ji)*, Economic Management Publishing House, Beijing.

Liu, Xiangdong, ed. (1994) *Handbook of China's Foreign Economic and Trade Policies 1994-1995 (Zhongguo duiwai jingji Maoyi zhengce shouce 1994-1995)*, Economic Management Publishing House, Beijing.

National People's Congress of the P.R.C. (1996) "The P.R.C.'s Ninth Five-Year Plan of National Economic and Social Development and the Guideline of the Long-term Development Targets toward the Year 2010", *People's Daily* (*Renmin Ribao*) March 20, Beijing.

State Statistical Bureau of the P.R.C. (1992) *Input-Output Table of China 1987* (*Zhongguo touru chanchu biao 1987*), China Statistical Publishing House, Beijing.

State Statistical Bureau of the P.R.C. (1993) *Input-Output Table of China 1990* (*Zhongguo touru chanchu biao 1990*), China Statistical Publishing House, Beijing.

State Statistical Bureau of the P.R.C. (1996), "A Statistical Communique on China's 1995 National Economic and Social Development", *People's Daily* (*Renmin Ribao*), March 7, Beijing.

Stone, Richard, (1961) *Input-Output and Natioan Accounts*, Organisation for European Economic Cooperation, Paris.

Sun Shangqing, ed. (1996) *The Chinese Economy in the Year 2000* (*2000 nian de zhongguo jingji*), China Development Publishing House, Beijing.

Zhang, Xiao-guang (1994) "A two-tier price general equilibrium model of the Chinese economy", Research Paper No.431, Department of Economics, University of Melbourne.

Zhang, Xiao-guang (1996) "A dynamic general equilibrium model of the Chinese economy", Research Paper, Department of Economics, University of Melbourne, forthcoming.

Zang, Xuheng (1994) *Analysis on Chinese Consumption Function* (*Zhongguo xiaofei hanshu fenxi*), Shanghai Sanlian, Shanghai People's Publishing House, Shanghai.

CHAPTER 8

RECENT CHINESE ECONOMIC PERFORMANCE AND PROSPECT

SIANG NG AND YEW KWANG NG*

ABSTRACT

The real GDP of China has more than quadrupled since the reform in 1978/9. Based on growth rates in the past 10 years, the Chinese GDP in PPP terms is projected to overtake that of USA (allowed to grow) before 2010. The rapid growth in China can be attributed to many factors associated with the reform, such as decentralization of decision making, the expanding role of the market mechanism and its openness to the world. However, China also enjoys many conditions favourable to growth at the beginning of the reform, such as political stability after the chaotic disturbance of cultural revolution, the lower stage of development and the associated relative importance of agriculture, absence of substantial external debts, the contribution of overseas Chinese, and high saving ratios. However, the fast growth is also accompanied by many economic problems, such as coastal-

---

*   Department of Banking and Finance, Monash University, Melbourne 3145 and Department of Economics, Monash University, Melbourne 3145

inland disparities, rural-urban, rich-poor differentials, and problems with state enterprises. Thus can we be optimistic about the future of China?

1. INTRODUCTION

Changes effected by economic reforms in China since the late 1970s have been quite phenomenal. The introduction of the open door policy has dramatically increased its external trade and direct foreign investments which in turn contributed to greater efficiency and growth. Since 1978, real GNP of China has been growing at an average rate in excess of 8% per annum. The real GNP in 1994 is more than four times that of 1978. Thus, the stated objective of quadrupling GNP by the year 2000 has been achieved six years ahead. In the last 2-3 years (1995-97), the economy has achieved the desired soft-landing, with real growth rates remaining high (1995: 10.5%, 1996: 9.7%) while the rate of inflation has been slashed continuously from 26% (Nov. 1994) to 1.1% (April 1997). (Figures based on comparison with the retail price level of the same month a year before. In comparison to March, the Aril 97 price level in fact fell by 0.6%, after a fall of 1% of the March figure over that of February. Source: Ming Bao, 20.5.97, p.A11 and *Hong Kong Economic Daily, 12.4.1997, p.A13.*) The growth in foreign trade is even more spectacular, as shown in Table 8.1. Moreover, the post-reform growth in China, unlike that of some Asian Tigers, has been accompanied by very high productivity growth (nearly 4% p.a. over the period 1979-94; see Hu and Khan 1996). Evidently, China has enjoyed sustained and higher (than pre-reform) economic growth, low inflation (single digit annual rates except 1988, 1989 and March 93 - Oct. 95), galloping exports, increased foreign reserves (expected to reach 120 billion US dollars in July 97, not including the US$70 billion of Hong Kong reserves) and improved standard of living. In fact, projecting at the average growth rate for the past ten years, China (without Hong Kong) can be expected to overtake the U.S. (allowing to grow) in GNP in PPP terms to become the largest economy in the world by 2010, as shown in Sub-section 4.2.

The rapid growth in China can be attributed to many factors associated with the reform, such as decentralization of decision making, the expanding role of the market mechanism and its openness to the world. However, China also enjoys many conditions favourable to growth at the beginning of the reform. Section 2 discusses these factors and their roles in contributing to the success of the reform. However, the fast growth is also accompanied by many economic problems, such as coastal-inland disparities, rural-urban, rich-poor differentials, and problems with state enterprises, which are discussed in Section 3. Thus can we be optimistic about the future of China? Section 4 tries to answer this question.

2. INITIAL FAVOURABLE CONDITIONS

2.1 Political and Structural Characteristics

First, probably foremost, China has largely enjoyed political stability at and since the time of the reform. When the reform was introduced in December 1978, the country had only emerged from the decade of the Cultural Revolution (1966-1976), the death of Mao (1976), the downfall of the Gang of Four (1976), and the transition of power from Hua (Mao's designated successor) to Deng (1978). With the effects and memories of the three disasters (the Anti-Right Movement in the mid 1950s, the Great Leap Forward 1958-1961, and the fairly recent Cultural Revolution) still freshly in mind, the Chinese people are much more anti-communist in heart and eagerly looking for a change. Though much weakened by the disillusionment associated with the three disasters, the Communist Party was still firmly in control. Furthermore, the country is also ethnically homogeneous. The predominant ethnic group, Han, accounts for 92% of the population. Thus, with the exception of isolated regions like Tibet, China is politically stable.

The importance of political stability for economic growth cannot be over-emphasized. Instability brings insecurity in properties. This increases transaction costs on the one hand and severely retards economic activities especially investments on the other. This impediment to investment is double-acting since the lenders require higher interest rates and the investors expect lower returns due to the instability. As illustrated in Figure 8.1, investment is reduced both by the upward shift of the supply curve of investment funds and the downward shift of the demand curve.

It might be queried that the alleged double-acting effects involve double-counting, since the risk to the property involved concerns the same property. There is really no double-counting since the higher uncertainty does apply to both the lender and the investor. If the investment is lost and the investor cannot pay the borrowed money back to the lender, it is not just the lender who loses (the money), the investor also loses. Not only does she/he lose the time and effort (which partly also applies to the case of a proprietor investor), she/he also suffers from the trouble of debt collection and the loss of reputation. With specialization, more people are doing different activities to achieve the same outcome. This taps the economies of specialization but also increases the number of linkages or steps necessary to secure the outcome, making the whole endeavour more vulnerable to risk, unless the riskiness of each step is substantially reduced. [For an analysis, see Yang and Ng 1993, Chapters 10 and 11. See also Ng and Ng, 1995, on the demonstration that an increase in the uncertainty in realizing future returns is more important than an increase in the rate of interest in reducing investment.]

Furthermore, the success of China's economic reforms may also be attributed to its more flexible decentralized system. Qian and Xu [1993] explain the relative ease of the Chinese transition by its more decentralized, multi-layer, multi-regional form of organizing the economy based on the territorial principle (M-form). It is not difficult to see that the less centralized M-form organization in China makes the transition to a market economy easier as it is less different from a market economy, more flexible, and more amenable to regional experimentation, competition, and emulation. Moreover, by the time of the reform in 1978, China had not quite completed its third

Table 8.1: Selected Macroeconomic Indicators for China
(Annual percent change, unless otherwise specified)

	Real Net Material Product[1]	General Retail Prices	Government Budget Balance[2]	Exports[3]	Imports[3]	Trade Balances[3]
1974	1.1	0.5	-0.3	6.9	7.6	-0.7
1975	8.3	0.2	-0.2	7.3	7.5	-0.2
1976	-2.7	0.3	-1.2	6.9	6.6	0.3
1977	7.8	2.0	1.1	7.6	7.2	0.4
1978	11.7	0.7	0.3	9.8	10.9	-1.1
1979	7.6	2.0	-5.1	13.7	15.7	-2.0
1980	7.9	6.0	-3.5	18.1	20.0	-1.9
1981	4.4	2.4	-0.6	22.0	22.0	-
1982	8.8	1.9	-0.7	22.3	19.3	3.0
1983	10.4	1.5	-0.9	22.2	21.4	0.8
1984	14.7	2.8	-0.8	26.1	27.4	-1.3
1985	12.8	8.8	0.3	27.4	42.2	-14.8
1986	8.1	6.0	-0.9	30.9	42.9	-12.0
1987	10.9	7.3	-0.9	39.4	43.2	-3.8
1988	11.3	18.6	-0.7	47.5	55.2	-7.7
1989	4.4	17.8	-0.7	52.5	59.1	-6.6
1990	4.1	2.1	-1.0	62.1	53.4	8.7
1991	7.7	2.7	-0.8	71.9	63.8	8.1
1992	13.0	5.3	-1.0	85.0	80.6	4.4
1993	13.4	13.7	-0.7	91.8	104.0	-12.2
1994	12.3*	21.7	-1.5	(8%)[4]	(29%)[4]	5.3
1995	10.5.	14.8	-1.08	121.1	115.6	
1966	9.7	6.1		(31.9%)[4]	(11.2%)[4]	16.7
				148.8	132.1	12.2
				(22.9%)[4]	(14.3%)[4]	
				151.1	138.8	
				(1.5%)[4]	(5.1%)[4]	

Source: *China Statistical Yearbook,* 1992. Figures for 1993 are from various Chinese publications; figures for 1994 are from *People's Daily,* 2 March and 7 March 1995, figures for 1995 are from *People's Daily, 7 March and 21 March 1996.*

[1] From 1978, the series is gross national product. [2] Revenue minus expenditure on the basis of the authorities' definitions in per cent of net material product or gross national product. [3]In billions of U.S. dollars, on a customs basis. [4] Growth rates over figures a year ago.* Growth rate of GDP. (Chinese GDP and GNP figures do not differ significantly.) * 1st half year, projected

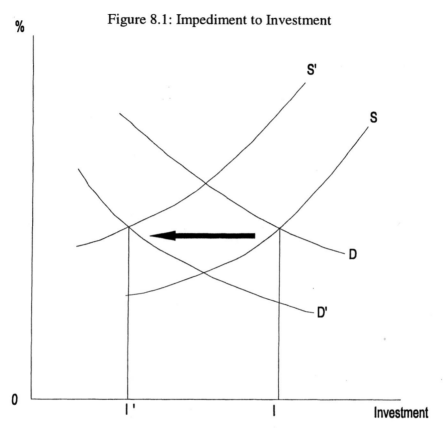

Figure 8.1: Impediment to Investment

decade under communism (since 1949), and some business related individuals in China had pre-communist experience. Thus, the entrepreneurial spirit and talents required for the market system emerge easily.

The different lengths of time after the communist revolution may however be a significant factor affecting economic growth according to Olson's [1982] institutional theory of sectional coalitions. Roughly, a major devastating event like a revolution or being conquered in a major war eliminates most of the interest groups of a country. These groups fight for their sectional interests and hence are usually counter-productive to economic efficiency and growth. As the organization of a group has the property of being a public good (for the group), it is difficult to form quickly due to the free-rider problem [Olson 1965]. It thus takes a fairly long period for such interest groups to become influential again after a major disturbance that destroys them. The theory has been used to explain the spectacular post-war growth in countries like Japan and Germany and the relative stagnation of countries like England. China did not just suffer the communist takeover in 1949, it also underwent eight years of Japanese invasion (1937-1944), and decades of civil wars before and after this invasion. For China, the Nationalist government had to surrender the capital Nanjing and moved right back to the southwest town of Chongqing. Practically the whole of China's northeast, north, central and coastal areas including most major cities like Beijing, Shanghai, Shenyang all fell. After the communist takeover, China suffered further devastating events, including the Great Leap Forward (1958-61) and the Cultural Revolution (1966-1975).

Another factor is the contribution of overseas Chinese. There are 6 million people in Hong Kong, 21 million in Taiwan, and over 23 million overseas Chinese in Southeast Asia alone. These economically very active people and their success not only is one of the factors contributing to China's transition but also serves to help in the development process of China since the reform. For one thing, these people provide significant amount of capital as well as entrepreneurial, technical and professional skills important for the development of China. This takes several forms, including investments (including joint ventures), remittances (such as contributions towards building a bridge in one's village of origin), and personal participation for various economic activities. (As may be seen in Table 8.2, Hong Kong and Macao, with the former accounting for the overwhelming majority of the total, alone accounts for roughly 44% and the Asian economies account for two thirds of the total foreign investment in terms of project number, contracted values, and realized values. (However, part of the investment from Hong Kong may originate from other parts of the world.) In recent years, Taiwan has also been increasing its share significantly. Hong Kong, Taiwan, and overseas Chinese are important not just in providing very significant amounts of investments. Due to language and cultural affinity, these entrepreneurial people are also

Table 8.2: Pattern of Source Countries of FDI in China (1990-94)
(Value: US$ Billion)

Source Countries	Realised Value	Share %	Ranking
Hong Kong & Macau	53.909	43.75	1
Taiwan	8.28	6.72	4
S.E. Asia:		2.04	8
Singapore	1.077	0.87	
Thailand	0.581	0.47	
Malaysia	0.320	0.26	
Philippines	0.290	0.24	
Indonesia	0.205	0.17	
Vietnam	0.039	0.032	
Japan	16.062	13.03	3
Korea	0.886	0.72	11
U.K.	2.619	2.13	7
France	3.718	3.02	6
Germany	1.758	1.43	10
U.S.	7.352	5.97	5
Canada	1.922	1.56	9
Australia	0.503	0.41	12
Other	23.698	19.23	2
Total	123.219		

Source: *Statistical Yearbook of China*

best suited to undertake successful business ventures in China and also to provide important links to the rest of the world. However, foreign investment is expected to moderate after the tariff reduction and the cancellation of certain tax concessions (including freedom from import duties on capital equipment) for foreign investment in 1996. (Controlling for its size, China has received very few foreign investment form the four major source countries, U.S. Germany, France, and U.K., although it may receive an average share from Japan; see Wei 1995.)

2.2 Agricultural and Rural Sector

Before the reform, agricultural production in China was organised by communes (corresponding to the township level) which were divided into brigades (villages) and production teams. A production team consisted of dozens or more of households and was the basic unit of production. Production decisions were decided from above and incentives were low. Growth in agricultural output barely kept up with population growth. After the disaster of Great Leap Forward and Cultural Revolution, the economic reform implemented at the end of 1970s overwhelmingly revitalises the rural sector. Pre-reform rural China had a very low extent of division of labour, making the creation of a market-based division of labour much easier. In 1978, China was still basically a peasant society with more than 70% of the employment in agriculture (See Table 8.3). The early success in the easier reform in agriculture also generates political dynamics in favour of further reforms. Within three years (1979-1982) in the initial period of the reform, the household responsibility system replaced the old system for virtually the whole country. This system emerged spontaneously from below but was subsequently given official sanction and encouragement. It effectively privatised agricultural production except that the land was still officially owned collectively and only on lease to individual household farmers (initially for five years but extended in 1984 to 15 years for annual crops and to 50 years for tree crops). As is well known, the household responsibility system led to immediate leaps in output. Lin et al [1993] estimated that almost half of the 42.2% growth of output in the cropping sector over 1978-84 was accounted by productivity change due to reforms. Yang, Wang and Wills [1992] show that the contribution of the reform on the property rights structure in rural China from 1979 to 1987 to economic growth via its effects on organisational efficiency accounts for 48% of total growth and the contribution of the reform to growth via its effects on allocative efficiency accounts for 52% of growth. However, after the mid 1980s, the rate of increase in agricultural output dropped to a low level. This may be due to the lack in outright ownership rights in land which retards long-term investments.

Table 8.3: Distribution of Employment by Sector, China, 1978

	Millions	%
Agriculture	283.7	70.7
Industry	60.9	15.2
Construction	8.8	2.2
Transport	7.4	1.8
Commerce	11.6	2.9
Other	29.1	7.2

Source: *Statistical Yearbook of China*

2.3 Macroeconomic Environment

When the reform was introduced at the end of 1978, substantial growth has been maintained after the initial chaotic years of the Cultural Revolution. More importantly, both inflation and the balance of payments had been kept under very tight control. The official statistics show some disinflation in the period 1963-67 and virtually no inflation since then up to 1978. An unnoted advantage of being at a lower stage of development and commercialisation is the bigger scope for non-inflationary expansion in money supply as the economy becomes more commercialised. Before 1978, the majority of people in China held very little amount of cash and bank deposits due to the small amount of cash exchanges. Since then, cash holding and bank deposits increased dramatically (See Table 8.4). This increased willingness to hold cash allows the central government to fund budget deficits by monetary expansion without adding to inflationary pressure.

Moreover, China had virtually no external debt at the introduction of the reform. This allowed China to benefit from substantial inflow of external resources without alarming either the external lenders and investors or the Chinese policy makers. The growth in foreign investment is shown in Table 8.5. However, this has been offset to a significant extent by the flight of fund abroad. (See Gunter 1996 for an estimate.)

Without attempting to emphasise the ethnic factor, completeness requires the mention of the high saving propensity (Table 8.6) and entrepreneurial ability of the Chinese people. It may not be an accident that three of the Four Asian Dragons (Hong Kong, Taiwan, Singapore) have overwhelming majority of their population being Chinese and the fourth (Korea) has been heavily influenced by the Chinese culture. The second group of the Asian Tigers (Thailand, Malaysia, Indonesia) have a sizeable minority of Chinese population who are disproportionately active in their commercial and industrial sectors. Moreover, their rates of economic growth are inversely related to the severity of their anti-Chinese policies.

Table 8.4: Growth in Saving Deposits

Year	Household Savings Deposits (RMB billion)	As % of GDP
1978[1]	21.06	5.87
1979	28.10	7.03
1980	39.95	8.94
1981	52.37	10.97
1982	67.54	13.03
1983	89.25	15.42
1984	121.47	17.53
1985	162.26	19.03
1986	223.76	23.10
1987	307.33	27.18
1989	514.69	32.17
1990	703.42	39.48
1991	911.03	45.13
1992	1154.54	48.07
1993[2]	1476.40	47.05
1994[3]	2151.88	49.13
1995[4]	2966.20	51.40

Sources: 1 *Statistical Yearbook of China*
2 *People's Daily, (International Edition), March*
3 *People's Daily, (International Edition), 3 February 1995*
4 *People's Daily, (International Edition), 7 March 1996.,*

Table 8.5: Growth in Foreign Investment Flow
(Billion of US$)

	Contracted Value	Realised Value	Growth Rate of Realised Value %
1979-1982	4.958	1.769	----
1983	1.731	0.915	----
1984	2.875	1.149	55.08
1985	6.333	1.956	37.84
1986	2.834	2.244	14.72
1987	3.709	2.314	3.12
1988	5.297	3.194	38.03
1989	5.600	3.393	6.23
1990	6.596	3.487	2.77
1991	11.980	4.366	25.21
1992	58.120	11.600	169.69
1993	110.800	25.759	122.06
1994*	---	35.00	39.90
1995**	---	48.40	48.30

Sources: *Ministry of Trade and Economic Cooperation, China*
* People's Daily, (International Edition), 2 March 1995.
** People's Daily, (International Edition), 7 March 1996.

Table 8.6: Gross Domestic Saving Ratios
(% of GDP)

	1980	1985	1990	1991	1992	1993	1994**
China*	31.5	35.0	32.8	32.8	34.3	38.7	44
Japan	31.1	31.7	34.6	35.1	34.0	32.5	32
USA	19.8	17.6	15.6	15.7	14.6	14.9	15
Australia	21.6	18.9	17.5	15.4	15.5	16.7	19
OECD	22.4	21.1	20.9	20.4	19.3	---	--

Sources: *OECD, Economic Outlook.* December 1995.
* *Statistical Yearbook of China.*
* *World Development Report, 1996.* (Figures are not perfectly comparable).

3. SOME CURRENT ECONOMIC PROBLEMS

While China has enjoyed spectacular growth in output, exports, and living standard, it is not without some serious problems, economically and politically. However, it is important to use economics to distinguish problems from non-problems. For example, Tao [1994] argued that GNP/TOV ratio "comprehensively reflects the total efficiency of economic development" [p.5], however, the falling GNP/TOV (total output value) ratio is not a problem. The level of transaction increases with the degree of specialization and the resulting enlargement of the extent of markets cause the falling of GNP/TOV ratio. Thus, the falling GNP/TOV ratio is a natural consequence of economic growth with specialization (See Yang and Ng [1993] for a modern classical analysis of the significance of specialization).

3.1 Three Big Differentials

3.1.1   Coastal-inland disparities

Visitors to China witnessing the spectacular spending abilities will find it hard to believe that it is a country with a per capita annual GNP (1996) of US$667. This is partly explained by the big disparities in per capita incomes between coastal and inland provinces, between cities and rural areas and between private proprietors, high officials, and those with lucrative sources of income over their formal salaries on the one hand and others who have to rely mainly on their low salaries on the other. However, it is difficult to believe that the understatement of the official GNP figure is not an important explaining factor.

Output disparities between China's coastal and inland regions are substantial. In 1995, the inland regions with 59% of the nation's population and producing 41.5% of GDP, had a GDP per capita of US$409. In contrast, 41% of the total population lives in the coastal regions producing 58.5% of GDP but with a per capita of US$820 which is much higher than the nation's average of US$579. In 1995, the average per capita income for China (excluding Tibet) was 3893 RMB, the province with the highest figure was Guangdong (6850 RMB). In 1995, the average wage in Shanghai was 9279 RMB which is the highest whereas Inner Mongolia had the lowest average wage of 4134 RMB; Guangdong and Beijing were below Shanghai with an average wage of 8250 RMB and 8144 RMB respectively while the national average was 5500 RMB. The disparities in per capita GDP between coastal and inland provinces are shown in Table 8.7. Coastal provinces had a higher GPD per capita with Shanghai (a city, not a province) as the leader.

Table 8.7: Per Capita GDP, 1993-1994 (Yuan)

	1994	1995	Ranking in 1995
Shanghai	15204	18943	1
Beijing	10265	13073	2
Tianjin	8164	10308	3
Liaoning	6103	6880	8
Guangdong	6380	7973	5
Zhejiang	6149	8074	4
Jiangsu	5785	7299	6
Fujian	5386	6965	7
Hainan	4820	5225	11
Shandong	4473	5743	9
Heilongjiang	4427	5465	10
Xingiang	3953	4819	12
Jilin	3703	4414	14
Hebei	3376	4449	13
Hubei	3341	4162	15
Inner Mongolia	3013	3639	16
Qinghai	2910	3430	20
Shanxi	2344	2843	27
Guangxi	2772	3543	18
Hunan	2701	3470	19
Ningxia	2685	3328	22
Jiangxi	2376	2984	26
Anhui	2521	3357	21
Sichuan	2516	3177	24
Yunan	2490	3044	25
Henan	2475	3312	23
Shaanxi	2819	3569	17
Tibet	1984	2392	28
Gansu	1925	2288	29
Guizhou	1553	1853	30

Source:　*Statistical Yearbook of China*
　　　　　Statistical Yearbook, various provinces, various years

We had the impression of an increase in the income disparity between provinces since 1978. However, this impression is not supported by our simple statistical analysis. We calculate the "relative standard deviation" or the "coefficient of variation" of provincial (including the Beijing, Tianjin, Shanghai, and autonomous regions) per capita national income as a summary measure of inequality between provinces. This is simply the standard deviation divided by the unweighted mean per capita income. As may be seen in Table 8.8, this measure of provincial inequality steadily decreased since the reform in 1978 until 1990 when a reversal started. But the reversal itself has been reversed over 1992-93. The inequality figure of 0.6387 in 1994 remains lower than that of 1992 and much lower than the figure of 1.0068 in 1978. Moreover, the relative liberalisation of inter-provincial migration since 1978 means that, while the poorer provinces remain relatively poor, a significant number of their former residents have been able to move to other provinces to earn higher incomes. However, the provincial inequality does not capture inequalities within each province. Moreover, in another paper that we have just started drafting (Ng and Ng 1997), we found that the provincial coefficient of variation increases a lot in recent years and in 1995 reached a level almost twice its 1978 figure if the per-capita disposable income of residents are used instead of per-capita GDP. The two differ mainly by personal income taxes/subsidies. Since income taxes were not important in 1978, interprovincial equalisation through the central government must have played a much more important role in 1978 than the recent years, probably due to the relative decline of the importance of central public finance. This indicates that, apart from certain forms of malpractice such as the abuse of power which need to be tackled urgently, the increase in provincial income disparity since the reform has been due to the decline of central redistribution rather than to the effects of reform or the functioning of the market economy. This has an important policy implication; see Ng and Ng 1997 for details. It is also reassuring to learn of a recent report (by New China News Agency, 3 May 1997, reported by *Cheng Ming,* June 1997, p.94) that in 1996, the trend in the past decade has been reversed, with rural net income increasing faster in inland (central and western) regions than the coastal (eastern) region.

We have seen researchers calculating the standard deviations of provincial per capita GDP overtime for China, showing an alarming increase. This we believe to be misleading. If relative shares remain absolutely unchanged, the standard deviation will increase through time as per capita incomes increase. Thus, the relative (to mean) standard deviation or the coefficient of variation is a more acceptable measure of regional inequality.

Table 8.8: Changes in Regional Inequality, 1978-1994
Standard Deviation of Per Capita National Income Between Provinces*
Divided by Mean

	Using National Income	Using GDP
1978	1.0068	
1982	0.8082	
1986	0.7117	
1988	0.6585	0.6585
1990	0.6078	0.6259
1991	0.6168	0.6387
1992	0.6480	
1993		
1994		

*   Including Beijing, Tianjin, Shanghai and autonomous regions and municipalities.

Sources: *Statistical Yearbook of China and Historical Statistical Data of Provinces, Autonomous Regions and Municipalities of China.*

3.1.2   Rural-Urban Differential

The success of reforms has led to rural-urban migration with huge impacts on the rural-urban segregation policy, calling for careful solution.

The consequence of the success of reforms is the increases in agricultural productivity and higher per capita income. As per capita income increases, demand for agricultural products increases but less than proportionately (Engel's law). Given an unchanged proportion of people engaging in agricultural production, the increase in demand falls short of the increase in supply of agricultural products. There is thus a pressure to transfer resources (including the agricultural labour force) from primary to secondary and tertiary production which concentrate in the urban areas. Thus, the rural-urban migration is a natural consequence of economic growth. The Chinese government attempts to address the problem by the development of rural industries. This has alleviated the problem to some extent but not completely. There are scale economies in cities and most people prefer to live in cities. In countries of high per capita income, only a few percent of people are engaged in agricultural production and the majority congregate in major urban areas.

On top of the above effect related to Engel's law, the policies of economic reforms and openness also lead to relaxation of control, availability of more information, and higher mobility. The occurrence of the rural-urban migration is thus not surprising. However, this does not mean that the migration can be permitted without control. There is some general agreement (including those who are against the rural-urban segregation policy) that a sudden complete elimination of control would lead to an unmanageable situation -- "the flooding of the cities by rural people".

Due to the existing big rural-urban disparity, a sudden and complete dismantling of the rural-urban segregation is infeasible. However, both to achieve efficiency and fairness and to avoid having the problem getting out of hand with the progress of further reforms and liberalisation, a policy of gradually narrowing the disparity is imperative. The success or otherwise in the implementation of this significantly affects the future political stability of China.

According to the source of the State Statistical Bureau, the average rural income for 1995 was $US190 compared with the average of urban income of $US609. Furthermore, the consumption disparities between rural and urban have also increased as shown in Table 8.9. The ratio decreased in the first few year of the reform due to the success of agricultural reform in implementing the household responsible system. However, the increase in agricultural productivity reached its limit in 1985, consequently the ratio rose and it is now well above that of the beginning of the reform. However, there was an encouraging reversal to the increasing urban-rural differential in 1995. Moreover, 1996 should see a further improvement as it was recently reported that "Rural residents on average saw greater improvement in their lot during 1996 than their urban counterparts, with upwards of 10% increases in real income" (Goldstein 1997, p.31).

For the disparity between groups of individuals, data are less readily available. However, the general consensus is that this has increased very substantially. (See Chen 1997, Cheng 1996, Rozelles 1996.)

Due to the conflicting figures and opposing effects of certain factors not reflected in official figures, it is difficult to judge whether income disparities now are greater than at the beginning of the reform. However, it is more certain that disparities have increased significantly in the last decade.

Table 8.9: Rural Urban Per Capita Consumption (Yuan)

Year	Rural	Urban	Urban/Rural
1978	138	405	2.9
1980	178	496	2.8
1985	347	802	2.3
1986	376	920	2.4
1987	417	1089	2.6
1988	508	1431	2.8
1989	553	1568	2.8
1990	571	1686	3.0
1991	621	1925	3.1
1992	718	2356	3.3
1993	855	3027	3.5
1994	1138	3979	3.5
1995	1479	5044	3.4

Source: *Statistical Yearbook of China*

3.2 State-owned enterprises

In contrast to the agricultural sector, the sector of state-owned enterprises is
the least satisfactory sector in the economy while the individual, the joint
venture, and foreign owned enterprises have achieved highest growth rates.
While the real growth rate of the individual owned enterprises has been very
much higher than that of the collective-owned enterprises, the latter's
performance has been better than the state-owned enterprises. This is well
known and officially acknowledged. Official Treasury's figures show that the
percentage of state-owned enterprises making losses has increased from 16%

in 1989 to 33% in 1994 and the figure for the first 10 months of 1995 was 41%. Unofficially, it has been estimated the real figures are about twice the official ones.

In May 1995, the National Economic Reform Committee reported the findings from a survey of the production activities of large and medium size of state-owned enterprises in 12 provinces (Shanghai, Tianjin, Liaoning, Sichuan, Guangdong, Zhejiang, Jilin, Henan, Hunan, Shanxi, Guizhou, and Yunan). The findings are summarised below:

Production Activities	% of Enterprises
Below 20%	18.3
Below 30%	36.0
Below 50%	41.7
Below 70%	62.3

As shown in Table 8.10, the production share of the state-owned enterprises fell from 77.6% in 1978 to 34.01% in 1995; the contributions of the collective-owned, the individual-owned and joint venture/foreign-owned enterprises increased from 22.4%, 0% and 0% in 1978 to 36.6%, 12.86% and 16.57% respectively. In particular, the dramatic decrease in the share of the state sector by more than 9 percentage points from 47.0% to 37.3% over one year 1993-1994 is remarkable. (It is probably related to the shift to the right following the speeches by Deng in the South in 1992). The trend is expected to continue.

The loss of assets and difficulties associated with transformation are problems facing the state-owned enterprises. Privatisation may on the one hand reduces some burden of the government, but on the other, will create unemployment and the problem of providing social security to workers affected by these changes. According to an official report [*Democracy and Law,* No. 2, 1996], the loss of assets of state-owned enterprises has been estimated as high as 500 billion RMB between 1982 to 1992.

Table 8.10: Industrial Production by Ownership of Enterprises (%)

Year	State	Collective	Individual	Joint/Foreign
1978	78.6	22.4	0.	0
1980	76.0	23.5	0.019	0.466
1983	73.4	25.7	0.116	0.78
1984	69.1	29.7	0.194	1.01
1985	64.9	32.1	1.85	1.20
1986	62.3	33.5	2.76	1.46
1987	59.7	34.6	3.63	2.02
1988	56.8	36.1	4.34	2.72
1989	56.1	35.7	4.81	3.44
1990	54.6	35.6	5.39	4.38
1991	56.2	33.0	4.83	6.01
1992	51.5	35.1	5.80	7.61
1993	47.0	34.0	7.98	11.06
1994	37.3	37.7	10.09	14.85
1995	34.0	36.6	12.86	16.57

Source: *Statistical Yearbook of China*

3.3 Political Stability

The widespread corruption and the abuse of power may to some extent damage the investment climate. With political reform lagging far behind economic reform, there was some concern as to whether the government will survive the possible disturbance following Deng's death. However, following the death of Deng in February 1997, nothing untoward has happened. In fact, the stock markets in China (Shenzhen and Shanghai) soared by more than 40% in the few months following Deng's death (with some corrections in

May/June 97). The stock market in Hong Kong have also been very bullish up to the transition in 1 July. Though the outcome of the forthcoming (October 97) major 15th Party Congress has yet to be watched, the present leadership appears to be very committed to further liberalisation and reform.

4. PROSPECTS

4.1 Recent Trends and Measures Towards Further Liberalisation

The move toward decentralization, the decrease in the scope of state control in international trade, and the allowance for direct contacts between domestic and foreign producers have lowered trade impediments and transaction costs. This, in turn, contributes to greater efficiency and growth. Early in January 1996, import restriction on 176 items has been cancelled. In April, it is announced that custom tariffs on 4962 products are reduced by an average of 23 %. Furthermore, it was announced that all enterprises will be allowed to import and export without government permission, though it is experimental. From 1 July 1996, the distinction of rural versus urban residency are to be abolished and replaced by a system of family versus collective households. However, to date of final revision (June 1997), we have not found any major changes. It appears that the transition is slow and few details have been announced.

The need for a better macroeconomic management of the economy is obvious following the increasing emergence of financial activities, restructuring of the banking and financial sector, and the opening up of the economy. The new economic environments enhance the important roles of monetary and fiscal instruments in maintaining macroeconomic stability. To this end, the RMB was made partially convertible (i.e. convertible in current but not in capital account) in 1996. In December 96, it was announced that foreign financial institutions would be allowed to do business involving RMB transaction in Pudong, Shanghai. By April 97, more than ten such institutions have been formally approved for such ventures (Pan 1997).

The inefficient and unprofitable state enterprises are still in need of reform. In 1996, the authority seemed to have decided to shed at least the smaller state enterprises. In the "Seize the Large and Release the Small" program, "up to 90,000 small and medium-size state-owned money-losing firms are being sold, leased or transferred to non-state sectors, with buyers promising to take responsibility for the workers" (China News Digest, *Global News,* 17 July 1996, on-line).

Fast economic growth in China has led to the bottlenecks in energy and transportation. However, the central and provincial governments have tackled this situation by increasing infrastructure investments. There is an increase in provincial economic power and a decline in regional protectionism together with further growth of the market and the expansion of the private sector.

4.2 Looking Ahead

Even growing at a little slower rate than the average over the last ten years, Chinese GNP in purchasing power terms can be calculated to surpass that the US (allowed to grow at its average rate) by the year 2010 to become the world's largest economy (see Figure 8.2). This is so before we include the sizeable GDP of Hong Kong (which is to be integrated into China on 1 July 1997). The general tendency towards further reforms and growth is almost assured. The scope for further growth is still enormous due to the relative low GNP per capita, high saving rates, the existence of huge inefficiencies, inventiveness and industriousness of the people.

Figure 8.2: GNP in Purchasing Power Parity, Projected from Average Growth
Rates in the Past 10 Years

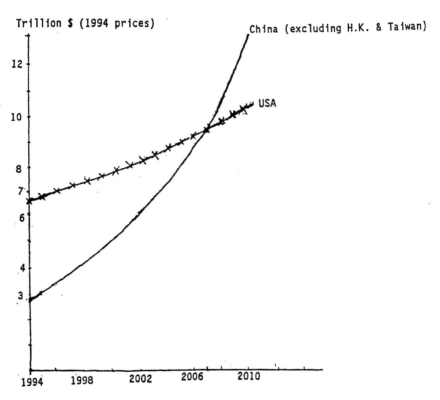

Many problems remained unsolved. Apart from the more economic ones
discussed above, there are problems of corruption, the unreformed political
system, increasing economic and violent crimes, increasing unemployment,
and others. Despite the existence of many difficult problems, we may be
cautiously optimistic about the likelihood of avoiding a chaotic disturbance
based on:

(a) Political forces/interest groups in favour of further reform and growth are overwhelming.
(b) The almost assured continuing high growth allows the reconciliation of conflicting interests.
(c) The traditional Chinese belief in "grand unification".
(d) The central control of the military.
(e) The general world-wide trend towards peace and mutual benefits through trade liberalisation.

REFERENCES

Chen, Z.S. (1997). "The Situation, Trends, and Influencing Factors in the Income Differentials of Urban Residents in China: A Case Study of Tianjin", *Economic Research* (in Chinese), 1997 (3): 21-31.

Cheng, Y.-S. (1996). "A decomposition Analysis of Income Inequality of Chinese Rural Households", *China Economic Review*, 7: 155-167.

Goldstein, A. (1997). "China in 1996", *Asian Survey,* 37: 29-42.

Gunter, F.R. (1996). "Capital Flight from the People's Republic of China: 1984-1994", *China Economic Review*, 7(1):77-96.

Hu, Z. and Khan, M.S. (1997) *Why Is China Growing So Fast?*, Washington, D.C.: International Monetary Fund.

Lin, J.Y., Burcroff, R. and Feder, G. (1993) "Agricultural Reform in a Socialist Economy: the experience of China", *The Agricultural Transition in East/Central Europe and the Former USSR,* Washington, D.C.: The World Bank.

Ng, S. and Ng, Y.-K. (1995) *The Rate of Uncertainty is More Important than the Rate of Interest in Affecting Investment,* Syme Department of Banking and Finance Working Paper Series.

Ng, S. and Ng, Y.-K. (1997) "Income Disparities in the Transition of China: Reducing Negative Effects by Dispelling Misconceptions", Paper to be presented to *International Conference on the Economic Development and*

Transformation of the East Asian Economies, Chinese University of Hong Kong, July 1997.

Pan, Z.Y. (1997) "The New Pattern of Chinese Banking Competition after Foreign Banks' Involvement in RMB Business", *Hong Kong Economic Journal,* 21(3): 63-66.

Olson, M. (1965) *The Logic of Collective Action,* Cambridge, Mass: Harvard University Press.

Olson, M. (1982) *The Rise and Declines of Nations: Economic Growth, Stagflation, and Social Rigidities,* New Haven: Yale University Press.

People's Daily

Qian, Y. and Xu, C. (1993) "Why China Economic Reforms differ: the M-form Hierarchy and Entry/Expansion of the Non-state Sector", *Economics of Transition,* 1(2): 135-170.

Rozelle, S. (1996). "Stagnation without Equity: Patterns of Growth and Inequality in China's Rural Economy", *China Journal,* 35: 63-92.

State Bureau of Statistics, *Statistical Yearbook of China.*

Tao, Z.P. (1994) "Commenting on the Chinese Development from the three Basic Relationships of National Economic Aggregates", *Hong Kong Economic Journal,* September.

Wei, S.-J. (1995) "Attracting Foreign Direct Investment: Has China Reached Its Potential?", *China Economic Review,* 6(2):187-199.

Yang, X., Wang, J. and Wills, I. (1992) "Economic Growth, Commercialisation, and Institutional Changes in Rural China, 1979-1987", *China Economic Review,* 3, 1-37.

Yang, X. and Ng, Y.K. (1993) *Specialization and Economic Organization: A New Classical Framework,* North Holland.

CHAPTER 9

CHINA'S MARKET REFORMS AND ITS NEW FORMS OF SCIENTIFIC AND BUSINESS ALLIANCES

C. HARVIE AND T. TURPIN*

ABSTRACT

During the past ten years China has embarked on a concerted program to link publicly funded research to the market demands of its rapidly expanding economy. Consequently research institutes and universities in China have become embedded in new alliances across a whole range business enterprises. Most significantly these alliances have incorporated a new and rapidly expanding industry sector known as township/village enterprises (TVEs).

With an annual growth rate of over 30% over the past 10 years, they comprise the fastest growing sector in China's economy. These enterprises are

* Department of Economics, University of Wollongong, Wollongong, NSW 2522, Australia and Centre for Research Policy, University of Wollongong, Wollongong, NSW 2522, Australia

predominantly collectively owned through a distribution of share holdings among villagers, however, an increasing number of TVEs are now privately owned. Many are now involved in alliances, through joint ventures with other TVEs, State owned enterprises, and foreign enterprises and have been built around a complex network of affiliations and alliances of scientists, engineers, academics and business entrepreneurs.

The status of firms is therefore highly dynamic. Some observers have raised questions about the longer term sustainability of the TVE sector. This chapter suggests that many TVEs are already undergoing significant organisational transformations. The question we ask is not the extent to which TVEs will survive as a significant sector, but the organisational forms that will enable them to do so.

1. INTRODUCTION

Recent developments in China's industrial sector indicate that one of the most distinctive features has been the major contribution of enterprises outside the state sector, the so called `non state sector', and particularly that of township/village enterprises (TVEs). The non state sector has attained major outcomes in terms of output and employment (see Table 9.1). Exports (including some non industrial goods) increased from US$3.9 billion to US$12.5 billion between 1985 and 1990, with the latter figure amounting to over one-fifth of China's total exports for 1990. Further, as Table 9.2 shows, the growth of output per worker (output per unit of capital and total factor productivity) especially among the TVEs has outstripped comparable measures for the state owned enterprises (SOEs). The rapid pace of growth of the non state sector has contributed to the share of SOEs in industrial production having fallen to less than half by 1992, despite steady state sector growth and the absence of significant privatisation.

Most of the output in the non state sector comes from collective firms, which are typically controlled by local governments. Although there are some definitional ambiguities, in the China situation these collectively owned firms can be considered to be part of the public sector. Hence despite the falling share of SOEs, publicly owned enterprises still dominate China's industrial production. The contribution of genuinely private firms is difficult to measure but has been estimated to be around 10% of total industrial production.

The TVEs expanded rapidly during the 1980s (see Table 9.1). Their foundations can be found from the contribution of the agricultural collectives or communes before this period, which established and promoted rural industry. However with the demise of the agricultural collectives in the early 1980s the responsibility for the TVEs was transferred to local government TVE industrial departments, which contributed start up funds, appointed managers and were ultimately involved in strategic decision making. The growth of the TVEs was also assisted by the success of China's agricultural reforms of the late 1970s and early 1980s, which greatly expanded rural savings, freed millions of workers to seek non farm employment and increased rural demand for consumer goods.

The role of China's TVEs and other collectives is unique in the context of an economy in transition. In no other such economy has public ownership played such a dynamic role, contributing the vast majority of industrial output (over 85%). However the collective ownership form does not have a precise definition in the country, leading to uncertainty about ultimate ownership rights. The literature would suggest that public ownership combined with vague ownership rights would present a recipe for economic disaster (see Weitzman and Xu, 1993). For them the success of TVEs arises from their internal institutional form, which facilitates cooperation through implicit contracts among community members. However Naughton (1994) argues that the success of the TVEs is largely due to a set of external conditions to which they have been an effective adaptation. They have been an effective response to a distinctive feature of the Chinese transition process which has seen the early development of product markets, without well developed markets for factors of production and assets. The latter in fact only developing gradually, or even in the 1990s being at a very early stage of development. Naughton therefore argues that the TVEs were a flexible and effective but basically ordinary adaptation to this environment.

Many of these enterprises have now developed to the extent that they have been able to challenge the heavily protected large SOEs. How has it been possible for these new enterprises to develop such technology capabilities in the absence of in-house R&D facilities and over such a short period of time?

Christerson and Lever-Tracy have argued that the impressive growth among Chinese rural enterprises reflects a pattern of development resembling the industrial districts of the `third Italy'. Their observation is that horizontal rather than vertical alliances, together with the involvement of local governments have enabled many rural industrial enterprises to become `globally competitive in producing for fast-changing fashionable market niches' (Christerson and Lever-Tracy, 1996). The emerging evidence certainly supports this conclusion.

On the other hand, others have suggested that TVEs may not represent an enduring organisational innovation in China's overall economy. Some authors have predicted that, as underlying economic conditions change, rural industry will lose ground to large domestic firms, enterprise groups, and joint venture companies during the course of the 1990s. However, although predominantly collectively owned through a distribution of share holdings by a group of villagers, an increasing number of TVEs are now privately owned. Many are now involved in joint ventures with State owned enterprises and foreign companies and a high proportion incorporate a complex network of affiliations and alliances involving scientists, engineers, academics and business entrepreneurs.

Table 9.1: Overview of Chinese Industrial Performance, 1980-1992

A. Real Output					
Ownership Type	Index of Real Output (1980 = 100)				Average Annual Growth 1980/92 (per cent)
	1980	1985	1990	1992	
State	100	148	210	257	7.8
Collective	100	247	554	914	18.4
Private^a	100	21752	126057	241455	64.9
Other^b	100	492	3530	8736	37.2

B. Shares of Various Types of Firms in Nominal Output					
	Shares of Nominal Output (%)				Percentage Share of Incremental Output 1980/92
	1980	1985	1990	1992	
State	76.0	64.9	54.6	48.4	43.6
Collective	13.7	13.3	10.3	11.8	11.5
Urban	9.9	18.8	25.3	26.2	28.8
Township-	0.0	1.9	5.4	6.8	7.9
Village	0.5	1.2	4.4	7.2	8.3
Private^a	100.0	100.0	100.0	100.0	100.0
Other^b					
Total					
Total Output (¥ billion)	515.4	971.6	2392.5	3706.6	

Source: Taken from Jefferson and Rawski (1994), p.48.

Note: Percentage totals may not check due to rounding error.

[a] Privately-owned firms employing less than 8 workers.

[b] Includes private firms employing 8 or more workers, joint ventures, foreign-owned firms, and other ownership forms.

Table 9.2: Estimated Rates of Annual Productivity Growth in Chinese
Industry (% change)

	1980-84	1984-88	1988-92
A. *Total Factor Productivity*			
State sector	1.8	3.0	2.5[a]
Collective sector	3.4	5.9	4.9[a]
Urban and township Township-Village	7.3[a]	6.6[a]	6.9[a]
B. *Labour Productivity (real terms)*			
State sector	3.8	6.2	4.7
Collective sector	8.6	7.0	13.8
Urban and township Township-Village	5.8	14.4	17.7

Sources: Taken from Jefferson and Rawski (1994), p.56.
         [a] Preliminary results.

As these smaller independent and flexible enterprises turn to science for
competitive advantage they are introducing new options, and new
imperatives, not only into collective relationships with industrial partners, but
also into R&D relationships with research institutes, universities and
government agencies. It is this horizontal connection between TVEs and
science based institutions that is likely to provide the organisational
capabilities for their sustainable development. There appear to have been
three important areas of reform that have contributed to these developments.
Firstly, state driven economic reforms have contributed to an environment
that has encouraged TVEs to move into new areas of industrial production
and trading. Second, science policy reforms have steered technological

alliances with public research institutions toward TVEs rather than toward state owned enterprises. Thirdly, reforms at local government levels have created an environment conducive to the formation of horizontal alliances among TVEs and with other enterprises. As future reforms in the state-owned sector deepen, it is likely that the long term survival of the TVE sector will rest even more on their capacity to build and maintain scientific and industrial organisational networks.

The chapter proceeds as follows. In section 2 a broad overview of the reform process in China is conducted focusing in particular upon those aspects which have encouraged the development of the non state sector and in particular that of the TVEs. Section 3 identifies developments in China's industrial sector. In particular the development and outcomes form reform of SOEs and reasons behind the success of the TVEs. Specific case study examples of TVEs and the alliances which they are developing are also presented. Finally in section 4 the major conclusions from this chapter are presented.

2. OVERVIEW OF CHINA'S REFORMS

Economic Reforms

Since the introduction of the economic reform process in 1978 China has achieved a remarkable economic performance, with the country experiencing a period of structural transformation and rapid economic growth. Real output of the Chinese economy has quadrupled over the period from 1978 to 1993. Major gains in productivity have enabled the improvement of real incomes and in the reduction of poverty. Many of the distortions and rigidities which existed in the previous centrally planned economic system have been alleviated, with economic agents increasingly making decisions on the basis of market signals. However in spite of the major improvements which have occurred, a number of problems still remain due to the partial nature of the reform process. This has contributed to the economy experiencing "stop-go" periods of macroeconomic instability, arising from the authorities having given up direct control over the economy while indirect instruments have remained ineffective because of the incompleteness of the reforms.

China's economic reform process contains a number of key features. Firstly, it has been both gradual and incremental unlike the "big bang" reforms implemented in certain Eastern European countries. Secondly, the economic reforms which have been implemented have not been obtained from a comprehensive blueprint, but rather have been firstly introduced on an experimental basis in some localities and if successful then introduced at the national level. Such a pragmatic approach to economic reform was designed to avoid major disruptions, and to gradually transform the economy from a predominantly centrally planned one to one in which the market mechanism played an important role. Thirdly, the reform process utilised intermediate mechanisms to enable the transition from one economic system to another to be a smooth as possible, thereby avoiding major disruptions that could arise from an abrupt shift. Specific examples of this process include: the dual-track pricing system to improve the allocation of resources at the margin; establishing a swap market in foreign exchange retention rights to improve the use of foreign exchange; establishing open economic zones to introduce foreign capital and technology to the country; using the contract responsibility system to encourage economic agents to behave in a market oriented fashion; and authorising some local governments to enact and experiment with market oriented legislation. The use of such mechanisms was a means of encouraging economic agents to behave in a way compatible with a market system, prior to the phasing out of central planning. Fourthly, the Chinese leadership has attempted to maintain the socialist character of the economy, focusing the public ownership of key sectors of the economy whilst encouraging the development of the non state sector.

Phases of Economic Reform (1978-Present)

The process of economic reform in China can be usefully broken down into a number of phases. The first phase covered the period 1978-84, the second phase from 1984-88, the third phase from 1988-91, the fourth phase from 1992-93 and the most recent phase from 1994 to the present.

First Phase (1978-84)

During this first phase emphasis was placed upon initiating a recovery of the economy, by overcoming the major obstacles to economic development in the pre-reform era which were: a deep mistrust of the market system; reliance on collective efforts and lack of individual work incentives; emphasis on self reliance bordering on autarky at all levels from the national to the provincial and commune.

Initially the reform policies pursued were similar to those adopted in the early 1960s after the period of the Great Leap forward, placing emphasis on material incentives and an expanded role for the market. Specifically procurement prices for agricultural products were increased, diversification and specialisation of crops were encouraged, restrictions on rural markets (trade fairs) were relaxed, and with the introduction of the household responsibility system the organisation of farming was decentralised from the collective to the household level. In the industrial sector the bonus system was reintroduced, the retention of depreciation allowance was permitted and the retention of profits by state owned enterprises on an experimental basis began. To encourage exports and the attraction of foreign investment and technology special economic zones were established, and were to be used as laboratories for bolder market economic orientated reforms.

Second Phase (1984-88)

The success of the rural reforms during the first phase of the reform process encouraged the authorities to expand such reforms to include the urban-industrial sectors in 1984. The major measures adopted included: the establishment of a dual-track pricing system; the introduction of enterprise taxation; the reform of the wage system linking in a closer way remuneration with productivity; breaking up the monobank system with the objective of creating a central bank.

Enterprises were encouraged to borrow from the banking system for their investment requirements rather than depending upon the state for such funds as in the past. Revenue sharing arrangements between the central and local governments was revised in favour of the latter. Fourteen major cities were "opened up" to encourage foreign trade and investment, including the accumulation of technical know how. Many of these measures were further expanded and revised in 1986 to include: the establishment of swap centres for trading in retained foreign exchange earnings; decentralising trade through the establishment of local foreign trade corporations; and the adoption of a contract responsibility system for SOEs similar to that adopted for the agricultural sector.

Third Phase (1988-91)

The success of the earlier reforms contributed to rising demand and production but also contributed to a sharp increase in inflation. Plans for a new round of price reforms were postponed and in fact some of the previous price reform was reversed with increased re-centralisation of price controls under a "rectification program", in conjunction with other strong measures designed to reduce the inflationary pressures within the economy. The country entered a period from mid 1988 to 1991 of retrenchment, in which further reform measures were delayed. While the retrenchment measures were successful in reducing the inflationary pressures, they contributed to a major reduction in the growth of the economy. This was felt particularly strongly in the industrial sector where the SOEs experienced a major increase in losses, inter-enterprise debt increased substantially and stock levels increased sharply. They were also felt by the TVEs who were deliberately starved of access to credit. Such developments contributed to a major economic crisis, resulting in the authorities in late 1990 deciding to stimulate the economy using monetary and investment policies. This contributed to a recovery of the economy in 1991. During this period generally stable prices encouraged the authorities to make substantial realignments in relative prices and liberalise certain other prices.

Fourth Phase (1992-1993)

By early 1992 the authorities had declared an end to the rectification program, announcing their intention to further accelerate the reform process and the opening up of the economy. This message became clear during Deng Xiaoping's tour of the prosperous coastal cities at this time, when he called upon the whole country to accelerate growth and to vigorously pursue the policy of reforming and opening up the whole economy. He prepared the ideological groundwork for the adoption of a more comprehensive reform strategy aimed at transforming the Chinese economy to a fully market based system, by announcing that the market mechanism was a tool for economic development and was consistent with socialism. At the Fourteenth National Congress of the Chinese Communist Party in October 1992 his views were formally endorsed, setting the establishment of a "socialist market economy" as the national goal. This goal was later included in the country's constitution during the first session of the Eighth National People's Congress in March 1993. A new reform strategy was later adopted during the Third Plenum of the Fourteenth Central Committee in November 1993.

Fifth Phase (1994-2000)

By 1994 China had entered a new phase of economic reforms aimed at overcoming the legacies remaining from the period of partial reform, with the objective of achieving by the year 2000 a "socialist market economy", where the market mechanism would play the primary role in the allocation of resources while public ownership (including in the form of corporatised enterprises and collectives) would remain at the core of the economy. The reform strategy would require fundamental changes in a broad range of important areas consistent with the development of a market economic system, and the mechanisms for indirect macroeconomic management of it. The latter would require reforms in the areas of the exchange rate and trade system, central banking and the financial system, the tax system and inter-governmental fiscal relations and the investment system. A further crucial area of remaining reform relates to that of the SOEs, and the need to transform these into autonomous, competitive and legal entities with full accountability for profits and losses. In addition there would be a need to fully develop the legal and regulatory system.

The reform measures were therefore to be comprehensive, far reaching and ambitious, with the objective of creating a competitive market environment in all sectors and throughout the country. These it is hoped will provide the basis for the future rapid, and sustained, growth of the economy. The role of the non-state sector had been crucial in the movement towards greater marketisation of the economy, and the provision of competition to the state sector. A key issue relates to the role and development of the non state sector during the current and future process of economic form, and the sustainability, in particular, of the growth of the TVEs.

Recent Science and Technology Policy Reforms in China

Since 1979 science and technology in China has become a dominant factor in the country's economic strategy for development. From the early 1980s the

Chinese Government began introducing reforms to encourage the formation of `high-technology' non-state owned enterprises, to reform the R&D funding system, to develop a legislative base for managing intellectual property rights, to develop a `technology market' and generally develop an economic and administrative environment favourable to the commercialisation of science and technology achievements.

Market principles and market forces have since come to have a significant influence on the production of science and technology in China's research institutions, and on the linkages between institutions and the rapidly growing industrial sectors.

Through the 1980s, China progressively implemented a series of Science and Technology development programs with specially designed objectives. These included the `Spark Program', intended to direct science and technology towards the development of township enterprises and the promotion of rural and local economic development;  the `863 Program' intended to promote China's high-tech R&D; the `Prairie-Fire Program' designed to guide agriculture technology training; `Harvest Program' aimed at diversifying agriculture, animal husbandry, and the fisheries; and `Torch Program' directed towards promoting new technologies in industry (State Science and Technology Commission of China, 1991).

Reforms in Universities and Research Institutions

Meanwhile, research institutes and universities, many with well established manufacturing capabilities, have been permitted and encouraged to trade independently. In 1992, for example, the China State Science and Technology Council issued regulations enabling research institutes, engaged in basic or applied research, to engage independently in export and trade - providing they have: industrial capacity to innovate; are internationally competitive; and are export oriented earning at least US$500,000 (China State Science and Technology Commission, 1993).

Factories and commercial enterprises, managed by universities and research institutes but highly regulated by the State, are undergoing major transformations. State controls are being relaxed and enterprises are entering a new phase of market control. Consequently, responsibility for management, production and marketing in these enterprises is in the hands of a new breed of enterprise managers, often senior academics, and key issues are usually concerned with efficiency and profit rather than the intrinsic problems of scientific research.

A consequence of the reforms has been that research institutes and universities in China have become embedded in new alliances that have produced not only new and economically powerful corporations, but have also led to the establishment of new institutions directed solely toward the production of trained technicians for the new enterprises.

Another feature of science policy reforms has been that the government has retreated from directly steering academic research. The gap has been filled by industry with the market becoming the dominant force. In 1986 government research grants accounted for 54% of university research funding. By 1995 this had fallen to only 23% (Institute of Policy and Management, 1995). Further, it appears that industry is now taking a more active role in initiating university collaboration. A recent study has shown that of technological innovations involving collaborative work between academic institutes and industry, over 48% were initiated by industry, compared to 32% by universities. (Institute of Policy and Management, 1995).

These science policy reforms, in the context of the broader economic reforms described above, have stimulated the development of new technological alliances between research institutions and the rapidly growing TVE sector.

3. DEVELOPMENTS AND NEW ALLIANCES IN CHINA'S INDUSTRIAL SECTOR

Industry is the largest sector of the Chinese economy, contributing some 50% of total output, employing some 104 million workers (17% of the labour force employed) and contributing 86% of total exports in 1993 (Asian Development Bank, 1995). This sector has achieved significant real growth during the period of economic reforms (1978-92), averaging some 10.8% annually (see Table 9.3), and providing the basis for the rapid overall growth of the world's most rapidly growing economy during this period. It stands at the centre of the country's reform initiatives, with efforts to revitalise and restructure domestic industry being closely linked to the reform of pricing, banking, public finance, ownership, social welfare and research and development. The contribution of SOEs to industrial production has declined during the period of economic reform but is still significant, hence further reform of the industrial sector implies further major reform of the SOEs.

In contrast, and of particular interest, is that the dynamism of the industrial sector has been provided from the non state sector (particularly that of the TVEs), which has achieved considerable growth during this equivalent period of time (see Table 9.1). The factors behind this and the sustainability of this, particularly for the TVEs, provides the major focus of this section. In doing so developments and reform of the SOEs, as well as the reasons behind the success of the TVEs with specific case study examples drawing upon the experiences of two of these, will be identified.

Table 9.3: China's GDP and its Components

	1978	1984	1988	1990	1992
GDP	669.4	1097.0	1625.9	1769.5	2162.9
(billion 1990 yuan)	695.0	1051.0	1464.0	1548.0	1846.0
- per capita	100.0	151.2	210.6	225.3	266.6
(1990 yuan)					
- per capita					
(index)					

Growth rates (in % per year)				
	1978/1984	1984/1988	1988/1992	1978/1992
Agriculture	7.3	3.1	4.3	5.2
Industry	8.9	14.2	10.4	10.8
Services	10.1	13.5	5.8	9.8
GDP	8.6	10.3	7.5	8.8

Sources: State Statistical Bureau, 1992, p. 6; State Statistical
    Bureau, 1991, pp. 33, 79; and "Statistical Communique of the State Statistical Bureau of
    the PRC on the 1992 National Economic and Social Development", February 18, 1993,
    Beijing Review, March 8-14, 1993, 36(10): 31-40; and State Statistical Bureau, 1993, pp.
    19, 21.
Note: The Chinese GDP figures were calculated by applying the indexes
    in "comparable prices" for 1978, 1984, 1988, and 1992 to the current price estimates of the
    three components of GDP in 1990. This produces rough constant price GDP figures for
    these years and an index that differs slightly from the official Chinese GDP index for this
    period

China's State Owned Enterprises (SOEs)

The relative contribution of the SOEs to industrial production has declined since the start of the reform process in the late 1970s. As Table 9.1 identifies, in 1978 the SOEs contributed some 76% of the gross value of industrial production but by 1992 this share had fallen to less than one half (48.4%). While the industrial production of SOEs increased during this period, the growth of production by the collectives (the township and village enterprises in particular), the private sector and other ownership types, which have provided competition or formed alliances with the SOEs, has been much more rapid. However the SOEs contribution to output remains large, it accounts for 50% of total urban employment (the SOEs are estimated to employ some 80 million people) and some one-third of GNP (Bell, M.W. et. al., 1993). In addition the SOEs are closely linked to the banking system through the credit plan, and are attributable for two-thirds of total domestic credit. They also play an important role in budgetary operations, contributing to about 25% of total revenue and receiving in return operating subsidies equivalent to two-thirds of the overall budget deficit. The latter is indicative of their overall weak financial performance and particularly so since 1988, although with the recovery of the economy after 1992 gross profits have improved. Losses have also remained high in absolute terms but improved noticeably in 1993. A sectoral disaggregation of losses indicates that these were about equally distributed between the industrial, foreign trade and commerce and grain sectors. In the industrial sector about one-half of the losses were concentrated in the coal and oil industries, primarily due to governmental control over related prices.

Reform of the SOEs

The reform of the SOEs has been a gradual and incremental process focusing mainly on a progressive increase in managerial autonomy, such that by the late 1980s major changes in the allocation of industrial products, the procurement of inputs, the character of incentives, and the degree of competition had occurred. Managers had gained control over most of the major business decisions, and even the largest SOEs were extensively involved in markets driven by decentralised forces of demand and supply, subject increasingly to competition from the non state sector.

This new structural environment facing the SOEs evolved from two distinct policy initiatives. The first reform effort, implemented around 1980, consisted of tentative steps to improve the performance of the SOEs within a framework of mandatory output planning and administrative allocation of inputs and products. On the domestic side, SOEs gained the right to retain a modest share of total profits. They also obtained unprecedented control over any output beyond mandatory plan targets. On the external side a new open door policy resulted in the dismantling of long standing barriers to international trade and investment, with the southern provinces enjoying special incentives to expand foreign economic contacts.

The second set of reforms dating from 1984 centred on two innovations: dual pricing and the enterprise contract responsibility system (CRS). Dual pricing divided the supplies of industrial products into plan and market components. Under the dual price regime, most state enterprises transacted marginal sales and purchases on markets where prices responded increasingly to the forces of demand and supply. At the same time, bank loans began to replace budgetary appropriations as the chief source of external funding for industrial enterprises, signalling the emergence of elementary factor markets. From 1986 under the CRS enterprise managers of medium and large sized SOEs, or sometimes the firm's entire work force, agreed to fulfil specific obligations, typically involving targets for total profit, delivery of profit to the state and productivity increases, in return for extensive control over enterprise operations including full or substantial retention of excess profits. Under the CRS, an enterprise's income tax liability was determined by the provisions of the enterprise's contract instead of by law, leading to a strong element of bargaining in the fiscal process. Also, a law permitting bankruptcy was enacted in 1986 and became effective in 1988.

In 1988 the Enterprise Law was enacted which legalised the measures of autonomy granted to enterprises in 1984. At the same time the CRS was extended to most SOEs on a nationwide basis. In 1992 the implementing regulations of the Enterprise Law of 1988 were issued by the state council. These regulations explicitly provided for noninterference by the government in the operations of the enterprises, which were endowed with a set of 14 rights over their operations[1]. In addition enterprises were expected to be accountable for their performance, with inefficient and loss-making ones to be restructured or closed down in accordance with the Bankruptcy Law. Although the reality is that the latter has hardly been used.

Since 1993 as part of a new phase of SOE reforms, focus has been placed upon changing enterprise governance with a view to establishing a "modern enterprise sector". This aim is to be achieved through the corporatisation of SOEs, that is the conversion of SOEs into shareholding companies through the implementation of a new Company Law. The aim being to achieve a separation of the ownership functions of the state from the management of the enterprises, within a framework of greater autonomy and accountability. Specifically the new framework will attempt to:

1. clarify the rights of enterprises as legal entities entitled to make decisions concerning assets entrusted to them by owners and investors;

2. separate government ministries and departments from enterprise management to eliminate government interference in enterprise management;

---

1   Enterprises would enjoy the following rights: to make production and business decisions; to set their own prices; to market their own products; to purchase materials; to import and export; to make investment decisions; to decide on use of retained earnings; to dispose of assets in accordance with production requirements; to form partnerships and mergers; to assign labour; to have personnel management; to set wages and bonuses; to determine internal organisation; to refuse arbitrary levies and charges.

3. relieve SOEs of the obligations to provide social services while expanding the government's role in the provision of these services;

4. establish market based relations between enterprises, so as to avoid the recent accumulation of inter-enterprise debt;

5. reduce the government's control over wage and employment policies while limiting its role in this sphere to a supervisory one. 1.2.

In this new framework, a system for the management of state owned assets by state holding companies, state asset management companies, and enterprise groups would be introduced.

Performance of the SOEs

These changes in industrial structure and enterprise conduct has noticeably affected industrial performance. The success of the reforms is demonstrated in a number of developments:

a) *Rapid Growth*

This is the most obvious feature of recent developments in China's industrial sector. Table 3 shows that China's real GDP grew at over 8% a year for 14 years (1978-82), or roughly 7% per capita. This rate is roughly double the GDP growth rate of the previous two decades 1957-78. While the share of the state sector in total industrial output has declined, the real product of state industry more than doubled during the 1980s and expansion is still continuing.

b) *Expansion of Exports*

China's foreign trade story is even more impressive (see Table 9.4). In the 1970s China's real exports grew by a modest 3.4% a year, rising to 14.1% a year during the first decade of reform. Some 70% of these exports were manufactures (petroleum and mining products by 1988 accounted for under 8% of exports, as contrasted to 25% in 1980). Available data shows that the combined exports of SOEs and urban collectives grew at an annual rate of about 16% during the period 1985-90, with the exports of SOEs growing rapidly during the latter half of the 1980s. Hence many of China's SOEs are gaining ground in the international marketplace. Connections with Hong Kong accounted increasingly for much of China's exports, and in the 1990s a similar exporting process seems to be happening through Taiwan. In effect the formidable marketing talents of Hong Kong and Taiwan are being grafted on to the manufacturing capacity of the Chinese mainland.

Table 9.4: Growth Rate of China's Foreign Trade (in per cent per year)

	Nominal		Real	
	Exports	Imports	Exports	Imports
1952/1972	7.4	4.8	–	–
1972/1978	19.0	25.0	3.4	13.0
1978/1988	17.2	17.6	14.1	10.2
1978/1992	16.7	15.4	–	–

Sources: Same as in Table 9.3 plus, for the real rates, China Foreign Trade Yearbook
   compiling committee, 1984, p. IV-5; and China Foreign Trade Yearbook Compiling
   Committee, 1989, p. 303.
   Appropriate price deflators were not available for the post-1988 period.

c) *Trends in Total Factor Productivity*

Evidence provided by Jefferson, Rawski and Zheng (Table 9.2) suggests that there have been noticeable improvements in total factor productivity in state industry, and that this was most apparent during the period 1984-88. Thereafter from 1988-92 it slowed but still showed impressive gains. However the major improvement in total factor productivity is to be found in the collective sector and most notably by the township and village enterprises. Improvement in labour productivity is also noticeable amongst the SOEs, with the most substantial improvements being once again with the township and village enterprises.

d) *Innovation*

Recent survey research confirms the acceleration of innovative activity within state industry. One study found that enterprises were focusing on "the development of new products and the abolition of old products" (Dong, 1992). Another survey found over 90% of large and medium sized enterprises engaged in some form of innovative activity, with 81% developing new products (Innovation, 1993). A third survey has shown that the output share of new products rose substantially during the 1980s (Jefferson, Rawski and Zheng, 1992b). Over 90% of the state owned, urban collective and township enterprises in the latter survey cited state owned enterprises as the principal innovators in their product lines.

Despite these successes a number of important weaknesses remain. Firstly official interference in credit decisions, weak control over lending leading to easy loans, and insufficient sanctions against insolvent enterprises have perpetuated the existence of a soft budget constraint for the SOEs. Arising from this firms often continue to supply non paying clients in the expectation that the banks will eventually commit funds to eradicate chains of inter-enterprise obligations. Secondly, and related to the first, about 90% of

Chinese industrial activity, including most of the output from non state firms, resides in the public sector. Current reform plans call for intensified efforts to restructure the governance of state owned enterprises by distributing shares among multiple owners-provincial and local governments, other state firms, banks, newly established asset management companies, and individuals-in the expectation that arms length relations between owners and managers will promote better performance. Ownership reform has the potential to stimulate further productivity gains in both state and collective industry. Thirdly, flexibility in the tax system has also contributed to the soft budget constraint facing state enterprises, since fixed tax rates are negotiable and a firm with losses or low profits can usually negotiate a lower rate. Fourthly there is a need to improve China's legal and regulatory law. The country lacks clear cut rules for the calculation of profits, and it has a bankruptcy law which is difficult to apply given the absence of a safety net for those losing their jobs. In practice it is not easy to decide which enterprises need to be closed down, given price distortions and inadequate accounting rules. Fifthly the SOEs have been responsible for the housing, health services, day care and much else of their workers. Eliminating surplus workers from SOEs, however desirable from an efficiency perspective, has meant depriving such workers from access to their homes and health care. Measures require to be implemented to separate the dependence of the unemployment insurance and the pension system on individual enterprises. Finally, factor markets for labour and capital require further development.

Township and Village Enterprises

Despite the "collective" label, TVEs themselves were never worker cooperatives, rather they were labelled "collective" because they were established and controlled by agricultural collectives. When these were dismantled in the early 1980s, their functions were either decentralised to individual households or else assumed by local governments. As a result, most TVEs became subordinate to the township and village governments that replaced the former communes and agricultural collectives, but the collective classification remained.

Township and village leaders are typically appointed from above by county administrators and, in turn, designate the managers of TVEs, and in effect possess all the key components of property rights: control of residual income; the right to dispose of assets; the right to appoint and dismiss managers; and assume direct control if necessary. Local residents possess no `right of membership' in the TVEs, nor do TVE workers possess any rights to participate in TVE management. Township and village officials' compensation is determined by a "managerial contract" with explicit success indicators covering economic and social objectives. TVE output and sales value, profits, and taxes enter into the compensation schedule, as well as family planning, maintenance of public order and education. However there are strong pressures to stress profits, since the township or village as a unit is subject to a fairly strong hard budget constraint. The successful township official maximises his own career prospects by producing economic growth during his term as a community leader, and this is likely to crucially depend upon maximising net revenue from the TVEs.

The importance of the TVE form of industrial enterprise can be seen to be as follows. Firstly the TVEs allowed rural communities to translate control over assets and resources into income, despite the absence of asset markets. The growth of product markets provided rural communities with the opportunity to realise value from locally controlled resources. Secondly TVEs provided a way to convert assets into income without solving the difficult problem of privatisation. The Chinese government then, and reconfirmed in 1993, was unwilling on ideological grounds to permit mass privatisation. The administrative difficulties involved with privatisation would have been immense due to the sheer size of China and the lack of administrative apparatus. The difficult problems of privatisation were probably insoluble in China during the 1980s. Hence the TVEs circumvented this difficulty while contributing importantly to competition and the opening up of markets. Thirdly with well functioning markets, urban firms would have purchased land and hired suburban labour. In the absence of such institutions TVEs represented an alternative solution. Urban SOEs could sub-contract to TVEs providing in the process technology and equipment, or rural governments could take the initiative in this regard themselves. Many TVEs grew up as complements to state run industry. The majority of TVE growth has been concentrated in advanced periphery-urban regions. For example in 1988 in the three provinces of Jiangsu, Zhejiang and Shandong, producing half of all TVE output, linkages with urban firms were central to TVE growth.

Finally, TVEs facilitated access to capital on the part of start up firms. In China local government ownership played a key role in the process of financial intermediation. Local governments could better assess the risks of start up businesses under their control, and were diversified and able to act as guarantors of loans to individual TVEs. By underwriting a portion of the risk of entry, local governments enabled start up firms to enter production with a larger size, starting with some mechanisation, and exploiting economies of scale. With local governments playing an important role in the flow of capital to rural enterprises, such firms were able to take advantage of China's relatively abundant household savings. In return, the profitable opportunities and reasonable risk levels in the TVE sector kept real returns high and contributed to the maintenance of high savings rates.

Reasons for the Success of the TVEs

A number of reasons have been advanced in the literature to explain the phenomenal success of the TVE. The major ones include the following:

- The TVEs faced cheap labour and expensive capital and natural resources, causing them to choose appropriate production technologies. As the reform process progressed prices were gradually liberalised reflecting more relative scarcity values, and the SOEs found themselves at a competitive disadvantage because of inappropriate capital and resource intensive technologies.

- The TVEs were highly profitable because of the distortions carried over from the formerly planned system. At the beginning of the reform process in 1978, the average rate of profit on TVE capital was 32% (capital being defined as depreciated fixed capital plus all inventories). Most of the new TVEs were in manufacturing, where state price controls kept profitability high so that the state could obtain high revenues from the SOEs. In addition the TVEs entered market niches for which the SOEs had either failed to produce or failed to innovate and improve quality control. The resulting high profits achieved by TVEs attracted further investment and rapid growth.

- Taxes on TVEs were low, requiring them to pay only 6% of profits as tax in 1980, climbing to 20% after 1985. Such low tax rates in China were primarily due to a policy driven desire to foster rural industrialisation.

- Information channels between the TVE managers and local government authorities tended to be both shorter and simpler compared to that for the SOEs, encouraging greater efficiency. Further, this greater flexibility and autonomy in management has meant that inter-firm alliances and technological alliances with universities and research institutes has produced a `networked' approach to innovation and industrial production.

- Local government officials and TVE managers had to focus more upon financial objectives (profit plus local tax revenues) because local governments lacked the borrowing capacity of higher levels of government. Hence the TVE enterprises under their jurisdiction faced harder budget constraints than SOEs, and were more likely to fall into bankruptcy. This focused upon the need for TVEs to be efficient, competitive and profitable in a period of a rapid opening up of markets. Meanwhile, managers of SOEs, having responsibility for housing and other social services as well as industrial operations, faced a more complex set of objectives and state obligations.

- A number of researchers have suggested that, despite the absence of well defined property rights, the demographic stability of China's rural communities promoted the emergence of "invisible institutions" to provide a "moral framework for rights" or a "cooperative culture" that served to reduce problems of shirking and monitoring found in most public enterprises (Byrd and Lin, 1990; Yusuf, 1993a, 1993b; Weitzman and Xu, 1993),

- The state sector also represents an important, and not sufficiently recognised, component in the successful development of TVEs and other non state firms. The TVEs and collectives in general rely on the state sector as a source of capital, materials, equipment, specialised personnel, technology, sub-contracting arrangements and sales revenue. For example in southern Jiangsu province near Shanghai, a centre of booming rural enterprise development, more than two thirds of TVEs have established various forms of economic and technical cooperation arrangements with industrial enterprises, research units, and higher educational institutions in larger cities. Local government officials attempting to develop industry in poor localities are encouraged to pursue joint operations with scientific research organisations or large and medium scale enterprises.

- The continual reduction of entry barriers associated with China's industrial reform created a domestic product cycle in which new products, materials and processes introduced by innovative state firms were adopted by TVE and other non state enterprises, which could use their cost advantages to erode state sector profits and force state industry toward fresh innovations.

The following case studies serve to illustrate the network of alliances that underpin the maturing of TVEs. In particular, they emphasise the extent to which TVEs have relied, for their development on three factors: economic reforms, science policy reforms and the role of governments in promoting industry and science cooperation. They provide examples of how cooperative arrangements between TVEs, science institutions, and other firms can produce organisational alliances with the capability to compete successfully with the larger and powerful state owned enterprises.

TVE Case Studies

The Kefu Cable Works[2]

An interesting case of emerging scientific alliances between TVEs and research institutions is embedded in the story of the Kefu Cable Works in China. This enterprise, a combination of academic and industrial interests, was the first to apply radiation cross-linked technology to produce high voltage cable for airport lighting, off-shore oil rigs and a wide range of electronic products. Although there were over 3,000 enterprises engaged in the production of electronic wire and cable in China in 1987, none of them were using radiation cross-linking technology. Production and markets were dominated by large state-owned enterprises.

Research on radiation processing technology in China began in the early 1950s and although low energy accelerators, developed for industrial use were capable of applying the technology to the production of cable, it was not

---

2   This case study was collected through collaborative research with colleagues at the
     Institute for Policy Management, Beijing, as part of a UNESCO sponsored project in 1995.

until the emergence of Kefu, as a post market reform structure in 1989, that it was ever applied beyond laboratory tests.

Kefu Cable Works has its origins in a joint venture between a commercial arm of the Chinese Academy of Science (CAS), operating under the name of the Kefu Corporation, and a township/village enterprise (Yantai Cable Works). Yantai Cable Works was seeking new technological capabilities to enable them to compete with their large state owned competitors. The technological innovation was primarily driven by one of the firm's new recruits whose previous work at a Harbin university had enabled him to grasp the potential of radiation technology. Such a major technological innovation, however, could only take place in China through collaboration with major Chinese science institutions. This collaboration was a direct consequence of the Chinese government's intention to commercialise its scientific institutions.

In order to develop the human resources for the complex plant operation both parties developed technical training programs for key personnel. In the course of establishing the production line, senior school graduates from the village were sent to an Institute of High Energy Physics to be trained for the regular operation and simple maintenance of the production line. In addition, a specialised research institute was set up jointly by Kefu Corp. and Yantai Cable Works to conduct further on-going research on radiation cross-linking cable and other potential new products.

Before its cooperation with the Chinese Academy of Science the Yantai Cable Works was a small township/village enterprise ranking towards the bottom of the 3,000 cable producers in the country. The radiation technology innovation enabled it to become a market leader in the Chinese cable industry. CAS, during its long experience of scientific research, had accumulated strong and comprehensive capability on the design and manufacture of accelerators and radiation chemical research. But it did not possess the manufacturing capability. Only through an alliance with a range of other enterprises could it generate commercial benefit.

The alliance was extended further, in 1990, when a second joint venture was established. This was formed with an additional US$1.3 million investment by the Qirong Company (Hong Kong). The Qirong investment created the Qirong-Kefu Cable Ltd, Yantai. The share distribution of the company was 25 per cent from Qirong Company and 75 per cent from Kefu Cable Works. The share distribution between the two parties inside Kefu Cable Works remained at 78% Yantai Cable Works (the original TVE) and 22% Kefu Corporation (the spin-of from the CAS).

The successful development of Kefu Cable Works and subsequent joint ventures required the integration of two separate sets of organisational strategies. First it required the collaboration between entrepreneurial scientists in CAS who were concerned to develop and diffuse the technology with scientists in the academy and its affiliated research institutes. Second it required the industrial entrepreneurs who were able to capitalise on market potential and incorporate technology to gain industrial leverage in the expanding township/village enterprise.

An interesting feature of this case is the flexibility and adaptive response to a technological opportunity from the TVE compared to the apparent inertia on the part of the state-owned enterprise. Under the planning economic system, the products of state-owned enterprises are sold in a planned way and controlled by the government. The inability of the State owned cable manufacturing enterprises to adopt the new technology contributed to the formation of alternative research alliances between the research institutes and the TVE.

Pressures from the market on the one hand is challenging the survival of these non-state-owned enterprises, but on the other encouraging their adoption of new technologies to overcome market competition. With pressures to open up market opportunities, research institutes and universities have therefore turned, more often, toward township enterprises as strategic partners in the commercialisation of science. Thus the combined effect of science and technology policy reforms and broader economic reforms have produced highly productive horizontal alliances among TVEs.

The Hengdian Group

In rapidly growing Zhejiang Province the Hengdian Group has emerged from being a small township enterprise in 1975, employing 53 workers and earning only 76,000 Yuan profit, to a powerful company in 1995 employing 20,000 persons and earning a profit of 92 million Yuan. In 1975 all assets were valued at 45,000 Yuan, in 1995 the groups assets were valued at 1.6 billion Yuan. A key factor in the group's development has been an aggressive approach to capturing a wide range of scientific knowledge and using it to develop new industrial opportunities.

In 1976 the Hengdian enterprise was solely engaged with the production of silk. Throughout the 1980s, it introduced a strategy of scouring the country, and later foreign countries, for potential technological advances and application. The group is now engaged as one of China's largest producers of products manufactured from third generation rare earth magnetic materials. At present 80% of their products in this area are exported. Other scientific applications developed by the group include the production of high pressure aluminium foil products and a range of electronic and chemical products.

The development of production capabilities for each new product emerged through the efforts of industrial managers to build formal linkages with universities and research institutes, either within China or internationally. In 1995 the group was engaged in 28 separate projects in collaboration with universities or research institutes with an investment of over 200 million Yuan. Approximately 60% of this investment was financed through state bank loans with the balance provided directly by the group. The company has now signed technical cooperation agreements with nine key universities and 20 research institutes. These agreements also include provision for key staff to engage in further technical training, thus providing not only further technical training but contributing to the endurance of the collaborative network.

The development of production capabilities for each new product at Hengdian emerged through the efforts of industrial managers to build formal linkages with universities and research institutes, either within China or internationally. In 1995 the group was engaged in 28 separate projects in collaboration with universities or research institutes with an investment of over 200 million Yuan. Approximately 60% of this investment was financed through state bank loans with the balance provided directly by the group. The company has now signed technical cooperation agreements with nine key universities and 20 research institutes. These agreements also include provision for key staff to engage in further technical training, thus providing not only further technical training but also serving to extend the industry and university alliances.

4. CONCLUSIONS

Despite the important contribution of non state firms to China's recent industrial achievements, it is too soon to conclude that China's collectives represent an enduring organisational innovation. The dependence of non state enterprises on resources from the state sector, the tendency for non state enterprise operations to cluster at the low end of the scale and technology spectrum, and the artificial nature of the domestic cost advantages enjoyed by non state firms all suggest that their rapid gains owe much to specific circumstances of China's economy in the 1980s. Some authors predict that, as underlying economic conditions change, rural industry will lose ground to large domestic firms, enterprise groups, and joint venture companies during the course of the 1990s.

The Chinese example of transition, in which the TVEs have played a central role, has demonstrated that a key component of this process is entry into markets rather than privatisation *per se*. Such entry creates competition and drives market development, which can lead to a decline in state control and monopoly. The existence of the TVEs and other collectives have in a sense simulated the existence of a private sector, seen as an essential ingredient in such a transition process and in sustaining rapid growth. China's

TVEs have effective incentive structures and reasonably hard budget constraints. They do go bankrupt and most TVEs do fire workers when required. In addition the flexible institutional form of TVEs is a crucial component of their success. With the existence of these preconditions, local government ownership of firms operating in an increasingly market environment was an alternative to early privatisation. This may also have been administratively less costly than early privatisation, enabling the avoidance of difficult and complex problems at an early stage of reform enabling managerial focus to be placed on more direct productive activities.

However, as we have sought to show here, many TVEs are transforming themselves into complex interconnected networks involving science, industry and local government. The status of firms is therefore highly dynamic in the present environment. The question we believe should be asked concerns not whether the TVEs will be able to maintain their industrial momentum, in the light of deepening reforms, but rather the organisational form that will enable them to do so.

During the 1990s as markets for assets and factors of production develop the "artificial" advantages which the TVEs possessed during the 1980s may be eroded resulting in them becoming less important. However their demonstrated flexibility and ability to solve problems of delegation and incentive design, together with capabilities for horizontal links to science based institutions suggest that they are likely to remain a significant feature of the Chinese economy, albeit in new organisational forms, for some considerable time.

REFERENCES

Asian Development Bank (1995) Key Indicators of Developing Asian and Pacific Countries, 26, Manila.

Bell, M.W., Khor H.E. and Kochhar, K. (1993) "China at the Threshold of a Market Economy", IMF Occasional Paper 107, IMF, Washington, September.

Byrd, W. A. and Lin, Q. (1990) "China's Rural Industry: An Introduction", in Byrd, W.A. and Lin, Q-S. (eds) *China's Rural Industry: Structure, Development and Reform*, New York, Oxford University Press, pp. 3-18.

Christerson, B. and Lever-Tracy C. (1996), "The Third China? China's Rural Enterprises as Dependent Subcontractors or as Dynamic Autonomous Firms?", Paper presented to The Asia-Pacific Regional Conference of Sociology, Manila, 28-31 May 1996.

China State Science and technology Commission (1993), *China S&T Newsletter*, (13) December.

Dong, F. (1992) "Behaviour of China's State Owned Enterprises Under the Dual System", *Caimao jingji* (Finance and Economics), (9): 3-15.

Innovation. (1993) "Technical Developments in Large and Medium Industrial Firms-Innovative Activity Develops Universally", *Zhongguo tongji* (China's Statistics), (4): 10.

Institute of Policy and Management (1995) *Study of Interface of Technology Transfer in Transition Economy,* Chinese Academy of Sciences, Policy Report, 95-001, Beijing.

Jefferson, G.H., Rawski, T.G. and Zheng, Y. (1992a) "Growth, Efficiency, and Convergence in China's State and Collective Industry", *Economic Development and Cultural Change*, 20(2): 239-266.

Jefferson, G.H., Rawski, T.G. and Zheng, Y. (1992b) "Innovation and Reform in Chinese Industry: A Preliminary Analysis of Survey Data (1)", Paper delivered at the annual meeting of the Association for Asian Studies, Washington DC, April.

Jefferson, G.H., Rawski, T.G. and Zheng, Y. (1994) "Enterprise Reform in Chinese Industry", *Journal of Economic Perspectives*, 8(2): 47-70, Spring.

Liao S-L. (1995) "The Development of Township Enterprises in Rural Fujian Since the Early 1980s", Paper presented to the International Workshop on South China, Nanyang Research Institute, Xiamen University, PRC, May 22-24th.

Naughton, B. (1994) "Chinese Institutional Innovation and Privatisation from Below", American Economics Association, *Papers and Proceedings*, 84(2) May.

Perkins, D. (1994) "Completing China's Move to the Market", *Journal of Economic Perspectives*, 8(2): 23-46, Spring.

Rawski, T.G. (1994) "Chinese Industrial Reform: Accomplishments, Prospects, and Implications, American Economics Association", *Papers and Proceedings*, 84(2) May.

Research Centre for Rural Economics (1995) "Case Study on Technology Transfer and Development of Township and Village Enterprises (TVEs)", Report to UNESCO, Beijing.

State Science and Technology Commission of China (1991), *White Paper on Science and Technology No. 4,* International Academic Publishers, Beijing.

Goh, K.S. (1994) "China - the New Capitalist Economy", *The Journal of the Securities Institute,* No. 4.

Tseng, W., Khor, H.E., Kocharm K., Mihajek, D., and Burton, D. (1994) "Economic Reform in China, a New Phase", IMF Occasional Paper 114, IMF, Washington, November.

Wietzman, M. and Xu, C. (1993) "Chinese Township Village Enterprises as Vaguely Defined Cooperatives", Mimeo, Harvard University, April.

Yusuf, S. (1993a) "The Rise of China's Nonstate Sector", unpublished manuscript, World Bank.

Yusuf, S. (1993b) "Property Rights and Nonstate Sector Development in China", unpublished manuscript.

ENVIRONMENTAL ISSUES

CHAPTER 10

CHINA'S ENVIRONMENTAL PROBLEMS AND ITS ECONOMIC GROWTH

CLEM TISDELL*

ABSTRACT

China has experienced outstanding economic growth in recent decades, but not without environmental problems and costs. China's environmental costs have included increased air and water pollution, loss of natural vegetation cover and deforestation, soil erosion and a decline in the fertility of its soil and biodiversity loss. Consequently, some writers have — questioned whether China's rate of growth is environmentally sustainable and doubt if China will attain middle-income status in the next century because of its environmental constraints. Some suggest that China has already reduced its natural environmental resources to the critical core, or nearly so, and that there is a high risk that further reduction will undermine its economic sustainability. Certainly the risks from greater intensification of land use in China are high and some examples of such risks are given, for example,

---

*   Department of Economics, The University of Queensland, Brisbane, 4072

intensified use of the Yangtze Valley as a result of the Three Gorges Dam project.

Market reforms in China provide greater scope for Chinese authorities to implement policies to deal with environmental problems by economic means, for example, to adopt the polluter-pays principles. However, market-based policies do not provide a complete answer to environmental problems in China. In response to environmental problems, Chinese authorities have drawn up *China's Agenda 21: White Paper on China's Population, Environment and Development in the 21st Century*. It is an important step in recognising China's environmental issues and suggesting policies to deal with these.

China's environmental problems involve several international dimensions. Some are of global concern such as China's greenhouse gas emissions and its loss of biodiversity. Some have impacts on its near neighbours, such as environmental deterioration in the headwaters of rivers which commence in China and flow into South-east Asia and South Asia, or acid rains originating from China and transported to Korea or Japan. Another international dimension is the attraction of China for investment in dirty industries from places such as Taiwan. China needs to make sure that the full social cost of such foreign investment is taken into account.

1. INTRODUCTION

China's outstanding growth in recent decades and its open-door policies have made it a growth pole in the Western Pacific. Higher income countries, experiencing sluggish economic growth, have been vying to share in China's economic growth. They are seeking to gain from this growth through increased trade with China and greater investment opportunities in China. Consequently, along with China's economic reforms, this growth has been welcomed in Western countries. On the other hand, less attention has been given in Western countries to the environmental problems and costs involved in China's economic growth, except in a few academic circles. Furthermore, it must be noted that China's improving economic strength has implications for its military power and its position in international political bargaining. China's advancing economic position increases its international strategic position because economic power and political power are closely intertwined. This is capable of producing some fear in Western countries as underlined by reactions to China's missile firings in the vicinity of Taiwan during Taiwan's elections in 1996. There are, therefore, two sides to the coin as far as the economic growth of China is concerned. This essay, however, concentrates only on the environmental aspects of China's economic growth.

Considerable debate exists in the literature about the relationship between economic growth and the state of the environment. The most optimistic view sees economic growth as leading to an improved environment whereas the most pessimistic view sees these two aspects as antagonistic. Differences of opinion exist both on the empirical and the theoretical plane. Using cross-sectional data, The World Bank (1992) for instance, suggests that with economic growth (or more particularly transition from low-income to high-income status) a country's environment at first deteriorates then improves. Economic growth is therefore seen as ultimately resulting in significant environmental improvement. Where is China currently placed on this U-shaped environmental quality curve? Is it still on its downward path and how much further will its environment deteriorate and in what ways? There is probably no easy answer to these questions.

One of the reasons why there is no easy answer to these questions is that environmental quality consists of multiple characteristics, so it consists of a number of variables. Some characteristics may improve with economic growth whereas others may decline and so it can be difficult to evaluate the resulting combination. Furthermore, very long-term environmental impacts may differ from short and medium-term ones and global environmental impacts may diverge from country-specific ones (cf. Tisdell, 1993a, Arrow et al., 1995).

On the theoretical level, most economists appear to agree that it is *possible* for economic growth to occur and for improved environmental quality to be achieved in the short to medium term, although some particular policy measures may be needed to make this a reality. However, there is considerable theoretical disagreement about the extent to which economic growth is sustainable in the long run. One school of thought sees economic growth as ultimately reducing the natural environmental stock and lowering it to a level where income can no longer be sustained. Advocates of this point of view argue that strong policy measures must be adopted to conserve the natural environmental stock if sustainable development is to be achieved. They are said to advocate strong sustainability conditions. (These conditions are outlined in Tisdell, 1995b.)

On the other side of the spectrum are those who advocate weak sustainability conditions. They see man-made capital as an adequate substitute for natural environmental capital. Basically, they are supporters of traditional recipes for economic growth, whereas the strong sustainability school sees these recipes as leading ultimately to economic disaster. It should not, however, be concluded that the strong sustainability school opposes all economic growth. It merely rejects the view that man-made capital is always a suitable substitute for natural environmental capital and advocates a cautious approach to reducing the stock of natural environmental capital. It is unclear where Chinese policy-makers stand in relation to this issue, but the general importance of sustainability issues in development have been officially recognised in *China's Agenda 21 - White Paper on China's Population, Environment and Development in the 21st Century* (State Council, 1994) and this document is discussed below.

This White Paper indicates that as a result of China's economic reforms, there is now more scope for using market-related instruments (such as taxes, tradeable permits) as a means of exerting environmental control in China. While up to a point these instruments are likely to be useful in balancing economic activities in a way which takes account of their environmental externalities, they may be of little value in addressing the level of environmental impacts from the scale of economic activity and on their own, may fail to conserve the natural environmental resource stock adequately. Price mechanisms do, it seems, have limitations in relation to environmental issues even when they operate extensively to take account of externalities (cf. Tisdell, 1990, Ch. 2).

China's environmental effects are not purely China's concern (Tisdell, 1993b). Environmental developments in China are capable of having global impacts, for example its increasing use of fossil fuels is likely to accelerate global warming and loss of biodiversity in China is to some extent a global loss. Furthermore, environmental changes in China can have international regional environmental impacts. Rivers from China flow into many nearby countries, and air bodies from China also circulate over nearby countries. Both have the potential of transporting pollutants to nearby countries. Such transboundary effects will be discussed later. Furthermore, given its eagerness to attract foreign investment, China has the potential to attract polluting economic activities which would not be tolerated in many higher income countries. Let us consider China's environmental problems with this background in mind.

2. The State of China's Environment and the Supply of its Natural Resources

Compared to the world as a whole, China seems to be a country relatively poor in natural resources in relation to its population. This is highlighted by Table 10.1. In terms of availability of land and water resources in proportion to its population, China is at a serious disadvantage compared to the world as a whole.

Table 10.1: Availability of Selected Natural Resources of China Compared on
a Per Capita Basis with those of the World in the early 1990s

	World	China
Population (person/km^2)	39	117
Arable land (ha/person)	0.26	0.08
Forest (ha/person)	0.77	0.13
Grassland (ha/person)	0.62	0.20
Fresh water (m^3/person)	7744	2484

Source: Based on Wu and Flynn (1995, Table 2).

In relation to water resources, the World Bank (1992) considers that
countries with less than 2,000 cubic metres per capita have serious problems
especially in drought periods and those with less than 1,000 cubic metres per
capita face chronic water problems. Given predicted population changes,
freshwater resources per capita in China are predicted to fall to less than
1,500 cubic metres by 2025 (World Bank, 1992). China's water availability
problem will undoubtedly worsen. Furthermore increasing industrial
production and higher income levels will add to the demand for water. The
geographical distribution of water resources in China combined with seasonal
variation in water availability is already causing severe problems in China
especially in parts of its northeast, for example in the Beijing-Tianjin area. It
might also be noted that given the high value placed on China's limited
freshwater resources, pollution of these can be expected to impose a heavy
economic cost on China.

Unfortunately many of China's water resources have become polluted.
Some lakes are reported to contain unacceptable levels of heavy metals
released from industry, e.g. those in the Wuhan area. The organic levels and

sediments carried in most rivers have increased significantly. Furthermore high rates of artificial fertilisers used in agriculture and inadequate treatment of sewage has significantly added to the nitrate and phosphorous levels in rivers. It has been suggested that the discharge of these nutrient-rich waters into the China Sea is a prime factor making for the periodic occurrence of red tides which kill fish *en masse* and/or make them poisonous for human consumption. It ought to be noted that all these types of water pollution threaten China's aquaculture industry which in terms of volume of production, is by far the largest in the world and a significant source of animal protein for China's population. Of course, the economic costs of water pollution are much wider than this example indicates and its health consequences and its impact in reducing biodiversity should not be ignored.

Air quality in China has deteriorated seriously with its economic growth. Excluding township enterprises (considered by some to be a source of serious pollution), sulphur dioxide remissions in China increased by more than one-third in the period 1982-1992 and other gases contaminating the air more than doubled (estimates from figures supplied by Wu and Flynn, 1995, p. 4). Most of China's large cities have air quality much lower than the standards set by the World Health Organization. For example, the air in Shenyang is heavily polluted and this has been proposed as a source of the high incidence of cancer amongst its population. Air pollution is responsible for a high incidence of respiratory illness in many of China's cities.

In fact because air quality is so poor, 26 per cent of all deaths in China are attributed to it, five times the U.S. level of such deaths (Bingham, 1993, p. 12). Respiratory disease is the biggest single source of death in China. Acid rains are a serious problem and sometimes cause pH levels in rivers south of the Yangtze to fall below 5.6 even though alkaline loess dust helps to reduce this acidity. Inefficient boilers and small power stations are a major source of this pollution (Bingham, 1993).

China is relatively rich in coal resources, and the burning of coal in China is a serious source of local air pollution. Furthermore, the burning of fossil fuels in China is adding significantly to greenhouse gases and China's emissions of such gases is predicted to rise significantly. In 1989, China ranked third in the world in terms of greenhouse gas emissions; after the U.S. and the Soviet Union. "However by 2020, China would be the world's largest producer of carbon dioxide, releasing three times as much as the US." (Bingham, 1993, p. 12).

Solid wastes create serious problems. About 55,000 ha of land is covered with untreated solid waste, most of it industrial and much of it contains heavy metals and toxic substances. Leaching from such waste dumps threatens aquifers and groundwater (Bingham, 1993, p. 14).

Loss of forests in China has occurred on a significant scale. Estimates of the World Resources Institute et al., (1994, Table 17.1) indicate that the area of forest and woodland in China decreased by 6.5% between 1979 and 1991. Consequently, in 1992 only 13.6% of China's area was covered in forest and woodland. This is one of the lowest percentages for Asian countries and is slightly less than the estimated percentage forest cover for Bangladesh (cf. Tisdell, 1995b).

While forest loss is not the only source of biodiversity loss, it can be a significant source. Like several countries in Asia, China has a large number of threatened species of mammals, birds and higher order plants. These are reported by the World Resources Institute et al. (1994, Table 20.4) to be 40, 83 and 3,340 respectively, and many of these species are unique to China.

Taking the situation overall, Chinese authorities estimate that almost 7% of China's GDP is lost due to environmental pollution, about twice the estimated percentage in high income countries (Bingham, 1993, p. 10). Chinese estimates put the annual economic costs of pollution (to China) at about 90 billion yuan, 40 billion of which is attributed to water pollution, 30 billion to air pollution and around 25 billion to pollution from solid wastes and pesticides. However, actual economic costs may be much higher than this when for example, full account is taken of the adverse impact of pollution on human health.

3. Environmental and Natural Resource Constraints on China's Economic Growth

In attempting to raise the income levels of its population to that of medium income countries in the 21st century, China faces many environmental and natural resource constraints. The question has certainly occurred to some Chinese policy-makers of whether these constraints will prevent China from achieving its goals for increasing incomes.

According to Wu and Flynn (1995, p. 5), who rely on statements in ZHN, 1992, p. 305, some policy-makers in the central government believe that it would be unwise or impossible for China to repeat the Western pattern of economic development involving in the first stage economic growth and environmental degradation and in the next stage, comprehensive `clean-up' of the environment. The reason is said to be "... China does not have sufficient natural resources and environmental capacity to absorb industrial pollution. It is also impossible for China to select the `high technology' route to control and treat industrial pollution due to its limited funding sources and great pressure for economic growth from population expansion. The best choice for China is to harmonize economic development and environmental protection to develop its economy as fast as possible under the condition of environmental stability (ZHN, 1992, p. 305)" (Wu and Flynn, 1995, p. 5).

Elsewhere Wu and Flynn (1995, p. 3) state that "... the relative shortage of natural resources constrains China's ability to copy the Western pattern of high-energy/resource consumption. Thus China must explore a new kind of development path to harmonize economic growth with environmental protection". This must be one that pays more attention to protecting the environment initially.

This basic policy is repeated in the preamble to *China's Agenda 21*, and has been contrasted with the approach of Taiwan to economic development. Taiwan has basically followed the Western pattern mentioned above (Tisdell, 1995a).

If the above is correct, then at least in principle major Chinese policy advisers lean more towards strong conditions for sustainable development in China rather than weak ones. However, in practice, China unfortunately does not have policies in place to enforce strong conditions effectively. There are many political reasons why practice differs from principles. These include the inability of central government to enforce central policies effectively at the local level. Politically China is very decentralised and provinces and localities compete with one another for investment sometimes resulting in considerable environmental concessions being made to investors at the local level. Furthermore, laws are often not enforced. In some cases this is due to bribery and corruption and in some other cases due to lack of application by administrators. As pointed out below, some pollution control measures are only put into effect in a few locations in China. Furthermore politicians are often keen to show quick economic results and are prepared to sacrifice environmental quality to achieve this, even though this might result in a worsened economic position in the long run. Political myopia is by no means peculiar to democratic systems. Hence, practice and principles of policy can diverge significantly.

The question should be pursued of whether China's situation is so different that it cannot follow the pattern of Western development which seems to have been imitated by Japan and is in the process of being copied by Taiwan and South Korea. The latter three countries, like China, might also be considered to be natural resource poor countries in relation to their population. However, like European countries, these countries have been able to overcome their natural resource constraints mainly by reliance on international trade. Japan has made considerable progress in improving its environment and Taiwan is now undertaking considerable investment with this aim in mind.

It is possible that China faces greater problems. It is a relative latecomer in international trade and it is a very large country which means that the expansion of its trade can bring adverse reactions from trading partners. Nevertheless, seeing that China is so short of arable land, it still has the option of importing food if it can export say manufactured products. It does not have to be self-sufficient in food. To some extent international trade can moderate China's environmental and natural resource constraints. Yet, its water shortage will continue and become more severe, and its air pollution and solid waste disposal problem will not be solved by international trade.

The global consequences of China's creation of pollution, e.g. its contribution to greenhouse gas emissions, may also place it in a different category to South Korea and Taiwan. Thus for environmental reasons, it may not be able to initiate blindly the economic growth strategies used by other Asian countries which have significantly improved their economic lot.

4. China's Agenda 21

In 1994, the Executive of the State Council of China adopted *China's Agenda 21 - White Paper on China's Population, Environment and Development in the 21st Century*. This is a wide-ranging document which, in English, consists of some 20 Chapters and is 244 pages in length. It is China's response to the United Nations Conference on Environment and Development held in Rio de Janeiro in 1992 which called on all nations to develop and put into effect their own strategies for sustainable development.

The preamble to this document states that "traditional ideas of considering economic growth solely in quantitative terms and the traditional development mode of "polluting first and treating later" are no longer appropriate when considering present and future requirements for development. It is now necessary to find a path for development, wherein consideration of population, economy, society, natural resources, and the environment are coordinated as a whole, so that a path for non-threatening development can be found which will meet current needs without compromising the ability of future generations to meet their needs" (State Council, 1994, p. 1). The document goes on to elaborate on this theme.

The white paper points out that China's economic growth is hampered by its large population, relatively inadequate natural resources and fragile environment as well as its low capabilities in science and technology. It suggests that this requires holistic co-ordination of China's economic growth. At the same time as China adopts growth measures to become a middle-income country in the 21st century, China's Agenda 21 states that "it will be necessary [for it] to conserve natural resources and to improve the environment, so the country will see long-term, stable development." Consequently, the development principles outlined above are articulated in China's Agenda 21.

Continuing market reforms and opening to the outside world are seen as an important part of China's Agenda 21 presumably because these can result in more efficient use of natural resources. Maintenance of population control is regarded as essential and measures to introduce technologies that are more environmental friendly than current ones are seen as desirable. Institution building and improvements in China's legal system are desired targets, as is continuing international cooperation. All of these factors are expected to contribute to China's sustainable development. The main policies recommended for China's sustainable development have been summarised as follows:

- "Carry forward reform and expand opening to the outside, and accelerate the establishment of the socialist market economy system, with the economic development as the central focus;
- Enhance capacity building for sustainable development, particularly standardize the establishment of the systems of policies, laws and regulations, and indicators of the strategic objectives. It is also important to set up a management system of resources, biological monitoring system, statistical system of social and economic development, and related system of information services, and to improve the public awareness of

sustainable development and the implementation of China's Agenda 21;

- Control population growth, enhance population quality, and improve population make-up;
- Popularize sustainable agricultural technology that suit local conditions;
- Develop clean coal technology, and other forms of clean and renewable energy sources;
- Adjust industrial structure and distribution, improve the rational utilization of resources, and reduce pressures on transportation and communication due to industrial development;
- Popularize cleaner production techniques, minimize the output of waste, encourage the conservation of resources and energy, and enhance the utilization efficiency;
- Speed up the construction of "better-off building", and improve residential environment;
- Develop and popularize key technology for environmental pollution control;
- Strengthen the protection of water resources and sewage treatment, protect and expand vegetation cover, rationally utilize biological resources to safeguard biodiversity, improve regional environmental quality, increase land productivity and mitigate natural disasters."

(Administrative Centre for China's Agenda 21, 1994, pp. 6-7)

The white paper (State Council, 1994) itself, however, gives little attention to possible conflicts between objectives and how these might be best resolved. Hence, it is doubtful if it provides a workable blueprint for development. To some extent this is understandable. However, it should be observed that if a holistic approval to economic development is adopted then trade-offs between objectives will be unavoidable. To a considerable extent, the various chapters of the white paper dealing with different sectors and spheres of development read as independent entities. There is therefore some concern that much of the white paper consists of `motherhood' statements and window-dressing. Furthermore, some may wonder if the English version of the white paper presented to promote China as an environmental leader of less developed countries and to allay the concerns of some Westerners about the environmental consequences of China's economic growth.

On the other hand, the positive side should not be forgotten. At least China's policy leaders do recognise that an economic growth dilemma may exist which calls for positive measures to conserve China's environmental resources even in its present economic growth stage. Recognition, while not sufficient, is necessary if concrete policy actions are to be taken to address the matter. Secondly, China appears to be one of the few countries to have followed up the UNCED resolution on Agenda 21 in a concrete manner. It is possible that China's Agenda 21 will become a catalyst for more workable policies for sustainable development in the future, and that China could become a leader in that regard.

In the past China was well known for its use of integrated diversified productive systems at the village level. These systems produced virtually no waste. Even today some of its integrated agriculture-aquaculture systems may be of this nature. Such systems basically incorporate balance, stability and harmony. In reality, however, China has increasingly abandoned such naturally balanced systems and has moved towards monocultures increasingly dependent on high energy inputs typical of Western productive systems. China has been moving towards productive systems dependant on high levels of external inputs typical of those in western countries. I have for example seen non-integrated aquaculture systems in China which involve the raising of a single species, e.g. white eels, using imported fish meal. Furthermore, it must be a matter for environmental concern that China's consumption of artificial fertiliser is now the largest in the world (Wu and Flynn, 1995, p. 4). Its application of manufactured fertiliser per hectare is now more than twice that in high income countries (Wu and Flynn, 1995, p. 4). Thus it seems that China has or is adopting production methods copied from the West which may be inappropriate to its environmental situation.

Economists who advocate market-making as the solution to society's ills will be pleased to learn that special mention is made in China's Agenda 21 of the desirability of making effective use of economic instruments and market mechanisms for promoting sustainable development. The Administration Centre for China's Agenda 21 (1994, p. 16) summarises the main points in this regard as:

- "Reform the unreasonable pricing system, and establish the paid use system for all kinds of resources and energy;
- Employ the taxation, financial and credit policies in promoting sustainable development;
- Endorse studies on economic policies to maintain sustainable development."

Despite this statement, reading of China's Agenda 21 white paper as a whole indicates a high degree of reliance on administrative measures rather than price-related strategies for environmental control.

5. CHINA'S ENVIRONMENTAL POLICIES IN PRACTICE

As mentioned earlier, principles and practice often diverge, sometimes sharply. China is continuing to lose natural resources and in several respects its environmental deterioration continues as its economic growth proceeds. The types of dilemmas that China faces are seen by its decision to proceed with the Three Gorges Dam. The dam will undoubtedly change the environment in the Yangtze Valley considerably even though it will bring economic advantages, at least in the short to medium term. However, it is hard to believe that the natural resource stock of this region will not be reduced and so one could say that China in making this decision is not acting in accordance with strong sustainability conditions said to be desirable in the preamble to its Agenda 21.

Possibly the first major moves by China to protect its environment in recent times began with the Second National Environmental Protection Work Conference in 1983. In 1984, following this conference, the Environmental Protection Commission was established under the State Council "to co-ordinate all ministries and agencies whose activities affect the environment. Similar organizations and institutions were set up at the local level" (Wu and Flynn, 1995, p. 5). Thus a relatively comprehensive administrative system for environmental management was established in China.

In the 1980s policy makers appear to have reached widespread agreement on:

(1) Use of the *precautionary principle*, that is avoiding environmental problems by means of prior planning and when necessary incorporating defensive environmental elements into projects.

(2) The importance of imposing greater responsibility and liability on polluters by using the *'polluter pays' principle* to internalise pollution costs which would otherwise be external to organisations.

(3) *Strengthening government administration* of environmental controls. Qu and Li (1994) claim that in fact strengthening of administrative management of the environment has been the main focus of the new policy.

China has considerably increased the number of persons employed in environmental protection. In 1981 only 22,000 were employed in this way but in 1992 the number was 74,898. Comparatively, however, it is still a low number and the number has failed to increase proportionately with China's

GDP because the growth in this employment has been linear rather than logarithmic (see Wu and Flynn, 1995, Table 2, p. 5). Nevertheless, in 1991 China is estimated to have spent 1 per cent of its GNP on environmental improvement compared to 0.7 per cent of GNP in the 7th Five Year Plan (1985-1990). The National Environmental Protection Agency's target is to increase this to 1.5 per cent (Bingham, 1993, p. 10) which for a less developed country is a substantial investment in environmental protection.

Coming to China's practice in using economic instruments to control pollution, there can be little doubt that China has made great progress in this regard, although much still has to be done. Discharge fees on pollutants were first imposed in one form or another and with varying degrees of coverage beginning in the late 1970s - basically at the same time as China's economic reform began. They have been widened in coverage and strengthened since then. Pollutants of water and air, solid wastes and noise creation incur discharge fees. However, discharge fees on sulphur dioxide and sewage have only been levied since 1992 in nine cities in two provinces on a trial basis.

In 1994, pollution discharge fees (including fines and related items) amounted to 3.097 billion yuan. Of this 2.355 billion yuan was obtained from regular pollution charges and 0.742 billion yuan from fines, penalties and related items (Mao, 1996, p. 1). Charges on emissions of water pollutants other than sewage were the major source of revenue, followed by charges on emissions of air pollutants, those on solid wastes, noise, and sewage.

Nearly all the revenue obtained from pollution charges was spent on treatment of pollutants and on administration. In 1994, 2.49 billion yuan was spent on the treatment of pollution and 0.54 billion yuan on government administration of pollution regulations. None of the income collected was used to compensate victims of pollution for damages caused. Nevertheless, in some cases victims can claim damages from polluters and this even when they are not fully compensated for its damage by the pollutor, the payment is often sufficient to moderate the behaviour of the polluter. Take the example of a non-ferrous smelter which was once a serious source of cadmium poisoning.

This plant located in Daye County emitted large quantities of cadmium into the air resulting in cadmium poisoning among nearby villagers. In the later part of the 1980s, it was required to compensate victims for their medical expenses. This was sufficient to cause the enterprise to install technology which reduced contamination of the air by cadmium. This extra investment in technology showed a substantial positive rate of social return (Zhiyong et al., 1991).

In relation to compensation of victims for environmental damage, there is still scope for strengthening China's laws and their application. There is still some doubts about whether China's discharge fees are fairly determined and consistently applied to individual enterprise in practice.

The National Environmental Protection Agency is intending to increase the level of pollution emission fees and to apply fees to emissions at all levels rather than to those exceeding some threshold quantity as is the case for a number of pollutants at present. Some of these extra funds will be used to provide loans to enterprises for environmental protection and for treatment of pollutants.

Overall China's performance in relation to protection of natural resources and environmental protection is mixed. Even in relation to pollution control, it seems that at least up to now less attention has been given to pollution prevention than to pollution treatment. So principles and practice still have yet to be brought fully into line.

6. China's Environment and the Outside World

Today the environment of most countries is not solely their own business. This is particularly so in China's case because of its immense size both in terms of population and land area. The main reason why a country's environment concerns the rest of the world is the presence of externalities from the state of its environment.

China's potential level of economic activity and its possible environmental impacts are so large that they cannot be ignored by the rest of the world. Some of its impacts are global. Its possible global impacts are not restricted to its large (and potentially much larger) addition to greenhouse gases. A recent additional example was its emissions of CFCs, a threat to the ozone layer. As a result of the Montreal Agreement and subsequent international meetings, arrangements have been made to phase out the use of CFCs in countries like China and an international fund has been set up to provide financial assistance for the phase-out (Litfin, 1994). China is one of the recipients of such aid.

Regionally China's environmental change has transboundary effects. It is the source of major rivers which are to a large extent the economic life-blood of Indo-China, Burma and Bangladesh. Environmental actions by China which pollute these rivers, reduce their waterflows, increase their sediment loads and vary the erratic nature of their flows can be expected to have considerable economic and environmental impact in China's neighbouring countries. Again, China's economic activity generates a considerable amount of acid rain. Some of this is transported to neighbouring countries. There have for example been complaints in parts of Japan that acid rains are responsible for the deaths of some trees in the vicinity of Hiroshima.

While not directly involving an international externality element, the environmental policies of a country can influence the international location of polluting industries and international trading. Countries which have low environmental standards may attract polluting industries from abroad and have an advantage in exporting goods the production of which generates pollution. The fact that those in polluting industries do not pay the full social costs of their economic activities means that in effect they are granted a subsidy. The 'concession' benefits special economic interests but often imposes greater costs on the community than the benefits received by these special interests. Therefore, extreme care is needed in making environmental concessions to particular businesses or industries. Some Taiwanese economic activities have, it is claimed, been located in China for environmental reasons.

In a relatively decentralised system particularly as in China, it is very difficult to prevent local authorities competing with one another by making environmental concessions to attract foreign investment. Increased central control may, however, be exerted as the National Environment Protection Agency becomes stronger.

7. CONCLUDING COMMENTS

China's growing importance in the world should not be judged purely in terms of its rapid and economic growth and the spin-off of economic benefits to the rest of the world. The environmental and social consequences of its economic growth must be considered including the sustainability of its growth. China does face considerable difficulties in achieving sustainable development. The Chinese themselves have posed the question of whether it is sensible for them to follow the Western and Japanese pattern of economic development which involves economic growth first and environmental clean-up later.

Although the Chinese have expressed doubts about the desirability of such a pattern of growth for China, there is little evidence that they have to date been following a different pattern. On the other hand, there are some signs that this could change. Consider the position outlined in *China's Agenda 21* and the increasing control of pollution by the National Environment Protection Agency. Nevertheless, politically and especially taking into account the influence of local politics, China will find it difficult to pursue an environmentally friendly development path. In addition, in order to follow this alternative path effectively, China may need new production techniques which are environmentally appropriate and must be careful to only transfer techniques from abroad which have suitable environmental and sustainability characteristics. Otherwise, articulation of China's *new development path* may amount to no more than lip service. On the other hand if the new path is earnestly sought and found, China's economic resurgence may not only be sustainable but China will re-emerge as a world leader, in technology and in intellectual thought, as it was in the Tang period.

REFERENCES

Administration Centre for China's Agenda 21 (1994), *Introduction to China's Agenda 21*, China Environmental Service Press, Beijing.

Arrow, K., Bolin, B., Costanza, R., Dasgupta, P., Fölke, C., Holling, C.S., Jansson, B., Levin, S., Mäler, K., Perrings, C., and Pimental, D. (1995) "Economic Growth Carrying Capacity, and the Environment", *Science*, 268: 520-521.

Bingham, A. (1993) "China's Phenomenal Growth has Environmental Tag", *Pollution Prevention* (Asia/Pacific edition) 1(4): 10-22.

Litfin, K.T. (1994) *Ozone Discourses*, Columbia University Press, New York.

Mao, Yushi (1996) "Economic Instruments adopted in China to Control Pollution", *Personal Communication*, March 26.

Qu, G. and Li, T. (1994) *Population and the Environment in China*, Paul Chapman, London.

State Council (1994) *China's Agenda 21 - White Paper on China's Population, Environment, and Development in the 21st Century*, China Environmental Science Press, Beijing.

Tisdell, C.A. (1990) *The Economics of Environmental Conservation*, Elsevier, Amsterdam.

Tisdell, C.A. (1993a) "Combining Biological Conservation, Sustainability and Economic Growth: Can We Overcome Potential Conflict?", *Discussion Paper No. 130*, Department of Economics, The University of Queensland, Brisbane, 4072.

Tisdell, C.A. (1993b) *Economic Development in the Context of China*, Macmillan, London.

Tisdell, C.A. (1995a) "Asian Development and Environmental Dilemmas", *Contemporary Economic Policy*, 13: 38-44.

Tisdell, C.A. (1995b) "The Environment, Biodiversity and Asian Development", *Biodiversity Conservation*, Working Paper No. 20, Department of Economics, The University of Queensland, Brisbane, 4072.

World Resources Institute, United Nations Environment Programme and United Nations Development Programme (1994) *World Resources 1994-95*, Oxford University Press, New York.

World Bank (1992) *World Development Report: Development and the Environment*, Oxford University Press, New York.

Wu, B. and Flynn, A. (1995) "Sustainable Development in China: Seeking a Balance Between Economic Growth and Environmental Protection", *Sustainable Development* 3(1): 1-8.

Zhiyong, H., Keguang, B. and Tisdell, C.A. (1991) "Cadmium Exposure in Daye County, China: Environmental Assessment and Management, Health and Economic Effects", *Environmental Management and Health*, 2(2): 20-25.

ZHN (1992) *Zhongguo Huanjing Nianjian* (China's Environment Yearbook), Chinese Environmental Science Press, Beijing.

CHAPTER 11

SUSTAINABLE LAND USE IN THE THREE GORGES AREA OF CHINA[1]

Y. ZHAI[**], S.R. HARRISON AND Q. XU[**]

ABSTRACT

The Three Gorges Area (TGA) covers a mountainous and hilly land surface of 54,00 km² with an average population density of 270 per km², 2.5 times the average throughout China. The enormous Three Gorges Project (TGP) with a total cost of US$25b will involve a major resettlement program of more than 1.1m people and impose severe pressures on land and environment. The government of China has decreed that some of the sloping land must be protected with forestry and pasture. The challenge will be to produce enough food such that the region will be near self-sufficient. Some of

1   The research was partly supported by the International Tropical Timber Organization (ITTO) through providing Dr Yushun Zhai a fellowship program to work as a visiting research fellow in Department of Economics, University of Queensland, Australia.

**   Institute of Soil Science, Chinese Academy of Sciences, Nanjing, Pr China and Department of Economics, the University of Queensland, Brisbane 4072

the measures which will protect the land while maintaining production and incomes include: integrating agroforestry, multiple cropping and sloping land terracing practices in farming systems; raising productivity of cropland; enhancing the forest coverage and building production bases of forestry products and other staples; and promoting the development of secondary and tertiary industries to arrange more resettlements beyond farmland.

1. INTRODUCTION

The controversial Three Gorges Project (TGP) is being built on the Yangtze River near Yichang, Hubei province of China. The Yangtze river is the longest river in China stretching 6,300km from Qinghai-Tibet Plateau to the East Sea in Shanghai with a drainage area of 1.8mkm^2, representing one fifth of the area of China. This region has contributed greatly to the national economy of China and the construction of the enormous hydro-electric project will have a great impact on the Chinese economy, society and environment. Electricity generation, flood control and improved navigation from Yichang to Chongqing are considered as the major three beneficial results from the dam. Disturbance to the environment and ecosystems and the resettlement of more than one million people are regarded as the negative impacts and, in fact, the displacement is now the key problem to the success of project as acknowledged by Chinese government. In spite of some international concern over social and environmental impacts (e.g. Barber and Ryder, 1993; Fearnside, 1994), the project commenced in 1993 after approved by China's National People's Congress, and the estimated completion date is 2010.

The TGP will create a 600km long reservoir affecting 54,000km^2 of land in 19 municipalities and counties and having more than 14m population, of which 90% are rural people. Therefore, it is obviously that land resource and its productivity will play important roles in the displacement of rural people whose household or farmland will be wholly of partly submerged after the construction of the dam. The reservoir region of the Three Gorges Project, namely the Three Gorges Area (TGA) is mountainous and hilly. The farmland availability on per capita base is no more than 0.1ha, much of which is steep and at present under dryland cropping. The area of unused land suitable for agriculture is very limited according the investigation of Chinese Academy of Sciences (CAS) from 1985 to 1990 (Xu and Liu, 1993). Also, the TGA is an environmentally sensitive area with serious soil erosion and the consequent mountainous disasters. It is, therefore, of crucial importance to improve the farmland productivity as well as to protect it from soil erosion and land degradation so as to increase the population carrying capacity. To achieve this goal, viable alternatives to the conventional agricultural systems needed to be adopted to combine the integrated utilisation of natural resources with ecological conservation and improvement of the environment.

2. LAND USE PATTERNS AND PRODUCTIVITY

Farm land. The total cropland area in the TGA is 1.15 million hectares representing 23% of the total land area and mainly distributed along the valleys of the Yangtze River and its tributaries, hilly tablelands and the basins among the mountains. There are 359,000ha of paddy land accounting for 31.2% of total farmland and 717,000ha of upland making up the remaining 68.8% of which 11.6% needs to be returned to forest or grassland (Xu and Liu, 1993). As for the vertical distribution, a large proportion of the farmland has elevation from 300m to 1000m with little difference between paddy lands and uplands (Figure 11.1). Due to the changes of physical (climate, soil, etc) and socioeconomic settings (irrigation, fertilisation and other external inputs) with vertical increase, the productivity of the farmland changes dramatically (Table 11.1), e.g. the productivity of cropping systems above 1,000m altitude is only 1/2 or 1/3 of that in the altitude of 300 - 500m (Xu, 1995).

Woodland and orchard land. The TGA belongs to mid-tropical evergreen broadleaved forest area with rich species diversity. The total wooded land area is 2.8mha but only 975,000ha are forest lands covering 19.5% of the total land surface, the remainder being bush lands, sparse wooded lands, non-mature planted forests and orchards. Of the wooded lands, natural and semi-natural forests make up 72.2% and artificial wooded land represents 27.8%, with typical annual productivity of 1.8 m³/ha/yr. The land cover of forest in the TGA has an uneven regional distribution. There is little forest in the river valley, normally no more than 10%, and relatively high forest cover in the remote mountainous area, normally 30-50%. In the 19 municipalities and counties of the TGA, the total percentage of forest cover is from as high as 31.6% (in Wuxi) to as low as 2.6% (in Baxian) (Figure 11.2). The orchard lands include mulberry, tea, citrus and other fruit lands which usually have high external inputs and productivity but are greatly affected by the market prices of the products. For example, the recent overwhelming increase of citrus planting has caused over-production of oranges and a drop of prices resulting in a dramatic decrease of the revenue from citrus production.

Figure 11.1: Vertical Distribution of Farmland in the TGA

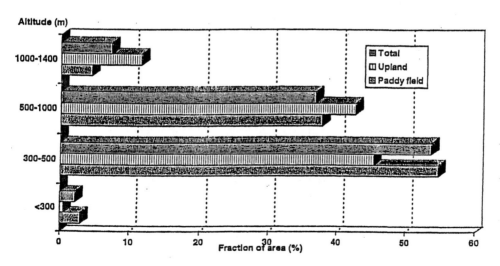

Table 11.1: Farmland Cultivation and Productivity in the TGA

Topography	Altitude (m)	Cultivation ratio (%)	Multiple cropping index (%)	Crop yield (t/ha/yr)
Basin	< 300	> 70	230	7.5
Tableland	300-500	68	190-230	6.0-7.5
Hill	500-1000	43	180	3.8-4.5
Mountain	1000-1400	14	80	3.3-3.8

Figure 11.2: Regional Distribution of Forest Cover Percentage in the TGA

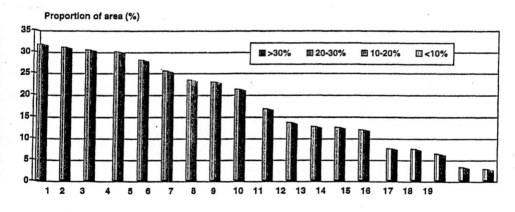

Code to counties: 1. Wuxi 2. Yichang 3. Xingshan 4. Wushan 5. Wulong 6. Fengjie 7. Shizhu 8. Badong 9. Zigui 10. Fengdu 11. Wanxian 12. Kaixian 13. Fuling 14. Yunyang 15. Jiangbei 16. Changshou 17. Zhongxian 18. Wanshi 19. Baxian

Grassland. The total grassland in the TGA is only 43,600ha, representing 0.9% of the total land area, of which about 70% is desert woodland with shadow top soil, low fertility and marginal development potential. The other 30% is meadow at the high elevation of 1,800 - 2,500m with quality grass species and having high development potential for livestock.

Uncultivated land. The uncultivated land base suitable for agriculture in the TGA is 19,700ha in accordance with the survey of CAS from 1985 to 1990 under the criteria of arable land evaluation, namely, under 25 degree of slope, at the elevation of 1400m or below, over 20cm of fine soil depth in the purple soil area and over 50cm in yellow-brown and limestone soil areas. This unused land has a remarkable vertical distribution in that only 17.2% is under the elevation of 500m (Figure 11.3).

Figure 11.3: Vertical Distribution of Unused Farmland in the TGA

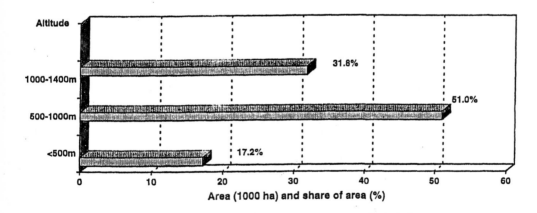

Most of the bush and sparse woodland could be converted to forest and grassland. The total area is 1.79mha with a vertical distribution as indicated in Figure 11.4. Nearly 80% is above 500m.

Figure 11.4: Vertical Distribution of Bush Land Suitable for Forest in the TGA

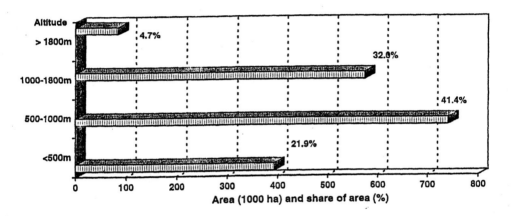

3. LAND USE - RELATED ENVIRONMENTAL PROBLEMS

Slopeland and soil erosion. The great pressure of population and inappropriate policies of agricultural development have resulted in over-reclamation of the TGA. At present, the cultivation ratio below the elevation of 300m is more than 70%, from 300m to 500m is 68%, from 500m to 1,000m is 43% and above 1,000m is 14%. The high cultivation ratio in this mountainous and hilly area has resulted in use of a high percentage of sloping land (Table 11.2). Intensive farming activities on the sloping land without protective measures have caused serious soil erosion (Figure 11.4) and related mountainous disasters. According to researches in the TGA, 80% of the TGA

Table 11.2: Distribution of Farmland by Slope Class

Slope (degrees)	Paddy field (%)	Upland (%)
0 - 7	33.3	4.7
7 - 15	39.8	23.8
15 - 25	21.5	46.5
> 25	5.4	25.0

is considered prone to soil erosion, of which three quarters falls in the moderate to high erosion classification (Xu, 1995).

Soil degradation. Because of the fragmentation of farmland (normally no more than 0.1ha per field plot) and the difficulty of slopeland management, a large amount of the farmland soils lacks basic nutrient elements and has low quality characteristics. According to the statistics of the local authorities, 37.9% of the farmland has top soil depth of less than 30cm, half of the farmland has less than 2% organic matter and 0.1% total nitrogen, and one third has less than 100 ppm K_2O in the top-soil. Overall, there are 22.0 %, 26.8% and 51.2%, respectively, of the soils showing high, medium and low productivity characteristics.

4. THE IMPACT OF THE TGP ON LAND USE

Inundation. The TGP will submerge a land area of 632km^2 including 7,380ha of paddy fields, 16,410ha of uplands and 4960ha of orchard lands. These lands are of high and stable productivity, and have been cultivated for centuries. It will not be possible to replace them with reclaimed land of the same productivity or stability, normally the productivity of the newly-

Figure 11.5: Grading and Area Composition of Soil Erosion in the TGA

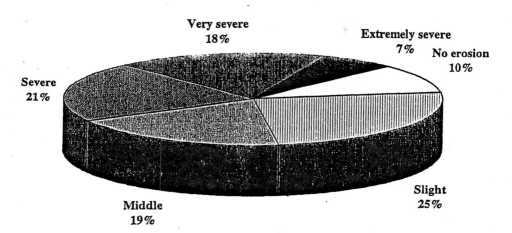

reclaimed land is only 1/3 - 1/5 to that of the inundated farmland. The number of people who need to be resettled in the reservoir region is about 860,000 and together with the secondary resettlement, the total relocated may reach 1.16 million. Nearly 50% of those to be resettled are farmers, who will move uphill in the resettlement, resulting in intense human activities and stronger impacts upon fragile ecosystems and environment.

Environmental carrying capacity of resettlement. The average population density in the TGA is about 275 persons per km^2, more than 2.5 times the overall density in China. The local resettlement will inevitably increase the population density in this area and increase the intensity of use of already over-loaded lands. Furthermore, in accordance with the stipulation of the Law of Soil and Water Conservation issued by the Chinese government, an area of 200,000ha, (25% of the total cropland in the TGA with slope gradient of more than 25) must be returned to forest or grass. By the end of year 2000, the population in the TGA will increase to 16.09 m but the cropland will decrease to 866,470ha (including the newly-reclaimed 16,330 hectares from the unused land suitable for cropping). Assuming an average yield of grain of 4.94 t/ha (following Xu and Liu, 1993), the grain production per capita will be as low as 266 kg. As a result, the grain needed, even if estimated at a modest average annual consumption of 300 to 400 kg per capita, will be far from satisfied even without allowing for return of land to forest and grass. Table 11.3 indicates estimates of the extent to which the TGA population will exceed that for which adequate locally-produced food supplies will be available up to the year 2000.

Ambient conditions. With the increase of water level and water body width, some biophysical conditions of the TGA will be changed including the air temperature and biogeochemical processes. The rise of annual mean temperature and extreme minimum temperature and the decrease of the extreme maximum temperature will improve the growing conditions and qualities of some kind of fruits, e.g. longan and citrus.

Table 11.3: Amount of Population Over-load in the TGA Relative to Grain Production

Grain consumption (kg/person/ year)	Population over-load in 1990 (1,000)	Population over-load in 2000 without slopeland reforestation and pasture (1,000)	Population over-load in 2000 with slopeland reforestation and pasture (1,000)
300	470	430	4318 - 4105
350	2440	2970	5875 - 5745
400	3900	4870	7035 - 6902

5. RURAL ECONOMY AND LAND USE IN THE TGA

Current situation of rural economy. The TGA is a relatively underdeveloped area in China with low income and low main staple food production on a per capita basis (Table 11.4). In particular, there are several counties in the TGA still in the absolute poor state without adequate food and clothing supplies. According to the statistics of 1991 of the local governments (Editorial committee of China Yearbook of Agriculture, 1991), 7.3% of rural people in the TGA had annual incomes of less than 250 yuan (about US$45 at that time), and more than one third earned less than 300 yuan (which is less than the self-support limit of living in China at that time) (Table 11.5). The rural economy of the TGA is dominated by primary industries, the relative shares of income from primary, secondary and tertiary industries being respectively 56.8%, 31.6% and 11.6% (Yearbook of Sichuan, 1991; Yearbook of Hubei, 1991).

Table 11.4: Income and Main Staple Food Production per Capita, Rural Area of the TGA, 1991

Region	Income (yuan)	Grain (kg)	Oil (kg)	Fruit (kg)	Meat (kg)
TGA	422	431	13	24	47
Sichuan	470	467	19	16	51
Hubei	532	533	25	11	38
All China	601	483	24	24	35

Table 11.5: Annual Income Grade in the Rural TGA in 1991

Income class (yuan/yr)	Number of counties and suburbs of cities	Rural population (1,000)	Proportion of the total population (%)
<250	1	1109.9	7.1
250-300	6	4392.0	28.2
300-400	6	4273.8	27.5
400-600	5	1821.4	11.7
600-800	6	3726.5	22.0
> 800	5	539.6	3.5

Underdevelopment of the rural economy has prevented farmers and the local governments from improving farming facilities and increasing external inputs (Table 11.6), and as a result, has hindered rise in productivity of land use patterns.

Table 11.6: Farming Facilities and Modernisation Factor Levels in 1991

Region	Cropland (ha/ head)	Machin-ery (mw/ha)	Chemical fertilisers (kg/ha)	Proportion of invest igated cropland (%)	Electricity consumption (kwh/ha)
TGA	0.0693	20.26	679.5	28.69	682.5
Sichuan	0.0680	21.08	750.0	45.00	765.0
Hubei	0.0820	32.42	1217.7	67.39	804.0
All China	0.1060	30.75	751.5	50.00	1006.5

Rural economy development strategies and impacts on land use options. The recent development of tertiary industry due to the incentives for tourism in the TGA has stimulated the investment in tourist facilities and other non-agricultural enterprises. Local governments have formulated non-agriculture-orientated economic development policies and development-resettlement strategies. These will not only increase incomes of local residents but also reduce population pressure on farmland. However, this kind of development strategy will encroach on arable land availability and impose incentives for alternative land use options.

6. SUSTAINABLE MANAGEMENT COUNTERMEASURES TO TGA LAND USE

The TGA has been confronted with an urgent requirement to increase agricultural production as well as to protect the ecosystems and environment. It is, therefore, of crucial importance to develop sound land use and management systems which will make maximum use of the biophysical potential and minimise adverse impacts on the environment, especially soil erosion. To achieve this goal, the following management strategies and countermeasures could be adopted:

Adjustment of the structure of rural industries. Since land resources in the TGA are already over-loaded, it is important to shift some people from farmland-related industries to other industrial involvements, namely to develop rural secondary and tertiary industries while raising the production of primary industries.

Establishment of rational cropping systems. Because slopeland cropping is popular in the TGA and soil erosion and consequent ecological and environmental problems have become a great concern of this region, it is vital to establish cropping systems not only with high and stable productive potential but also with soil erosion control and other protective characteristics. Multiple cropping systems, agroforestry systems, slopeland terracing and reafforestation systems have potential to maintain output while protecting or restoring land.

Improvement to medium and low-yield farmland. Because a large part of the farmland in the TGA is suffering from various ecophysical constraints and has low to medium productive characteristics, the development of these into high and stable productive farmlands will increase the total agricultural production in the TGA and improve the environmental situations. Furthermore, with respect to the fact that most of the unused land in the TGA is bush and shrub land with little vegetation cover and low biomass productivity, reforestation and development of agroforestry systems will bring great potential to the land use systems.

Establishment of production base of special and key products. The TGA has rich and diversified biogenetic resources, and it is the main production base of various famous and special fruits and cash crops, such as oranges, tung oil tree, lacquer tree and some Chinese herb medicines. Moreover, the region has a great positional preponderance for developing commercialised and foreign exchange-earning agricultural and forest products. It is therefore paramount to take viable measures to make maximum use of the advantage and potential.

7. CONCLUDING COMMENT

The TGA has been attracting world wide attention with controversies on the resettlement and ecological and environmental impacts. Sustainable use and management of the scarce land resources will play an important role in the resettlement of the enormous population and the development of the whole economy as well as the protection of the environment in that remote and underdeveloped area.

REFERENCES

Barber, M. and Ryder, G. (eds) (1993) *Damming the Three Gorges: What Dam-Builders Don't Want You to Know* (2nd edition). Probe International, Toronto.

Editorial Committee of China Yearbook of China (1991) *China Yearbook of Agriculture*, China Agriculture Press, Beijing.

Editorial Committee of Yearbook of Hubei Province (1991) *Yearbook of Hubei Province*, Hubei Science and Technology Press, Wuhan.

Editorial Committee of Yearbook of Sichuan Province (1991) *Yearbook of Sichuna Province*, Sichuan Science and Technology Press, Chengdu.

Fearnside, P.M. (1994) "The Canadian Feasibility Study of the Three Gorges Dam Proposed for China's Yangzi River: A Grave Embarrassment to the Impact Assessment Profession", *Impact Assessment*. 12(1): 21-57.

Xu, Q. (1995) "The Ecological and Environmental Impact of the Three Gorges Project", *Bulletin of the Chinese Academy of Sciences*, 9(4): 341-347.

Xu, Q. and Liu, Y. (1993) *Environmental Carrying Capacity of Resettlement in the Reservoir Region of the Three Gorges Project*, Science press, Beijing.

Zhang, T., Zhao, Q., Zhai, Y. Chen B. and Sun B. (1995) "Sustainable Land Use in Hilly Red Soil Region of South-eastern China", *Pedosphere*, 5(1): 1-10.

CHAPTER 12

COMMUNITY-BASED FORESTRY IN YUNNAN: DICTATES OF ENVIRONMENT AND SOCIO-ECONOMICS

ZHUGE REN AND CLEM TISDELL*

ABSTRACT

Yunnan is a mountainous region of Southwest China and six large rivers flow through it - the Mekong, Salween, Irrawaddy, Yangtze, Song Hong and the Pearl. This means that the environmental conditions of uplands in Yunnan have significant environmental consequences, not only in China, but also in Indo-China. Silt loads, water quality and variability of waterflows in these major rivers are greatly influenced by conditions in rural Yunnan. The rural natural environment in Yunnan is being degraded by cultivation on steep slopes, shifting agriculture and deforestation. It is estimated that only 2.8 million hectares of land in Yunnan are suitable for cropping, but it has a population of 40 million. Furthermore, 67 per cent of this arable land is on slopes. In addition, 70 per cent of its forest resources are located in

---

*   Department of Forestry, Southwest Forestry College, Kunming, China and Department of Economics, The University of Queensland, Brisbane 4072

mountainous areas. Consequently, Yunnan's hilly areas are under pressure both from agriculture and logging.

Yunnan contains 25 minorities and some, such as the Dai, have traditionally adopted forestry practices which have helped to conserve the rural natural environment, reduce soil erosion and biodiversity loss and promote sustainable livelihoods. However, this is not true of all minorities. Some minorities practice slash-and-burn agriculture and engage in cultivation of crops on steepland, such as maize, with no attention to soil conservation. In practice, Yunnan's environment is deteriorating as cultivation of its lands intensifies and extends and forests are destroyed or overexploited. About 25 million people live on the mountainous land in the province.

The possibility of using community forestry as a solution to the present environmental problems of upland Yunnan is explored. Community forestry can help in reducing shifting agriculture, cropping on steep slopes, desertification of river valleys, soil erosion, biodiversity loss and rural poverty. It may, for example, provide a more effective approach to establishing shelter belt forests in Yunnan for the Yangtze River than the present one. The present one involves forcibly trying to prevent local people from cultivating steeplands and the mass planting of steeplands with trees by a central agency. Without decentralisation and community support, this shelter-type reforestation project may fail, or be less economic and environmentally effective than would be community-based forestry.

1. INTRODUCTION

This chapter stresses the importance of community-based forestry for the conservation of natural resources and alleviation of poverty in upland Yunnan. In contrast with state-managed forests, which account for the bulk of forested land in many countries, including China, community-based forestry is a decentralised form of forestry which empowers local people to manage and establish forests. Forestry based in local communities can take many forms. It can involve forestry, including agroforestry, on the private land of individual villagers, or it can entail communal or social forestry, for example, the communal establishment and management of forests on wasteland, or on degraded land.

Communal forestry has been practiced in parts of India for more than 20 years and was first adopted in West Bengal. It has been observed that in villages where community forests have been established, biodiversity has increased and the extent of poverty appears to have been reduced. While China has less experience with community-based forestry than India, some minorities in China, such as the Dais, have engaged in silviculture for centuries. There is growing interest in community-based silviculture in China, particularly in Yunnan, the prime region of interest in this contribution.

Yunnan, a frontier province in South-west China, has a long history of upland cultivation. Today, the inhabitants of its upland areas are demanding improvements in their environment and in their living standards. The simultaneous achievement of these objectives requires strategies to be found for environmentally sustainable development. There is worldwide interest in discovering strategies to achieve this and in particular China has adopted its *Agenda 21* (State Council, 1994) with a view to achieving such development.

Over the past decades, human exploitation has almost exhausted forests in upland Yunnan and the area has fallen into a vicious circle of poverty and environmental deterioration. Researchers in the province have been searching for a way to reverse this trend and have now concluded that the expansion of community forestry might be the most effective way to develop the area's rural economy and improve its environment. This can be seen as a new policy in China, where it is hoped that the establishment of community forestry will accelerate forest rehabilitation and foster environmental improvements.

In implementing this program, the benefits to the local area and its population are of prime concern, and local customs and beliefs will receive full consideration. Community forestry has been extremely successful in the developing countries of South and South-east Asia where these factors have been given priority. In view of this, it is felt that the advantages of community forestry far outweigh its disadvantages and that community forestry has great potential to help solve the development problems of upland Yunnan.

A feature of this chapter is its emphasis in its discussion of community-based forestry on: (i) the state of the environment, and (ii) the significance of institutional structures for appropriate economic decision-making and for the optimal use and conservation of resources. Decentralised governance structures linked with appropriate economic incentives to local communities can be a powerful force for improvements in decision-making about resource use and conservation. Nevertheless, they should not be regarded as a panacea for effective governance. The situation is more complicated than some advocates for the empowerment of local communities realise.

2. BACKGROUND

Yunnan is a mountainous province. Of the province's total land area of 394,000 km², 94% is categorised as mountainous. Elevations in the province range from 6,740 m above sea level in the north-west down to 76.4 m above sea level in the south-east. Six famous rivers - the Lancangjiang (Mekong), Nujiang (Salween), Dayingjiang (Irrawaddy), Jinshajiang (Yangtze), Yuanjiang (Song Hong), and Nanpanjiang (Pearl) - and over one hundred of their tributaries, pass through Yunnan to the mainland of South-east Asia and the coastal provinces of China.

Yunnan has distinctive climatic conditions: climate in its west is controlled by the plateau climate from Tibet and in the east is subject to the wet monsoon from East Asia; the central region is influenced by the South Asia tropical monsoons. The pattern of mixing of the west winds with monsoonal air currents causes considerable oscillation of climatic conditions. A dry season occurs in winter and spring and the wet season is in summer and autumn.

The diverse topography of high mountains, deep river valleys and steeply sloping land in Yunnan produces varied climatic patterns throughout the province such that almost every type of climate in China can be found within Yunnan. Consequently the province contains a very wide range of vegetation types with over 17,000 higher plant species being found in the upland region.

Yunnan has a population of 40 million people but has only an area of 2.8 million ha. suitable for crop cultivation and 67% of this arable land lies on the mountain slopes. In addition, 70% of the forest resources are confined to the north-western highlands and southern remote areas of Yunnan (Xue, 1984). Consequently, Yunnan's shortage of arable land and its lack of accessible forest resources greatly intensifies conflicts between the demands of the human population on its natural resources and the conservation of those natural resources.

3. TRADITIONAL PRACTICES INVOLVING RURAL LAND USE AND COMMUNITY FORESTRY IN YUNNAN

During several thousand years of agricultural production in Yunnan, local people have developed many effective methods of cultivation. The following are the major types:

3.1 Trees for Commercial Non-Timber Products

Originally for self-consumption, the native people traditionally planted trees for fruits, spices, oils and fibres near their houses or on the corners of their fields. Through selective breeding of varieties which adapted most successfully, some areas gradually became known for particular local products. For example, Funing county is today one of the major anise-producing areas of China. Although the county's yield of anise ranks second in China, its quality is ranked first. However, it was not until 1675 that the first anise tree was introduced into Funing by a refugee from Guangxi province. It thrived in the county and the scattered plantings developed into mass production. The county is also renowned for its anise by-products. Similarly successful local products in Yunnan include Baozhu pear, Mixiang pear, Hongxie pear, Dapao walnut, early maturing chestnut, Fengdong orange, Zhongpai orange, seedless persimmon, Diao plum, sweet pomegranate, sour pomegranate, Yanshui pomegranate, Nuomi pomegranate, three-year mango, fingered citron, prickly ash, tung oil, lac, natural silk, palm fibre and lacquer.

3.2 Home Gardening

Home gardening is a traditional activity in the villages of Yunnan. Fruit trees, bamboos, spice trees, vegetable trees (for example, the sprouts of Chinese mahogany *Toona sinensis* from which a delicious dish is made from a traditional recipe) and other trees are commonly cultivated in the gardens. Dai people are particularly successful in managing their own gardens. They often plant trees, shrubs, vegetables, vines and epiphytes together in one patch of ground, each plant positioned to make the most efficient use of the sunlight. It is possible for home gardens to meet all the needs of the local people for fruit, wood, vegetables, spices, flowers and medicinal herbs. (Yu et al., 1985).

3.3 Fuelwood

Dai people have traditionally cultivated the senna tree *Cassia siamea* for the production of fuelwood. At five years old, a tree can be coppiced with a stump of 0.5-1.5 m remaining and it will sprout two to three new shoots the following year. Then shoots can be cut from the tree for fuelwood at three yearly intervals. One stump at between thirty and fifty years of age has over twenty shoots. Dai people usually divide a block of senna trees into three sectors so that they can rotate the collection of fuelwood each year. Some Dai people originally cultivate senna trees for timber and then switch to their use for fuelwood.

Many other minority groups are experienced in managing natural fuelwood resources. They identify the trees which provide good fuelwood and ensure that these remain dominant in their woodlands.

3.4 Village Woodlands

In rural areas of China, there are widely held beliefs that the forests guarantee favourable weather and bumper harvests, and that the trees ensure the prosperity of a village or community. Tree covered hills around a village are often called "dragon hills" or "holy hills". In Chinese folklore, "dragon" is a monster that takes charge of rainfall. Another kind of protected woodland near villages is called "water source forest". These woodlands help to maintain a continuous supply of water flowing into the villages and farmlands. Therefore, villagers always ensure that great care is taken of the local woodlands. The indigenous knowledge of trees and the traditional management of woodlands have ensured that woodlands have flourished near villages for thousands of years. Unfortunately, a lot of protected woodlands were destroyed during the "Cultural Revolution" when beliefs associated with them were seen as a kind of feudal superstition.

3.5 Agroforestry

Agroforestry is an ancient practice which has existed for several thousand of years. In China, there are well-known examples of the intercropping of both *Paulownia* trees and Chinese wood oil trees with crops. A less well-known example is that of the intercropping of alder trees *Alnus nepalensis* and upland rice which has been practised in the south-western part of Yunnan for several centuries. In this system, upland rice and alder trees are intercropped in the first year. After the rice harvest, the alder trees are left to grow for fuelwood and for supply of green manure. Usually the alder trees can provide green manure of 1.5-2.5 tons per ha. by the fifth year. After seven to ten years, the alder trees can be felled for timber and fuelwood and the next rotation of crops and trees can commence (Xue, 1984). Besides providing timber and fuelwood, the nitrogen-fixing capabilities of alder trees are beneficial for soil fertility. This system is very similar to the "Taungya System" first practised in Burma.

In central Yunnan, soybean, maize, wheat, buckwheat and radish are traditionally intercropped between rows of pine trees *Pinus armandi* for the first two or three years, after which the pine trees continue to be managed alone for timber. The edible seeds of the pine trees are sold for food. In addition, space and sunlight are used effectively in orchards, where various winter crops are planted under deciduous fruit trees.

In Southern Yunnan, the local people cultivate tea bushes under natural forest. Ethnic minorities such as Jino, Hani and Dai people have practised this kind of agroforestry for at least 400 years. In Menghai county, there are intercropped camphor-tea plantations (*Cinnamomum porrectum + Camellia sinensis* var. *assamica*). It is believed that the oldest tea bush in this area is over 800 years old. In earlier times, the Dai people occasionally planted tea seedlings under the natural camphor forests. Then they found that the most successful method was to create artificial mixed forests by intercropping camphor seedlings in the tea plantations. To date, more than 1,200 ha of camphor-tea plantations have been established. Farmers can get 0.8-0.9 tons of tea and 0.2-0.3 tons of camphor from one ha of camphor-tea plantation. In addition, the chemicals secreted by the camphor trees protect the tea trees from pests, resulting in higher quality leaves and shoots (Zou, 1995).

In South and South-east Yunnan, a shade-loving spice and medicinal plant, Tsao-ko, *Amomum tsao-ko* is widely cultivated in the forests near streams at an altitude of 1,000-1,500m. The Tsao-ko fruit is harvested in the third year and provides a good income. It is thought that this type of cultivation has been practised for over 300 years (Zou, 1991).

3.6 Non-Timber Products of Forests

A rich knowledge of the non-timber products of forests, such as edible mushrooms, wild fruits, wild vegetables, bamboo shoots, spice and medicinal herbs, is held by almost all nationalities living in the forest areas of Yunnan. Other non-timber forest products include raw materials such as tannin, lac, aromatic oil, resin, cork, gum, fibre, dyes, starch, forage and green manure. In the spring of 1995, a research team led by Zhuge Ren conducted an investigation at the local vegetable markets in Dehong Prefecture of Southwest Yunnan and collected 56 kinds of wild vegetables in this single season, including trees, shrubs, vines and herbs. Some of these wild vegetables have been introduced into home gardens, for example, *Erynigium foetidum, Solanum indicum, Oenanthe javanica, Gynura crepidioides, Acacia intsia* var. *caesia, Houttuynia cordata,* and *Solanum nigrum* var. *photeinocarpum.*

Another interesting aspect is indigenous knowledge of natural food additives and dyes. Dai people in South Yunnan mix the pulverised dried flowers of *Gmelina arborea* with glutinous rice to steam yellow-coloured "Baba Cake" for their New Year Festival. The flowers of *Buddleja officinalis* are widely used by the minorities in Yunnan as a food colouring. One plant used for food colouring, *Peristrophe baphica*, changes its colour from red to purple or black depending on the ash content of the plant. Yao people in South and South-east Yunnan use dye from this plant to colour rice for the celebration of their grand "Panwang Festival" (Tao *et al*, 1993).

3.7 Handicrafts Based on Forest Products

People from twenty-six different nationalities live in upland Yunnan and over thousands of years, the various cultures have developed a variety of arts and crafts based on the rich resources of the land. Handicrafts based on forest products are commonly found in the countryside. The best known of these are Jianchuang wood carvings, Tengchong rattan wares, Dali wood-marble furniture, Heqing white tissue paper and Dali knot-dyed cloth (APCYP, 1990).

As far back as the Ming Dynasty (A.D. 1368-1644), Jianchuang wood carving was renowned throughout the country. The artisans from Jianchuang county were selected to build the Beijing Imperial Palace. In the Qing Dynasty (A.D. 1644-1911), the famous Yuanming Palace (destroyed by the Eight-Power Allied Expedition in 1900) was an outstanding example of the exquisite craftsmanship of Jianchuang artisans. Many ancient temples in Yunnan still preserve the consummate artistic handicraft in classical Chinese style of the Jianchuang carpenters who participated in their construction.

Tengchong county was renowned for its rattan wares during the Song Dynasty (A.D. 960-1279). "Teng" in Chinese means "rattan" and "chong" means "strategic pass". The hand-made rattan wares of Tengchong are both beautiful and durable. The high quality raw materials come from the native rattan plants, *Clamus spp.* and *Daemonorops margaritae*.

Dali wood-marble furniture is made by hand using local timber and marble. Tables, chairs and beds are decorated with wood carvings of flowers and birds and embellished with the natural patterns of the marble. Natural Chinese paint is used on the surface of the furniture.

Tissue paper of Heqing county was in common use during the period of the Dali Kingdom (A.D. 937-1253). This white, soft and durable paper, made from the strong fibred bark of the daphne tree, was one of the earliest artificial papers.

Dali knot-dyed cloth uses dye from the cultivated "blue-dye plant". White cloth is tied and sewn according to the pattern desired, then dyed in a vat and finally rinsed well to achieve the special print effect.

The abundance of natural resources of bamboo in most parts of Yunnan has led to the development of crafts utilising the bamboo for hand-made wares, for example, Eshan bamboo work. In addition, a market has been developed in processed bamboo shoots - dried, slivered, pickled and so on. Zhaotong Qiongzhuea bamboo shoots, Xishuangbanna sweet bamboo shoots and pickled bamboo shoots are well known in the province.

4. COMMUNITY-BASED FORESTRY, A SOLUTION FOR THE PRESENT PROBLEMS OF YUNNAN

An area of about 346,000 km² of the province is mountainous and contains a population of some 25 million people. Over the past decade, the increasing pressures from harmful agricultural practices, such as shifting cultivation based on short and shortening cycles of cultivation, cropping on steep slopes and so on, have led to a significant worsening of the ecological environment in Yunnan's mountainous areas. Introduction of community forestry to such areas could well alleviate these problems. Furthermore, the development of community forests in Yunnan is seen as essential if the urgent problems of desertification of dry-hot river valleys, reduction of biodiversity, and other forms of environment deterioration and rural poverty are to be solved.

4.1 Diversion of Shifting Cultivation

Shifting cultivation, or slash and burn agriculture, produces food by simple techniques and minimum use of labour. It has been practised effectively by the upland local people for over ten centuries under conditions involving low population density and rich forest resources, and is still practised in some remote areas of South Yunnan. However, with the current increase in population and decrease in forest areas, shifting cultivation has become a problem which is threatening the limited natural resources of Yunnan. Shifting agriculture has become an environmental problem because the length of cultivation cycles has become very short, and an increasing proportion of land is under cultivation at any one time. Consequently, more land is exposed to erosion and biodiversity is reduced. Furthermore, with shortening cultivation cycles the productivity of the soil declines and cultivation becomes less economic (CF. Ramakrishnan, 1992). Government attempts to control the practice by legislation have generally been unsuccessful. Since forests provide local people with items to meet their basic needs, an alternative means of providing support must be found before the inhabitants can be persuaded to change their way of life. Community-based forestry encourages local people to depend on permanent forest land for their livelihood and conserves forest resources. The most successful way is to replace the simple agricultural system with a more diversified economic system involving trees of commercial value as a complement to food production. For example, the local people living in a mountainous Aini village have practised shifting cultivation for many generations. In 1976, they were given help to establish a tea garden and as a result, their tradition of shifting cultivation has gradually changed. For nearly twenty years now they have lived on the same land in order to manage the tea garden and their living conditions have quickly improved (Long et al., 1985).

4.2 Restriction on Steep Slope Cropping

The cultivation of grain crops on steep slopes is a major problem in upland Yunnan. In Nujiang prefecture of West Yunnan, 42.2% of ploughed land is on slopes in excess of 25 degrees (Gao et al, 1992); the Yangtze River valley of North Yunnan also has about 40% of its ploughed land on slopes exceeding 25 degrees (He, 1991). In some places, people even cultivate grain crops on slopes of 50 degrees. Today, the pressure of the increasing population on the land is leading to slope cultivation in most areas of the province. In addition, the lower productivity of steep slopes compared to flatter land requires the utilisation of a larger area of such land to yield the quantity of production from grain crops. Soil erosion, mountain torrents, mud-rock flows, landslides and collapse of embankments frequently result from steep slope cultivation.

In the Yangtze River area of Yunnan, an ongoing project to establish protected forests is now addressing the reforestation of steep slopes. The main problem is to continue to satisfy the population's requirement for arable land when such a plan is put into practice in a highly populated area. A successful technique for slope cultivation which could be considered is agroforestry. This technique involves the planting of multipurpose trees along the terrace ridges with crops being planted in the "alley". By this means, not only can people obtain food, fuelwood, fodder and other living materials, but the tree lines help prevent soil erosion. In addition, if nitrogen-fixing trees are cultivated, this will improve the fertility of the soil. Where such an alternative is offered, it will be much easier to reforest the steep slopes, than by merely forcing people to stop the cultivation of steep slopes.

4.3 Reforestation in the Dry-Hot River Valleys

Over 800,000 ha. of dry-hot river valleys are scattered along the Yangtze, Mekong, Salween and Song Hong rivers. The primary forest vegetation of these areas has been utterly destroyed and today it has been replaced by savanna-like woodland. The dry-hot climate of the dry season causes water shortages for living things and for farming, yet the heavy rain of the wet season frequently washes the soil from the bare land. From the 1950s through to the end of the 1970s, local governments implemented programs for the mass afforestation of these areas using both pine trees and broad leaved trees, but all failed (Du, 1994).

Actually, there are many plants, both native and domesticated, which adapt well to the unique ecological conditions of the area. Coffee, mango, pear, orange, pomegranate and tamarind *Tamarindus indica* are commonly planted in the dry-hot habitat; *Phyllanthus emblica, Ziziphus mauritiana, Jatropha curcas, Calotropis gigantea* and *Dodonea viscosa* can be used as industrial raw materials; *Acacia farnesiana, Bombax malabarica, Bischofia javanica* and *Ficus lacor* grow quickly; *Toona cilicata, Schima wallichii* and *Pistacia chinensis* produce high quality timber. The exotic multipurpose trees, such as *Leucaena leucocephala* and *Eucalyptus spp.* are cultivated widely and are well received by the local people. In addition, the introduction of tropical crops into these areas has proved very beneficial and many spring or summer vegetables can be grown in winter due to the high winter temperatures. It would also be advantageous to develop agroforestry systems by intercropping trees and crops or vegetables in the lower valley and to plant native cash trees or shrubs for reforestation of the slopes above the valley.

4.4 Conservation of Biodiversity

Yunnan is famous for the abundance of its species of animals and plants. A total of 1,638 species of vertebrates, 261 species of mammals, 779 species of birds and 13,000 species of insects have been identified. Of these, 164 species of wild animals are regarded as rare and endangered and are under protection. There are about 14,000 seed plants, of which 5,300 are trees. 145 rare and endangered plants have been listed in the first edition of the State Red Data Book. Since 1981, Yunnan has established 105 natural reserves covering over 2 million ha. However, shifting cultivation, the use of woodlands for crops and felling of trees for fuelwood have been threatening the conservation of biodiversity in the protected areas. Moreover, only about 70% of those botanical species has been included in reserves. According to an inventory of forest resources in the province, during 1985-1992, the area of woodland decreased at the rate of 50,000 ha per year. Inevitably, if this rate of decrease continues, many living species will eventually disappear. The best method for conserving the biodiversity is to develop rural industries and handicrafts to release people from the land and, at the same time, increase production of forest resources in order to meet the demands of local people for them. The development of community forests fulfils these requirements.

4.5 Improving the Agricultural Environment

According to official statistics, during the period 1950-1990, there were 297 disasters involving mud-rock flows, landslides and other types of geological destruction in Yunnan. As a result, 14,000 ha of farmland were destroyed resulting in a reduction of 14.51 million kg in grain supplies (Liu et al., 1993). This decade has seen an increased frequency of major droughts and floods. Serious soil erosion now extends over an area of 140,000 km^2 (Kang, 1991).

Deforestation is the link between increased soil erosion, desertification, reduced water supplies, mud-rock flows, landslides, drought and flood. Forests are the basis of mountain agriculture. It is clear that any measures other than reforestation will only alleviate the symptoms of the "diseases". But reforestation can no longer be undertaken by the simple government initiative of mass plantings. The traditional method of reforestation is centred on the establishment of large tracts of forestland, usually including few tree species. The essence of the modern community forestry is that it considers the needs of each individual and community in reforesting a region, which is where it differs from traditional forestry. The current project establishing the Yangtze River Shelter Forests in Yunnan has involved a massive labour force, considerable material resources and the expenditure of large sums of money. Little attention has been given to arousing the enthusiasm of the local people and to utilising their initiative. If the ideas of community forestry are to be incorporated into this project, the prime consideration in plans for reforestation and selection of trees must be the needs of the local people.

4.6 Poverty Alleviation

In Yunnan today, nearly seven million people, or one-sixth of the total population, are classified as living in poverty. Serious poverty occurs in mountain regions in 73 counties containing over 3,500 administrative villages. In poor areas, the traditional agricultural economy usually involves food production depending solely on cropping systems with simple techniques, and extended areas of cultivation giving poor yields. It is exactly as described by Dr Nancy Peluso (1988) in her famous PhD dissertation: "Rich Forests, Poor People....". Forestry policy also has a critical influence on the economy of rural areas. In China, all large forests belong to the state and local people are regarded as outsiders to be excluded. Even in the 1990s, many reports can still be found in official documents regarding the hostilities between government and local people concerning the use of forest resources.

Rural poverty has complicated roots some of which are linked with local conditions and customs and hence any solution requires integrated measures. Community forestry focuses on the coordination of government forest resource management and use in conjunction with local people, thus diminishing conflict between the government and the local people. Furthermore, community forestry is designed to take account of the cultural and economic activities of local people and help them to select the best options for the development of diversified land-use systems.

5. PERSPECTIVES ON COMMUNITY FORESTRY IN UPLAND YUNNAN

Upland Yunnan has similar natural and social conditions to those of the countries of South and South-east Asia. Therefore, concepts and methods of community forestry being applied in these countries can also be introduced and developed in upland Yunnan. In fact, initial results from the practice of community forestry have been very good.

5.1 Adjustment of Development Policies

The provincial government of Yunnan has recently adopted a development plan for the economy. The tobacco industry, which is currently the cornerstone of the province's economy, will be gradually replaced by industries based on forestry, flowers and plants, tourism, sugar, tea, and processing industries. In China's ninth "Five Year Plan" starting in 1996, the alleviation of poverty and the exploitation of biological resources will be a prime focus. The Eighteen Exploitation Projects of Biological Resources mainly include the comprehensive utilization of forest products and economic plants as a basis for rural development.

Tourism is a new and expanding "smokeless industry" in Yunnan. At the end of 1992, the development of tourism became one of the most important items on the agenda of the provincial government and soon afterwards, special policies for promoting tourism were instigated. In October 1994, the provincial government convened a province-wide Tourism Program meeting in Lijiang, a city in North-west Yunnan. At the meeting, the governor of the province requested that the speed of construction should be increased for communication facilities, such as high-grade highways, new main line railways, new airports and other tourist infrastructures. Along with community forestry, tourism may provide a basis for conservation of natural resources. Tourism can contribute significantly to rural development and yet be environmentally friendly.

5.2 Education

Since the end of the 1980s, Yunnan has sent dozens of researchers abroad to study community forestry and other areas related to rural development. Most of them have now resumed work in these fields. In addition, several training courses for community forestry and agroforestry, sponsored respectively by the Ford Foundation (FF) and the Worldwide Fund for Nature (WWF), have been conducted at various academic institutes in Yunnan. The Southwest Forestry College offers a course in community forestry. One of the aims of the FF-supported project is to train government officials and foresters "on-the-job". As a result of the training of policy-makers and forestry technicians in community forestry, it will be much easier to introduce concepts and methods of community forestry into traditional forestry activities. The 1995 academic year saw the introduction of a three year course in community forestry at the Southwest Forestry College. All students accepted for enrolment have at least two years' experience in the forestry branch of the Ministry of Forestry and will return there after completing their studies. Subjects from the community forestry course are also available to students completing other specialisations at Southwest Forestry College.

Plans for technical training for farmers are going ahead. The provincial government is sending scientists and technicians to poor areas to help educate local farmers in improved agriculture and forestry techniques. It is hoped that this will help to alleviate the poverty of seven million poor people.

5.3 Potential of Natural Resources for New Uses

To date, only a few hundred species of plants have been cultivated in upland Yunnan, but thousands of wild plants, from which fruits, oils, tannin, fibre, starch, gum, resin, lac, dyes and drugs can be obtained, remain to be exploited. For example, according to recent research, there are 28 genera and 215 species of bamboo widely distributed in Yunnan, but only a few have traditionally been utilised. Researchers at the Bamboo Research Institute at Southwest Forestry College, have developed processing techniques for local factories to enable them to produce plywood and plywood flooring from a variety of bamboos. They also developed a new technique for preserving bamboo shoot products. This has improved the economics of large scale production of bamboo shoot products and has brought profound changes to mountain regions. Another example is the production of soft drink from the wild plant, *Phyllanthus emblica*, which is found as a small tree in most parts of the province. During the 1980s, scientists discovered that the fruit of *Ph. emblica* is rich in vitamins and also contains a beneficial amount of selenium, which can help to protect the human body against carcinogens. Since then, large investments have been made in rural areas in the production of *Ph. emblica* and soft drink products based on it. It has become an important source of income for some rural communities.

The province of Yunnan has six state nature reserves, 99 local nature reserves, 17 national forest parks and over one hundred local forest parks. These reserves and parks represent diverse patterns of forests, ecological systems, climates and geographical conditions. Most of these are located in rural areas remote from cities and have been opened, or are to be opened, for forest recreation. Tourism in rural areas can bring many benefits: first of all, economic prosperity from tourism can bring improvements to local communications and to the rural economy. Secondly, the varied commercial demands of tourists can propel minority groups into a commercial world and make them less dependent on subsistence activities. Nevertheless, negative social and other impacts from tourism development are possible and these need to be guarded against. Tourism and rural development will be closely connected in the future of upland Yunnan.

5.4 Exploration of Indigenous Knowledge

It has been found that the traditional practices of community forestry which have been developed in local areas by local people are most successful. In addition to providing local people with supplementary incomes, cash tree planting and home gardening, community forestry provides a basis for cottage industries and handicrafts, and leads to increased food production thereby assisting rural development. Traditional local products, especially handiworks of minorities, such as Dali knot-dyed cloth and Banna Tongpa (a small satchel made by the Dai people) are very popular purchases by tourists. It is an important undertaking to find and develop products with local characteristics.

Fuelwood from village woodland management will relieve the threat of insufficient energy for cooking and community forests can also help meet the demands of local people for wood for the building of houses and the production of furniture. The successful Taungya system in upland Yunnan is particularly practicable for the upland cultivation systems. Multi-purpose trees not only retard soil erosion and improve soil fertility, but also supply fodder, fuelwood, timber of short length and other forest by-products for local people. In developing community forestry and village silviculture it is of great importance to tap indigenous knowledge about traditional production practices involving trees.

5.5 Extensive International Cooperation

The natural advantages and special geographical position of Yunnan province have attracted much attention from international organisations in the past decade. The FF, WWF, World Bank, FTPP, UNFAO, UNESCO, IDRCC, RECOFTC, VSO, ICRAF, CARE, WINROCK and many universities in the developed countries, such as the United States, Canada, Australia, Germany, Britain and Holland, have all been involved directly or indirectly in projects concerning rural development of upland Yunnan. Government departments, research institutes and universities of Yunnan have worked with these international organisations towards the goal of poverty alleviation.

6. CONCLUDING COMMENTS

Community-based forestry has the potential to remedy unsustainable land-use practices in much of upland Yunnan and can help alleviate poverty in many areas. In fostering community forestry, it is important to take account of indigenous knowledge about land-use involving trees and create ecologically balanced land-use systems incorporating a variety of species. The development of these systems should draw on the traditional practice of community forestry in parts of Yunnan. Unlike in the case of traditional state-based forestry where local communities have mostly been ignored, consultation with and responsiveness to the needs of the local community are paramount in community-based forestry. Because of their lack of attention to local communities, many state-sponsored reforestation schemes are in danger of failing and are creating much rural hostility.

Community-based forestry can have favourable environmental and social effects: it can divert farmers from practising shifting cultivation, reduce environmental problems arising from the cropping of steep slopes, help the afforestation of dry-hot river valleys, conserve biodiversity, and generally improve environmental conditions for the practice of agriculture, and as well can alleviate much poverty. Community-based forestry together with rural-oriented tourism can provide a basis for sustainable development in upland Yunnan. Programs for educating the rural people in Yunnan about new sustainable land-use practices are increasing the likelihood of such developments. Furthermore, international co-operation and recent progress in community forestry and in ecotourism at Southwest Forestry College are bringing these goals closer to fruition.

ACKNOWLEDGMENTS

We would like to thank Professor Xue Jiru of Southwest Forestry College for his suggestions, and Dr Liu Dachang, Faculty of Arts, Deakin University, Australia, for his constructive comments.

REFERENCES

Agriculture Program Committee of Yunnan Province (APCYP), 1990, *Yunnan Special Local Products*, Yunnan People's Press, Kunming.

Du, Tianli (1994) "The orientation of exploitation and utilization of dry-hot river valley in Southwest China", *Natural Resources* (1): 41-45.

Gao, Yingxin et al. (1992) "An opinion on the ecologically based development of the economy in Nujiang Prefecture of Yunnan Province", *Ecological Economics* (1): 44-49.

He, Yinwu (1991) "On soil erosion and sloping fields returned to forest in shelter forest region of middle-upper reaches of the Yangtze River", *Ecological Economics* (4): 18-20.

Kang, Yunhai (1991) "On the methods of integrated irrigation in farmland", *Ecological Economics* (4): 46-49.

Liu, Xiaohai et al. (1993) "The calamity forecast about destruction of the ecological environment of Yunnan", *Yunnan Environment Sciences* (1): 42-45.

Long, Yiming et al. (1985) "The significance of expanding the rubber-tea community in the border villages", *Ecological Economics* (2): 26-28.

Peluso, Nancy Lee (1988) *Rich Forests, Poor People, and Development: Access Control and Resistance in the Forests of Java*, Ph.D. dissertation, Cornell University.

Ramakrishnan, P.S. (1992) *Shifting Agriculture and Sustainable Development: An Interdisciplinary Study for North-Eastern India*, UNESCO, Paris and Parthenon, Carnforth, UK.

State Council (1994) *China's Agenda 21 - White Paper on China's Population, Environmental Development in the 21st Century*, Environmental Science Press, Beijing.

Tao, Guoda et al. (1993) "Ethnic food pigments", *Botanical Magazine* (2): 13.

Xue, Jiru (1984) *Yunnan Forests*, Yunnan Science and Technology Press, Kunming.

Yu, Pinghua et al. (1985) "The study on traditional cultivated plants in Dai villages of Xishuangbanna", *Acta Bot. Yunnanica* 7 (2): 169-186.

Zou, Shouqing (1991) "Amomum cultivation in tropical forests", *Chinese Jour. Ecol.* 10 (1): 37-39.

Zou, Shouqing (1995) "The patterns and the assessment of some traditional and newly developed agroforestry systems in Southern Yunnan", Prepared for the "Workshop on Ethnobotany and the Cultural Context of Natural Resource Use and Agroforestry Management", held 16 March - 3 April 1995, at Chiang Mai, Thailand and at Xishuangbanna, China.

SOCIAL AND REGIONAL DIMENSIONS AND MORE ON EFFICIENCY: GROWING DISPARITIES

CHAPTER 13

IMPLICATIONS OF ECONOMIC PERFORMANCE AMONG CHINA'S MINORITIES

COLIN MACKERRAS[*]

ABSTRACT

China has fifty-five state-recognised minority nationalities, most of which live near or along China's borders. Many are extremely different ethnically and culturally both from the dominant Han and from each other. Some are very well integrated with the Han, while others have shown secessionist tendencies, especially the Tibetans and Uygurs.

The chapter will take up a dominant question concerning the economic performance of the minorities: does the current economic modernisation of China act as an integrating force among the minorities of China?

To answer this question, reference will be made to the differing economic levels and styles among the minorities and their very different interest in

[*]   Faculty of Asian and International Studies, Griffith University, Nathan, Queensland, 4111

economic matters. Several of the most populous minorities, including the Tibetans, Uygurs, Kazaks, Mongols, Miao and Koreans, will be taken as examples to illustrate the ways in which economic modernisation favours or disfavours Chinese national integration. Considerable attention will be devoted to how these peoples interrelate with co-nationals or culturally similar nationalities on the other side of national borders. Examples are the Koreans of Jilin and the Turkic minorities of Xinjiang.

In addition, this chapter considers how the minorities have performed economically in comparison with the dominant Han population and the implications for cohesion among the various parts of China, especially the coast and the inland.

This chapter will thus draw attention to some serious problems of national integration. It will also make some evaluation of how the Chinese authorities have coped with these problems and conclude with some discussion of the prospects for Chinese national integration in the coming years.

1. INTRODUCTION

China has fifty-five state-recognised minority nationalities. According to the 1990 census their overall population was 91,200,314, or 8.04 per cent of China's total.[1] Although they are so small a proportion of the total, the absolute figures are nevertheless large if the comparison is with the population of almost any other country. Moreover, the places where they live or form a high or dominant proportion of the local population make up well over half China's total area. From a strategic point of view another factor increasing their significance is that most of China's border areas are minority regions, and some of the borders are extremely sensitive. As one

---

1   The sample census taken on 1 October 1995 showed that the proportion of minority
     nationalities had risen to 8.98 per cent. See Population Grows Slower, 1996, 6. Probably
     the main reason for the rise, a very substantial one for so just over five years, was
     reregistration. See also Mackerras, 1994, 243-4.

contemporary authority has put it, "The importance of the minorities to China's long-term development is disproportionate to their population" (Gladney, 1994, 185).

Many of the minorities are very similar ethnically and culturally to the Han. These include the Zhuang, the most populous of all the minorities, living in China's southwest, especially in Guangxi which borders Vietnam. Others are extremely different both from the dominant Han and from each other, examples including the Tibetans and the Uygurs, living respectively in China's far southwest and northwest. While many of the minorities are very well integrated with the Han ethnically, socially and politically, others have shown secessionist tendencies, especially the Tibetans and Uygurs. Since the 1980s, there has been a general rise of national consciousness among virtually all the nationalities, although some much more than others, again with the Tibetans and Uygurs at the leading end of the spectrum (Mackerras, 1995, 208-10).

This chapter will take up a few questions concerning China's minority economies in the 1990s. It will focus some attention on various kinds of inequalities relating to the minorities, including both those between the dominant Han people and those of the minorities in general. In addition, the chapter will address a related but yet distinct question: does the current economic modernisation of China act as an integrating force among the minorities of China? Given the importance of both modernisation and national integration and cohesion for contemporary China, this is a question of considerable moment, and can only gain in significance as China enters the twenty-first century.

The policy of the Chinese government towards the minorities is autonomy. This concept of autonomy has been defined quite specifically in the 1982 Chinese Constitution, as well as in the Law on Regional Autonomy for Minority Nationalities, adopted on 31 May 1984. Among the essential points are that the government leaders of the autonomous places must belong to the particular nationality exercising autonomy and that each should have the right to use its own language in governmental, legal processes. However, the Chinese notion of autonomy does not allow for any possibilities of secession, which is always suppressed firmly whenever and wherever it occurs.[2] In the 1980s and 1990s the most serious cases of such secessionism were in Tibet in 1987 and 1989 and in Xinjiang in 1990.

2. HAN-MINORITY ECONOMIC INEQUALITIES

It is not my intention in this chapter to give an overall analysis of economic performance in China's minority areas, a task attempted elsewhere.[3] The overall picture is of impressive growth in many ways, but with serious problems remaining, some of them getting worse as a result of economic growth. In the pastoral areas, according to one recent study, "the long-standing threat of the loss of natural pastures has become progressively more serious" as the number of sheep has increased, becoming "the most obvious constraint to further progress" (Longworth and Williamson, 1993, 336).

One issue for the minority economies has been widening inequalities by comparison with the Han areas. The minority areas began from a generally much lower base than the Han both when the Chinese Communist Party (CCP) came to power in 1949 and when the Cultural Revolution ended in 1976. In addition, the rates of growth have almost always been higher in the Han than the minority areas.

In economic terms the policy of the government is to give preferential treatment to the minority areas, the main reason being to allow them the opportunity of closing the widening gap. An official update on human rights in China, dated December 1995, gives some specific examples of this policy.

---

2   The issues of autonomy are discussed in range of works, in greatest detail in Mackerras, 1994, 145-66 and Heberer, 1989, especially 40-53.

3   Among accounts of the minority economies are Mackerras, 1994, 198-232 and Longworth and Williamson, 1993, which deals in enormous detail with the pastoral regions.

In December 1991 the State Council issued a document requesting governments at all levels to increase input to the autonomous areas and to speed up the aid scheme whereby economically developed areas give aid to ethnic minority areas. It required banks at all levels to give appropriate preferential treatment to autonomous areas in terms of loans for projects of investment in fixed assets. More funds and materials allocated for assisting poor areas should be directed to poor ethnic minority areas. (Information Office, 1996, 22-23.)

A range of statistics have been published which assist in making comparisons between the Han and minority areas. The following table shows rates of growth relevant to the 1990s in the agricultural, industrial and education sectors comparing China as a whole with the nationality areas.

The figures suggest that for agriculture the minority growth rates are very slightly higher than the Han. Since most of the minority areas are still dominated by agricultural or pastoral production, this is an important factor. But the clear implication is that the kinds of modernised economic pursuits characteristic of cities are still rather or very backward. It is in the field of industry that the Han areas dominate in the field of growth rates. Moreover, it is likely that the disparities between Han and minority are actually greater than the statistics show for industry, because of a tendency for Han people to dominate industry even in minority areas.

It should be noted that the education enrolment figures specify that the students are members of a minority nationality, whereas the agriculture and industry figures are specific to minority areas, not to nationality. The figures for education show that in the 1990s there has been actually a *greater* rate of

Table 13.1: Selected Growth Rates in the Chinese Economy[4]

Item	1994 as percentage of 1990	1994 as percentage of 1993	Average percentage increase 1986-94
Total National Agricultural Output Value	129.2	108.6	5.6
Total Agricultural Output Value in Nationality Areas	128.9	107.6	5.9
Total National Industrial Output Value	236.3	126.1	17.9
Total Industrial Output Value in Nationality Areas	182.6	113.2	14.0
National Primary School Enrolments	104.7	103.2	-0.5
Primary School Enrolments of Minorities	107.5	100.8	2.1
National Regular Secondary School Enrolments	108.6	105.1	0.6
Secondary School Enrolments of Minorities	117.2	103.4	5.0

4   The figures come from State Statistical Bureau, 1995, 20-6, 48.

increase among the minorities at both primary and secondary levels. This has been due both to government policy and also to the recently developed charity program called Project Hope (*Xiwang gongcheng*), designed to provide education to the children of impoverished families,[5] and to United Nations funding. According to my travels in minority areas in many parts of China in the 1990s, these efforts have made substantial differences in the educational levels of the minorities. It hardly needs emphasis that rising educational standards not only assist, but are even a prerequisite for a modernising economy, especially in the cities.

These affirmative action efforts should be seen against the background of a considerably higher illiteracy rate overall among the minorities than the Han. For instance, the 1982 census, which counted semi-literates and illiterates as those persons twelve years of age and over who could read or write very little or not at all, then the rate of semi-literacy and illiteracy for all China was 31.87 per cent in 1982, while the corresponding rate among the minority nationalities was 42.54 per cent (Research Institute, 1991, 62, 67-68).

Another factor is that illiteracy is much more pronounced in rural areas, precisely those where the great majority of minorities lives, with more than 90 per cent of China's illiterate people living in the countryside in 1993. Moreover, this figure disguises the fact that the standard for literacy it measures is actually different in the urban and rural district. According to these 1993 figures, knowledge of 2,000 characters is necessary to count as literate in the cities, but only 1,500 in the countryside (*Guangming*, 1994).

Educational authorities have made some attempts in recent years to come to grips with the serious shortage of teachers among the minorities, especially

---

5   The main donors to Project Hope are the Chinese themselves, including those in Hong Kong, and the main beneficiaries are poverty-stricken children in China. One part of the Project allows individual people in China, including foreigners, to sponsor specific children by paying for their education. Project Hope encompasses both boys and girls, while the similar Spring Bud Project (*Chunlei gongcheng*) is open only to girls.

those belonging to the minorities themselves. For example, Northwest Normal University in Gansu Province set up a teacher training centre especially to cater for people of minority nationalities in 1985 and another such centre for Tibetans. From 1978 to 1994 it trained nearly 5,000 Han and minority teachers for the minority regions of western China, including China's first Tibetan holder of the Ph.D. degree (NCNA, 1994).

One of the areas of inequality which the education system exemplifies is that between male and female, and it is especially pronounced among the minorities. In 1993, the illiteracy rate among all women aged 15 and over in China was 30 per cent, as against 15.5 per cent for the total population, the latter figure having fallen from 16.1 in 1990. In 1992 the number of girls going to school was lower than boys, with 2.1 million girl absentees from school, or two-thirds of all child absentees. Absenteeism was especially serious among girls in the more remote western and southern provinces of Tibet, Gansu, Ningxia, Qinghai and Guizhou, all of them areas where minority peoples are much more populous than the average for China.

Chinese authorities plan to wipe out illiteracy among people aged 15 to 40 by the year 2000. To do this it will need to educate three million younger women a year, a formidable although not necessarily impossible task. One way that is planned is to establish more informal methods of educating women, including half-day classes and boarding schools, as well as allowing pupils to work in the fields for part of the day (*Guangming*, 1994). These methods will be appropriate for minority populations, because among the great majority of them, women traditionally take on just as much rural labour as men, and in most cases more (Mackerras, 1994, 108-9).

3. INEQUALITIES AMONG THE MINORITIES

As well as inequalities between Han and minority, including subsets such as gender inequities, there are considerable variations among the minority areas themselves. The Koreans have always been particularly progressive economically, indeed in some ways the most of any Chinese nationality, including the Han. On the other hand, among the most populous minorities, the Tibetans are traditionally less concerned about economic matters and more so about religious, with a slower and weaker economy. However, this is beginning to change in the 1990s.

Table 13.2 shows some 1993 official figures for a few of the main nationality areas in China.

Table 13.2: Some 1993 Figures for the Nationality Areas[6]

Nationality Area	1993 Population	Proportion Minority (per cent)	Total Industrial and Agricultural Value per person (RMB *Yuan*)
Tibet AR	2 288 800	98.0	1 208
Ningxia Hui AR	4 908 600	33.8	3 138
Xinjiang Uygur AR	16 052 600	61.9	4 028
Yanbian Korean AP (Jilin)	2 138 400	42.9	4 249
Southeast Guizhou Miao and Dong AP (Guizhou)	3 791 400	74.9	1 113
Xishuangbanna Dai AP (Yunnan)	798 100	74.1	2 155
Nujiang Lisu AP (Yunnan)	446 700	92.1	996
Diqing Tibetan AP (Yunnan)	321 300	83.9	1 282
Yushu Tibetan AP (Qinghai)	232 900	97.0	826
Kizilsu Kirgiz AP (Xinjiang)	397 800	94.9	1 053
Yili Kazak AP (Xinjiang)	3 496 200	55.4	2 182

6   These figures are based on State Nationalities Commission, 1994, 138-41.

What becomes clear from these figures, which measure agricultural and pastoral value in a few selected minority areas, is just how great the disparities among the nationalities themselves. The figures do not show just how much of the value comes from the labour invested by the minorities themselves, but the population proportions do cast light on the extent to which the relevant areas are dominated by minority or Han.

Clearly the figures suggest that the Koreans stand at the top in terms of agricultural value, with the Uygurs and possibly one or two peoples of Xinjiang a little below. At the lower end of the scale are the Tibetans and the Lisu of Yunnan. Examples of peoples in the median position include the Kazaks of Xinjiang and the Dai of Yunnan.

The reasons for this diversity are very complex and detail is outside the scope of this chapter. However, there are geographical, historical and cultural factors, and probably political as well. Among the reasons why the Koreans stand at the top is the more fertile land they occupy. They are among the few nationalities in China whose territory includes low-flying fertile plains suitable for agriculture. Although the Japanese occupation of their land was generally negative and cruel, it did promote economic development to an extent greater than almost any other in China. By tradition the Koreans have laid great emphasis on education, in part because of the strength of Confucianism among them, and their history in the last century has strengthened their dedication to education. Many people I interviewed in Yanbian emphasised how strong was the Koreans' insistence on education, and the 1990 census showed their rate of illiteracy and semi-literacy at only 7 per cent (Chen, 1993, 15), by far the lowest of the most populous nationalities, including the Han. The same count showed that 822.54 per thousand of Koreans had graduated from primary school or higher, this being by far the highest of any nationality in China (State Statistical Bureau, 1993, 91-92).

Similar reasons explain why the Uygurs do comparatively well. Their Muslim religion encourages hard work and a dedicated attitude to labour. Although parts of Xinjiang are mountainous and much is desert, there are also quite good plains, some of them very good agriculture or pasture land. The rule of Sheng Shicai in the 1930s is nowadays excoriated by Uygurs and others in Xinjiang, but in my opinion he does deserve credit for some of the economic development found in Xinjiang.[7]

In the 1990s, especially since the fall of the Soviet Union at the end of 1991, most of the nationalities of Xinjiang have given a good deal of attention to developing good trading relations to conationals on the other side of the border. The central government has been very keen to strengthen good political relations with the newly independent states of Central Asia which once belonged to the Soviet Union. Kazak trade with Kazakstan and Kirgiz with Kyrgyzstan have picked up substantially, especially the former. On the other hand, the border between Tajikistan and the Tajik area of China remained closed when I visited the area in October 1994, due to severe political turmoil in Tajikistan, amounting at times to civil war, which had begun in 1991 at about the time the country declared its independence of the Soviet Union on 9 September that year.[8]

The territory of the minorities in Yunnan is extremely mountainous. Modernisation has hardly begun in the rural productive methods of many, including the Lisu. The Dai of the same province do have the benefit of some plains, where agriculture is easier and more productive. The Dai are the same ethnically as the Shan of Burma and the Thai of Thailand. Trade along the borders between Yunnan and Burma has increased enormously over the last few years, another reason why the economy of the Dai, who inhabit extensive territory along that border, has improved over that period.

The Tibetans deserve more detailed treatment. This is because of their enormous political sensitivity and their unique and powerful cultural tradition.

---

7   For some comments on Sheng Shicai's performance in the realm of education, and current reaction, see Mackerras, 1995, 44-45.

8   For an account of the first years of Tajikistan as an independent country see Atkin, 1994, 211-31.

For years economic and educational levels remained pitifully low, while the traditional education system was geared far more towards religious devotion than economic development (Mackerras, 1995, 40-43). For various reasons secessionism has been stronger among the Tibetans than any other of China's minorities, a factor diluting enthusiasm for economic growth. Although the standard of living has risen quite a bit over the years of CCP rule in Tibet, the fact is that traditional Tibetan dedication to a rather fatalist form of Buddhism and hatred for the Han are among reasons why Tibet's economy has been notable for its slow growth by comparison with other populous nationalities in China.

After very slow progress in the early 1990s, the Tibetan economy has definitely picked up in the mid-1990s. The Chinese government has obviously decided to do something drastic about the economic situation there, in the hope of integrating Tibet better into China and for fear of facing drastic political consequences. It inaugurated 62 construction projects, including mainly infrastructure, such as water supply, electricity, roads, power, telecommunications, schools and hospitals. In July 1994 the Central Government decided that the rest of China should give help to Tibet with these projects (Information Office, 1995, 23). Gyaincain Norbu, Chairman of the Tibet Autonomous Region, claimed at a press conference in Beijing on 8 March 1996 that 42 of these 62 were already completed, and that the remainder would follow suit by the end of the same year. Policies adopted in the 1990s or of longer standing aimed at accelerating economic growth in Tibet include a flexible and light taxation system, exemption from taxation for the region's agriculture and township industries, refunding some taxes, price subsidies, and giving priority to Tibet in central governmental appropriations (Chen and Yin, 1996, 32).

How much of this has translated into reality? At his March 1996 news conference Gyaincain Norbu gave a very rosy picture of developments so far and even more for the future. He noted that the average annual income of urban dwellers in Tibet has reached 4,000 yuan, exceeding the national average, figures confirmed by the State Statistical Bureau.[9] Gyaincain Norbu claimed that Tibet would achieve a 10 per cent annual economic growth rate over the next 15 years, that Tibet would be freed of poverty in the next five years, and most of its farmers and herdsmen would lead a fairly comfortable life by the year 2010. He said that during the Ninth Five-Year Plan period (1996-2000) Tibet's annual gross product would reach ¥10.8 billion, quadrupling the 1980 figure (Tibet, 1996, 5). The growth rates would be about equal to China's national average over the last decade and more and would be both very high and unlikely, although not impossible.

The claim of freeing Tibet from poverty within five years from 1996 is of course highly laudable but on the basis of what I have seen in Tibet it would be impossible unless the poverty level were placed so low as to be meaningless. Although the figures which Gyaincain Norbu gives for urban living standards are impressive, it should be noted that the cities are precisely where most of the non-Tibetans live, especially the Han and the Hui. The 1993 figures given above suggest that rural Tibet is still extremely poor. Moreover, figures for Tibet as a whole, not just the urban areas, suggest that the income per capita there were only 51.68 per cent of the Chinese national average, as compared with 68.25 per cent in 1978 and 66.02 in 1989 (Dawson, 1996, 71). What this indicates is that the rural areas of Tibet have declined significantly relative to the country as a whole in the 1990s, although not in absolute terms. However, it is quite possible that rural living standards will improve as the flow-on from the intensive economic investment itself.

The year 1993 was stipulated as Tibetan Education Year. According to an article in the *People's Daily* (*Rr* 1994) the year forced the government in Tibet to fast-track education there and to pump considerable sums of money into it, as well as seeking funds from Project Hope and encouraging better off private individuals to invest some money in education. Over the following

9   According to State Statistical Bureau, 1995, 266, the annual real income of urban households in Tibet was ¥4,025.04 in 1994, the national average being ¥3,402.31.

two years, a total of 523 new schools were built, with an additional 50,000 pupils enrolled, with the enrolment rate for school-age children rising to 67 per cent. Local education authorities were asked to develop plans and implement concrete measures to bring about compulsory education. It hardly needs to be added that this thrust towards greater education includes a strong component of pressure to make students willing to stay within the PRC and avoid the separatist tendencies for which Tibet has become known in the last few years.

The question of inequalities among the minorities has been given a good deal of attention by China authorities. In June 1995 there was a major conference on disparities between the minority nationality districts and the eastern seaboard. Some 127 cadres from nationality regions all over the country took part. A survey was taken on their views (Hu, 1995, 33). Among its major findings were the following:

- 98.2 per cent believed that the disparities between the economies of the minority nationality regions and the eastern seaboard had got wider since the 1980s;
- 89.1 per cent of the cadres believed the disparities excessive, only 10 per cent normal;
- 85 per cent expected the disparities to continue widening over the next decade, while only 11.8 per cent thought they would diminish;
- 93.5 per cent believed the government should play a leading role in solving the problem of disparities;
- 40.6 per cent believed that, compared with the eastern seaboard, the marketisation of the minority nationality regions was sluggish while 56.6 per cent believed it was very sluggish;
- 89 per cent believed that main responsibility for universalising education by the year 2000 lay with the central government, only 11 per cent specifying reliance on Project Hope; and

- 62.2 per cent believed the disparities were creating a serious impact on relations among the nationalities, 35.1 per cent an impact and only 2.7 per cent no impact (Hu, 1995, 34-5).

Nearly all the cadres, that is 95.2 per cent, saw the issue of disparities as essentially a question of development. The Conference's major conclusion could be summed up as follows:

The problem of nationalities is essentially that the development of the minority nationalities is inadequate, and will remain relatively backward over a long period. Because of this, the first way out for solving the nationalities problem is to help and support the minority nationality regions to accelerate their economic development... Just as some leaders have said, economic backwardness begets further backwardness, and eventually affects social stability; but economic development can bring with it further development, which is favourable to social stability (Hu, 1995, 35).

4. Conclusion: Identity, Modernisation And Integration?

What appears to emerge from the above material is that the disparities between the Han and minority areas, as well as among the minority areas themselves, have widened in the 1990s at the same time as the economy has grown. The government is aware of this tendency and is trying to counter the trend by injecting money and personnel into the minority areas, by strengthening the allocation to them of a preferential or "affirmative action" policy. Once again Tibet has received even more preferences than the other areas. The government is aware that the cost of ever widening disparities could easily be social instability and unrest in the minority areas, especially in Tibet and Xinjiang.

It is also clear that China has indeed put a great deal of effort in the 1990s to developing the economy in the minority areas. It has done this through an infusion of funds and exerting itself to enhance the education system to raise the skills of the minorities in human resource terms and to integrate the country from a political point of view. Not surprisingly a significant proportion of the effort has been invested in Tibet. the reason for that is that Tibet is the most sensitive minority area of China politically, the one where secessionist tendencies are strongest and most obvious, and have the greatest international support, and where the economy has traditionally been most backward by comparison with most other minority areas, let alone the Han areas.

The big questions to emerge are: what chance of success does the Chinese government have in solving either of these two apparently interrelated questions, namely disparities and secessionist tendencies. The evidence suggests that it cannot solve either, but has a good chance at least of coping with the second.

The disparities between the minorities and Han have tended to widen, simply because both are doing quite well, but the minorities from a considerably lower base and not as well as the Han, anyway. The policy of affirmative action might help to assuage the disparities, by making them less serious than they would be without it, but the only way of truly solving them is by holding the advanced ones back. This was what Mao's government did in effect and it failed hopelessly. There is absolutely no possibility that the present government would repeat such a mistake in the foreseeable future. My suspicion is that the cadres cited above from the June 1995 Conference are right in their perceptions: government intervention will lessen the effects of the market, but they will not solve the problems. The basically free economy which now prevails in most parts of China, including most of the minority areas, is the only viable option today. The inequalities will probably result in a degree of social instability.

But the question is how much? This brings us to the second, and more important, question, the political one.

What frightened the government into taking action concerning the minorities was basically two secessionist uprisings. One occurred in the Tibetan capital Lhasa in March 1989, on the thirtieth anniversary of the 1959 rebellion which forced the Dalai Lama to flee to India. The uprising drove the central government to send troop reinforcements to Tibet and to declare martial law on 7 March 1989, the first time this had ever happened in the history of the PRC, and it was not lifted for over a year. The second occurred in Akto County in southern Xinjiang in April 1990. Over two days, secessionist forces battled Chinese government troops. The result was a devastating defeat for the former, with their leader being among the people killed. At the same time, Xinjiang television stations showed footage from the uprising, including the defeated but defiant secessionists. Sources in nearby Kaxgar told me, during my visit there in 1994, that ordinary people had been cowed by seeing the footage but nevertheless reacted to the secessionists with both sympathy and admiration for their courage in taking on the overwhelmingly more powerful Chinese forces.

Since these two events, there have been further incidents in Tibet and Xinjiang. In Lhasa there were anti-government demonstrations late in May 1993, especially on 24 May when up to 3,000 Tibetans rioted (Clashes in Lhasa, 1993, 23202). On 17 June 1993 two bombs exploded in the Oasis Hotel in Kaxgar which succeeded in seriously damaging the building and killing three people, a separatist group claiming responsibility for the explosion (Gladney, 1994, 183). In May 1996 the official press both in Xinjiang and Tibet called for increased crackdowns on armed terrorism carried out on behalf of secessionism. In the case of Tibet, the call was prompted by clergy-led demonstrations earlier the same month which had followed local officials' attempts to ban the display of pictures of the Dalai Lama in temples (CND, 1996, 60).

Reports have also persisted of disturbances in Muslim areas of China outside Xinjiang. In the summer of 1993, unrest followed the publication in Sichuan of a book from Taiwan which showed a pig near a mosque. In February 1994 a court in Ningxia handed down stiff sentences on twenty people for organising gang fights which had left nearly fifty people dead since 1992. In May 1993, the central government even sent in the People's Armed Police to suppress such riots, as a result of which twenty people were killed. In the middle of 1994, the Ningxia government acted to reduce Muslim influence in politics and social affairs. In defense of this action the head of the region's Religious Affairs Bureau argued that some clerics, acting "under the cover of religion", had been "unduly meddling in education, marriage and family planning" (AFP, 1994).

What is most striking is that most of these disturbances are fundamentally social. The 1993 demonstrations in Tibet began as a protest against inflation (Clashes in Lhasa, 1993, 23202). Despite some commentary in the Western press at the time, my sources during visits to various Muslim areas of China in 1993 and 1995 suggested most strongly that secessionism was totally peripheral to the Ningxia riots.

At the same time, it is very clear that in both Xinjiang and Tibet religious issues have become bound up with political, separatism being a function of religious devotion. The 1996 reports that authorities are accusing clergies and other religious followers of armed terrorism can only be a cause for concern. They suggest that the social and political problems are both long-term in those two parts of China.

Authorities have improved their methods of handling riots, at least by comparison with 1989. During the demonstrations of 24 May 1993 police "kept their distance" until "slogans changed into calls for Tibetan independence" and even then used tear gas, not lethal weapons, to disperse the crowds (Clashes in Lhasa, 1993, 23202). In 1987 and 1989 not even the Chinese were denying that some people were killed. But in 1993 and 1996 the number of confirmed deaths was much smaller. In addition, Chinese authorities are trying to avoid social problems through attempts at showing sensitivity towards the religiously dedicated minorities. In April 1996 they decided against screening the Australian film *Babe* in China, in which the star is a talking pig; it was reported that the reason may have been fear of upsetting the Muslims (Hutcheon, 1996).

In 1995, when serious disturbances in Tibet itself were predicted over the Chinese acceptance of the Tashilhunpo Monastery's designation of the Eleventh Incarnation of the Panchen Lama in preference to the Dalai Lama's. Most of the argumentation about Chinese iniquity in the affair took place outside China, and especially outside Tibet. Inside, serious consequences were predicted by the Dalai Lama's supporters but never eventuated.[10] The Dalai Lama has been saying for years that the Chinese are trying to destroy Tibetan culture. What is happening instead, according to my experiences in various Tibetan areas of China, is that Tibetan identity and culture are on the rise. Indeed, I have argued elsewhere that the identities of virtually all the minorities have increased over the last decade and more in China (see Mackerras, 1995). Although nationalities with strong clergies, such as the Tibetans and the Muslim minorities, are preeminent in this factor of increased national consciousness, they are certainly not the only ones.

So given this tendency towards social instability and a rise in minority consciousness, as well as an apparent rise in secessionist activity in Xinjiang and Tibet, should we conclude that China faces disintegration? And what is the effect of modernisation? Does it hinder or assist this process? Are the cadres of the June 1995 Conference right to assert that economic development helps "the unity of the nationalities"?

The answer to that question is not at all easy. In some respects economic development has assisted stability and national integration. It has given many members of the minorities, even most in all but a few of the nationalities, a stake in China's development. The rise in the standard of living inevitably makes most people less dissatisfied with the political situation in which they

---

10   For an account of the controversy over the enthronement of the Eleventh Panchen Lama, written essentially from the Dalai Lama's point of view, see Powers, 1996, pp. 4-11. This article argues that China's motivation in choosing its own candidate as the Eleventh Panchen Lama is to control the selection of the successor to the present Fourteenth Dalai Lama when he dies, thus leaving it with compliant people in both top positions (p. 11). The article claims that, fearing a public outcry over their choice of Panchen Lama, the Chinese leaders "moved quickly to prevent opposition" (p. 8).

find themselves. As one Mongol writer, commenting on his own people but with much more general application, has stated: "Mr Deng's economic strategy has outmanoeuvred ethnic consciousness and nationalism" (Naran Bilik, 1996, 10). In the last few years, the improvements in the economic lot of most Chinese nationalities has been considerably greater than most conationals on the other sides of borders. Illustrative examples would include the Koreans, the Mongols, the Tajiks, the Kirgiz and even the Kazaks. It is not obvious that those countries which have split apart have benefited from the experience economically, and in some cases the lessons are profoundly negative. Tajikistan, which borders the Tajik area of China and is the heartland of the Tajiks, has been in a state of civil war for much of the period since 1991. A BBC report, broadcast over Australia's Radio National on 18 April 1996, claimed that food shortages had reached critical proportions in parts of Tajikistan, with outright starvation threatening.

There are respects, however, in which the opposite case could be made, in other words that economic modernisation assists secessionism. By educating leaders countries such as China may actually be assisting their enemy. Education given to Tibetans may have the effect of integrating Tibet into China in some ways, but it may also train some Tibetans anxious to give leadership to the creation of their own independent homeland. The increasing flow of young Tibetan men into monasteries could easily end up providing a core of leaders for Tibetan independence. Certainly the Chinese authorities are worried about this possibility, to judge from their statements on the direction of Tibetan education.

One such was part of a speech by Tibet Chairman Gyaincain Norbu at the Fifth Regional Meeting on Education on 26 October 1994. He said:

> We must educate students to clearly understand the political face
> of Dalai and his clique, as well as the essential point of our struggle
> against the Dalai clique; namely, it is not a matter of religious belief
> or autonomy, but a matter of safeguarding the unification of the
> motherland and opposing splittism, and its nature is a struggle

between us and an enemy. We must educate students to have a profound understanding that Tibet is an inalienable part of China and that the principle - "minority nationalities are inseparable from the Han nationality and vice versa" - is the foundation stone for the prosperity and powerfulness of the whole Chinese nation as well as the objective necessity for and inevitable trend of economic and social development, unity among nationalities and their progress (Gyaincain Norbu, 1994).

What he is saying is that further and more intensive training in seeing the virtues of economic growth, as part of the People's Republic of China, with a rising standard of living, including better health, more comfortable housing and greater availability of consumer goods and entertainment from outside Tibet, will tend to quieten the desire of many Tibetans for the Dalai Lama's rule, as long as their traditional culture and religion are to be tolerated to a certain extent. He may well be right. It is extremely doubtful if anything could help secessionism in Tibet or Xinjiang more than a major slowdown in economic growth or a major decline in living standards.

What does this tell us about the future of China as a united country within its current boundaries? Although conditions in the minority areas are relevant to the question, the question of Chinese integration or disintegration is fundamentally one depending on the central Chinese government and international developments. In my judgement, while the central government remains reasonably strong, its armies would have no difficulty in suppressing any social disruption or secessionism which might occur in Tibet or Xinjiang. The only possibility for either place to secede from China would be the collapse of the central Chinese government and massive international support, including military aid, for Tibetan or East Turkestan independence from China.

The reason why the countries bordering China, such as Kazakhstan, Tajikistan and Kyrgyzstan, became independent was because the Soviet Union split apart under circumstances showing economic decline. There is a tendency towards economic autonomy of the richer regions in China at the moment, but they are not such as to lead to political or military fragmentation of the sort which will tear the country apart in the foreseeable future. Although Deng Xiaoping cannot live long, the trends in the mid-1990s are for Jiang Zemin to consolidate his leadership. Social disruptions, due in part to widening inequalities, are occurring not only in the minority areas, but elsewhere as well. They are no more likely to tear China apart than are similar developments in the United States or elsewhere.

One of the ways China has tried to counter threats to its unity is by strengthening its friendly relations with its neighbours to the west, in particular those Central Asian states which once belonged to the Soviet Union. The peoples of the three states of Kazakhstan, Kyrgyzstan and Tajikistan are Muslims, which poses a threat to China if Muslim extremists were able to stir up separatist trouble in Xinjiang. As of 1996, all these three countries and Russia are very enthusiastic to maintain friendly relations with China, and on 26 April the Presidents of China, Russia, Kazakhstan, Kyrgyzstan and Tajikistan signed an agreement in Shanghai aimed at building mutual trust in military affairs along their borders, representing a step towards resolving border problems.

And what of the question of foreign intervention in China? The Chinese government appears to me to have become convinced that the United States wants the overthrow of the CCP and China to follow the Soviet Union into disintegration. Their statements include numerous slighting references to American interference in China's internal affairs. It was the question of national unity which lay at the heart of the Chinese military exercises over Taiwan in March 1996.

There is a group within the American government which expects and hopes for the disintegration of China, for the very simple reason that it does not welcome the economic and political challenge which a rising China poses in the Eastern Asian region. There is known to be very strong support for the Dalai Lama both among the American public and within the American Congress. But that is a very different matter from that kind of formal and large-scale military intervention which would be necessary for Tibetan or Xinjiang independence to succeed unless the central Chinese government suffered total collapse.

What would be the impact on Chinese unity were Taiwan formally to declare itself independent? Would such an event signal the secession of Tibet, Xinjiang and Inner Mongolia from China? Many have raised the possibility of Chinese military intervention to thwart Taiwanese independence and American military response on Taiwan's side. Such a possibility is well beyond the scope of this chapter, and I say only that I doubt very much that China will recognise Taiwanese independence in the foreseeable future. On the question of whether Taiwan's declaration of independence would lead to the withdrawal from China of Tibet and other territories, I suspect that China would cling even more strongly than ever to preserve its view of its sovereignty. A war leading to a general disintegration in China and possibly other parts of East Asia is not out of the question but does not appear at all likely.

A far more probable scenario is for the rise of China to continue. Social and political tensions are not going to decline, let alone disappear. But they are not likely to lead to China's overall disintegration. Rather, I suspect that, even if the CCP is overthrown within the next decade, the territory which now makes up the People's Republic of China will remain politically united for the foreseeable future. If history is any guide, a fragmentation would be followed by a reintegration later on. China has a far longer and stronger history of unity than any other continental country in the world, a tradition which is likely to continue to weigh heavily for the indefinite future.

REFERENCES

Agence France Press (AFP) English Wire, 17 July 1994, in *China News Digest Europe/Pacific Section*, 1 August 1994, item 5. *China News Digest* is published several times weekly on the Internet.

Atkin, Muriel (1994) "The Politics of Polarisation in Tajikistan", pp. 211-31 in Hafeez, Malik (ed.), *Central Asia, Its Strategic Importance and Future Prospects*, St Martin's Press, New York.

Chen, Hanchang and Yin, Qingyan (1996) "Historical Jump of Tibetans' Human Rights", *Beijing Review*, 39 (special issue) (January), 30-34.

Chen, Qiuping (1993) "Progress Seen in Minority Population", *Beijing Review*, 36(29) (19-25 July): 14-17.

China News Digest (CND), Global News, no. GL96-068, 20 May 1996.

Clashes in Lhasa (1993) *Asian Recorder*, 39(25) (18-24 June), 23202.

Dawson, Bonnie, comp. (1996) "Provincial China: statistics, The 1995 Statistical Yearbook in Provincial Perspective", *Provincial China, A Research Newsletter*, 1 (March), 34-73.

Gladney, Dru C. (1994) "Ethnic Identity in China: The New Politics of Difference", in Joseph, William A. (ed.), *China Briefing, 1994*, Westview Press, Boulder, San Francisco, Oxford, pp. 171-92.

Guangming ribao (*Guangming Daily*), 23 November 1994.

Gyaincain Norbu, in *Xizang ribao* (*Tibet Daily*), Lhasa, 30 October 1994.

Heberer, Thomas (1989) *China and Its National Minorities, Autonomy or Assimilation?* M.E. Sharpe, Armonk, N.Y. and London, England.

Hu Angang (1995) Tebie guancha - Guanzhu zhongxi bu, Minzu diqu, chaju daodi you duodao? (Special survey - solicitude for the Central West, Just how big are the disparities in the nationality areas?), *Minzu tuanjie* (*Ethnic Unity*) 294 (10 November), 32-6.

Hutcheon, Stephen (1996) in *Sydney Morning Herald*, 9 April.

Information Office of the State Council of the People's Republic of China (1996) The progress of human rights in China, *Beijing Review*, 39 (special issue) (January), 4-29.

Longworth, John W. and Williamson, Gregory J. (1993) *China's Pastoral Region, Sheep and Wool, Minority Nationalities, Rangeland Degradation and Sustainable Development*, CAB International, Oxford.

Mackerras, Colin (1994) *China's Minorities. Modernisation and Integration in the Twentieth Century*, Oxford University Press, Hong Kong.

Mackerras, Colin (1995) *China's Minority Cultures, Identities and Integration Since 1912*, Longman Australia, Melbourne, St Martin's Press, New York.

Naran Bilik (1996) "Mongol-Han Relations in a New Configuration of Social Evolution", Paper Presented at the Association of Asian Studies Annual Meeting, held in Honolulu in April 1996.

New China (Xinhua) News Agency (NCNA) (1994), Beijing, in English, 0829 GMT, 2 November.

Population Grows Slower (1996) *Beijing Review*, 39 (11) (11-17 March), 6.

Powers, John (1996) "Opiate of the Atheists? The Panchen Lama Controversy", *The Asia-Pacific Magazine*, 1(1) (April), 4-11.

Renmin ribao (People's Daily, Rr) (1994) Beijing, in Chinese, 1 November.

Research Institute of All China Women's Federation Research Office of Shaanxi Provincial Women's Federation, comp. (1991) *Zhongguo funü tongji ziliao (1949-1989) (Statistical Material on Chinese Women, 1949-1989)*, Chinese Statistics Press, Beijing.

State Nationalities Affairs Commission Economics Office and State Statistical Bureau National Economy Comprehensive Statistics Office, comp. (1994) *Zhongguo minzu tongji nianjian (1949-1994) (China's Nationalities Statistics Yearbook, 1949-1994)*, Nationalities Press, Beijing.

State Statistical Bureau, comp. (1993) *Zhongguo tongji nianjian 1993* (Zhongguo tongji chubanshe, Beijing, 1993) *(Statistical Yearbook of China 1993)*, China Statistical Publishing House, Beijing.

State Statistical Bureau, People's Republic of China, comp. (1995) *Zhongguo tongji nianjian 1995 (China Statistical Yearbook 1995)*, China Statistical Publishing House, Beijing.

Tibet quickens development (1996) *Beijing Review*, 39(13) (25-31 March), 5.

CHAPTER 14

TOURISM AND THE REGIONAL DEVELOPMENT OF CHINA: ITS ROLE AND THE EXPERIENCE OF YUNNAN

JIE WEN*

ABSTRACT

Despite rapid growth in tourism for almost two decades in China, a regional imbalance has been observed in both demand and supply of tourism with the bulk of tourism skewing toward the 12 coastal localities. Domestic tourism and ecotourism are expected to reduce regional inequality in tourism and provide more economic opportunities for both non-coastal and economically disadvantaged areas containing rich tourism resources. Tourism in Yunnan Province shows significant potential in promoting regional development and conservation of both the natural environment and ethnic culture, especially if the multiplier effect is taken into account. The State Nature Reserve in Xishuangbanna needs to play a more pivotal role in ecotourism promotion. Better management of tourism markets accompanied

* Department of Economics, The University of Queensland, Brisbane 4072, Australia

by efficient coordination of sectors involved and improvement in infrastructure are essential for further expansion of tourism in Yunnan. Links with Southeast Asia promise attractive prospects for Yunnan's share in this tourism market but raise the need for more competitive tourist products and quality control of service.

1. INTRODUCTION

Because of rapid tourism development since 1978, China has become one of the world's most popular tourist destinations. It received 43.7 million inbound tourists in 1994 and earned US$ 7.3 billion in income from international tourism, reaching 2.08 per cent of the world's total tourism receipts, plus Yuan 102.351 billion from domestic tourism (National Tourism Administration of China, 1995). The direct output from its tourism industry accounted for 3.78 per cent of China's total GNP in 1994, and 6.1 per cent of its total export income (National Tourism Administration of China, 1995). However, analysis of both the demand- and supply-side of inbound tourism to China indicates a predominant concentration along the east coast of China, including as generally agreed such 12 localities as Liaoning, Hebei, Beijing, Tianjin, Shandong, Jiangsu, Shanghai, Zhejiang, Fujian, Guangdong, Guangxi, and Hainan, especially in coastal cities, with more imbalance in its regional distribution than the already regionally concentrated general economy (Wen and Tisdell, 1996). So far the contribution of international tourism in promoting economic and social development in the non-coastal and rural regions lags seriously behind it is in the coastal areas of China.

Nevertheless, against the trend of divergence of general economy between the coastal and interior China, international tourism has shown a degree of convergence in regional distribution from the mid-1980s, indicating its potential for promoting economic growth in some inland areas.

This discussion starts from the regional inequality of general economy as well as tourism in China. The trend of regional convergence in tourism is then discussed. As an emerging major tourism destination for domestic tourism and ecotourism, Yunnan Province in southwest China is selected as a case study for analysis to demonstrate the importance of tourism in regional development and decentralisation of economic activities.

2. BACKGROUND ON REGIONAL INEQUALITY OF TOURISM IN CHINA

Inequality in the distribution of both personal income and regional economic welfare between the coastal and inland areas in China, especially in the post-Mao era, has been a focus of multi-disciplined studies (Chen and Fleisher, 1996; Wen and Tisdell, 1996). With growth and decline of regions immediately translated into changes in regional income inequality, regional divergence and convergence in per capita income across regions, usually referring to increase and decrease in regional inequality respectively, thereby tends to occur over time in light of regional dynamics, urbanisation, and growth in service sector. Divergence seems to have occurred since the early 1980s principally as a result of the widening gap separating the high income region, located in the coastal areas, from the poor, even though there is conditional convergence of per capita production across China from 1978 to 1993, but the income differential between the coast and interior is likely to increase in the near term (Chen and Fleisher, 1996). Convergence is conditional on physical investment share, employment growth, human-capital investment, foreign direct investment and coastal location. Other research has shown that regional income in China converged from 1978 to 1984 with the rise in rural productivity, but started to diverge again from around 1984 because the coastal areas grew markedly faster than the interior even though the convergence continued within the coastal localities (Jian et al, 1996).

Classical economic theory assumes that income distribution will correct itself through market forces to reflect the marginal productivity of factors of production. But studies have indicated that this does not always happen

(Kaldor, 1955). A 'steady state' of income distribution which does not reflect marginal productivity can exist as a result of market imperfections, social systems, regional imbalances or other reasons. Hence policies for tourism development may target not only income generation but normative goals of income distribution as well (Lin and Sung, 1984). Rampant regionalism and growing regional economic inequality in China may jeopardise the interests of China as a whole and affect social stability. Decentralisation of economic power and development of non-coastal areas have become major issues in China. Nonetheless, instead of taking such radical steps as stripping privileges from special economic zones as suggested by Hu Angang, an outspoken Chinese economist (McGregor, 1996), at the risk of slowing growth along the coast without necessarily improving performance of the inland, encouraging those industries in which non-coastal areas have a relative economic advantage, may serve as a better solution.

Tourism is regarded as an industry that promotes economic growth in the periphery areas (Weiler and Hall, 1992). However, study into the regional distribution of international tourism in China reveals that the coastal areas obtain a dominant portion of gains from international tourism. Gini ratios are calculated for major economic and tourism indicators.

Table 14.1: Gini Ratios for Selected Economic and Tourism Variables in China, 1995

	GDP	GDP Per Capita	Number of Tourists	Tourism Receipts	Number of Hotel Rooms	Number of Hotel Employees
Gini ratio	0.407	0.311	0.6704	0.7439	0.5204	0.5813

Source: Based on data in National Tourism Administration of China (1996) and SSB (1996)

Often used to measure income inequality, Gini ratio has a value of zero for absolute equality and unity for complete inequality. Analysis of Gini coefficients in Table 14.1 reveals that even though general economic activities are already unevenly distributed in China as indicated by fairly high Gini ratios for GDP and GDP per capita, tourism exhibits an even higher regional disparity. But Gini ratio does not indicate where the concentration is. Lorenz curve analysis reveals a overwhelming concentration of international tourism in the Chinese coastal areas (Wen and Tisdell, 1996). In addition, higher Gini ratios for tourism demand than those for tourism supply combined with higher proportion of the coastal areas in the demand-side variables indicate that coastal areas obtain a larger fraction of tourism receipts compared to the quantity of their inputs than interior areas, and economic gains from tourism are more concentrated on the coastal localities than is the supply of hotel rooms and hotel staff.

Table 14.2 indicates that the distribution of China's economy is significantly biased in favour of the coastal area compared to the inland. When demand-side tourism indicators are examined, the bias is even more marked. Percentages for tourism receipts, hotel income and tourist arrivals are around double that of the population accounted for by the coast and are in excess of the percentage of GDP earned by the coast. Thus, the direct economic impact of inbound tourism to China is to favour the coastal area most markedly (Wen and Tisdell, 1996).

The high concentration of tourism on the coastal areas and their higher economic gains from tourism mean that inland areas are less able to profit from their rich tourism-resources and the efficiency of their hotel operations is lower, leaving them even more disadvantaged than their coastal competitors. Consequently in China international tourism has not necessarily helped the rural areas and inland areas catch up with more developed coastal

Table 14.2: Economic, Demographic, Demand- and Supply-side Indicators for 12 Coastal Regions in China with Comparisons for the Whole of China, 1995

	China Total	Sum of the Twelve Coastal	The Proportion
Socioeconomic indicators:			
GDP	4,558 (Yuan b)	2,661 (Yuan b)	0.584
Population	1,199 (m)	489 (m)	0.408
GDP per capita	3,804 (Yuan)	5438 (Yuan)	1.193
Tourism indicators on the demand side :			
Tourism receipts	7,323 (US$ m)	6,335 (US$ m)	0.865
No. of inbound tourists	16,211,200	13,194,000	0.812
Hotel income	54,830 (Yuan m)	47,788.8 (Yuan m)	0.872
Tourism indicators on the supply side :			
Hotel rooms	486,054	336,907	0.693
Hotels with more than 500 rooms	73	67	0.918
State-owned hotels	2,478	1,534	0.619
No. of hotel employees	868,600	662,800	0.763
No. of travel agencies	3826	2,384	0.623
1st category travel agencies	360	257	0.714

Source: Based on data in National Tourism Administration of China (1996) and SSB (1996)

areas. However, study of the trend of international tourism reveals a decreasing regional concentration for such major tourism variables as tourism receipts, arrivals, hotel rooms and employees since the mid-1980s, as manifested by decreasing Gini ratios for China as a whole, the coastal and inland areas respectively, principally as a result of the growing 'opening up' of China that offers progressively more entry points to the interior, improvement of tourist supply and productivity of tourism industry in the interior, and changes in tourism demand and tourist mix, especially the increasing status of ecotourism. This trend in regional convergence in international tourism is combined with growing domestic tourism, which reached 524 million trips and Yuan 102.4 billion in revenue in 1994 and is more dispersed in China than international tourism (National Tourism Administration of China, 1995), casting more light on the role of tourism in stimulating economic growth in some inland areas and hence contributing to the reduction of regional inequality in China. Careful analysis of the local economic structure, especially the backward and forward linkage of tourism industry, needs to be conducted before targeting tourism as a key industry or growth pole for any economy. Yunnan Province, as an inland destination for ecotourism and domestic tourism, serves as an example of how tourism promotes economic development and contribute to conservation.

3. TOURISM IN YUNNAN PROVINCE

Tourism has been targeted by Yunnan Province since middle 1980s as a leading industry, together with mineral production, tobacco and forestry industries, in the economic development in Yunnan. Tourist arrivals in Yunnan have been increasing on average by 30 per cent annually since 1978 (Wen, 1996). In 1994, overseas arrivals in Yunnan reached 522,059, or 39 times that in 1979. Receipts from international tourism totalled US$ 124.4 million in 1994, a 20 per cent increase over that in 1993, and Yuan 3.1 billion was received from Chinese travellers (Travel & Tourism Bureau of Yunnan Province, 1995). There were more than 1,000 tourist enterprises in Yunnan at the end of 1994, with fixed assets of Yuan three billion and 60,000 employees. With 258 travel agencies and 171 hotels till 1994, Yunnan's goal for international tourism is to receive over one million arrivals and to attain receipts of US$ 300 million in the year 2000 (Travel & Tourism Bureau of Yunnan Province, 1995).

Yunnan has become a major tourist destination in China specialising in tourism based on nature and ethnic cultures. Compared with other provinces in China promoting city-based tourism, tourism in Yunnan is more scattered spatially. Tourism operations in Yunnan are less affected by seasonality and attract more diversified clients from both China and abroad than other parts of China. Ecotourism shows undoubtedly great potential for further development. Figure 14.1: shows the location of major tourist centres in Yunnan, namely Kunming, Dali, Lijiang and Xishuangbanna.

3.1 Spatial and seasonal distribution of tourism in Yunnan

Singled out in 1991 by the State Council of China for quick tourism development, Yunnan is endowed with diversified tourism resources, providing four of the 14 special tourism itineraries in China designated by the state. The spatial distribution of tourist resource is relatively more scattered compared with other major tourist destinations in China.

Figure 14.1: Major Tourist Destinations in Yunnan

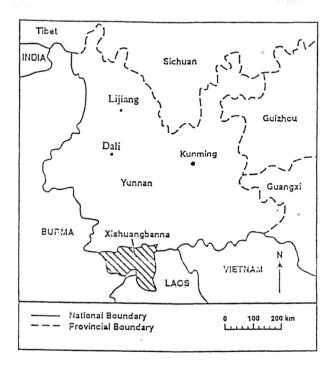

Table 14.3 compares both economic and tourist indicators for four major tourist areas in Yunnan in 1994. Kunming is the economic and political centre of Yunnan and the most popular tourist destination in this province. Nonetheless, Dali, Lijiang and Xishuangbanna are attractive for both overseas and Chinese tourists. The average length of stay of tourists in these centres is longer than that in Kunming, and there is great potential for further tourism growth in these three areas with improvement in transportation, given the increasing demand for ecotourism. Domestic tourism in northeast and southeast Yunnan is also on the increase. Instead of concentrating tourism in the capital city as it is common in other provinces (Wen and Tisdell, 1996), Yunnan is able to present at least four major tourism centres at Kunming,

Dali, Lijiang, and Xishuangbanna with both natural and cultural attractions, making its tourism relatively more decentralised throughout the province. Therefore tourism in Yunnan contributes more economic benefits to areas outside the central city than in other provinces where usually only the capital cities serve as a major attraction.

The multi-centred distribution of tourism in Yunnan makes it easier to extend the average stay of tourists and to decentralise tourism operation. But the fact that tourists with restricted availability of time find it impossible to visit all the attractions within this Province suggests the need for better travel arrangement on the basis of more efficient transportation. Given the scarcity of available funds for investment in tourism, tourism projects need to be carefully planned in an effort to concentrate on sites with unique characteristics. Close contacts between tourists and local people raise the issue of conservation of both natural environment and ethnic communities with insufficient preparation, which have been exposed to large volumes of tourists. Personnel training in tourism sector is still inadequate in Yunnan. Macro-control over both hardware (such as hotels and tourist vehicles) and software (mainly tourist services) in tourism is also essential to ensure the satisfaction of tourists.

Another feature of tourism in Yunnan is that seasonality does not affect tourism as much as it does in northern China mainly due to the mild climate throughout the whole year. Slight difference in the number of monthly tourist arrivals is, nonetheless, still observed. Higher monthly arrivals occur in December, January and February in Yunnan when it is dry season and when holidays including the Chinese New Year and winter vacation for schools occur. Some special occasions also influence the number of tourists in a particular month to a great extent. In Dali City, March is the month with the highest tourist arrivals when the March Street Fair is held, accounting for 4902 of Dali's 34,579 tourists in 1994 (Travel & Tourism Bureau of Yunnan Province, 1995). The highest daily arrivals in Xishuangbanna occur in April during the Water Splashing Festival.

Table 14.3: Economic & Tourist Indicators for Yunnan Province and its
Major Tourist Areas, 1994

	GDP (Yuan 000000)	GDP from Tertiary Industries (Yuan 000000)	Area (sq. km)	Pop-ulation (000000)	No. of Hotels	No. of Travel Agencies
Total	97397	30680	394,13	39.39	171	258
Kunmin	26813	10554.77	15,942	3.71	42	119
Dali	5342.	1675.03	29,459	3.13	19	14
Lijiang	1479.	493.29	21,219	1.05	5	3
Xishuan	2283.	775.77	19,700	0.81	14	47

	No. of Overseas Tourists	No. of Domestic Tourists (000000)	Domestic Tourism Income (Yuan 000000)
Total	522,059	14.58	3077.98
Kunmin	378,672	4.83	1019.66
Dali	34,579	2.49	525.66
Lijiang	16,885	0.2	42.22
Xishuan	15,312	1.25	263.89

Source: Statistics Bureau of Yunnan, 1995; Travel & Tourism Bureau of Yunnan, 1995

3.2 Ecotourism in Yunnan, especially in Xishuangbanna

Ecotourism is defined as 'nature-based tourism that involves education and interpretation of the natural environment and is managed to be ecologically sustainable' (Commonwealth Department of Tourism, Australia, 1994: 17). Here 'natural environment' includes cultural factors and local benefit as well as resource conservation. As a type of tourism that does not alter the integrity of the ecosystem while providing economic opportunities that make conservation of natural resources financially beneficial to local communities, ecotourism is an alternative to traditional high impact, exogenously controlled mass tourism. The call for alternative tourism coincides with the increasing switch from mass tourism in traditional Caribbean and Mediterranean resorts to tourism satisfying increasingly diversified tastes of western travellers. Nevertheless, the out-of-the-way experiences demanded by ecotourists often introduce intensive human activities to inherently fragile environments, and choice of destination is a minor consideration if ecotourism is controlled by companies owned by outsiders. The balancing of economic growth and environmental conservation is still an important matter. Ecotourism is expected to contribute to economic development of its destination areas especially in its role of earning foreign exchange, diversifying regional economies and in providing income directly to regional and local economies (Boo, 1990; Commonwealth Department of Tourism, 1994). At present, China's tourism is in fact concentrated in cities with more than 90 per cent of tourism receipts being earned by cities (Wen and Tisdell, 1996). Consequently diverse natural attractions and cultures in rural areas are not obtaining a large share of tourism in China.

Ecotourism is promoted in China as a means to conserve biodiversity and nature generally and pilot projects are to be developed for this purpose (State Council, 1994: 177). This direction is not only indicated in China's Agenda 21 but it is followed up in China: Biodiversity Action Plan (National Environmental Protection Agency, 1994).

Yunnan is rich in both natural tourism attractions and ethnic cultures. It has 30 nature reserves at provincial level and 40 reserves at county level with tremendous potential for ecotourism. By giving the minority communities and the traditional land users of the region the privileged use of the buffer zone areas, it is expected to integrate them into the conservation system and stop more dangerous encroachment while developing agroforestry to replace the traditional shifting cultivation, and to provide the opportunity "to demonstrate how the development of appropriate forms of ecotourism can generate substantial earnings for nature reserve bureaus and local communities" (Anon, 1993: 41). Xishuangbanna Prefecture, an area internationally recognised as being very rich in biodiversity, has been targeted as one of the areas for ecotourism development.

Situated in the south of Yunnan Province, Xishuangbanna came to be known as the "green gem in southern China" in the 1950s when former premier Zhou Enlai took part in the Water Splashing Festival and held functions to host his overseas guests here. The attractiveness of tropical rainforests, flora and fauna in wild state, combined with the multifarious minority life-styles and cultures make this place a significant tourist attraction. However, Xishuangbanna was not targeted as a major tourism destination until the 1980s for the reasons of both ultra-leftist concern about national security at border areas and transport difficulties in this area. Yunnan decided in the middle 1980s to expedite tourism development in Xishuangbanna by motivating investment in tourism as a response to both congestion of mass tourism in Kunming and strong demand for visiting Xishuangbanna.

Tourism in Xishuangbanna Prefecture has been growing at an average annual rate of 20 per cent since the mid 1980s. It received 15,312 overseas tourists plus 1.25 million domestic travellers in 1994 and obtained tourism receipts of US$ 4.29 million and Yuan 264 million respectively, together accounting for 26 per cent of its total GDP, and 50 per cent of the income from tertiary industries in Xishuangbanna (data collected from the Tourism Bureau of Xishuangbanna; Statistics Bureau of Yunnan Province, 1995). The number of travel agencies jumped from 22 in 1992 to 44 in 1993, and to around 50 in 1994. Besides more than 1,000 rooms provided by 14 hotels with sufficient quality to cater for overseas tourists, many more rooms are supplied by hotels and guest houses operated by non-tourist sectors (Wen, 1996). Tourist arrivals in Xishuangbanna are expected to reach 50,000 from overseas and 2 million from China by the year 2000 as indicated by the Tourism Bureau of Xishuangbanna. A brief overview of tourism in Xishuangbanna is given in Table 14.4.

Table 14.4: Tourism Data for Xishuangbanna Prefecture, Yunnan, 1991-1994

	International	tourism	Domestic	tourism
	Arrivals	Receipts (US$ m)	No. of tourists	Income (Yuan m)
1991	8,460	0.37	600,000	30
1992	13,609	0.8	900,000	100
1993	14,305	1.17	1,000,000	180
1994	15,312	4.29	1,250,000	264

Source: data collected by the author from the Tourism Bureau of Xishuangbanna, 1995

Rich ecotourism resources are found in the State Nature Reserve of Xishuangbanna, an area of 240,000 hectares with well-preserved tropical forest and rich biodiversity, including the last remaining Asian elephants. Major ecotourism sites in the Reserve include Sanchahe, Bubang and Menglun. The WWF, World Bank, together with other international organisations have recognised its importance in the worldwide campaign of preserving biodiversity by providing soft loans and technology to help with its conservation programs. From the 1000-foot-long and 125-foot-high treetop footpath aided by the National Geographic Society of the USA in Bubang, visitors may sometimes spy such severely depleted animals as mouse deer, gibbons, hornbills and peacocks.

A major problem with observation of wild animals lies in not being able to find them. Although birds and butterflies can be easily observed in the Reserve, it is rare for daytime visitors to see wild animals except that elephant droppings and their damage to vegetation and track can be seen occasionally. This is one of the reasons why travel agencies are not enthusiastic about bringing tourists to the Reserve. Consequently, although Xishuangbanna is known for its forests and wildlife, tourism at this stage in Xishuangbanna concentrates mainly on ethnic cultures. Encounters with nature in a typical tour of three or four days include a two hour visit to the Menglun Botanical Garden and three hour trip walking along the mountain tracks at an average height of 500 metres in Mandian, a site financed by the Forestry Department and the Planning Committee of Xishuangbanna, to watch two waterfalls, where some plants and 'plant-strangling' flora can be observed on the way.

The Reserve is facing impending encroachment from both inside and outside. More than 10,000 villagers live within the Reserve, 300,000 people live around it, and some busy roads pass the Reserve. It has long been the custom for some nationalities to carry some kinds of arms, and young people are often seen entering the Reserve with firearms. Satellite imagery shows that natural vegetation cover on land outside of protected areas has been severely reduced (Tisdell and Zhu, 1995), while pressure from increasing population and industries requiring raw materials is on the rise. Therefore, there is a danger that nature reserves will be degraded and biodiversity values reduced.

Although it would be ideal to have as big an area protected as possible, it does not appear feasible to enlarge nature reserves to a great extent since both human and financial resources are limited, especially in China where most nature reserves are located in poor areas with limited opportunities for economic development (National Environmental Protection Agency, 1994). The ultimate solution for the Reserve in Xishuangbanna is to convince people through the process of education and appreciation of nature conservation. In the mean time, ecotourism is expected to play a leading role in both conservation education and bringing income for the Reserve to finance more conservation projects even though how much it may achieve is still doubtful (Tisdell, 1996). The limitations to making quick profit from ecotourism owing to the nature of its low-effect on its resources as well as its requirement on the economic capability of the immediate society arise whilst constraints of infrastructure and expertise exist in most rural tourist destinations in China.

Some traditions of the Dais, the major ethnic group in Xishuangbanna, help with conservation. They plant fast growing trees called Heixinmu (Cassia siamea), a nitrogen-fixing species which enriches the soil, along the roads as fuel wood for domestic needs rather than chopping down trees from the rainforest. It is estimated that each Dai uses 1.0 to 1.5 cubic metre of fuel wood a year and 0.1 hectare of land on average is enough to meet the fuel wood needs of one person annually (Wen, 1996). Some hills are reserved for hundreds of years as Longshan (Dragon Hill) or Shengshan (Holy Hill) for burials, collecting of medicinal plants and religious reasons. Woodchipping, vegetation removal or hunting are prohibited in those areas. The 'holy hill' concept is beneficiary to conservation in the buffer zone areas in the Reserve.

Relying on small-scale, locally managed facilities and activities, ecotourism is supposed to be able to avoid the commonplace negative effects of mass tourism on destinations but to promote a balanced growth in tune with local, environmental, social and cultural concerns. However, ecotourism needs to be an integral part of the regional planning network and to be supported by the local communities in order to survive in the long run. Failures have been observed in ecotourism because local residents are not involved in the decision-making process (Tisdell, 1996). Ecotourism resources are threatened by encroaching agriculture, forestry and other economic activities which benefit from the same resource bases. Pollution and deforestation due to low efficiency of energy use is another danger because China uses over three times as much as energy as the United States per dollar of output, and eight times as much as Japan (Bingham, 1993). Ecotourism faces the pressure of both financing itself and conserving the natural resource base (Tisdell, 1996). Income collected from entrance fees to national parks is sometimes hardly enough to cover operation expenses and expenditure by tourists in natural areas may be low. For example, average daily expenditure for foreign visitors in Khao Yai National Park in 1987 was US$ 10, which was in sharp contrast to US$ 100 of average daily expenditure for foreigners in Thailand (McNeely and Dobias, 1991). It is conservatively estimated that $27 million of tourists' total expenditure in Nepal were attributable to the protected area network in 1988, when the costs of managing the parks were almost US$ 5 million but direct fees collected from tourists visiting the protected areas amounted to less than US$ 1 million (Wells, 1993). To facilitate further tourism growth, Xishuangbanna still needs to find a solution for financing ecotourism resources. Improvement in infrastructure, staff training, more efficient administration, and better coordination of related sectors are also important issues that have to be attended.

Ethnic and cultural aspects in Dali and Lijiang are promising attractions for tourists with higher education and budgets. However, commoditisation of ethnicity has been observed in Yunnan (Swain, 1990) in the selling of the material culture of minorities and in the mass marketing of pseudo-artefacts to tourists. How to prevent ethnic culture becoming commercialised in the process of tourism growth remains to be tackled in Yunnan. The fragility of tropical environment and minority cultures requires careful planning of tourism in Yunnan if its tourism is to be sustainable in the long term.

3.3 Tourism in regional development of Yunnan

The contribution of tourism to the regional economy and the distribution of returns to factors of production in tourism depend not only on the marginal productivity or efficiency of factors, but on the type of tourism principally practised in a specific area. The tourism multiplier, based on largely Keynesian principles that a proportion of income is recirculated into consumption spending, engendering further income and employment (Keynes, 1936), has been one of the most extensively discussed areas in relation to the economic effect of tourism on local economy (Archer, 1977; Holloway, 1989).

Owing to leakages on imports, taxation, savings and so on, the tourism income multiplier (TIM) is expressed by Bull (1995) as:

TIM = 1 / leakages, or, TIM = (1-MPM) / leakages

where MPM stands for marginal propensity to import goods.

Other tourism multipliers, such as those for employment, output, transaction, and so on, can be considered along the same lines. There is evidence that tourism is a capital - intensive industry on the whole when its social infrastructure requirements are taken into consideration (McKee and Tisdell, 1990), and its employment generating effect is much less than expected in some developing countries (Mishra, 1982; Dwyer, 1986) because tourism requires skills in short supply, such as foreign languages and management, in those countries.

The scarcity of data at the regional level of China and the difficulty of what is or what is not part of the tourism sector make it difficult to determine tourism multipliers. Unpriced environmental costs are not taken into account in multipliers. An income multiplier in excess of unity has been observed in countries such as the United Kingdom, Canada and Australia, and lower in Less Developed Countries and small island states ranging from 0.7 to 1.2 (Bull, 1995).

Table 14.5 shows that tertiary industry has accounted for over one third of the total GDP in Yunnan since 1992. It shows that tourism in Yunnan contributes a significant portion to the regional economy, especially if domestic tourism is also taken into account.

Table 14.5: Comparison of tourism with other sectors in Yunnan

	Tertiary industry (yuan b)	Tertiary industry as proportion of GDP (%)	Export (US$m)	Tourism receipts (US$m)	Inbound tourist arrivals (000)
1980		17.1	NA	1.16	20.5
1985	3.35	20.3	129	9.71	72.2
1990	12.57	27.9	434.5	16.4	148.2
1991	16.8	28.1	NA	63.13	212.1
1992	21.3	30.3	NA	67.27	313.5
1993	26	33.4	522.9	102.73	405.2
1994	30.7	31.5	910.2	124.4	522.1

Source: Statistics Bureau of Yunnan Province (1995), Travel and
        Tourism Bureau of Yunnan Province (1995), and National
        Tourism Administration of China (various years)

Compared to export income as a whole in Table 14.5, receipts from inbound tourists do not seem a large proportion, but their importance will be magnified if the multiplier effect is taken into consideration. It is reasonable to conclude that tourism has become a major contributor to this regional economy as a whole, and more so in popular tourist destinations.

Studies have shown that the tourism income multiplier is higher in diversified economies with capability to supply most factors in tourism itself (Burkart and Medlik, 1981). As a consequence, Kunming benefits more than proportionally from tourism than other areas of Yunnan due to its higher capability of supplying commodities and services for tourists not only to Kunming but to other areas within Yunnan as well (Wen, 1996). By contrast, areas importing tourist supplies suffer higher leakages and lower economic benefits from tourism. It is estimated by the Tourism Bureau of Xishuangbanna that 15 to 40 per cent of goods supplied for tourism are purchased from outside of the Prefecture. Income from long-distance transportation to and from Xishuangbanna goes mainly to the Yunnan Airlines and other coach services whose headquarters are located outside of Xishuangbanna. It is estimated by the Tourism Bureau of Xishuangbanna that the multiplier effect of tourism in Xishuangbanna averages around 1 to 2 for GDP and 2 to 3 for employment, and it is higher in sites popular with tourists. A unified multiplier is usually applied to different rounds of tourist consumption, but in fact it may be higher for the subsequent rounds of consumption once main imports have been computed at the first round. More detailed research is necessary into tourist multipliers in Xishuangbanna.

Although tourism within Yunnan is relatively scattered with multiple popular regions, tourism is distributed unevenly within each region with concentration in regional cities. In Xishuangbanna, a tourist spends normally 3 nights and four days with an average daily expenditure of Yuan 200 to 400, and 99 per cent of tourists make Jinghong City - the centre of the Prefecture- their base during their stay. Most travel agencies and hotels are located in Jinghong. Hence other popular tourist areas in Xishuangbanna can only obtain tourism income from lunch and entry fees plus small sales of tourist commodities from tourists taking day trips, and areas rarely visited can hardly benefit from tourism at all. Therefore, tourism may enlarge economic inequality within a local region with severe economic and social consequences. Although tourism is proposed as a means of decentralisation to promote rural development (Forsyth and Dwyer, 1991; Commonwealth Department of Tourism, 1994), rural areas find it difficult to benefit from tourism as a result of short-stay of tourists and high leakages. Regionally differentiated incentives such as higher grants and interest rate subsidies for remote areas could be designed to disperse tourism development and to ultimately help them really benefit from tourism (Chiotis and Coccossis, 1992).

Average length of stay may influence the number of places a tourist visits within a country or region, and Pearce (1990) suggests that an increase in "length of stay results in more places being visited, not more time being spent in the same number of places". He argues that visitors who stay shorter "opt for the most accessible sites and what are perceived to be the main tourist attractions. Those on longer visits take in other secondary and small centres and attractions". It may be practical to extend the stay of tourists in Xishuangbanna to 6 to 8 days through more diversified tourist activities so that tourists stay at places other than Jinghong, such as within the Reserve. As a result more economic gain for local community may be obtained.

Average expenditure is influenced by the level of tourist consumption, and expenditure shopping has good potential for increase. Nationwide average expenditure on shopping was 16.9 per cent of total tourist expenditure in 1994 (National Tourism Administration of China, 1995). It was estimated that the average percentage of total tourism expenditure on shopping was 18.5 by overseas tourists in Xishuangbanna (Tisdell and Zhu, 1995). Visitors sometimes complain about the limited design, availability and chaotic prices for tourist products in Yunnan. While increase in the number of tourist may bring more income, it is desirable to improve both average length of stay and average spending of tourists by providing attractive tourist activities as well as commodities at competitive price. Quality commodities with unique ethnic and tropical characters at reasonable prices are promising channels for increasing income from tourism.

Petty traders such as handicraft sellers are said to be in the informal sector as compared to the well established tour businesses in the 'formal sector' in tourism (Drakakis-Smith, 1980). This informal sector offers economic participation to many low skilled or unskilled individuals, and ultimately it may offer more secure employment and participation in the economy through upward links with the formal sector (Wu, 1982). In many southeast Asian nations, there is an increase in the number of tourists who share the same ethnic background with the host as it is happening in Yunnan. They may behave differently from the Westerners in shopping, dining and recreation, and they may also be treated differently by the local residents (Wahnshafft, 1982). Still much remains to be achieved for the informal sector of tourism in Yunnan to meet the demands from different market segments.

Investment decisions are not always rational so may incur an economic loss. Some tourism projects in Yunnan are running at a loss due to improper investment decision and mismanagement. Sites not close to major roads or without close connection to tour organisers often suffer unsatisfactory visitation levels, such as the Dai Culture Garden at Ganlanba, Xishuangbanna. Coordination between travel agencies and other tourist sectors is also crucial for tourism in Yunnan. Basic maintenance and hygiene of tourist sites need improvement. Further tourism development must be based on careful planning, taking account of the carrying capacities dependent on social, ethnic and environmental factors.

3.4 Domestic tourism in Yunnan and its prospects

It has been commonly recognised that expanding domestic tourism is an unavoidable phenomenon with increasing income and leisure time (Smith, 1989). Although the Chinese government gave no clear encouragement to the development of domestic tourism because it was not considered to contribute to foreign exchange earnings and was viewed as a competitor for the supply of transportation and accommodation for inbound tourism, it has been growing at an average annual rate of over 10 per cent since early 1980s with increasing living standards in China (National Tourism Administration of China, various years). A national tourism conference held in Tianjin in 1987 emphasised the importance of domestic tourism and recommended its further development (Gerstlacher et al, 1991). Although the policy on domestic tourism has since then alternated between allowing it to grow in order to direct individual consumption and discouraging it to curb trips paid by public funds and to reduce pressure on transportation, it has been recognised that there is no channel similar to tourism to disperse the strong consumption potential in China, the pressure on commodity market would undermine inflation control if Chinese people try to spend their private deposits of around Yuan 2,700 billion on commodities, which are sometimes in short supply. In 1994, total domestic trips reached half a billion with expenditure of

Yuan 102.4 billion (National Tourism Administration of China, 1995). Yuan 30 billion was absorbed by domestic tourism from 1985 to 1992, and it is forecasted that Yuan 120 billion will be spent on domestic tourism by the year 2000 (Anon, 1992), alleviating excess demand on commodity market in China.

The prospects for domestic tourism in Yunnan are promising due to its image as an affordable holiday destination with diverse features. 11.12 million Chinese visited Yunnan in 1992, spending Yuan 1.1 billion (Travel & Tourism Bureau of Yunnan Province, 1995). In 1994, Yunnan received 14.58 million domestic tourists and earned an income of Yuan 3.08 billion from them (Table 14.3).

Analysis using market segmentation suggests that destination choice of tourists from overseas differs from that of Chinese tourists in Yunnan. Yuxi and Honghe in the southeast of Kunming received 2.97 million domestic tourists in 1994, making 20 per cent of the Province's total domestic arrivals, but they accounted for only 6.5 per cent of the overseas arrivals to Yunnan Province (Travel & Tourism Bureau of Yunnan Province, 1995). Lijiang and Xishuangbanna received almost the same number of overseas tourists in 1994, but the number of domestic tourists to Xishuangbanna was six-fold of that for Lijiang (Table 14.3). Different from western tourists who tend to observe the sensation of scenic landscape individually, travel is sometimes a social event for Chinese. Tourist activities differ as well. The overall pattern for tourists in Xishuangbanna is that Chinese hardly miss the cross-border trips, whereas Japanese are interested in the Lesser Vehicle Buddhism, Europeans and Americans seek more adventure in the forest. More careful analysis on tourism market segmentation in Yunnan is necessary for better-orientated marketing and for further development of tourist sites.

The destination choice of Chinese tourists is different from international tourists in that the former have more chances to visit rural areas while the latter usually visit popular cities in the coastal areas due to limited time allowance. Therefore Chinese domestic tourism may play a more important role in contributing to rural development than inbound tourism (Wen and Tisdell, 1996) as is the case in Xishuangbanna.

Cross-border tourism in Yunnan is attractive to Chinese. As the first travel agency in Yunnan permitted to organise tours to the Laos, Mengla Travel Agency in Xishuangbanna arranged for more than 32,000 Chinese to visit Laos from 1991 to 1993 (Travel & Tourism Bureau of Yunnan Province, 1993). Visiting Burma, the Laos or Vietnam has become essential part of travel itinerary for Chinese tourists in Yunnan. The simple procedure to go abroad as cross-border travellers in Yunnan provides undoubtedly a good chance for Chinese who usually face a tedious process when applying to go abroad.

The Nature Reserve of Xishuangbanna is upgrading its tourist facilities in order to expand ecotourism within this area. More marketing is required to promote ecotourism because ecotourism is still new to the majority of Chinese tourists, who from their trips expect such tangible cultural remnants as a temple, stone inscriptions from famous people, or steps leading to the top of a mountain. They usually regard thick forest and wild animals as dangerous, and their average holiday is short except for students and teachers who may have longer vacations. Consequently ecotourism in the Reserve has to provide enough interpretation and activities to make visitors interested in the forest while marketing itself through multiple channels. Ecotourism has great potential in opening up new tourist routes and in adding the content of education and adventure to recreation while extending average tourist stay.

4. INTERNATIONAL TOURISM IN THE ASIA-PACIFIC REGION AND IN YUNNAN

East Asia has had the longest sustained period of economic growth in postwar history, accompanied by significant increase in per capita income and leisure time (World Bank, 1992). The economic growth in the Asia - Pacific region has been associated with increased ratios of foreign trade to output, rapid structural change in response to changing economic conditions, and specialisation in export and production (Garnaut, 1990). International tourism has grown rapidly since the 1960s in the Asian-Pacific region primarily because of increased intra-regional travel among Asia-Pacific residents (Mak and White, 1992), accounting for 73% of total arrivals in the region in 1990 (WTO, 1991). Regional specialisation and market segmentation have been observed in the world tourism market as a result of resource distribution and local economic structure (Lewis and Williams, 1988).

Japan provided the first wave of outbound travel in this region. The second wave of Korea, Taiwan and Hongkong commenced in the late 1980s, while the third wave from the ASEAN is underway. The fourth will occur around the turn of the century when China has further expanded its rapidly growing market economy (Hall, 1994).

Nevertheless, most attention has been paid to the economic dynamism of the East and Southeast Asia rather than the environmental lessons that those countries need to learn (Giok, 1994). More than 8 million acres of Asia's tropical forests are destroyed annually and millions of additional acres are degraded (Anon, 1994). Environmental pollution in China causes Yuan 95 billion in economic loss per year - 6.75 per cent of its GNP (Bingham, 1993). Deterioration associated with both pollution of general environment and mass tourism has threatened the long-term development of tourism in this region. Lessons of Thailand tourism may assist destinations in this region in avoiding further detrimental damage to their tourism. After four years of mass tourism growth from 1987 which brought forth deterioration and disorderliness, tourism in Thailand started to decline in 1990 as a result of political instability, soaring prices, environmental degradation, and ill planning (Chon and Singh, 1994). It has been suggested that tourists are seeking travel alternatives and are prepared to pay extra to obtain the desired 'green' travel experience (Millman, 1989). A US travel data centre survey found in 1992 that travellers would be willing to spend on average 8.5 per cent more for both travel services and products provided by environmentally responsible suppliers, including transportation, accommodation, food services, and sightseeing trips, and that 43 million American travellers would take ecotourism trips from 1992 to 1995 (Wight, 1994). It has been noticed that special interest tourism has become a major feature of travel to east Asia with emphasis on nature-based tourism (Weiler and Hall, 1992). Measures targeted at conserving tourism resources have become essential for continuous development of tourism in this region.

China unveiled the Environment Protection Law and the Forest Law in 1979, specifying goals of maintaining 30 per cent of its forest cover and prohibiting logging in protected areas. There were 630 reserves with an area of 30 million hectares, 3 per cent of China's land area. It has been planned to set up 800 reserves to cover 6 per cent of China by 2000 (Anon, 1993), providing more opportunities for ecotourism development.

The fact that two provinces in China's inland area abundant in cultural and natural tourism resources became top ten earners of tourism receipts in 1994 - Yunnan as the eighth and Shannxi as the tenth (National Tourism Administration of China, 1995) - indicates that inbound tourists to China have paid attention to non-coastal areas and they are looking for touristic experience with new content. With novelty of China waning from the late 1980s (Roehl, 1995), it is important for China to improve its tourist products to compete with other destinations.

Half of foreign visitors to Yunnan come from Asia, particularly southeast Asia. Thailand was the biggest single source country in 1994, generating one-fifth out of Yunnan's 402,332 foreign visitors (Travel & Tourism Bureau of Yunnan Province, 1995). A road connecting Kunming and Rangoon in Burma is to be finished in 1998, allowing annually at least one million vehicles to come from southeast Asia to Yunnan and providing expanded opportunities for regional tourism. Note that more than two million cross-border day visitors to Yunnan annually are excluded from international visitors' statistics. The future of international tourism in Yunnan lies in expanding its market in southeast Asia. A tourism cooperation conference for China, Burma, Thailand, and Laos was held in 1993 in Thailand to plan for the regional tourism development. Burma established a special zone in Mengla area mainly for tourism development to promote cross border tourism from Daluo Town in southwest Xishuangbanna.

The bottleneck for tourism in Yunnan is still transportation although there has been improvement. Tourism transportation is often in short supply, and tickets for planes and trains coming to Yunnan are hardly available in the peak season. Road conditions within Yunnan still need improvement.

5. CONCLUSION

Tourism is expected to be a major force in promoting economic development in rural areas where most economic resources are inadequate but where tourism attractions, generally in the form of well-preserved natural environments or rich cultural heritage, as is the case of Yunnan, are outstanding. Promotion of ecotourism and domestic tourism may facilitate greater convergence of tourism in China and ultimately contribute to reducing inequality between the coastal and inland areas through multiplier effect.

Tourism has been growing rapidly in Yunnan for more than 15 years. Its international tourist arrivals in 1994 ranked seventh among all the 30 localities in China and its receipts from international tourism ranked the 8th (National Tourism Administration of China, 1995). The future for tourism in Yunnan lies in intensive development rather than in expanding its present scale. Efforts are required to complete the existing tourist sites and to improve the quality of tourist services. Average stay of international tourists in Yunnan was only 1.59 day in 1994, less than the nationwide average stay for overseas travellers of 2.39 days (National Tourism Administration of China, 1995). Extending the stay of both international and domestic tourists and increasing the average expenditure of tourists may be more promising in raising tourism income than simply trying to raise the tourist volume. Factors such as transportation, staff training, coordination among industries and regions within Yunnan Province are all essential for further tourism development in Yunnan. Ecotourism in Xishuangbanna has just begun to develop and scope for further growth exists.

REFERENCES

Anon (1992) China Tourism News, 1 December 1992, Beijing.

Anon (1993) Environment in China, Ministry of Forestry of China, Beijing.

Anon (1994) Saving Asia's Forests: A New Approach, Asia Pacific Observer, 1(1): 1.

Archer, B. (1977) Tourism Multiplier: the State of the Art, University of Wales Press, Bangor.

Bingham, A.(1993) China's Phenomenal Growth has Environmental Price Tag, Pollution Prevention, 1(4):10-14.

Boo, E. (1990) Ecotourism: The Potentials and Pitfalls, WWF, Washington, D. C.

Bull, A. (1995) The Economics of Travel and Tourism, Longman, Melbourne.

Burkart, A. J. and Medlik, S. (1981) Tourism Past, Present, and Future, Heinemann, London, 2nd edn.

Chen, J. and Fleisher, B. (1996) "Regional Income Inequality and Economic Growth in China", Journal of Comparative Economics, 22: 141-164.

Chiotis, G. and Coccossis, H. (1992) Tourist Demand and Environmental Protection in Greece, Pp. 132-143 in H. Briassoulis and J. van der Straten (eds.) Tourism and the Environment, Regional, Economic and Policy Issues, Kluwer Academic Publishers, Dordrecht.

Chon, K. S. and Singh, A. (1994) Environmental Challenges and Influences on Tourism: The Case of Thailand's Tourism Industry, Pp. 81-91 in C. P. Cooper and A. Lockwood (eds.) Progress in Tourism, Recreation and Hospitality Management, Volume 6, John Wiley & Sons, New York.

Commonwealth Department of Tourism (1994) National Ecotourism Strategy, Australian Government Publishing Service, Canberra.

Drakakis-Smith, D. (1980) Urbanisation, Housing, and the Development Process, St. Martin's Press, New York.

Dwyer, L. (1986) Tourism, Islands / Australia Working Paper No. 86/3, National Centre for Development Studies, Australian National University, Canberra.

Forsyth, P. and Dwyer, L. (1991) Impacts of Foreign Investment in Australian Tourism: Report to the Department of the Arts, Sport, the Environment, Tourism and Territories and Queensland Treasury, Bureau of Tourism Research, Canberra.

Garnaut, R. (1990) Australia and the Northeast Asian Ascendancy, AGPS, Canberra.

Gerstlacher, A., Krieg, R. and Sternfeld, E. (1991) Tourism in the People's Republic of China, Ecumerical Coalition on Third World Tourism, Bangkok.

Giok, Ling Ooi (1994) A Centralised Approach to Environmental Management: the Case of Singapore, Sustainable Development: 2(1) 17-22.

Hall, C. M. (1994) Tourism in the Pacific Rim, Development, Impacts, and Markets, Longman Cheshire, Melbourne.

Holloway, J. C. (1989) The Business of Tourism, 3rd edn, Pitman, London.

Jian, T. L., Sachs, J. and Warner, A. (1996) "Trends in Regional Inequality in China", China Economic Review, 7(1): 1-21.

Kaldor, N. (1955) Alternative Theories of Distribution, Review of Economic Studies, 23(2): 83-100.

Keynes, J. M. (1936) The General Theory of Employment, Interest and Money, Macmillan, London.

Lewis, J. and Williams, A. (1988) Portugal: Market Segmentation and Regional Specialisation, Pp. 101-122 in A. Williams and G. Shaw (eds.) Tourism and Economic Development: Western European Experiences, Pinter, Belhaven Press, London and New York.

Lin, T. B. and Sung, Y. W. (1984) Tourism and the Economic Diversification in Hongkong, Annals of Tourism Research, 11(1): 231-247.

Mak, J. and White, K. (1992) Comparative Tourism Development in Asia and the Pacific, Journal of Travel Research, 31(1): 14-23.

McGregor, R. (1996) China 'Threatened' by Upstart States, The Australian, 16 April, 1996, Sydney.

McKee, D. and Tisdell, C. (1990) Development Issues in Small Island Economies, Praeger, New York.

McNeely, J. A. and Dobias, R. J. (1991) Economic Incentives for Conserving Biological Diversity in Thailand, Ambio, 20(2):86-90.

Mishra, R. H. (1982) Balancing Human Needs and Conservation in Nepal's Royal Chitwan National Park, Ambio, 11(5): 246-251.

Millman, R. (1989) Pleasure Seeking verses the 'Greening' of World Tourism, Tourism Management, 10(4): 275-278.

National Environmental Protection Agency (1994) China: Biodiversity Conservation Action Plan, National Environmental Protection Agency, Beijing.

National Tourism Administration of China (1986, 1991, 1992, 1995 and 1996) The Yearbook of China Tourism Statistics, Beijing.

Pearce, D. G. (1990) Tourism, the Regions and Restructuring of New Zealand, Journal of Tourism Studies, 1: 33-42.

Roehl, W. (1995) The June 4, 1989 Tiananment Square Incident and Chinese Tourism, Pp. 19-40 in A. Lew and L. Yu (eds.) Tourism in China: Geographic, Political, and Economic Perspectives, Westview Press.

Smith, S. L. J. (1989) Tourism Analysis: A Handbook, Longman Scientific & Technical, Harlow.

Statistics Bureau of Yunnan Province (1995) Yunnan Statistics Yearbook 1995, State Statistical Publishing House, Beijing.

SSB (State Statistical Bureau) (1995 and 1996) Statistical Yearbook of China, State Statistical Bureau (ed.), State Statistical Publishing House, Beijing.

State Council of the People's Republic of China (1994) China's Agenda 21: White Paper on China's Population, Environment and Development in the 21st Century, China Environmental Press, Beijing.

Swain, M (1995) A Comparison of State and Private Artisan Production for Tourism in Yunnan, Pp. 223-236 in A. Lew and L. Yu (eds.) Tourism in China: Geographic, Political, and Economic Perspectives, Westview Press.

Tisdell, C. (1996) Ecotourism, Economics and the Environment: Observations from China, Journal of Travel Research, 34(4): 11-19.

Tisdell, C. and Zhu, Xiang (1995) Tourism Development and Conservation of Nature and Cultures in Xishuangbanna, Working Paper No. 15, Biodiversity Conservation: Studies in its Economics and Management, Mainly in Yunnan, China, the Department of Economics, University of Queensland, Brisbane.

Travel & Tourism Bureau of Yunnan Province (1991) A Tourist Guide to Yunnan, Kunming.

Travel & Tourism Bureau of Yunnan Province (1993) Rising Tourism in Yunnan, Kunming.

Travel & Tourism Bureau of Yunnan Province (1995) Yunnan Tourism Statistics 1994, Kunming.

Wahnshafft, R. (1982) Formal and Informal Tourism Sectors: A Case Study in Pattaya, Thailand, Annals of Tourism Research, 9: 429-452.

Weiler, B and Hall, C. M.(eds., 1992) Special Interest Tourism, Belhaven Press, London.

Wells, M. P. (1993) Neglect of Biological Riches - The Economics of Nature Tourism in Nepal, Biodiversity and Conservation, 2(4): 445-464.

Wen, J. (1996) Tourism in Yunnan Province and the Xishuangbanna Prefecture of China: Achievements and Prospects, Working Paper No. 30, Biodiversity Conservation: Studies in Its Economics and Management, Mainly in Yunnan, China, the Department of Economics, University of Queensland, Brisbane.

Wen, J. and Tisdell, C. (1996) "Spatial Distribution of Tourism in China: Economic and Other Influences", Tourism Economics, 2(3):235-250.

Wight, P. (1994) Environmentally Responsible Marketing of Tourism, Pp. 39-55 in E. Cater and G. Lowman (eds.) Ecotourism: A Sustainable Option?, Wiley, Chichester.

World Bank (1992) World Development Report 1992, World Bank, Washington, DC.

WTO (World Tourism Organisation) (1991) Tourism Trends Worldwide and in East Asia and the Pacific 1950-1991, WTO Statistics Section, Madrid.

Wu, Chong-Tong (1982) Issues of Tourism and Socioeconomic Development, Annals of Tourism Research, 9: 317-330.

Yang, Liuli (1988) History for the Economic Development of Nationalities in Yunnan, Yunnan Nationality Publishing House, Kunming.

CHAPTER 15

INTER-VILLAGE INCOME INEQUALITY IN CHINA*

CHENG YUK-SHING AND TSANG SHU-KI**

ABSTRACT

There has been a growing interest in the impact of China's economic reform on income inequality. While an increase in inequality in the reform era is expected and may be acceptable, excessive polarisation could also jeopardise healthy socio-economic development. Changes in income inequality at various levels, such as inter-province, inter-county and inter-household, have been examined in recent years. Few studies, however, focus on inter-village income inequality. Since the mid-1980s, administrative villages have replaced production brigades and become the basic governmental bodies that organise socio-economic affairs for the rural community. A peasant household's well-being can be significantly affected by

* This paper is part of the output of a project entitled "The Behavioural Changes of Chinese Farming Units under the Economic Reform" funded by the Research Grants Council of Hong Kong Government (HKBC 168/92H). The authors would like to thank Woo Tun-oy for stimulating discussions during the process of writing this paper.
** Department of Economics, Hong Kong Baptist University, Kowloon Tong, Hong Kong

which village it is living in. Comparison of income levels across villages thus bears distinct importance.

This chapter evaluates the changes in inter-village inequality during 1978-92. Data of 280 villages were collected from four provinces in China, including Fujian, Hubei, Jiangsu, and Sichuan. We have computed indicators including the Gini coefficient and Theil's Entropy and performed decomposition exercises. Major findings include: (1) Inter-village income inequality exhibited a U-shape pattern of change. It fell initially to a trough in 1984, and then increased sharply till 1992. (2) The increase in inter-village inequality after 1985 was due to the steep rise of inter-village inequality in Jiangsu, while inter-village inequality in other provinces remained roughly stable for most of the time in the period. (3) Inter-provincial contribution to overall inequality was less than 20% before 1985, but it rose to 35.8% in 1992. In contrast, intra-provincial contribution to the overall inequality fell from the peak of nearly 90% in the late 1970s to less than 80% in 1985, and further down to 64.2% in 1992. (4) At the beginning of the reform, inter-village income inequality within county accounted for the major part of the overall inter-village inequality. However, inequality between counties grew rapidly after 1985 and explained 79.3% of overall inequality in 1992. (5) The increase of inequality of the whole sample after 1985 can mostly be explained by the growth of non-agricultural activities. In 1992, as much as 98% of inequality in our Jiangsu sample was attributable to the contribution from the non-agricultural sector; nevertheless, the contribution of agriculture to inequality was still very significant in the sample of the other three provinces.

1. INTRODUCTION

There has been an increasing concern of the impact of China's economic reform on income inequality. At the beginning of the reform, the official slogan was to "let some people become rich first". The egalitarian principle of income distribution was to be abandoned. An increase in income distribution could be expected and was deemed reasonable. In recent years, however, there were more reflections on the growing inequalities from both the Chinese leadership and academics. The extent of inequality and the mechanism that has generated unequal distribution of income have become a focus of studies. Top Chinese officials are apparently wary of the further widening of income gaps in the country. Greater emphasis, for instance, has been placed on the development of rural industries in interior provinces so as to raise the incomes of rural residents in those areas.

The western literature on China's inequalities has been growing since the late 1980s, thanks to the release of a large volume of official statistics by the Chinese government.[1] Many of the studies of inequalities in China tackle inter-provincial and inter-regional disparities. Tsui (1991) pioneers in applying rigorous techniques to measure regional inequality in China. He utilises provincial output data to investigate changes in China's inter-provincial inequality from the fifties to the mid-eighties. Lyons (1991) examines inter-provincial disparity in output and consumption during the same period. Tsui (1992) extends his studies to the reform period and finds that changes in inter-provincial inequality experienced an U-shape pattern during 1978-89. Tsui (1993), on the other hand, employs a complete set of data from all counties and cities of China in 1982 to study interesting issues such as the relative importance of inter-provincial and intra-provincial inequalities, intra-rural, intra-urban and rural-urban inequalities. Both Rozelle (1996) and Cheng (1996a) concentrate on disparity in rural income across provinces, while Cheng (1996b) further probes into the impact of taxes and transfers on inter-provincial rural inequality. Knight and Song (1993), on the other hand, study spatial contribution to rural income inequality in China by regressions using county-level data of 1987.

On the other hand, the collection of micro-level data of households by Chinese and western researchers in recent years has also facilitated studies of inequality at the household level. Knight and Song (1991) utilise data of 1986

---

1   Earlier studies of interprovincial inequality before reform include Lardy (1980) and Paine (1981).

to examine the determinants of urban income inequality. Khan et al. (1992, 1993) use household-level data of 1988 to compute the Gini coefficient for rural and urban areas respectively. Cheng (1996c) provides an analysis of income inequality based on survey data of 1000 households in grain-producing areas of five provinces.

All these previous studies provide a better understanding of the inequality issue in China. Yet not much effort has been spent on inter-village inequalities. The only exception is Rozelle (1994), who probes into the linkage between rural industrialisation and income inequality among villages in Jiangsu Province in the mid 1980s. Since mid-1980s, the Chinese government has established administrative villages, which replaced the production brigades (shengchan dadui)[2] and have become basic governmental bodies that organise socio-economic affairs of the rural community. As argued by Zhu and Jiang (1995), although the institutional changes create increasing opportunities for farmers to engage in individual economic activities, the reform also provides a socio-economic framework for a type of village-level community-based development. The village itself has sponsored essential public activities, such as providing social security for the aged, improving school facilities and maintaining basic health care.

Most villages are performing important distributive functions and a peasant household's well-being can be significantly affected by which village it is living in. Comparison of income levels across villages thus bears distinct importance. The study of inequality across villages has been constrained by data availability. This chapter attempts to examine the changes in inter-village income inequality in China in the reform period. A unique data set of 280 villages selected from 4 provinces is used. Apart from the concentration on village-level data, our data set has several advantages. First, we have a complete series of data over the whole reform period. While there are a number of studies that depict the inequality situation in China for a specific

---

2   At the same time, people's communes were replaced by township governments. At the lowest level, farmers of production teams (shengchan dui) were organised in villager groups (cunmin xiaozu) which formed the basic administrative units in rural regions. (Zhu and Jiang, 1993)

time point, the changing pattern over different stages of the reform period has not been captured (except for highly aggregate data at provincial level). Second, the data have been collected from four provinces that apparently have gone through different paths of development. This enables us to demonstrate differing changes in inequality in various provinces. In particular, we illustrate that the pattern of changes as shown in Rozelle (1994), who utilises village data collected from Jiangsu province only, is only one of many cases. Furthermore, the village-level data can be grouped by county and by province, from which we can examine inter- and intra-location inequalities.

The rest of the chapter is organised as follows. In section II, we describe some basic features of our data set. In particular, we compare our sample with national and provincial averages to see how representative our sample is. Section III presents the changes of inter-village income inequality over the period of 1978-92. Decomposition of the overall inequality into inter- and intra-provincial and into inter- and intra-county contribution will be conducted in Section VI. In Section V, the contribution to inequality by each of the sectors (agriculture and non-agricultural activities) will be examined by another decomposition exercise. The concluding section summarises the results.

2. THE DATA SET

We choose to collect village-level data from four provinces, namely, Fujian, Jiangsu, Hubei and Sichuan. The data were collected through the State Statistical Bureau (SSB) of China. In the SSB's own survey system, there are 26 counties in Fujian, 31 counties in Hubei, 34 counties in Jiangsu, and 49 counties in Sichuan. For our project which we commissioned the SSB to collect data, ten counties were randomly chosen from each of the provinces. Questionnaires were sent to the 40 counties. 28 counties responded before the specified time. Among them, ten counties were from Fujian, and six counties from each of the other three provinces. In each of the chosen counties, ten villages were randomly selected. Thus data from a total of 280 villages were collected. As there was some inconsistency in the figures of some villages, 16 villages were deleted from the data set. Consequently, our sample has 94 villages from Fujian, 57 from Hubei, 56 from Jiangsu and 57 from Sichuan.

Each of the four provinces has obviously distinct characteristics. Both Fujian and Jiangsu are located in the coastal region, while Hubei and Sichuan are situated in middle and western regions respectively. Jiangsu was famous for being a strong base for township industries even before reform, and its rapid development in the reform period has been a much discussed model of growth. The developmental level of Fujian is lower than that of Jiangsu, but still quite high compared with interior provinces. On the other hand, the income level of Sichuan is among the lowest while that of Hubei is roughly at the middle level.

Figure 15.1 shows the provincial and sample averages of per capita total rural income. In the mid 1980s, the income level of our sample was a bit higher than or the same as the provincial averages. However, since the later half of the 1980s, the sample averages appeared to be lower than the provincial averages in the cases of Fujian, Hubei and Jiangsu. As for Sichuan, the average income level of our sample villages was very close to the provincial average. In fact, as can be shown by the slope of the curves, the sample villages had a lower growth rate than the respective provincial averages in Fujian, Hubei and Jiangsu. Nevertheless, the deviations of the income levels of our villages from the provincial averages were not large. The relative ranking of income levels of the sample villages in various provinces remains the same as the four provinces.

Apart from the income level, we may also have a look at the difference in the development paths of the four provinces, which can be shown by the growth of non-agricultural activities. Panel (a) of Figure 15.2 shows the share of non-agricultural incomes in total rural incomes of the four provinces during

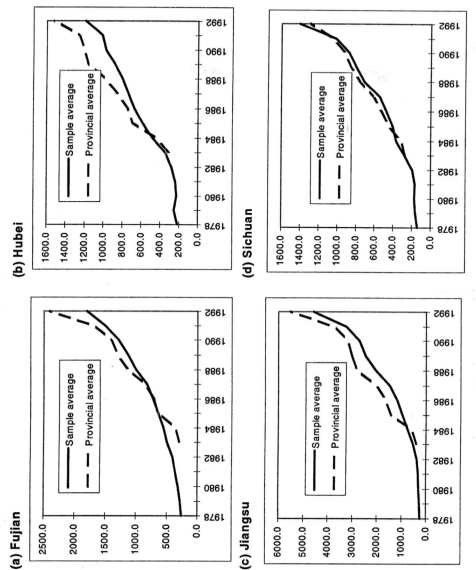

(a) Fujian

(b) Hubei

(c) Jiangsu

(d) Sichuan

Figure 15.1: Provincial and sample averages of per capita total rural income (Rmb)

(a)   National and provincial averages

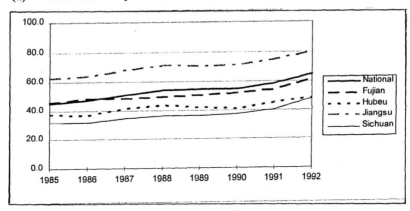

(b)   Sample averages

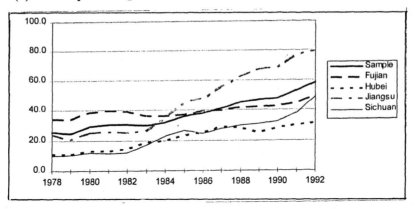

Figure 15.2: Share of non-agricultural activities in total rural income (%)

1985-92.[3] It can be seen that the development of non-agricultural
activities was the most rapid in Jiangsu. In fact, it was the only one among the
four chosen provinces that exhibited a non-agricultural share consistently

---

[3]   There were some changes in the statistical definitions of non-agricultural activities that
       rendered the figures before and after 1985 not directly comparable. Thus we only show the
       figures for the share of non-agricultural incomes after 1985.

higher than the national average. In 1985, the share of non-agricultural income in total rural income in Jiangsu already amounted to 62.6%, and it rose to the height of 80% in 1992. In contrast, the expansion of non-agricultural activities in Sichuan was the slowest. Nevertheless, its share in total rural income rose from less than 32% in 1985 to 48% in 1992. One interesting fact is that the level of 48% in 1992 was almost the same as that of Hubei. In fact, the share of non-agricultural activities in Sichuan rose very dramatically in 1992 by 40.5% over 1991. This probably reflects some new growth momentum of non-agricultural activities in western China.

As to our sample, the income shares of non-agricultural activities were basically lower than the respective provincial averages (see Panel (b) of Figure 15.2). This seems to be consistent with the fact that the income levels of our sample villages were lower than provincial averages, as `non-agricultural sectors had been the major forces behind growth in many areas. Our sample in Jiangsu had the same level of non-agricultural development as the provincial average, albeit starting from a much lower level of 45.2%. in 1985. Similarly, our sample in Sichuan also started from lower-than-average level of non-agricultural development but achieved the provincial average in 1992. In the cases of Hubei and Fujian, the level of non-agricultural development of our sample was considerably lower than the provincial level.

One concern is of course whether the observed deviations of our sample villages from the provincial averages would significantly affect the measurement of inequality in our analysis. Since we have a below-average income level for the high income group (Jiangsu and Fujian) and an up-to-average for the low income group, our measurement of inequality is probably biased downwards.

3. CHANGE OF INEQUALITY DURING THE REFORM PERIOD

Figure 15.3 shows the trend of inequality as measured by two different indicators, namely, the Gini coefficient, and Theil's entropy. Per capita total

Figure 15.3: Inter-village inequality in our sample

(a) Gini coefficient

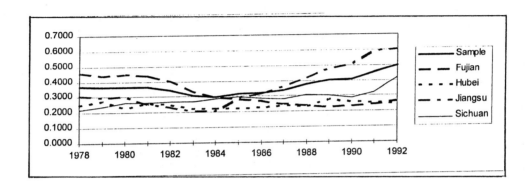

(b) Theil's entropy

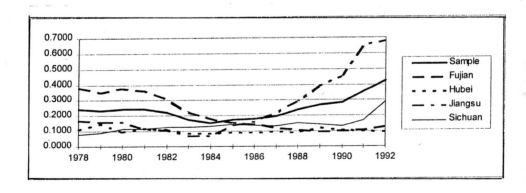

rural income is used in our analysis. Both indicators for the whole sample (represented by the bold line) exhibit similar patterns: income inequality declined in the early stage of rural reform and then went up after 1985. More precisely, both indicators did not change much during 1978-1981, but fell to a trough in 1984, and then increased steeply till 1992. The Gini coefficient, for instance, was 0.371 in 1978, but fell to 0.296 in 1984. It gradually rose to 0.500 in 1992.

The result of a decline in inequality during the early stage of reform is consistent with other studies. For instance, a household analysis conducted by the World Bank (1985) shows that the rural Gini coefficient fell during 1979-82, while Tsui (1992) indicates that inter-provincial output inequality (as measured by GDP and net material products) declined in the early years of reform before going up in the latter stage. In a similar study, Cheng (1996b) also shows that inter-provincial inequality of average net income of peasants had a U-shape development since 1978. Our result here confirms that this pattern of change is also true for inter-village inequality.

This result is important because, as pointed out by Tsui (1992), the conclusion drawn in some studies that are based on comparison of inequalities at the starting and the end points may be misleading (e.g. Tang 1991; Yang, 1992). As far as inter-village inequality is concerned, the result of Rozelle (1994) has it that inequality increased substantially during 1983-1988. We do have a similar increase in income inequality in that period, but we also show that there was a substantial decline prior to that period.

A further scrutiny of the pattern of income inequality in each province indicates that the overall trend we found above was not a national phenomenon. The only province with a sharp increase in inequality after 1985 was Jiangsu. Again, our result for Jiangsu is consistent with that of Rozelle (1994).[4] However, our sample shows that the patterns were rather different in

---

4   The figures of Rozelle (1994) show that there were ups and downs in the inter-village inequality level in the short-period of 1983-88. His inference that inequality (particularly intervillage inequality) increased by 15% is based on a comparison of the average of the final two years and that of the first two in the period. The rise of inequality in Jiangsu

other provinces. Indeed, when the inequality level of the whole sample exhibited an increase after the 1985, those of the sample villages from Fujian showed a decline. The inequality level of our Hubei sample fluctuated around a low level (0.22-0.27) of the Gini coefficient in most of years in the 1980s but fell in the early 1990. On the other hand, the inequality level of our Sichuan sample rose only slowly in the 1980s but jumped up drastically in the early 1990s.[5]

The pattern of changes in income inequality can be decomposed into various components, from which we can have a better understanding of the sources of the changes. Now we turn to the decomposition exercises.

4. INTER- AND INTRA-LOCATION INEQUALITIES

One convenient way to investigate the source of changes in inequality is by decomposing the overall inequality into contribution from inter-subgroup and that from intra-subgroup inequality. In our case, it is interesting to know the relative changes in the inequality among the villages within a location (a county or a province) and the inequality among the averages of the locations.

In this regard, Theil's entropy has the nice property of being additively decomposable. Let us use the unweighted version of the index:

$$I(y) = \frac{1}{N} \sum \log \frac{\mu}{y_i}$$

---

since the mid 1980s are shown to be more conspicuous by our data.

5   In another study of peasant household income inequality based on a survey of 1000 households in five provinces, Cheng (1996c) finds that the inequality of peasant households in Guangdong in 1994 was much higher than the results of other studies conducted in the 1980s while those of Jilin and Shangdong were respectively the same and lower. Cheng (1996c) conjectures that the growing rural inequality in China mainly comes from some specific provinces, which is consistent with the results of our present study.

where y_i = per capita income in village i, μ = mean income of the villages, N = number of villages.

It can be shown that

$$I(y) = \sum_{g=1}^{G} w_g I_g(y_g) + I(\mu_1 e_1, \mu_2 e_2, \ldots, \mu_G e_G)$$

where $I_g(y_g)$ is Theil's entropy index for location g, $g = 1, 2, \ldots, G$, representing the provinces/counties; w_g = number of villages in location g divided by the total number of villages; and e_g is a N_g vector of one's, with N_g equals the number of villages in location g. The last term is the entropy measure of inter-location inequality, as the income levels of all villages in a region are set to mean level of the location. The first term on the right hand side is the weighted sum of intra-location inequality. Contributions of inter- and intra-location inequalities can thus be found be dividing the respective terms by the overall inequality. (For further explanations, see Tsui, 1992).

(a) Inter- and intra-provincial inequalities

Figure 15.4 shows the results of the decomposition of inequality into inter- and intra-provincial contributions. Two major points should be noted. First, we can see that inter-provincial inequality in our sample had an increasing trend in the reform period. There was slight fluctuation in the early stage of reform (small increase in 1978-80 and slight decline in 1981-84), but the rise after 1985 was very sharp. The contribution share of inter-provincial contribution to overall inequality was less than 20% before 1985, but it rose to 35.8% in 1992. Second, intra-provincial inequality first fell but then picked up again in the mid 1980s. One notable finding is that the enlargement of intra-provincial inequality in Jiangsu was a key contribution to overall inequality after 1985. In terms of percentage contribution to the overall

Figure 15.4: Intra- and inter-province inequality (measured by Theil's entropy)

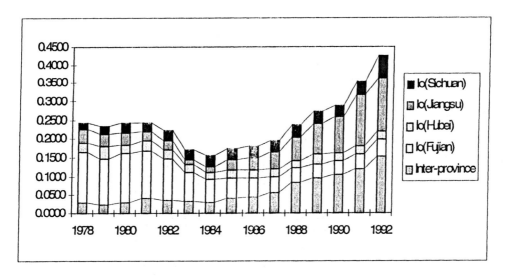

inequality, however, it declined from the peak of nearly 90% in the late 1970s to less than 80% in 1985, and further down to 64.2% in 1992.

From these results, we can see that the initial decline in the inequality in the reform period was attributable to the decrease in intra-provincial inequality. As mentioned in the previous section, some studies found that inter-provincial inequality followed a U-shape in the reform period. It has been postulated that it was because the poorer provinces were allowed to implement reforms first and thus benefited more in the initial stage of reform (Tsui 1992). Our result here indicates that even within provinces, poorer areas seemed to have grown faster in the initial stage of the reform period.

Figure 15.5: Intra- and inter-county inequality (measured by Theil's entropy)

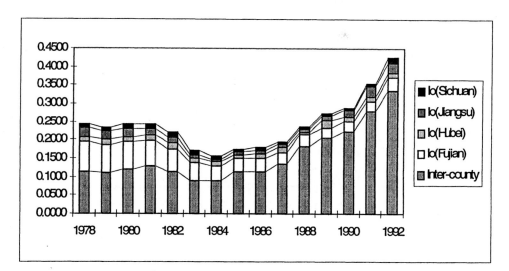

(b) Inter- and intra-county inequalities

As for inter- and intra-county inequalities, Byrd and Gelb (1990) believe that income inequality within counties is usually much less than inequality among counties. They reason that resource endowment for communities within a county are generally more equal and county governments try to hold down the gap between leading and lagging townships. They do not specify the time frame that they are referring to. Our result shows that there had been significant change in the relative importance of the inter- and intra-county inequalities. As shown in Figure 15.5, inter-county inequality contributed to less than half (47.1%) of the overall inter-village inequality at the beginning of the reform. In other words, intra-county inequality accounted for a major part of the overall inter-village inequality as measured by Theil's entropy.

This result throws some doubts on the equalisation hypothesis of Byrd and Gelb (1990).

However, the contribution of the inter-county component to the overall inequality expanded to 79.3% in 1992. Its rise was particularly drastic after 1985. The other side of the coin is that intra-county inequality contributed less. One implication is that in the competition to reform and grow, different counties faced varied fortunes. However, the fruits of success were distributed in a more equal manner to the members with each county.

5. INEQUALITY DECOMPOSITION BY FACTOR COMPONENTS

In this section, we try to decompose the Gini coefficient into the inequality contribution of each of the income sources (factor components). The method we use is developed by Lerman and Yitzhaki (1985).

Let $x_1, \ldots, x_K$ be the components of total income x. Denote the cumulative distribution of x as F, and correspondingly those of x_k be F_k. Lerman and Yitzhaki (1985) show that the Gini coefficient of total income, G, can be expressed as:

$$G = \sum_{k=1}^{K} \left[\frac{cov(x_k, F)}{cov(x_k, F_k)} \cdot \frac{2 \, cov(x_k, F_k)}{m_k} \cdot \frac{m_k}{m} \right]$$

$$= \sum_{k=1}^{K} R_k \, G_k \, S_k$$

where R_k is called the Gini correlation between the income component k and the rank of total income, G_k is the Gini coefficient for income component k, S_k is the share of k in the total income, and K is the number of income sources.

Dividing each of the terms on the right-hand side by G, we have

$$\frac{R_k \, G_k \, S_k}{G} \qquad \text{for each k,}$$

Figure 15.6: Agricultural and non-agricultural contributions to inequality
(measured by Gini coefficient)

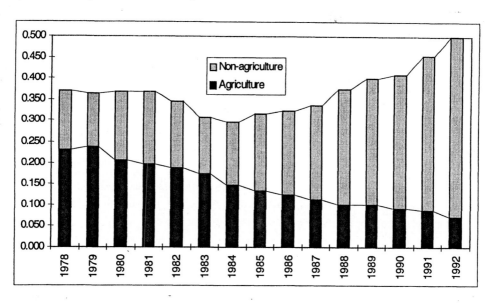

which can be interpreted as the inequality contribution of component k (I_k) as
a proportion of the overall Gini coefficient G. Thus, the contribution of a
component to the overall Gini is determined not only by the Gini of the
component, but also the share of the component in total income and the
correlation term R_k.

Furthermore, denote e_k as the percentage change in income source k that
is identical across the households, Lerman and Yitzhaki (1985) show that

$$\frac{\partial G/\partial e_k}{G} = \frac{R_k \; G_k \; S_k}{G} - S_k \; ,$$

which represents the marginal effect (measured in percentage change in G) of a percentage change in income source k. Some call it the "elasticity of inequality" (Rozelle,1994). It can be used to determine the distributional effect of imposing a percentage tax (or increasing the tax rate) on an income source where the tax leads to a change in that income source. A positive value of the elasticity of inequality means that taxing the income source will decrease the overall inequality level.

Figures 15.6 shows the Gini of per capita total income for the whole sample and Figure 15.7 for each of the provinces. Seen from the result of decomposition of inequality by factor component for the whole sample, the contribution of agriculture had been declining throughout the reform period. In contrast, the contribution of non-agricultural activities had been basically constant in the early stage of the reform, but rose drastically after 1985. This appears to be consistent with the results of other studies that find the growth of non-agricultural activities to be the major driving force of growing inequality (e.g. Rozelle, 1994) Among the three elements of the inequality contribution of non-agricultural activities, the Gini of non-agricultural activities did not show any increase. (See Table 15.1) However, the correlation term R had been increasing considerably since 1983, which implies a closer relationship between the level of total income and the level of non-agricultural income. The biggest increase had come from the third term, that is the share of non-agricultural activities in total income. Finally, the positive sign of the elasticity of inequality of the non-agricultural sector means that taxing it will lower the overall inequality. Conversely, the negative sign of the elasticity of inequality of agriculture indicates that subsidising the sector will alleviate inequality.

Table 15.1: Decomposition of Gini coefficient of per capita total rural income

	Rural	Agriculture					Non-agricultural				
	Gini	S(k)	R(k)	Gini(k)	SRG(k)/G	Elasticity	S(k)	R(k)	Gini(k)	SRG(k)/G	Elasticity
1978	0.371	0.782	0.936	0.316	0.623	-0.159	0.218	0.837	0.767	0.377	0.159
1979	0.364	0.792	0.939	0.319	0.652	-0.141	0.208	0.822	0.742	0.348	0.141
1980	0.368	0.751	0.916	0.299	0.559	-0.192	0.249	0.851	0.767	0.441	0.192
1981	0.368	0.742	0.890	0.299	0.537	-0.206	0.258	0.846	0.783	0.463	0.206
1982	0.347	0.742	0.860	0.294	0.540	-0.202	0.258	0.821	0.752	0.460	0.202
1983	0.308	0.735	0.831	0.287	0.569	-0.165	0.265	0.720	0.693	0.431	0.165
1984	0.296	0.707	0.781	0.268	0.500	-0.207	0.293	0.756	0.668	0.500	0.207
1985	0.316	0.657	0.744	0.274	0.424	-0.233	0.343	0.808	0.656	0.576	0.233
1986	0.323	0.636	0.728	0.270	0.387	-0.249	0.364	0.827	0.657	0.613	0.249
1987	0.337	0.598	0.721	0.263	0.336	-0.262	0.402	0.853	0.653	0.664	0.262
1988	0.374	0.551	0.708	0.262	0.273	-0.278	0.449	0.892	0.679	0.727	0.278
1989	0.401	0.528	0.700	0.274	0.252	-0.276	0.472	0.900	0.707	0.748	0.276
1990	0.409	0.507	0.677	0.269	0.226	-0.281	0.493	0.908	0.707	0.774	0.281
1991	0.456	0.451	0.682	0.284	0.192	-0.260	0.549	0.930	0.722	0.808	0.260
1992	0.500	0.397	0.643	0.287	0.146	-0.251	0.603	0.948	0.747	0.854	0.251

Yet, a closer look at the patterns of each of the provinces shows that the above conclusions are not necessarily true for all of them (see Figure 15.7). In the case of Fujian, the contributions of both agriculture and non-agricultural activities declined during the reform period. This is why the overall inequality in the province narrowed. Contrary to the conventional belief, even the Gini for non-agricultural activities in Fujian had been decreasing. As for Hubei, the inequality contributions of both agriculture and non-agricultural activities fluctuated during the reform period. Nevertheless, a trend of slowly increasing importance of non-agricultural activities can still be discerned. In the case of Sichuan, the increase in the contribution of non-agricultural activities had been roughly offset by the decrease in the contribution of agriculture, except in 1991-92. Again, Jiangsu is the major driving force

Figure 15.7: Agricultural and non-agricultural contributions to inequality - province
(measured by Gini coefficient)

(a) Fujian

(b) Hubei

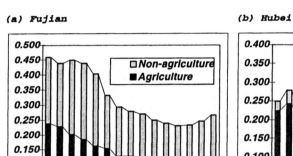

(c) Jiangsu

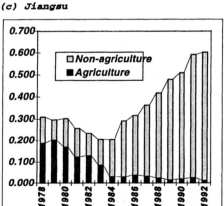

(d) Sichuan

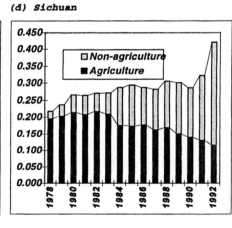

behind the pattern of the whole sample. The contribution of non-agricultural activities since the mid 1980s had been so tremendous that it reached 98% in 1992. Interestingly, the increase in the contribution of non-agricultural activities had been caused by increases in all the three elements (the correlation term, the Gini of the sector and the share of the sector).

6. SUMMARY

In this chapter, we have studied the changes in China's inter-village income inequality in the reform period, on the basis of a set of sample data in four selected provinces. Here we summarise the major findings of the chapter :

(1) Inter-village income inequality exhibited a U-shaped pattern of change. It fell initially to a trough in 1984, and then increased sharply till 1992.

(2) The increase in inter-village inequality after 1985 was due to the steep rise of inter-village inequality in Jiangsu, while inter-village inequality in the other three provinces remained roughly stable for most of the time in the period.

(3) Inter-provincial contribution to overall inequality was less than 20% before 1985, but it rose to 35.8% in 1992. In contrast, intra-provincial contribution to the overall inequality fell from the peak of nearly 90% in the late 1970s to less than 80% in 1985, and further down to 64.2% in 1992.

(4) At the beginning of the reform, inter-village income inequality within county accounted for the major part of the overall inter-village inequality. However, inequality between counties grew rapidly after 1985 and explained 79.3% of overall inequality in 1992.

(5) The increase of inequality after 1985 can mostly be explained by the growth of non-agricultural activities. In 1992, as much as 98%

of inequality in our Jiangsu sample was attributable to the contribution from the non-agricultural sector; nevertheless, the contribution of agriculture to inequality was still very significant in the sample of the other three provinces.

Most of these results appear to be consistent with those of other published studies. However, the patterns in each of the provinces in our sample have shown remarkable differences. This suggests that the applicability of the results of previous studies that relied purely on macro data may be very limited. Future analyses of income inequality in China should therefore be more conscious of the peculiarities of the localities under investigation so that accurate conclusions and meaningful policy implications can be drawn.

REFERENCES

Byrd, William A., and Gelb, Alan (1990), "Why industrialize? The incentives for rural community government," in Byrd and Lin (1990).

Byrd, William A., and Lin Qingsong (eds.) (1990), *China's Rural Industry: Structure, Development, and Reform*, Oxford University Press (published for the World Bank).

Cheng Yuk-shing (1996a), "Peasant income in China: the impacts of rural reforms and structural changes," *China Report*, Vol.32, No.1 (January-March 1996), pp.43-57.

---------- (1996b), "Inter-provincial rural income inequality in China," mimeo, Department of Economics, Hong Kong Baptist University, May 1996.

---------- (1996c), "A decomposition analysis of income inequality of Chinese rural households," *China Economic Review*, 7(2):155-167.

Hare, Denise (1993), "Rural non-agricultural activities and their impact on the distribution of income: evidence from farm households in southern China," *China Economic Review*, 4(1):59-82.

Hsiung, Bingyuang and Putterman, Louis (1989), "Pre- and post-reform income distribution in a China Commune: the case of Dahe Township in Hebei Province," *Journal of Comparative Economics*, 13:406-445.

Khan, Azizur Rahman, Griffin, Keith, Riskin, Carl, and Zhao Renwei (1992), "Household Income and its distribution in China," *The China Quarterly*, No.132 (December): 1029-1061.

--------- (1993), "Sources of income inequality in post-reform China," *China Economic Review*, 4(1): 19-35.

Knight, John, and Song, Lina (1991), "The determinants of urban income inequality in China," *Oxford Bulletin of Economics and Statistics*, 53: 123-154.

-------- (1993), "The spatial contribution to income inequality in rural China," *Cambridge Journal of Economics*, 17: 195-213.

Lardy, Nicholas (1980), "Regional growth and income distribution in China," in Robert F. Denberger (ed.), *China's Development Experience in Comparative Perspective*, pp.153-190. Cambridge, MA: Harvard University Press, 1980.

Lerman, Robert I. and Yitzhaki, Shlomo (1985), "Income inequality effects by income source: a new approach and applications to the United States," *Review of Economics and Statistics*, 67(1):151-156.

Lyons, Thomas (1991), "Interprovincial disparity in China: output and consumption, 1952-1987," *Economic Development and Cultural Change*, 39: 471-506.

Paine, Susan (1981), "Spatial aspects of Chinese development issues, outcomes and policies," *Journal of Development Studies*, 17(2): 133-195.

Rozelle, Scott (1994), "Rural industrialization and increasing inequality: emerging patterns in China's reforming economy," *Journal of Comparative Economics*, 19:362-391.

--------- (1996), "Stagnation without equity: patterns of growth and inequality in China's rural economy," *The China Journal*, No.35 (January):63-92.

Tsui, Kai-yuen (1991), "China's regional inequality, 1952-1985," *Journal of Comparative Economics*, 15:1-21.

------------ (1992), "Economic reform and interprovincial inequalities in China," mimeo, Department of Economics, Chinese University of Hong Kong, September 1992.

------------ (1993), "Decomposition of China's regional inequalities," *Journal of Comparative Economics*, 17:600-627.

Zhu Ling and Jiang Zhongyi (1993), "From brigade to village community: the land tenure system and rural development in China," *Cambridge Journal of Economics*, 17:441-461.

CHAPTER 16

THE POLITICAL ECONOMY OF CHINA'S NEW REGIONAL DEVELOPMENT POLICY IN THE NINTH FIVE-YEAR PLAN (1996-2000): A CONCERN OVER SOCIO-POLITICAL INSTABILITY

PAK K. LEE[*]

ABSTRACT

During the fifteen years from 1981 to 1995, particularly between 1986 and 1990, China's Five-Year Plans had steadfastly emphasised the importance of the economic development of the coastal provinces. Starting from the Ninth Five-Year Plan period (1996-2000), however, China seeks to adjust the balance between the booming coast and the less fortunate interior provinces.

*   Faculty of Social Sciences and Humanities, University of Macau, Macau

This chapter addresses the following questions: what accounts for this shift in the orientation of the regional policy? Why does the central government attach great importance to the problem of the regional gap? What measures will be adopted by the central government to assist the poorer regions? And, do the inland leaders feel satisfied with the central measures?

This chapter argues that the change in the regional policy is largely driven by the central perception of an imminent socio-economic crisis. There is thus a reordering of the goals of the macroeconomy. The values of stability and justice are placed on the top of the priorities of the country's macroeconomic policy. Theoreticians have second thoughts on the trade-off between the goals of economic efficiency and equity, calling for a less inequitable regional economic development. Moreover, in the light of the tendency that regional inequality becomes excessive and permanent, leaders in interior China do not offer normative support to the uneven regional development strategy. Achieving common prosperity rather than promoting the productive forces is now said to be the fundamental principle of socialism. A theory of coordinated regional development (*xietiao quyu fazhan*) is then advocated.

The gravity of the socio-economic situation has been borne in on the central leaders by the negative outcomes of uneven regional economic development strategy, such as the continuation of the "cellular structure" of regional economies as evidenced by the rise of regional economic protectionism and duplication of industrial pattern across provinces, since the late 1980s. The persistence of economic backwardness in the resource-abound interior provinces is believed to be a drag on the long-term economic development of the coast. The negative consequences of large-scale "random" labour movements to large cities and coastal areas from less well-off regions are also sources of particular concern to central and eastern coastal leaders.

Politically, the central government is worried about the adverse impact of economic backwardness on the stability of the impoverished inland areas, where China shares border with foreign powers, in the early post-Deng era. Beijing leadership is concerned with the possibility that in the wake of the death of the supreme leader of Deng Xizoping, unfriendly foreign powers would exploit the discontent among the poorer people, particularly the ethnic minorities, in western China to foment discord inside the country. In essence, the new focus of the Chinese central leadership in the late Deng era is on the possible effects of economic restructuring on social stability and geographical fragmentation of China.

In the fifth plenum of the 14th Central Committee of the Chinese Communist Party in September 1995, the General Secretary, Jiang Zemin, spelled out that the central authorities would adopt standard payment transferring system and straighten out price systems of resource-bonded products to bolster up the economies of the interior. It seems, however, that inland leaders demand more from the central government than the latter is willing to give. Inland officials call for preferential treatments to inland regions in the areas of industrial development, bank loans, capital investment, and enterprise taxation. They vow to achieve an economic growth rate higher than the central government-set target.

1. INTRODUCTION

During the fifteen years from 1981 to 1995, particularly between 1986 nd 1990, China's Five-Year Plans had steadfastly emphasised the importance of the economic development of the coastal provinces. A corridor of rapid growth along the coast stretching from Shandong in the north to Guangdong in the south has emerged. Starting from the Ninth Five-Year Plan period (1996-2000), however, China seeks to adjust the balance between the booming coast and the less fortunate interior provinces.

When the General Secretary of the Chinese Communist Party (CCP), Jiang Zemin, addressed the closing session of the fifth plenum of the 14th Party Congress in September 1995, he stated that the Party "will seriously deal with and correctly handle the problem of the widening gap between the eastern and central-western regions in the central-western regions in the course of economic development" (*Beijing Review*, 6-12 November 1995, p. 10). In Premier Li Peng's annual address to the National People's Congress in March 1996, a narrowing of the income gap between the booming coastal areas and the paupered hinterland provinces was suggested as a main theme of the government's Ninth Five-Year Plan. Deng's remarks that "achieving common prosperity is a cardinal principle and an essential characteristic of socialism and should never be shaken" have been frequently cited to justify the shift in the regional policy.[1]

To view from the perspective of political economy, this chapter intends to address the following questions: what accounts for this shift in the orientation of the regional policy, or what are the political determinants of the policy change? What specific measures will be adopted by the central government to assist the poorer regions? And, is it likely that the poorer inland leaders feel content with the central measures?[2]

This chapter will be divided into four parts. First, it will discuss the assessment of the regional policy of the 1980s by the central leadership in the early years of the 1990s. The second part is devoted to the discussion of the reordering of the priorities of the national economy policy, followed by an outline of the policy measures of coordinated regional development. The feedback from the poorer provinces will be discussed in the fourth part.

2. PERCEPTION OF THE PAST

A change in state policy is often preceded by an assessment of the past policy, and accompanied by a reordering of the values of the macroeconomic policy. The author's central concern is with the deliberate efforts on the part of the central government to redress perceived errors in the previous or existing

1   See, for example, the remarks made by Jiang Zemin in the fifth plenum of the 14th CCP Central Committee on 28 September 1995 (*Beijing Review*, 6-12 November 1995, p. 10).

2   The perspective of political economy is one that broadly takes into account the impact of economic events on social and political structures and attitudes, and vice versa (Riskin, 1991, p. 1). In the case of China, it studies the ways in which politics and economics interact in the causes, content and consequences of economic reforms (Perry and Wong, 1985, p. 2).

policy. The post-1978 lopsided regional policy reflected, first of all, an adjudication on the part of the post-Mao Chinese leadership of the Maoist regional policy as a premature attempt to realise socialism in a backward society such as China, and secondly, an emphasis on efficiency and openness to the outside world at the expense of equity and self-reliance.

By the same reasoning, an understanding of how the Chinese leadership perceives the consequences of the regional policy in the 1980s and what values they rate the highest is required for us to comprehend the logic behind the new regional development policy in the 1990s. Also, the perception of the past and a reappraisal of the goals of macroeconomic policy serve to legitimise a new path of development.

The doctrine of step-by-step diffusion (*tidu tuiyi lilun*) and a three-economic-belt model, which was guided by Western neoclassical theories, served as the blueprint for China's regional policy in the 1980s.[3] Investment resources were allocated to where they would maximise the total available income. A series of lopsided preferential policies was implemented in favour of coastal provinces and cities to enhance their abilities to generate, retain and reinvest profits and revenues. But unanticipated negative outcomes of local economic protectionism, the ever-widening income gap between the coast and the interior, and the concomitant movement of migrant labour from the poorer hinterland provinces to the coastal provinces and cities prompted the central leaders to reconsider the feasibility of the uneven regional policy.

Neoclassical economic theory takes the position that the market will reallocate factors of production such that factor prices will equilibrate across regions in the long run. While this may not immediately lead to a regional equalisation of per capita incomes, such a trend is believed will take place eventually (see Kuznets, 1955). The assumed perfect or high level of factor

---

3   The most influential of these theories was perhaps the inverted-U model suggested by Jeffrey Williamson (1965). Williamson's model suggests that in the process of a country's economic development, uneven regional development is inevitable in the short term, and inequality decreases in later stages as diffusion effects come into play. Chinese regional economists had cited Williamson's work to justify the logic of the coastally biased regional policy. See Zhang Wenhe (1989), Jiang (1990, pp. 106-197, 284-84) and Yang (1991).

mobility, however, did not come into being in China. The cellular structure of
the pre-reform Chinese economy and the preferential policies granted to the
coastal provinces and cities worked in the opposite direction to preserve or
even exacerbate regional inequalities.[4] Income differentials between the coast
and the interior widened greatly during the Eight Five-Year Plan period
(1991-95). It is predicted that the level of regional disparity will not be
improved by the year 2000. The extent of regional inequality in the reform era
is shown in Table 16.1.

The plight of the interior provinces was compounded by the "unequal
exchange" between them and the coastal manufacturing provinces. Because of
price scissors, hinterland provinces sold primary and agricultural products at
low prices to the resource-poor coastal areas and bought manufactured goods
at high prices from the latter. There has been widespread perception in
Xinjiang that Beijing milks Xinjiang's petroleum, coal, aluminium, wool and
cotton for the coastal provinces and cities without adequate compensation.
The Xinjiang Science and Technology Information Research Institute raised
an issue of equity of energy consumption. The Institute found that in 1979, a
Shaihaiese consumed 700 kilograms of standard fuel equivalent per year in
daily living at a charging rate of 0.67 yuan per kilogram. A poor person in
Xinjiang consumed only 242 kilograms, yet at a rate of 0.79 yuan per
kilogram, and a wealthy person consumed 361 kilograms at a rate of 0.83
yuan per kilogram (Christoffersen, 1993).

The coastally biased development policy has led to tensions between
coastal and inland governments. Officials of inland governments and state-
owned enterprises have responded in two ways. On the one hand, they tried to
thwart opening up. For instance, to reduce the leakage of value to the east,
governments in hinterland provinces increased efforts to process the primary
and agricultural products within their environs, and to forestall the influx of
final industrial goods into local markets from the east. This gave rise to local
economic protectionism and the break-up of the national market. They also

---

4   See Donnithorne (1972) for a discussion of the cellular structure of the Moaist economic
     system.

Table 16.1: Provincial Distribution of Per Capita Gross Domestic Product,
1980, 1985, 1990, 1994 and 2000 (projection)(percentage of national average)

Province	1980	1985	1990	1994	2000
East (Mean)	127.5	127.9	130.0	142.3	141.2
Beijing	354.2	331.8	305.5	251.6	303.5
Tianjin	311.7	269.8	232.8	202.5	235.0
Hebei	95.7	88.4	89.8	87.8	80.4
Liaoning	172.2	164.2	161.1	165.9	152.1
Shanghai	613.6	474.2	368.6	379.7	361.1
Jiangsu	122.2	129.6	128.7	150.9	149.2
Zhejiang	105.2	126.4	132.9	162.2	145.1
Fujian	77.0	86.9	100.1	116.6	113.0
Shandong	91.0	101.4	103.9	116.6	113.0
Guangdong	106.0	120.9	153.5	165.5	204.8
Guangxi	62.0	57.8	61.0	72.2	53.9
Hainan	70.3	89.5	94.8	121.6	192.8
Central (Mean)	87.1	86.8	83.6	76.1	73.9
Shanxi	98.1	99.5	91.3	73.2	78.0
Inner Mongolia	78.3	88.5	87.7	78.8	81.2
Jilin	100.6	107.8	105.0	98.3	105.9
Heilongjiang	153.6	124.3	123.0	115.1	112.0
Anhui	63.7	75.3	70.7	65.3	58.8
Jiangxi	76.7	74.0	72.9	67.1	66.4
Henan	70.9	72.1	68.5	63.6	57.7
Hubei	96.0	99.3	96.3	85.8	83.2
Hunan	81.9	76.9	75.9	69.6	68.1
West (Mean)	70.8	70.5	71.3	62.7	65.9
Sichuan	70.9	70.9	70.1	64.7	66.8
Guizhou	48.9	51.6	51.6	39.4	45.3
Yunnan	59.9	59.7	70.2	64.6	66.1
Tibet	n.a.	110.1	72.9	50.7	65.0
Shaanxi	75.9	74.7	74.7	63.5	66.9
Gansu	86.9	74.7	68.7	49.6	59.6
Qinghai	106.4	100.3	98.0	76.1	80.7
Ningxia	91.0	86.0	86.0	69.4	88.1
Xinjiang	92.5	100.5	109.0	107.8	97.5

Note: n.a. = not available. Sources: 1980 and 1985: *Guangxi tongji nianjian* (Guangxi Statistical
Yearbook), 1995, pp. 21, 27 (for Guangxi); Hseuh, Li and Liu, 1993, p. 365 and *Hainan tongji nianjian*
(Hainan Statistical Yearbook), 1995, pp. 17, 31 (for Hainan); *Jilin tongji nianjian* (Jilin Statistical
Yearbook), 1995, pp. 56, 74 (for Jilin); *Quanguo gesheng zhizhiqu zhixiashi lishi tongji ziliao huibian*
(1949-1989). (A Compilation of Historical Statistical Materials on Provinces, Autonomous Regions and
Centrally-administered Municipalities, 1949-1989), various pages (for others).
1990:   *Zhongguo tongji nianjian* (China's Statistical Yearbook), 1991, p.81; 1994, p. 35.
1994:   Ibid., 1995, pp. 33,60. 2000:   Guowuyuan faxhan yanjiu zhongxin ketzu, 1994, pp. 125-26.

lent support to campaigns against economic crime and "spiritual pollution" in 1985. On the other hand, they have lobbied for an extension of preferential policies to the interior since the mid-1980s. There were demands for the establishment of special economic zones in interior provinces such as Sichuan (Howell, 1993, pp. 22-23). In the light of the tendency that regional disparity becomes excessive and permanent, leaders in interior China have repeatedly criticised the uneven regional policy and called for the central government to offer preferential treatment similar to that enjoyed by coastal areas to inland provinces (Jiang, 1995).

Furthermore, the ever-widening income disparity between the better-off coastal and the impoverished inland areas induced an outpouring of a sizeable group of transient labourers, estimated at 80 million, into the economically more advanced regions, such as the Zhujiang (Pearl River) delta, the Changjiang (Yangtze River) delta, Beijing and Tianjin from Sichuan, Hunan, Guangxi, Guizhou, Hubei and other inland provinces.[5] It is clear from Table 16.2 that unemployment in the western part of China was much more severe than in the rest of the country.[6] The pool of labour reserve induced migration flow.

Vice-premier Wu Bangguo noted that China's rural labour force now numbered 450 million, of whom 120 million were in surplus (it was expected to rise to 200 million by the year 2000).[7] While he acknowledged that migration was an inevitable consequence of the prevailing economic reforms,

---

5   This figure was suggested by Luo Gan, vice-chairman of the Central Committee Commission for Comprehensive Management by Public Security, at a national conference on administering floating population in China in July 1995 in Xiamen, Fujian. British Broadcasting Corporation, *Summary of World Broadcast*, Part 3: Asia-pacific (hereafter *SWB-AP*), No. 1913/G/9, 4 February 1994; No. 2351/G/11,21 July 1995.

6   Chai (1996) notes the virtually unchanged ability of secondary industry in the western region to absorb labour from the primary sector during the economic reform.

7   A group of experts from the State Commission for Restructuring the Economy estimates that China's surplus labour in the countryside will amount to nearly 200 million by the end of the century (*SWB-AP*, No. 2365/S1/3, 26 July 1995).

Table 16.2: Provinces with Urban Unemployment Rate Above the National Average, 1990-94

1990	1991	1992	1993	1994
Qinghai (224)	Ningxia (209)	Ningxia (187)	Ningxia (146)	Qinghai (214)
Nigxia (216)	Qinghai (191)	Sichuan (165)	Gansu (138)	Guizhou (196)
Gansu (196)	Gansu (183)	Qinghai (161)	Sichuan (135)	Gansu (189)
Guizhou (164)	Guizhou (165)	Gansu (157)	Guizhou (131)	Ningxia (189)
Guangxi (156)	Inner Mongolia (152)	Inner Mongolia (148)	Hunan (131)	Sichuan (136)
Inner Mongolia (152)	Sichuan (148)	Guangxi (148)	Guangxi (112)	Hunan (136)
Sichuan (148)	Xinjiang (130)	Hunan (130)	Anhui (104)	Inner Mongolia (132)
Henan (132)	Henan (126)	Xinjiang (126)	Xingjiang (104)	Guangxi (129)
Shandong (128)	Hunan (126)	Anhui (122)		Hainan (129)
Hainan (120)	Anhui (126)	Hebei (113)		Shaanxi (125)
Xinjiang (120)	Hainan (113)	Henan (113)		Xinjiang (114)
Shaanxi (112)	Jiangxi (104)	Zhejiang (109)		Zhejiang (111)
Anhui (112)	Shandong (104)	Hainan (104)		Anhui (111)
Tianjin (108)	Shaanxi (104)			Shandong (111)
Hunan (108)				Hubei (107)
Fujian (104)				

Note: Figures in parentheses are percentage of national average.

Sources: *Zhongguo tongji nianjian*, 1993, p. 120; 1995, p. 107.

he warned that unless properly managed, the movement of such large numbers was bound to threaten social stability (*SWB-AP*, No. 2361/G/11, 21 July 1995).

In Beijing, the number of "transients" was said to have reached 3.3 million, of whom about 70 per cent were engaged in trade or in search of jobs, by mid-1995. Against this background, it was announced that from 15 July 1995, all units and individuals in the capital would be required to obtain permits from "designated job introduction agencies" before being allowed to hire people outside the city (ibid., No. 2346/G/2, 4 July 1995). On the other hand, local governments in the origins of labour migration, which benefited from the migration, took pains to assist the mobility of labour. They provide information about jobs all over the country to their local workforce, or make contacts with other areas and employment units, or even provide training courses to potential migrants for their future jobs (Mallee, 1995-96; Han and Li, 1994).[8]

Ren Jianxi, the president of the Supreme People's Court, pointed out that migrant workers had generated negative effects to the social order of the richer cities. He cited statistics showing that a considerable number of crimes in some cities were committed by rural labourers.[9] The influx of migrant labourers to urban areas also worsened unemployment there (*SWB-AP*, W/0403/WG/1-2, 27 September 1995). The rate of urban unemployment in China was 2.89 per cent in 1949, a 0.2 percentage point increase over 1993.[10]

---

8   For poorer regions, labour migration was an important source of capital accumulation. A study in southern Shaanxi revealed that of the increase in peasant income in the 1980s, 60 percent came from agriculture, 24 percent from labour export and only 10 percent from employment in rural enterprises (Han and Li, 1994).

9   *SWB-AP*, No. 1930/G/9, 24 February 1994; No. 1959/G/9, 30 March 1994; No. 2325/G/6, 9 June 1995; No. 2330/G/8-9, 15 June 1995. See also Jiang (1995).

10   China's official statistics of urban unemployment do not include a group of "resting" employees who are sent home because of the dire financial situation at the overstaffed enterprises. Technically the "sent-home" workers are still on the books of the factories. Take Beijing's No. 2 Knitwear Factory as an example. About one-third of its workforce were sent home in 1995. They received a monthly subsistence wage of 170 yuan, which

The Labour Ministry admitted that the situation was rather grim. The authorities reportedly intend to make strenuous efforts to keep the urban unemployment rate within 5 per cent during the Ninth Five-Year Plan period (*Beijing Review*, 29 April-5 May 1996, p. 19; *Eastern Express* (Hong Kong), 8 April 1996). Under the condition that target cities are not suffering unemployment problems, the Ministry of Labour will allow only 30 million rural labourers to seek jobs legally in urban areas in 1996. The quota will be raised to 40 million by the year 2000. To enforce the quota system, rural workers will be required to obtain a relocation permit from local government, and a separate permit must be obtained from the government of the destination (*Eastern Express*, 11 and 15 April 1996). In the light of the grim employment situation in urban centres, further population inflow would therefore be likely to increase investment expenditure in social capital and this might well outweigh any increase in output which the inflowing labour could contribute.

Although the original view was that after the coastal region had achieved a high level of development towards the end of the 1990s, it would be able to provide economic assistance to the interior and thereby correct the disparities, the negative impact of the a really biased regional policy commanded the attention of central leaders by the end of the 1980s and then constituted a strong pressure for policy change in the 1990s.[11] A policy that directs economic activity to underdeveloped regions has become evidently necessary. Since the early 1990s, a theory of coordinated regional development *(xietiao quyu faxhan)* policy that calls for national development with less regional inequality has been advocated (see Jiang, 1993, 1995; Wei and Liu, 1994).

according to a "sent-home" employee, was not enough to live on (*South China Morning Post* (Hong Kong), 15 June 1996).

11   Chai (1996) addresses the issue why trickle-down effect has not taken place in China's regional development during the economic reform.

3.A REORDERING OF THE PRIORITIES OF THE NATIONAL MACROECONOMIC POLICY

On entering the 1990s, the values of equity and stability are placed at the top of the priorities of the country's macroeconomic policy. The reordering of the values is caused by the perception of an imminent socio-economic crisis on the part of the central leaders. In other words, concern about social stability tends to dominate the deliberations of the policy change.[12]

Equity, however, is interpreted in the crisis-ridden 1990s in a way that is different from the previous decade. Under the influence of neoclassical theory, the CCP, throughout the 1980s, reiterated the long-term goal of common prosperity for all but argued that in the process of reaching that goal, it is desirable to let some people and regions get rich first, thereby creating the examples and the wealth to help make the others wealthy. Inequality in income was of a "temporary" nature. The CCP theoreticians asserted further that public ownership of the means of production would ensure that the "temporary" inequality will not become excessive or permanent. In other words, the CCP interpreted equality as equality of wealth and perceived that

---

12 A clear indication of the stress placed on public order by the Chinese leadership is shown in the leitmotif of the annual session of the National People's Congress (NPC) in March 1996. The focus of the session was on maintaining economic stability and tackling crime. A month before the session, Li Peiyao, a vice-chairman of the NPC Standing Committee was murdered by one People's Armed Policy officer in his Beijing home, strengthening the fear of a deteriorating law and order across the country (*Eastern Express*, 5 March 1996). for fear of aggravating the unemployment problem, the Chinese state is not to liquidate the state enterprises running in the red. Instead, it will encourage profit-making domestic and foreign enterprises to take over the debt-ridden firms. The central government made it clear in the session that it would spend more than ever to prop up the loss-making state-owned enterprises. A total of 280 billion yuan will be pumped into the state-owned enterprises to reduce the liabilities to assets ratio from the prevailing 84 percent to 70 percent over the Ninth Five-Year Plan period. Cai Lulun, the director of the Hunan branch of the People's Bank of China, was quoted by the Xinhua news agency as saying that bank loans account for more than 80 percent of working capital of state-owned enterprises. If enterprises deliberately evade debt payment by declaring bankruptcy, the biggest loser will be state banks (ibid., 11 and 12 March 1996; *Far Eastern Economic Review* (Hong Kong), 21 March 1996, p. 54.

inequality itself was conducive to efficiency, and that there was no insoluble conflict between efficiency and equality under socialism. It was also prepared to see inequality continue to increase. In discussing the guiding principle of regional policy, the CCP had emphasised that equality must be gained on the basis of efficiency (HSU, 1991, p. 108).

As the widening regional income gap (inequality of the outcome) was generally attributable to the unequal opportunities to develop as a result of the coast-led development policy, the conception of equality that enjoys the most popularity in the 1990s is equality of opportunity (Guo, Yan and Cheng, 1995). It is now admitted that the relationship between equity and efficiency is never an economic concept, it itself is concerned with social, political and ethical considerations (Jiang, 1995). the central government has been exposed to demands from the inland provinces, which have blamed the system and shown a strong sense of grievance of relative deprivation, for institutional changes to create greater opportunities to develop. Equality of opportunity to develop, as proponents suggest, promises that the doors to success and prosperity will be open to all areas, and rewards those who have ability and will to achieve in a competitive situation. The principle of equality of opportunity does not assume *a priori* that the poor are necessarily less productive than the rich. There are talented individuals among the poor, and providing such individuals with adequate resources will actually and possibly add to national production. However, the advocates did not call for an equality of condition, i.e. all competitors in the race should start at the same point with appropriate handicaps, to get rid of inherited inequalities in order to bring about a meaningful equality of opportunity. The advocates for an equality of opportunity also suggest that the cost of achieving this type of equality is less than the cost of social and national instability caused by growing income inequality.

Hu An'gang, a senior research fellow of the Research centre for Eco-Environmental Sciences of the Chinese Academy of Sciences and an alleged policy advisor to Jiang Zemin and Vice-premier Zhu Rongji, cites the disintegration of the former socialist country of Yugoslavia as a cautionary lesson for China. He attributes the break-up of the Yugoslavian federation to two economic conditions, namely a relative decline in the central government's fiscal extractive capability and growing regional inequalities. His study finds that in 1988, the average per capita income in Slovenia, the richest republic in Yugoslavia, surged to 7.5 times that of Kosovo, the poorest republic, from a multiple of five in 1965. Thus, development disparity may put national unity in peril. He also argues that the phase of letting some people and regions to get rich fist is over (*Beijing Review*, 22-28 January 1996; *Eastern Express*, 14 March 1966).[13] A survey done by Hu to a group of more than thirty provincial and prefectural cadres in June 1994 shows that more than 80 per cent of the cadres suggest that an excessive regional inequality would lead to social disorder.[14]

Hu's analysis came to the attention of the senior Party leadership. After reading Hu's report, Song Ping, a former member of the Politburo Standing Committee, echoed by suggesting in a "Support-the-Poor" meeting, organised by the Organisation Department of the Central Committee, in June 1994 that unless regional disparities were under control, national economic development, even social stability and national unity, would be undermined. Song Ping criticised those officials who reduced the essence of socialism to the development of the productive forces alone. He argued that socialism would not spontaneously come whenever the productive forces were developed. To achieve common prosperity on the basis of the development of productive forces is the only way for China to achieve socialism with its own characteristics (*Renmin ribao* (People's Daily) (Beijing), 13 October 1994).

Xiao Gongqin (1995), a historian in Shanghai, notes that on entering the 1990s, China is in the intermediate stage of economic reforms, and this stage is characterised by, among others, a polarisation of wealth and a "soft state" engendered by the market-oriented reform measures implemented in the first stage of economic restructuring (1978-89). Therefore, there are lively debates

---

13 See also the interview of Hu An'gang in *Xianggang lianhe bao* (Hong Kong United Daily), 12 September 1995.

14 The survey was done when the provincial and prefectural cadres attended a religious seminar in the Central Party School. See Hu An'gang (1994).

about the suitability of egalitarianism and centralisation in the academic and policy circles in China.

Moreover, central leaders have perceived the danger posed by the relatively low level of economic development in inland provinces, particularly those inhabited by national minorities, to the unity of the nation. Xinjiang is a case in point.[15] Beijing-Xinjiang relations have deteriorated since mid-1989.[16] In early 1990, Premier Li Peng warned in a National Conference on Nationalities Affairs that "reactionary and splittist forces would carry out their infiltration activities while hoisting the nationality banner and donning religious outer garments" (Harris, 1993; Postiglione, 1992). Deputies from the region too advantage of the third session of the Seventh National People's Congress in March 1990 to lobby the central government for more autonomy and development aid. Senior regional officials asked Beijing to let them keep more local earnings and grant them autonomous powers in the formulation of the region's own foreign trade policy (*South China Morning Post*, 26 March 1990). A vice minister of State Nationalities Affairs Commission, Jiang Jiafu (of the Zhuang minority), urged the central government to abolish the "East-Central-West" strategy favouring east China over western provinces in the allocation of development funds (Postiglione, 1992). Less than one month later, a separatist armed uprising, in the form of jihad or "holy war", broke out in Baren township, Akto county (seventy-five kilometres south of Kashgar), in the Kizilsu Kirgiz autonomous prefecture. Subsequently, Chinese troops were deployed in the cities of Kashgar, Hoton and Kuqa.[17] The disintegration of the Soviet Union brought further problems to the region's relations with the central government (Harris, 1993).

---

15   The central government is also concerned with the separatist movement in Tibet and Inner Mongolia (see *South China Morning Post*, 30, 31 May, 7 June 1996).

16   On the "most-wanted" list of the twenty-one students identified as ringleaders of the 1989 pro-democracy movement, two were national minority students (Postiglione, 1992).

17   *Summary of World Broadcast*, Part III: Far East, 0745/B2/8-9, 23 April 1990; Foreign Broadcasts Information Service, *China: Daily Report*, 10 April 1990, pp. 48-49.

At a rally celebrating the 40th anniversary of the founding of Xinjiang Uighur Autonomous Region in Urumqi on 1 October 1995, vice-premier Jiang Chunyun said that the central government would augment fiscal support for the region. He, however, emphasised that the central government would expect loyalty in return and that all separationist forces in the region had to be combated (*Xinbao caijing xinwen* (Hong Kong), 2 October 1995; *South China Morning Post*, 2 October 1995). Wang Zhaoguo, head of the CCP United Front Work Department, noted at a meeting in Beijing in October 1995 marking the anniversary of Xinjiang that "some hostile forces in the world have supported activities aimed at splitting China and have carried out religious infiltrations, hoping it will lead to China breaking up and becoming Westernised" (*Beijing Review*, 16-22 October 1995, pp. 6-7). The governor of Xinjiang, Abdulahat Abdurixit, views foreign influence in the region negatively and warns that some unidentified unfriendly foreign powers look for opportunities to exploit the uneven regional development to undermine Xinjiang's integration into Han China (*Wen hui bao*) (Hong Kong), 18 March 1996). The Party Secretary of Xinjiang, Wang Lequan, also identifies nationalist separatism as the greatest threat to stability in the region (*South China Morning Post*, 17 May 1996). The central government ordered strict punishment for party cadres in the region who were sympathetic to the separatists.[18]

---

18 *Xinjiang ribao* wrote on 22 May 1996 that "Party members and officials ... implicated in political bombings, assassinations or other violent terrorist activities, must be immediately investigated and punished with due severity" (cited in *South China Morning Post*, 28 May 1996). Xinjiang was the last of China's outlying areas that was incorporated into the Qing dynasty's formal administrative system. After the fall of the dynasty in 1911, a succession of autonomous Chinese warlords which culminated in Sheng Shicai, a pro-Soviet leader who promoted Uygurs and Kazaks to high posts, controlled Xinjiang. In 1942, Sheng turned against the Soviet Union and committed himself to the Guomindang. However, the Russians still remained in control over three districts in the province (Ili, Tarbagatai and Altai). During the revolutions of 1944-45 in the Ili region, the Soviets set up an East Turkestan Republic at Ining (Barnett, 1993, pp. 343-45; Moseley, 1966, chapter 2).

4. POLICY MEASURES OF COORDINATED REGIONAL DEVELOPMENT

A coordinated regional development policy has the following general goals:

(1) Income gap between coastal and inland China is to be diminished or at least not the be widened by the end of the century (Jiang, 1993); and

(2) An integrated domestic market, which allows free circulation of production materials and final goods, is to be established. The Decision of the CCP Central Committee on Some Issues Concerning the Establishment of a Socialist Market Economic System, adopted by the third plenum of the 14th CCP Central Committee in November 1993, suggested that regional and departmental barriers must be broken down and unfair competition eliminated - all in the interests of creating a "unified, open, competitive and orderly integrated market" (*Beijing Review*, 22-28 November 1993, p. 17).

In order to achieve the abovementioned goals, some more concrete measures are suggested for implementation. Provinces are to compete on equal footing. The preferential status of the five special economic zones (SEZs) - Hainan, Shantou, Shenzhen, Xiamen and Zhuhai - will be limited to be the "testing ground" for China's reform measures. The import duty exemption on self-used equipment and materials will be gradually phased out in five years (*Eastern Express*, 23-24 March 1996; *South China Morning Post*, 19 March 1996).[19] During an inspection tour of Yunnan in October

---

19 According to Liu Xiaohua, department director of the State Council's Special Economic Zones Office, enterprises in the SEZs will continue to enjoy a preferential corporate income tax of 15 percent, although it is China's long-term policy to unify the income tax rate throughout the country (*Eastern Express*, 23-24 March 1996; *South China Morning Post*, 19 March 1996). See also the remarks made by Premier Li Peng in a meeting on the SEZs in Zhuhai in early April 1996 (*Eastern Express*, 6-7 April 1996; *Far Eastern Economic Review*, 18 April 1996, p. 87).

1995, Zhu Rongji stressed that while it was true that Deng Xiaoping had said that "we have to let some get rich first", nevertheless Deng also said that "we have to walk the road of common prosperity. This is socialism." Zhu added that if some had become wealthy, it was "thanks to Party policies and state support". It is now their duty to help the poor (*Renmin ribao*, 16 October 1995; *China News Analysis* (Taiwan) No. 1548, 1 December 1995, p. 9).

It is proposed that prices of agricultural and primary goods will be straightened out. In the meantime, resource-producing areas are allowed to retain a higher proportion of resources for local processing. In February 1993, the State Council issued a "Decision on Accelerating Development of Township Enterprises in Central and Western Areas". According to the Decision, the state plans to allocate five billion yuan per annum from 1993 to 2000 to support the development of rural enterprises in inland China. Specialised banks and local fiscal departments are required to inject capital in the rural enterprises in the inland areas (ibid., 20-26 December 1993, p. 23).

Division of labour among provinces or regions is to be established. Some labour-intensive productions, such as textiles, are to be shifted from coastal areas to the interior, with coastal regions concentrating on developing more sophisticated, higher value-added products. According to Xu Kuangdi, mayor of Shanghai, the municipality will transfer its labour- and resource-intensive industries westward to exploit the natural resources in inland China at low costs (*China Daily Business Weekly*, 24-30 March 1996).

In addition, seven cross-provincial economic regions are to be established to foster economic cooperation among provinces. The plan for setting up seven economic regions throughout the country was first released by vice-premier Zou Jiahua in mid-1992 and confirmed in the Ninth Five-Year Plan and the Long-Term Target for the Year 2010. The seven economic regions are: (a) the area along the Changjiang (Yangtze River), with Pudong in Shanghai playing the leading role; (b) the area encircling the Bohai Sea, which includes Beijing, Tianjin, Hebei, Shandong and Liaoning; (c) the Zhujiang (Pearl River) delta; (d) select provinces and regions in southwest and southeast China, which include Yunnan, Guizhou, Sichuan, Hainan, Western Guangdong, and the coastal areas of Guangxi; (e) northeast China;

(f) the five provinces in central China; and (g) northwest China (ibid., 3-9 August 1992, pp. 14-18; *Jingji ribao* (Economic Daily) (Beijing), 20 March 1996).

More investment and financial resources are to be poured into inland China to speed up the development of infrastructure and energy.[20] A system of transfer payments which the central government will use to provide conditional fiscal support to regions where the per capita gross domestic product is under the national average. Migration of labour force from less to more developed areas is to be encouraged, yet better guided. It is hoped that while emigration help relieve population pressures in the poorer areas, migrants will earn higher incomes and receive technical training in the better-off regions (*Beijing Review*, 22-28 January 1996, p. 21; *Jingji ribao*, 20 March 1996).

5. FEEDBACK FROM THE CENTRAL AND WESTERN PROVINCES

In response to the "blessing" from the central government regarding alleviating regional disparities, central and western provinces have vowed to achieve a higher-than-national economic growth rates in the Ninth Five-Year Plan period in order to catch up the bustling coastal regions. For example, Shaanxi's governor, Chenge Andong, said in the third session of the Eighth National People's Congress in March 1996 that the provincial government set the prevailing year's annual growth target of gross domestic product at 10.5 per cent, i.e. 2.5 per cent above the national goal. Chen explained that because the central and western provinces had long fallen far behind the eastern provinces in the pace of economic growth, they need to achieve a faster-than-national rate of economic growth to reduce the income disparity with the coastal areas. Change's views were echoed by Song Baorui, governor of Sichuan, and Gao Yan, Party secretary of Yunnan. Sichuan's and Yunnan's

---

20   The share of investments in central and western regions in the 1990s is suggested to be 44.4 to 48.8 percent of the total. See Wei (1990).

targets of GDP growth were set at 9-10 per cent and 10 per cent per annum respectively. Shanxi vows to play an exemplary role in the development of inland areas as well (*Ming bao* (Hong Kong), 6 March 1996; *Wen hui bao*, 17 March 1996).

Inland provinces do not anticipate that the central government will significantly increase fiscal support to the hinterland areas in the Ninth Five-Year period. Yunnan and Guizhou in the southwest were even resentful of the tax-sharing system (*fen shui zhi* which was supposed to increase the central share of the national budgetary revenue. This was because as a result of the implementation of the tax-sharing system in 1994, most of the taxes levied on the production, circulation and consumption of tobacco and liquor would go into central coffers. These two provinces specialise in the production of cigarettes and liquor. In Guizhou, before the implementation of tax-sharing system, 50-60 per cent of provincial revenues came from the taxes on these products (Chung, 1995; *Wen hui boa*, 19 March 1996).

Instead, inland provinces call for increased investment and receiving preferential policies that had been given to the areas along the coastline. They demand that profits of the joint ventures, cooperatives and sole-foreign investment enterprises (*sanzi qiye*) in the west be taxed by the same rate as their counterparts in the coastal SEZs, i.e. 15-24 per cent. Some inland leaders propose establishing a central-west development bank to give financial support to the region, and suggest that eastern regions must also play a role in helping the impoverished parts of the country. Yang Rudai, a former Party secretary of Sichuan and a member of the Politburo, now a vice-chairman of the National Committee of the Chinese People's Political Consultative Conference (CPPCC), even proposes that each eastern province and city should establish direct economic relations with a province or region in the hinterland to raise the aim of "rich aiding poor". Hu An'gang asserts that China should gradually channel about two-thirds of all investments for public projects into the less developed inland regions, which are home to two-thirds of China's population (*China Daily Business Weekly*, 24-30 March 1996). Li Dongfei (1995) argues that the central government should relax its control over investment projects in inland provinces. Investment projects which are supposed to be curtailed by the prevailing industrial policy should be allowed to be undertaken in hinterland regions as long as they serve to expedite economic growth.[21]

Some regional economists sympathetic to the plight of inland provinces argue that the central government's macroeconomic regulation measures must not be implemented uniformly across the country; and the measures must take into account the difficulties of the provinces and cities in question. The economists complain that the state stipulates equal requirements for coastal and inland areas in the proportion of self-raised funds (*zichou zijin*) in bank loans for investment and in the proportion of regional auxiliary funds in state key construction projects. They contend that these equal requirements effectively undermine the investment capabilities of interior regions (Wei and Liu, 1994).

6. CONCLUSION AND DISCUSSIONS

The first conclusion that may be drawn from the foregoing discussion is that it is wrong to regard regional policy as if it is purely an economic issue. This chapter argues that the shift in China's regional policy in the 1990s is principally brought about in response to political and social factors. They are the central concerns over the disintegration of national economy and unity and over social chaos brought about by regional differences in income. When confronted by the pressing need for maintaining national unity and social stability, Chinese leaders in the transition to the post-Deng era refine the priorities of the macroeconomic policy and opt for efficiency *not* at the expense of equity and stability. In other words, the reform measure is driven by a central perception of an imminent crisis in the country. This helps explain why the central leadership and even leaders in coastal provinces and cities are committed themselves to tackling the issue of uneven regional

---

21   Li is a vice-governor of Xinjiang.

development. An, the disputes surrounding the proper measures to tackle the issue is not a reformist-conservative disagreement, but a different region of the country. As many of the policy measures are still new, much remains to be learnt about their effectiveness.

Nevertheless, the shift in the regional policy may serve to stimulate overheating of the national economy in the Ninth Five-Year Plan period. This is because all interior provinces see the Plan as giving them a golden opportunity to catch up with the booming east while the coastal areas try to maintain their leading positions in the country by vowing to speed up economic growth.[22] Hinterland provinces in general do not feel content with the central policy measures designed to promote coordinated regional development in the country. Unbridled investment, which has long been a chronic problem in China since the launch of Economic reforms, tends to be increasingly difficult to be under central control in the Ninth Five-Year Plan period.

This study also sheds some light on the nature of the Chinese "socialist market economy". Chinese leaders and their advisors have come to an understanding that market mechanisms serve better than planning in stimulating economic dynamism at the micro (enterprise) level, but that market forces often generate at the same time outcomes contrary to the established goals of socialism such as equality. Learning from China's East Asian neighbours, Chinese leaders tend to rely on market forces to guide production at the micro level and on state-led macroeconomic control to achieve the values of equality and social stability. This chapter reaffirms the case that the role of the state in its socio-economic context should not be ignored or downplayed in understanding China's economic policy change. A study of the interaction of economics and politics as a mode of identifying and interpreting the political determinants of economic policy is likely to heighten our understanding of China's development issues.

---

22   Coastal leaders argue that their regions have had the conditions to go faster. Some claim that the growth rate of individual province should be set according to the actual conditions of individual provinces.

A relatively bold move to alleviate regional inequality notwithstanding, whether the new regional policy can proceed smoothly to reduce regional disparity remains to be seen. An interesting question that merits further research is: what the Central government can do to mitigate uneven regional development if it cannot increase fiscal support to the less well-off provinces?

REFERENCES

Barnett, A. Doak (1993) *China's Far West: Four Decades of Change*. Boulder, CO: Westview Press.

Chai, Joseph C.H. (1996) "Divergent development and regional income gap in China", *Journal of Contemporary Asia*, 26(1): 46-58.

Christoffersen, Gaye (1993) "Xinjiang and the great Islamic circle: the impact of transnational forces on Chinese regional economic planning", *China Quarterly*, 133: 130-51 (March 1993).

Chung, Jae Ho (1995) "Central-provincial relations", in Lo Chi-kin, Suzanne Pepper and Tsui Kai-yuen (eds), *China Review 1995*, Hong Kong: Chinese University Press, Chapter 3.

Donnithorne, Audrey (1972) "China's cellular economy: some trends since the Cultural Revolution", *China Quarterly*, 52: 605-19 (October-December).

Guo, Zhiyi, Yan, Qian and Cheng, Jiyuan (1995) "A reconsideration of east-west relationship under the conditions of market economy", *Lanzhou daxue xuebao (shehui kexue ban)* (Journal of Lanzhou University) (Social Sciences), 27(2): 3-7.

Guowuyuan fazhan yanjiu zhongxin ketizu (1994) *Zhongguo quyu xietiao faxhan zhanlue* (China's Coordinated Regional Development Strategy) Beijing: Zhongguo jingji chubanshe.

Han, Jun and Li, Jing (1994) "The labour migrant wave': a topic for China extending into the next century -- summary of the Conference on the phenomenon of the labour migrant wave'", *Zhongguo nongcun jingji* (China's Rural Economy), 5: 3-11.

Harris, Lillian Craig (1993) "Xinjiang, Central Asia and the implications for China's policy in the Islamic world", *China Quarterly*, 133: 111-29 (March).

Hsu, Robert C. (1991) *Economic Theories in China, 1979-1988*, Cambridge: Cambridge University Press.

Hsueh, Tien-tung, Li, Qiang, and Liu, Shucheng (eds) (1993) *China's Provincial Statistics 1949-1989*, Boulder, CO: Westview Press.

Howell, Jude (1993) *China Opens Its Doors: The Politics of Economic Transition*, Hertfordshire: Harvester Wheatsheaf.

Hu, An'gang (1994) "East-west inequality in the eyes of provincial and prefectural cadres", *Zhanlue yu guanli* (Strategy and Management) 5: 88-90.

Jiang, Qinghai (1990) *Zhongguo quyu jingji fenxi* (An Analysis of China's Regional Economies), Chongqing: Chongqing chubanshe.

Jiang, Qinghai (1993) "On coordinated regional economic development", *Kaifa yanjiu* (Development Studies), 1: 37-40.

Jiang, Qinghai (1995) "Coordinated regional development: an analysis and consideration of regional disparity", *Guizhou shehui kexue* (Guizhou Social Sciences), 2: 7-14 and 19.

Kuznets, Simon (1955) "Economic growth and income inequality", *American Economic Review*, 45(1): 1-28 (March).

Li, Dongfei (1995) "Some understanding of the problem of reducing east-west inequality", *Zhanlue yu guanli* (Strategy and Management), 4: 42-45.

Mallee, Hein (1995-96) "In defence of migration: recent Chinese studies of rural population mobility", *China Information*, 10(3/4): 108-40 (Winter/Spring).

Moseley, George (1966) *A Sino-Soviet Cultural Frontier: The Ili Kazakh Autonomous Chou* (Harvard East Asian Monograph, No. 22), Cambridge, MA: East Asian Research Center, Harvard University.

Perry, Elizabeth J. and Wong, Christine (1985) "The political economy of reform in post-Mao China: causes, contents and consequences", in idem (eds), *The Political Economy of Reform in Post-Mao China*, Cambridge, MA: The Council on East Asian Studies/Harvard University Press, pp. 1-27.

Postiglione, Gerald A. (1992) "China's national minorities and educational changes", *Journal of Contemporary Asia*, 22(1): 20-44.

Riskin, Carl (1991) *China's Political Economy: The Quest for Development Since 1949*, Oxford: Oxford University Press.

Xiao, Gongqin (1995) "Social contradictions and political stability in the intermediate stage of reform", *Zhanlue yu guanli* (Strategy and Management), 1: 1-9.

Wei, Houkai (1990) "An evaluation of the outcome of regional policy and its new directions", *Jingji lilun yu jingji guanli* (Economic Theory and Economic Management), 6: 57-62.

Wei, Houkai and Liu, Kai (1994) "The goals and policies of China's Coordinated regional development", *Jingji zongheng* (Economic Strategies), 3: 5-9; 4: 19-20.

Williamson, Jeffrey G. (1965) "Regional inequality and the process of national development: a description of the patterns", *Economic Development and Cultural Change*, 13(4): 3-84 (Part II, July).

Yang Kaizhong (1991) "Several theoretical problems in the development of regional economies", in Chen Dongsheng (ed), *Quyu jingji yanjiu de xin qidian* (New Starting Point of Regional economic Research), Beijing: Jingji guanli chubanshe, pp. 55-66.

Zhang, Wenhe (1989) "Regional economy: a retrospect and reassessment of ten-year reforms", *Gaige yu zhanlue* (Reform and Strategy), 4-5: 78-83.

CHAPTER 17

THE USE OF CAPITAL AND LABOUR IN TOWNSHIP-VILLAGE INDUSTRIES IN CHINA

FUNG KWAN*

ABSTRACT

The greatest change in China's countryside, since the economic reform, has been the rapid expansion of *rural township-village industries (TVIs)*. It accounted more than 10 per cent of the rural employment from 1978 to 1993. This chapter addresses to the following issues: (1) how the TVIs' capital is estimated; (2) to evaluate the TVIs' labour employment at the national level by applying the *Critical Minimum Effort Criteria (CMEC)*; (3) to determine the appropriate level of capital and labour use of TVIs through a decomposition analysis; (4) to suggest the reasons for (2) and (3). Labour absorption due to capital increase is estimated to be about 95 million from 1978 to 1993 while the actual labour employed by TVIs was around only 56 million. The result indicates that the *theoretical labour absorption* due to

---

•   Faculty of Social Sciences and Humanities, University of Macau, Macau

capital accumulation was much higher than the actual labour absorption *after 1984*. In other words, a capital-using strategy was adopted by the TVIs after 1985 whereas the labour-using strategy was prevalent at the early stage of TVIs development. Possible reasons for the continuous decline of labour absorption of TVIs could include an increase in labour productivity; a rise of labour costs in TVIs; and a shift of TVI's output from use of labour-intensive to capital-intensive methods due to the changing international market.

1. INTRODUCTION

The greatest change in China's countryside, since the economic reform, has been the rapid expansion of rural township-village industries TVIs. Its output share to the rural output has increased from 19 per cent in 1978 to 58 per cent in 1994 (*ZGNCTJNJ*, 1995, p51). It accounted for 5.5 per cent and 15.3 per cent of rural employment in 1978 and 1994 respectively (*ZGNCTJNJ*, 1995, p51, 335). This chapter has the following purposes: (1) to estimate the TVIs' capital; (2) to evaluate the TVIs' labour employment at the national level by applying the *Critical Minimum Effort Criteria (CMEC)*; (3) to determine the appropriate level of capital and labour use of TVIs through a decomposition analysis; (4) to suggest the reasons for (2) and (3). We are particularly *interested in why the TVIs have employed more capital in light of the fact that labour is abundant in rural China.*

2. ESTIMATES OF TVIS' CAPITAL

The original data of TVIs' capital employed is the 'Township-village Industrial Enterprises Original Values of Fixed Assets (TVIGK), which is part of the 'Township-village Enterprises Original Values of Fixed Assets (TVEGK) (shown in Column TVEGK of Table 17.1) at current market prices from 1984 to 1993.

Figures between 1984 and 1986 refer only to village-run industries and *a 15 per cent more*[1] is added to derive the TVIs' original values of fixed assets for this period. Since the ratio of TVIGK to that of TVEGK is 0.95171 between 1984 and 1993, *this ratio* is multiplied by the TVEGK from 1978 to 1983 in order to derive the TVIGK employed for this period. The whole series for TVIs' capital at nominal values from 1978 to 1993 is therefore shown under the column TVIGK in Table 17.1.

The 'Industrial Products Rural Retailing Prices Index (1978 = 100)' (IPRRP) is used to deflate the TVIGK and the constant TVIs' capital is shown in the column TVIGK78 in Table 17.1.

The after-depreciation 'Township-Village Enterprises Net Values of Fixed Assets at current market price (TVENK) is available from 1978 to 1993. The ratio of TVENK to TVEGK is calculated throughout the period and is approximately 0.78 (shown under the column TVENK/TVEGK in Table 17.1). Finally, the TVIs' net capital values 'Township-Village Industries Net Values of Fixed Assets (TVINK) at 1978 constant prices are estimated by applying this ratio and it is indicated under the column TVINK78 in Table 17.1.

Figure 17.1 indicated that other than 1984, the growth of TVIs' capital (TVINK78) is higher than that of labour (TVIL), with the average growth rate of capital being 16.24 per cent and the average growth rate of labour being 10.95 per cent. The TVINK78 was RMB17.3 billion in 1978 and rose to RMB159.3 billion in 1994.

---

[1]   In general, township-run industries was about 15 percent of total TVIs in the middle of the eighties.

Table 17.1: Estimated TVI's Capital Employed in China (1978-1993)

Year	IPRR P	TVEG K	TVIG K	TVIG K78	TVEN K	TVENK/TV EGK	TVINK 78
1978	1.000	229.6	218.5	218.5	181.8	0.791811847	173.02
1979	1.001	280.2	266.7	266.4	226.1	0.806923626	214.97
1980	1.009	326.3	310.5	307.8	266.0	0.815200736	250.90
1981	1.019	375.4	357.3	350.6	304.0	0.809802877	283.93
1982	1.035	429.3	408.6	394.8	342.4	0.797577452	314.85
1983	1.045	475.6	452.5	433.1	373.0	0.784272498	339.70
1984	1.077	575.0	422.2	484.8	445.7	0.775130435	375.82
1985	1.111	750.4	686.9	618.3	589.7	0.785847548	485.86
1986	1.147	946.7	873.6	761.6	743.2	0.78504278	597.91
1987	1.202	1226.6	1169.3	972.8	959.8	0.782488179	761.19
1988	1.385	1574.3	1545.9	1116.2	1234.5	0.784158038	875.28
1989	1.644	1920.7	1885.	1146.6	1486.2	0.773780393	887.21
1990	1.720	2202.0	2191.6	1274.2	1668.6	0.757765668	965.54
1991	1.772	2626.3	2618.4	1477.6	1959.3	0.746030537	1102.36
1992	1.827	3490.8	3483.1	1906.5	2607.1	0.74684886	1423.84
1993	2.043	5160.9	4459.6	2182.9	3768.0	0.730105215	1593.71

IPRRP: Industrial Products Rural Retailing Price Index - 1978 = 100, *ZGTJNJ 1995* (P. 233); TVEGK: Township-Village Enterprises Original Values of Fixed Assets, current 100 million RMB, *ZGNCTJNJ 1994* (P.352); TVIGK: Township-Village Industry Original Values of Fixed Assets, current 100 million RMB, 1984 - 1986: *ZGXZQYTJZY 1993* (P.40), The original figures are for village industry only. A 15 % more is adjusted to obtain the TVI capital. 1987: *ZGXZQYNJ 1978-1987* (P. 594), 1988: *ZGXZQYNJ 1989* (P.102), 1989: *ZGXZQYNJ 1990* (P.149), 1990: *ZGXZQYNJ 1991* (P.161), 1991: *ZGXZQYNJ 1992* (P.161), 1992: *ZGXZQYNJ 1993* (P.182), 1993: *ZGNCTJNJ 1994* (P.349); 1978-1983: the average share of TVI fixed assets to TVE fixed assets between 1984 and 1994 is 0.95171. This ratio is used to derive the data from 1978 to 1983; TVIGK78: Township-Village Enterprises Original Values of Fixed Capital, constant 100 million RMB 1978=100, TVIGK/IPRRP; TVENK: Township-Village Enterprises Net Values of Fixed Assets, current 100 million RMB, *ZGNCTINJ 1994*, (P.352); TVINK78: Township-Village Enterprises Net Values of Fixed Assets, constant 100 million RMB, 1978 = 100, TVIGK78*(TVENK/TVEGK)

Figure 17.1: Growth Rate of TVIs Capital and Labour in China (1978-1993)

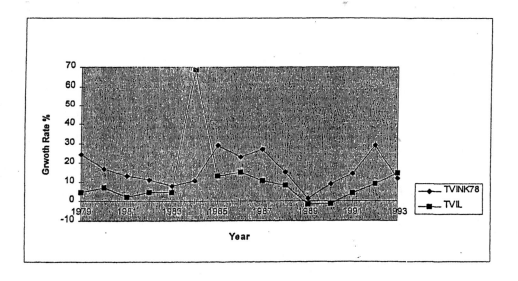

3. THE *CMEC* ANALYSIS AND DECOMPOSITION ANALYSIS

The CMEC and decomposition analysis are shown in Table 17.2, supplemented by Figure 17.2. The total labour force (P) at national level grew by 2.55 per cent per annum[2] from 1978 to 1993 while the TVI labour (L)

---

2   (2.17 + 3.26 + 3.22 + 3.59 + 2.52 + 3.79 + 3.48 + 2.83 + 2.93 + 2.94 + 1.83 + 2.55 + 2.86
     + 1.84 + 1.33)/15 = 2.55%

expanded by 10.95 per cent.[3] In general, the growth rate of TVI labour (L) were *much larger* than the total labour force (P), except for the years 1981, 1989, 1990 and 1994. That means the conditions of critical minimum effort (Fei & Ranis, 1964) are met,[4] i.e. the growth rate of industrial labour η_L is higher than the growth of total labour force η_P. China in some extent is a success case of shifting labour from low value-added to high value-added production.[5]

If the total industrial labour force is considered, its growth rate was 3.70 per cent[6] per annum from 1978 to 1993. The growth rates were higher than that of total labour force throughout the period except 1989, 1990 and 1991. Since the total industrial labour includes all types of ownership (state ownership in majority) and its growth rates were *much lower* than that of only township-village industry (3.70 per cent vs. 10.95 per cent), we could preliminary argue that *all forms of industrial establishment in China met the CMEC but the township-village industries employed more labour than the others*. This could be further proved by the increasing share of TVI labour to total industrial labour, from 28.47 per cent in 1978 to 64.61 per cent in 1994, shown in Column L/L1, Table 17.2.

---

3 (4.61 + 7.05 + 1.98 + 4.65 + 4.6 + 68.63 + 13.15 + 15.11 + 10.6 + 8.29 - 1.39 - 0.93 + 4.34 + 8.99 + 14.57)/15 = 10.95%

4 The critical minimum effort asserts that to avoid the Malthusian underemployment equilibrium (low income level and constant population growth), the minimum necessary investment to be raised so that further development becomes easier.

5 The other two cases are stagnation case, where the growth of industrial and total labour are the same, and failure case, where the industrial labour force grows slower than the total labour force.

6 (3.4 + 6.61 + 3.89 + 3.28 + 2.68 + 7.21 + 5.28 + 7.56 + 4.04 + 3.4 -0.96 + 1.35 + 2.58 + 2.73 + 2.43)/15 = 3.70%

Figure 17.2:TVIs Labour Growth nL, Labour Growth Due to Capital
Accumulation nR, Labour Growth Due to Innovation nH (1979-1993)

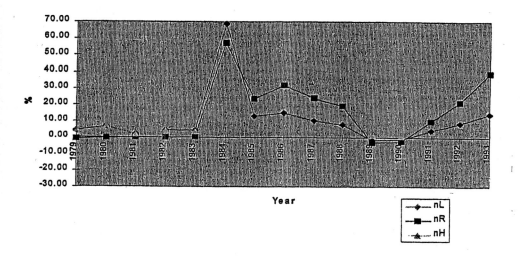

In terms of absolute value, the capital-labour ratio has been increased
from RMB998 in 1978 to RMB1,594 in 1993, the trend of *K/L* ratio
throughout the years of study is a little bit complicated and unclear. 1984, the
year of official recognition of TVE, experienced a sharp decrease of the ratio,
mainly due to a sudden increase in TVI labour by 68.6 per cent while the TVI
capital only increased by 10.6 per cent. Only in 1979, 1985, 1987, and 1992
TVIs *K/L* ratio enjoyed a double-digit growth rate.

Table 17.2: Critical Minimum Effort Criteria Analysis and Decomposition Analysis of the TVIs (1978-1993)

Year		[Critical Minimum Effort Analysis]				[Input Ratio Analysis]			[Decomposition Analysis]		
		P [10,000]	L1 [10,000]	L [10,000]	L/L1	X [10,000]	TVINK78 [100 million]	TVINK78/L	nL	nR	nH
1978		40152	6091	1734.36	28.47	28313	173.0209	997.6066			
	[%]										
1979		41024	6298	1814.38	28.81	28629	214.9667	1184.794	80.02	-9.12691	89.14691
	[%]	2.17	3.40	4.61			24.24	18.76	4.61	-0.53	5.14
1980		42361	6714	1942.3	28.93	29117	250.8968	1291.751	127.92	-5.7432	133.6632
	[%]	3.26	6.61	7.05			16.71	9.03	7.05	-0.32	7.37
1981		43725	6975	1980.8	28.40	29771	283.9253	1433.387	38.5	0.627269	37.87273
	[%]	3.22	3.89	1.98			13.16	10.96	1.98	0.03	1.95
1982		45295	7204	2072.81	28.77	30853	314.8459	1518.933	92.01	6.273656	85.73634
	[%]	3.59	3.28	4.65			10.89	5.97	4.65	0.32	4.33
1983		46436	7397	2168.14	29.31	31145	339.7013	1566.787	95.33	14.14246	81.18754
	[%]	2.52	2.68	4.60			7.89	3.15	4.60	0.68	3.92
1984		48197	7930	3656.07	46.10	30862	375.8199	1027.934	1487.93	1238.216	249.7143
	[%]	3.79	7.21	68.63			10.63	-34.39	68.63	57.11	11.52
1985		49873	8349	4136.7	49.55	31105	485.8557	1174.501	480.63	864.1922	-383.562
	[%]	3.48	5.28	13.15			29.28	14.26	13.15	23.64	-10.49
1986		51282	8980	4761.96	53.03	31212	597.9097	1255.596	626.26	1319.715	-694.455
	[%]	2.83	7.56	15.11			23.06	6.90	15.11	31.90	-16.79
1987		52783	9343	5266.69	56.37	31614	761.1878	1445.287	504.73	1139.111	-634.381
	[%]	2.93	4.04	10.60			27.31	15.11	10.60	23.92	-13.32

	P [%]	L1 [%]	l [%]		X		TVINK78	nR [%]	nH	nL [%]
1988	54334	9661	5703.39	59.04	32197	875.2789	1534.664	436.7	1014.328	-577.628
[%]	2.94	3.40	8.29			14.99	6.18	8.29	19.26	-10.97
1989	55329	9568	5624.1	58.78	33170	887.2089	577.513	-79.29	-175.662	96.37227
[%]	1.83	-0.96	-1.39			1.36	2.79	-1.39	-3.08	1.69
1990	56740	9697	5571.69	57.46	34049	965.5424	1732.944	-52.41	-116.046	63.63617
[%]	2.55	1.35	-0.93			8.83	9.85	-0.93	-2.06	1.13
1991	58360	9947	5813.55	58.45	34876	1102.358	1896.187	241.86	555.7435	-313.884
[%]	2.86	2.58	4.34			14.17	9.42	4.34	9.97	-5.63
1992	59432	10219	6336.4	62.01	34769	1423.843	2247.085	522.85	1256.013	-733.163
[%]	1.84	2.73	8.99			29.16	18.51	8.99	21.60	-12.61
1993	60220	10467	7259.6	69.36	33966	1593.714	2195.319	923.2	2335.371	-1412.17
[%]	1.33	2.43	14.57			11.93	-2.30	14.57	36.86	-22.29
1994	61470	10774	6961.6	64.61	33386					
[%]	2.08	2.93	-41.10							

P: total labour force in 10,000 persons, *ZGTJNJ 1995* (p.83), *ZGTJNJ 1993* (p. 101); L1: total industrial labour force, in 10,000 persons, sum of excavation, manufacturing, power generation, gas and water production and supply, *ZGTJNJ 1995* (p. 86), *ZGTJNJ 1993* (P.98); 1: industrial labour of township-village enterprises, in 10,000 persons, *ZGTJNJ 1995* (P.364), *ZGTJNJ 1993* (p.395); X: labour in primary production in 10,000 persons, *ZGTJNJ 1995* (p. 83), TVINK78: TVIs net capital refer to Table 11; TVINK78/L: capital labour ratio; nL: growth rate of TVIs labour, same as column L; nR: radial effect; nH: horizontal effect; %: percentage growth rate.

Regarding the decomposition analysis,[7] the radial effect (nR) (Column nR, Table 17.2) is calculated based on the following regression:

$$Capital = 444.0919 - 0.196382 \ Labour + 0.0000506 \ Labour^2 \quad (1)$$
$$\underset{(3.4954)}{} \quad \underset{(-2.7223)}{} \quad \underset{(5.8129)}{}$$
$$\bar{R}^2 = 0.968 \qquad D.W. = 1.342$$

The regression estimates produce a very significant adjusted correlation of determination, i.e. 96.8 per cent of the result can be explained. In addition, the individual student t statistics are very high.

The growth rate of radial effect showed double-digit increase from 1984 to 1988, 1992 and 1993. In particular, the nR was less than 1 per cent between 1978 and 1983. The horizontal effect (nH) is the difference between nL and nR, which was negative for the period 1985 to 1988 and 1991 to 1993.

This result indicates that the theoretical labour absorption due to capital increase (nR) is much higher than the actual labour increase after 1984 except 1989 and 1990. This analysis contrasts a different view of the state industrial enterprises (Zhang, 1990), (Guo and Hu, 1991), and (Guo, 1993):[8] *the capital-using strategy was adopted by the township-village industry after 1985 while the labour-using strategy was prevalent at the early stage of TVI development.*

The relations between capital and innovation are clear in Table 17.2. Firstly, the theoretical labour absorption due to capital employed was *94.371 million* in total from 1978 to 1993 while the actual labour employed in TVIs was *55.252 million* for the same period. Therefore, the process of TVI

---

7   It is an attempt to decompose any given total observed labour absorption into the horizontal effect, which is the labour absorption due to innovation, and radial effect, which is the labour absorption due to capital accumulation.

8   Studies show that state industrial enterprises have employed more capital than labour for the last four decades.

Figure 17.3: The Organic Composition of TVIs in Rural China (1987-1993)

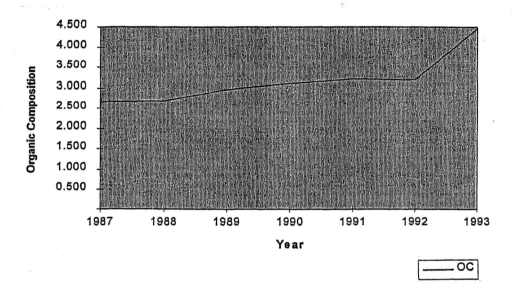

development has absorbed *39.119 million less* during this period. Secondly, these results indicate that the reform era and the process of rural industrialisation has adopted a more *capital-intensive* approach and the technological innovation is more *capital-biasing* rather than labour-biasing.

Indeed, the scenario is quite different even within these 16 years with the following breakdowns:

1978 - 1984 :	+ 6.77 million
1985 - 1988 :	- 22.9 million
1989 - 1990 :	+ 1.6 million
1991 - 1993 :	*- 24.59 million*
1978 - 1993 :	- 39.12 million

The "+" indicates more labour has been absorbed in comparison to the theoretical labour absorption due to capital accumulation.

4. DIMINISHING LABOUR ABSORPTION

Han (1995) offers several explanations on the continuous decline of TVEs labour absorption. First of all, the organic composition of capital (OC) was relatively low in the early stage of TVEs due to cheap and less-productive labour was largely available but capital and technology were scarce. Table 17.3[9] shows that the values of OC were about 2 to 2.3 between 1978 and 1984. In 1984, the official establishment of TVEs, marked the lowest OC value in the reform era, i.e. 1.863. Later on in the next half of 1980s, the OCs were increased from 1.957 to 2.75. Since the early 90s, they have rapidly risen from 2.773 to 3.148. Figure 17.3 depicts the values of OC of TVIs from 1987 to 1993. They were generally around 3 with 4.5 in 1993.

These data confirm the overall trends of TVEs: as labour was abundant in Chinese rural areas, most of output was from labour-intensive handicraft and

---

9   Since TVIs data are not available from 1978 onwards but only after 1987. We use TVEs
     data first and in Figure 3 TVIs data are analysed.

processing industry in nature. The increase of capital, thus, led to speedy increase in labour demand. However, at the later stage, with the increase in market competition and diversification of industrial output, TVIs tended to produce more technology-based output, for instance, energy, chemicals, machinery, electronics and biotechnology. It is found that the technical innovation contributed 35 per cent to the TVEs' output in 1990 but drastically rose to 50 per cent in 1994 (Han, 1995). This change of output orientation required higher organic composition of capital. Relatively, demand for labour became smaller.

However, another study (Chen, Findlay, Watson & Zhang, 1994) found that the product diversification of TVIs exports is not clear. The labour intensive products[10] shared about 81 per cent, 78 per cent, 71 per cent, 79 per cent, 79 per cent and 81 per cent of the total TVIs exports from 1986 to 1991 respectively; while the capital intensive products[11] was about 7 per cent, 10 per cent, 9 per cent, 10 per cent, 11 per cent and 11 per cent respectively[12]. On average, the capital intensive exportables were about 10 per cent of the TVIs export but the labour intensive had been more than 70 per cent: what a huge share! The only reservation of these data is that they were exports but the product diversification of TVIs output might be somewhat different.

---

10   include textiles, silk textiles, clothing, food processing, light manufactures, handicrafts and others.

11   include chemicals and machinery.

12   The remaining are the natural resource based products.

Table 17.3: Trends of TVEs' Organic Composition in Rural China (1978-1994)

Year	TVENK	TVEW	OC
1978	181.10	86.60	2.091
1979	226.10	103.80	2.178
1980	266.00	119.40	2.228
1981	304.00	130.60	2.328
1982	342.40	53.30	2.234
1983	373.00	175.80	2.122
1984	445.70	239.30	1.863
1985	589.70	301.40	1.957
1986	743.20	355.50	2.091
1987	959.80	427.70	2.244
1988	1,234.50	541.20	2.281
1989	1,486.20	580.70	2.559
1990	1,668.60	606.80	2.750
1991	1,959.30	706.50	2.773
1992	2,607.10	957.10	2.724
1993	3,768.00	1,323.90	2.846
1994	5,196.25	1,650.54	3.148

TVENK: TVE net value of fixed asset in current RMB100 million, 1978-1993: *ZGNCTJNJ 1994*, 1994, p. 352: *ZGNCTJNJ* 1995, p. 348; TVEW: TVE wages in current RMB100 million, 1978-1992: *ZGTJNJ* 1993, p. 397: *ZGNCTJNJ* 1994, p. 348; *ZCNCTJNJ* 1995, p. 347; OC: Organic composition, TVENK/TVEW.

Secondly, there has been substantial increase in labour productivity. In terms of per capita output,[13] the agricultural productivity had increased by 8.5 per cent during the first half of 1980s, 42 per cent in the second half of 1980s,

---

13   Value-added of constant priced per capita output.

Table 17.4: Growth of Agricultural Productivity in Rural China (1978-1994)

	1978	1980	1985	1990	1994
L	3.1349	3.2506	3.7708	4.2804	4.5354
Y	1,018.4	1,359.4	2,541.6	5,017.0	9,457.2
P	1.0000	1.0460	1.5540	1.9070	2.1960
Y78	1,018.4	1,299.6	1,635.5	2,630.8	4,306.6
Y78/L	324.86	399.81	433.74	614.62	949.54

L: rural labour force in 100 million, *ZGNCTJNJ* 1995, p. 51; Y: value-added of agricultural output in current prices, *ZGNJTJNJ* 1995, p. 51; P: index of value-added of agricultural output 1978=100, *ZGNCTJNJ* 1995, p. 123; Y78: value-added to agricultural output in constant 1978 price; Y78/L: per capita value-added agricultural output 1978=100.

and by 55 per cent in the first half of 1990s. Details are shown in Table 17.4. Calculated by average product, per capita TVIs output was RMB2,221, RMB3,162.72, RMB6,213.32 and RMB19,402.35 in 1978, 1984, 1990 and 1994 respectively. This is shown in Table 17.5.[14] Han (1995) suggested that the increase in labour productivity would have created less demand for labour from the middle of 1980s onwards. In fact it could be the case where the MP_L has increased due to more capital being employed.

Thirdly, most of TVEs (99 per cent) were located in towns/villages and they were highly separated geographically. This reduced the possibility of the expansion of tertiary production (services, commerce, and the like). Since many servicing industries require a relatively low level of skilled labour, the underdevelopment of services in rural areas would reduce the employment creation for labour surplus.

---

14   In constant market prices.

Table 17.5: Growth Rate of TVIs Labour Productivity in Rural China (1978-1994)

Year	TVIL	Y	IPRRP	Y78	PY78	GPY78
1978	1,734.36	385.26	1.000	385.26	2,221.34	
1979	1,814.38	423.52	1.001	423.10	2,331.91	4.98
1980	1,942.30	509.41	1.009	504.87	2,599.32	11.47
1981	1,980.80	579.34	1.019	568.54	2,870.24	10.42
1982	2,072.81	646.02	1.035	624.17	3,011.25	4.91
1983	2,168.14	757.09	1.045	724.49	3,341.52	10.97
1984	3,656.07	1,245.35	1.077	1,156.31	3,162.72	-5.35
1985	4,136.70	1,827.19	1.111	1,644.64	3,975.72	25.71
1986	4,761.96	2,413.40	1.147	2,104.10	4,418.55	11.14
1987	5,266.69	3,243.88	1.202	2,698.74	5,124.16	15.97
1988	5,703.39	4,529.38	1.385	3,270.31	5,733.98	11.90
1989	5,624.10	5,244.11	1.644	3,189.85	5,671.75	-1.09
1990	5,571.69	6,050.25	1.720	3,517.59	6,313.32	11.31
1991	5,813.55	8,708.61	1.772	4,914.57	8,453.64	33.90
1992	6,336.40	13,635.40	1.827	7,463.27	11,778.41	39.33
1993	7,259.60	23,446.60	2.043	11,476.55	15,808.80	34.22
1994	6,961.60	32,336.10	2.394	13,507.14	19,402.35	22.73

TVIL: TVIs labour employed in 10,000 persons, 1978-1992: *ZGTJNJ*, 1993 p. 395, 1993-1994: *ZGTJNJ*, 1995 p. 364; Y: TVIs output in current RMB100 million, 1978-1992: *ZGTJNJ*, 1993 p. 396, 1993-1994: *ZGTJNJ*, 1995 p. 365; IPRRP: Industrial Products Rural Retailing Prince Index, 1978 = 100, *ZGTJNJ 1995*, p. 233; Y78: TVIs output in RMB100 million (1978-100), Y/IPRRP; PY78: Per capita TVIs output in RMB (1978=100), Y78 / TVIL; GPY78: Annual growth rate of per capita TVIs output (1978-100) in percentage.

Fourth, the labour cost of TVIs has been kept on growing. Data indicate that per capita cost was RMB810 during the late 1970s, RMB1,280 in the mid-1980s and was RMB5,370 in 1993 (Han, 1995). The labour surplus in rural area is generally regarded as an unskilled workforce while most of TVIs

rural area is generally regarded as an unskilled workforce while most of TVIs require more management-oriented and technically-oriented personnel. In order to improve the labour quality, TVIs have to increase the education/training expenses. As the opportunity cost increases, TVIs might tend to employ more capital than labour.

Fifthly, the TVEs have shouldered increasing financial burdens as a result of the implementation of tax reform and fiscal reform initiated by the central government. The newly created tax sources (such as resource tax, consumption tax, value-added land tax) and the increase in some tax rates, together with the cancellation of some preferential treatment on taxes and loans for TVEs, reduced the possibility of offering larger bank credits to TVEs. This in turn reduced the labour demand of TVIs. It is observed that the total tax paid to the government was about RMB2,200 million in 1978 for all TVEs but increased to RMB10,860 million in 1985 (Table 17.6, Column TVET). Data for TVIs in detail are available after 1988. Table 17.6 shows that TVEs' tax-gross-profit ratio has been increasing. However, TVIs' financial burdens[15] has been confusing. The debate of this explanation lies in that even TVEs and TVIs financial burdens have been increasing, and the expansion of production scale may have been reduced, it is difficult to explain why the capital used has been increased in the past years.

Other possible reasons include the labour movement to the urban informal sectors rather than job opportunities in TVIs. On the other hand, the higher capital injection to TVIs maybe the profit differentials between SOEs and TVIs.

---

15   Including income tax, business tax, net profit appropriated to township/village government, net profit appropriated to collective welfare and education (1989-1992), value-added tax, business tax, consumption tax, resource tax, other tax, special funds and support funds (1994-).

Table 17.6: Trends of Non-Production Burdens of TVEs and TVIs (1978 - 1994)

Year	TVET	TVEP	TVET/TVEP	TVIT	TVIP	TVIT/TVIP
1978	22.0	110.1	20.0			
1979	22.6	127.1	17.8			
1980	25.7	144.1	17.8			
1981	34.3	147.1	23.3			
1982	44.7	160.2	27.9			
1983	58.9	176.7	33.3			
1984	79.1	207.8	38.1			
1985	108.6	279.9	38.8			
1986	137.3	298.3	46.0			
1987	168.1	355.9	47.2			
1988	236.5	495.7	47.7			
1989	272.5	512.6	53.2	305.9	428.1	71.5
1990	275.5	508.2	54.2	316.7	529.9	59.8
1991	333.8	618.5	54.0	388.9	543.3	71.6
1992	470.2	947.8	49.6	558.5	1,225.5	45.6
1993						
1994				828.8	1,077.2	76.9

TVET: Government tax paid by all TVEs, in current RMB100 million, *ZGTJNJ*, 1993 p. 396; TVEP: Gross profit of all TVEs, in current RMB100 million, *ZGTJNJ*, 1993 p. 396; TVIT: TVIs' non-operational expenses, in current RMB100 million, including income tax, business tax, net profit appropriated to township/village government, net profit appropriated to collective welfare and education (1989 - 1992), value-added tax, business tax, consumption tax, resource tax, other tax, special funds and support funds (1993 -), *XZQYTJZL*, 1989 p. 353, *XZQYTJZL*, 1990 p. 463, *XZQYTJZL*, 1991 p. 359, *XZQYTJZL*, 1992 p. 499, *XZQYTJZL*, 1994 pp. 12-14; TVIP: Gross profit of all TVIs, in current RMB100 million, *XZQYTJZL*, 1989 p. 353, *XZQYTJZL*, 1990 p. 463, *XZQYTJZL*, 1991 p. 359, *XZQYTJZL*, 1992 p. 499, *XZQYTJZL*, 1994 pp. 12-14.

5. LABOUR ABSORPTION IN DIFFERENT STAGES

The labour absorption rates are also presented in Figure 17.2 with explanations given below. During the initial stage of economic reform (1978 - 1984), more labour was successfully absorbed from cropping sectors to the rural industry. The main reason for this transfer was *the continuous decline in agricultural resources*, mainly in terms of the arable land. China has decreased the arable land by 4.5413 million hectares or 4.6 per cent between 1978 and 1994 (Table 17.7, Column L). In terms of per rural labour arable land, its absolute value has decreased from 0.32 hectare in 1978 to 0.26 in 1985 and 0.21 in 1994 (Table 17.7, Column L/P). The rate of declining per labour arable land reveals that it had increased from 1978 till 1984 with 4 per cent the highest decline in the reform era; the decline rate dropped from 4 to 2.2 per cent between 1985 and 1989 and it further reduced to around 1 per cent in the 1990s. Figure 17.5 shows these trends.

With limited land, peasants were looking for the best alternative (the lowest opportunity cost), provided that they were granted higher autonomy in using resources. The reform programme after 1978 furnished such an environment by changing the institutional settings in the rural economy, including the abolishment of commune system and the re-establishment of xiang Ïç and zhen Õò. Since labour was the principal resource other than cultivable land at that period and the TVIs were those with less technology-oriented production, TVIs have enjoyed a profound growth and labour surplus was the main contributor during the time 1978 - 1984.

In addition, the labour surplus during this period almost carried zero opportunity cost on transferring to TVIs because of the huge wage differentials between urban and rural areas. Furthermore, the entrepreneurs of TVIs originated from hard-working personnel, rather than capable managerial technocrats. All these contributed positively to the development on the labour-intensive production during 1978 - 1984.

Figure 17.4: Growth Rate of TVIs Labour Productivity in Rural China (1978-
1994)

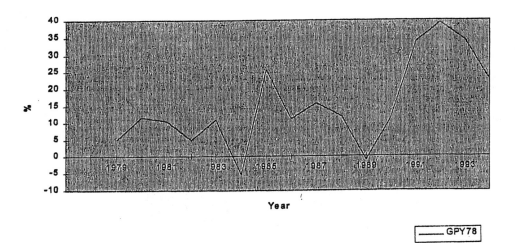

The second period (1985 - 1988) marked a decline in labour absorption by
22.9 million. After development for a number of years, many TVIs
experienced a higher growth in output and a greater production scale. As the
government increased the procurement price of agricultural products together
with the expansion of non-crop production, peasants started to move back to
agricultural production, and therefore, the labour surplus declined gradually.

Figure 17.5: Per Labour Arable Land and Growth of Per Labour Arable Land
in Rural China (1978-1994)

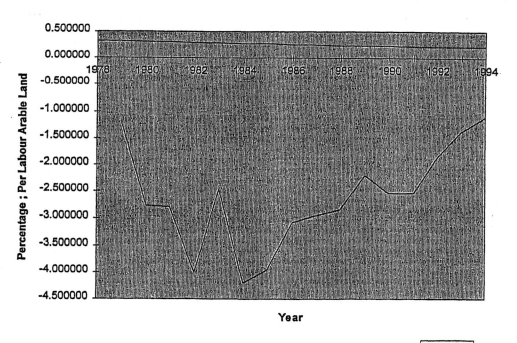

Table 17.7: Change of Arable Land in Rural China (1978 - 1994)

Year	L	P	L/P	G
1978	99.448	306.38	0.324590	
1979	99.527	310.25	0.320796	-1.17
1980	99.306	318.36	0.311930	-2.76
1981	99.096	326.76	0.303268	-2.78
1982	98.602	338.67	0.291145	-4.00
1983	98.506	346.90	0.283961	-2.47
1984	97.855	359.68	0.272061	-4.19
1985	96.848	370.65	0.261292	-3.96
1986	96.229	379.90	0.253301	-3.06
1987	95.889	390.00	0.245869	-2.93
1988	95.722	400.67	0.238905	-2.83
1989	95.656	409.39	0.233655	-2.20
1990	95.6729	420.10	0.227738	-2.53
1991	95.6538	430.93	0.221971	-2.53
1992	95.4258	438.02	0.217857	-1.85
1993	95.1014	442.56	0.214889	-1.36
1994	94.9067	446.54	0.212538	-1.09

L: Arable land - in million ha., 1978 - 1998: Walker, K.R. "Trends in Crop Production" in Kueh, Y.Y. & R.F. Ash (eds.), *Economic Trends in Chinese Agriculture* Oxford: Clarendon, 1993, pp. 189-190 (originally in the *China Quarterly* No. 116, 1988), 1989-1994: *ZGTJNJ*, 1995, p. 331; P: Rural labour force - in million persons, 1978-1992: *ZGTJNJ*, 1993, p. 97 1993-1994: *ZGTJNJ*, 1995, p. 329; L/P: Per labour arable land; G: Growth rate of L/P.

As more training was needed in order to cope with the continuous sophisticated production processes, labour cost was increasing. This decrease in demand for labour in TVIs explains why growth of the labour involved in TVIs contracted between 1985 and 1988. There had been a trend on the change from labour-using strategy to capital-using production.

The third period (1989 - 1990) was mainly an exceptional and unstable political era. This implies that the economic performance had been highly

influenced by the June Fourth Event. Li Peng, the Chinese premier[16] blamed
Zhao Ziyang for having contributed to China's economic difficulties by
'inappropriately exaggerating' the role of town and township enterprises (CQ
121, p.170). During this retrenchment period, the indiscriminate development
of private and individual economic activities was warned and 'it would be
necessary more strictly to control labour movements from agricultural to non-
agricultural occupations ...' (CQ 121, p.171).

The final stage, from 1991 onwards, 24 million less labour had been
shifted to TVIs and in 1994 alone the TVIs absorbed *14.1 million less* (Table
17.2). This records further indicate that the TVIs enterprises were more
willing to use capital rather than labour during the 1990s. There could be a
number of reasons. The market economy in rural China became more mature
than before and the 'market' were more *competitive* than 15 years before.
Many small scale firms were more difficult to be alive under this
environment. Together with high labour cost, firms tried to develop higher
technology basis production, which effectively meant that less labour was in
demand. In addition, most TVIs' product were export-oriented. Since high-
technological output could earn more foreign exchange for further investment
in TVIs, most of TVIs in the nineties produced more technical product rather
than labour-based product. Therefore, the labour absorption in the early 1990s
were very slow.

6. POLICY IMPLICATIONS

The labour absorption of TVIs are bounded by several assumptions. In a
labour surplus economy like China with about 90 million to 130 million

---

16   In fact, there were a number of occasions for him making comments on the economy after
      the June Fourth event. The example shown here is the address in a national industrial
      conference on 11 October 1990.

agricultural labour surplus,[17] labour transfer to other non-agricultural sectors will not reduce total agricultural output because the MP_L is approaching zero. In addition, there exists high labour demand (labour absorption) in TVIs partly because of the wage differentials due to the higher value-added production of the TVIs. Furthermore, the base for higher TVI labour demand is the conventional neoclassical capital accumulation while the later comes from re-investable profit.

Soon after the founding of the People's Republic, the government imposed a Hu Ji Zhi (fixed household system) to restrict permanent movement of rural population to urban areas for strategic rationales. They include large cities have already congested, large cities have insufficient infrastructural development and housing, large cities' employment opportunities are limited, environmental and social costs of migration are very high, and the difficulties of monitoring huge mobile population.

However the three decades development in both rural and urban areas witnesses a greater income differential between the two. Moreover the population policy aimed at more people, together with the cultural factors in countryside, in the middle of 1970s, China's population had been more than double that in 1949. To rectify this problem, the Chinese government has been finding alternatives to allow movement of people but without causing too much trouble to the cities.

The objective of rural industrialisation policy after 1978, according to the Chinese leaders, has been to develop higher value-added non-crop and/or non-agricultural production in order to *resolve the huge rural population pressure.* This has been proved successful at least up to the mid-1980s. Our analysis displays that the growth of labour absorption in the late 1980s, and well into the early 1990s, has been decreasing. In view of this, does it imply the rural industrialisation policy is not a successful one? Alternatively, should the

---

17   There are many estimates of the rural/agricultural labour surplus. For a summary revision
     and estimates, see Kwan (1995).

Chinese government modify its policy in light of the decline in labour absorption? We have no intention to underestimate the contributions of TVIs in absorbing labour surplus. Perhaps the rural unemployment would be even *greater* without the present policy.

Some estimates on the rural labour surplus in 2000 will be about 200 million.[18] If the rural labour surplus cannot be transferred to other meaningful productions properly, what would be the impact on rural China in terms of social stability and economic efficiency of resource allocation?

7.CONCLUDING REMARKS

This chapter first estimates the TVIs capital. Secondly, the *CMEC* and decomposition analysis are applied to TVIs at national level to examine the degree of labour absorption of the rapidly growing township-village industries. The result shows that although TVIs contributed much to absorb rural labour surplus, many more rural workers should be *theoretically* employed by the TVIs. It is also clear from our analysis that the capital deepening did happen in the later stage of the TVI development, i.e. in the early 1990s. Further research should concentrate on the development of regional/provincial TVIs and various models[19] of TVIs in examining the labour absorption and the reasons for growth of TVIs, so as to illustrate the process of Chinese rural industrialisation.

---

18   See *NMRB* 30 March, 1995, p. 4.

19   The commonly quoted models include *Sunan Model, Wenzhou Model, Zhujiang Model, Gengche Model, Minquan Model, and Baoji Model*

References

Ash, R.F. (comp.) 'Quarterly Chronicle and Documentation' *The China Quarterly*, No. 121, 1990 [CQ].

Chen, Chulai, Findlay, Christopher, Watson, Andrew & Xiaohe Zhang. "Rural Enterprise Growth in a Partially Reformed Chinese Economy" in Findlay, C., Watson, A. & H.X. Wu (eds.), *Rural Enterprises in China*, St. Martin, 1994.

Fei, J.C.H. & G. Ranis. *Development of the Labour Surplus Economy Theory and Policy*, Illinois: Irwin, 1964.

Guo, Qin & Angang Hu. Zhongguo Gongyehua Wenti Chutan, Beijing: Zhongguo Kexue Jishu Chubanshe, 1991.

Guo, Qin. Xiangdaihua zhongde Nongcun Shengyu Laodongli Zhuenyi Beijing: Zhongguo Shehui Kexue Chubanshe, 1993.

Han, B.J. "Xianzhen Qiye Xina Laodongli Bianji Dijian Yu Shengyu Liaodongli Fantidu Zhuangyi, Vol. 7, 1995.

Kwan, F. 'Labour Surplus in Rural China' paper presented at the 4th Biennial Conference of the Chinese Studies of Australia Association, July 1995.

State Statistical Bureau, Zhongguo Nongcun Tongji Nianjian 1995, Beijing: China Statistical Publishing House, 1996 [ZGNCTJNJ].

State Statistical Bureau, Zhongguo Tongji Nianjian 1995, Beijing: China Statistical Publishing House, 1996 [ZGTJNJ].

Township-Village Enterprises Division, Xinagzhen Qiye Tongji Ziliao 1989, [XZQYTJZL].

Zhang, Yong-Feng. Zhongguo Dalu Ziyuan Leizhi Moshe yu Jingji Fazhen zhi Yanjiu (1953 nian zhi 1978 nian), (Jingji Zongshu 19), Taipei: Chung-Hua Institution For Economic Research, 1990.

CHAPTER 18

PROPERTY RIGHTS AND PERFORMANCE OF CHINA'S TOWNSHIP-VILLAGE ENTERPRISES

CHARLES C.L. KWONG*

ABSTRACT

It is evident that the development of township-village enterprises (TVEs) is one of the most momentous segment of China's economic reform programme. Their numbers soared from 1.5 million in 1978 to 24.9 million in 1994 and the workers employed escalated from 28.3 million to 120.2 million (25.0% of China's rural labour force) for this period. In terms of output value, the figure jumped from 49.3 to 1,464.0 billion yuan in 1978 and 1994 respectively. Its performance is comparable to its private counterparts and much better than the state-owned enterprises (SOEs) (Svejnar, 1990; Pitt and Putterman, 1992). Under a communal ownership with ill-defined property rights, the growth and performance of TVEs seem to pose a paradox on

---

* School of Arts and Social Sciences, Open Learning Institute of Hong Kong, Kowloon, Hong Kong

standard property rights theory (Alchian and Demsetz, 1972; Demsetz, 1967; Furubotn and Pejovich, 1974; Cheung, 1982) which states that a well-defined private property rights system is a pre-condition for eliminating disincentive and free rider problem as well as other opportunistic behaviour. This chapter argues that the seemingly paradox can be resolved by analysing the regional property rights structure of the TVEs in the context of a multiple principal-agent hierarchy. It is revealed that the agents are less inclined to opportunistic behaviour and perform relatively well mainly because:

(1) the residual benefits and control rights of the retained profits are assigned to the agents of the locality. Though such rights are not assigned to a individual, agents involved have received increasing benefit in the past years;

(2) the principal and agents have less conflicting objective functions;

(3) the repeated games played between the principals and agents maintain a cooperative equilibrium; and

(4) the fiscal requirement, market competition and the absence of government subsidy facing the TVEs further press the TVEs to be efficient.

1.INTRODUCTION

It is evident that the development of township-village enterprises (TVEs) is one of the most momentous segment of China's economic reform programme. Their numbers soared from 1.5 million in 1978 to 24.9 million in 1994 and the workers employed escalated from 28.3 million to 120.2 million (25.0% of China's rural labour force) for this period. In terms of output value, the figure jumped from 49.3 to 1,464.0 billion yuan in 1978 and 1994 respectively. Its performance is comparable to its private counterparts and much better than the state-owned enterprises (SOEs) (Svejnar, 1990; Pitt and Putterman, 1992).

Under a communal ownership with ill-defined property rights, the growth and performance of TVEs seem to pose a paradox on standard property rights theory (Alchian and Demsetz, 1972; Demsetz, 1967; Furubotn and Pejovich, 1974; Cheung, 1982) which states that a well-defined private property rights system is a pre-condition for eliminating disincentive and free rider problem as well as other opportunistic behaviour. This chapter argues that the seemingly paradox can be resolved by analysing the regional property rights structure of the TVEs in the context of a multiple principal-agent hierarchy.

This chapter begins with a brief overview of the TVEs in terms of its growth and performance. It follows with a discussion of the core of standard property rights theory. The chapter then raises the seemingly paradox and shows how it can be resolved by looking at the residual income (benefit) and control rights of the TVEs from a regional property rights perspective. It further points out that other constraints such as the tight budget constraints, market competition, fiscal contract system, labour surplus pressure and the enhancement of local welfare press the TVEs to operate efficiently. The final part concludes the discussion.

2. CHINA'S TOWNSHIP-VILLAGE ENTERPRISES (TVEs): A BRIEF OVERVIEW

The growth of TVEs is spectacular since the 1980s. Table 18.1 shows the output value, number of establishments and the level of employment of the TVEs. It is noted that the growth is particularly evident after 1984. The growth rate of TVEs' gross output value (GOV) soared from 17.8 per cent in 1983 to 63.2 and 49.2 in 1984 and 1985 respectively. Except the negative growth rate recorded in 1989, the GOV of the TVEs for most of the years demonstrates a double digit growth. The number of establishments also exhibits a drastic jump from 1.35 million in 1983 to 6.07 and 12.22 million in 1984 and 1985. Since then, this figure has steadily increased. In terms of employment creation, the TVEs employ 28.3 million of workers in 1978

Table 18.1: Growth of TVEs 1978-1994

Year	Gross Output Value (billion yuan)	Number of TVEs (million)	Workers Employed (million)
1978	49.3	1.52	28.3
1979	53.8 (9.0)	1.48	29.1
1980	61.7 (14.7)	1.43	30.0
1981	68.6 (11.1)	1.33	29.7
1982	77.1 (12.5)	1.36	31.1
1983	90.9 (17.8)	1.35	32.3
1984	148.3 (63.2)	6.07	52.1
1985	221.3 (49.2)	12.22	69.8
1986	273.4 (23.6)	15.15	79.4
1987	346.2 (26.6)	17.50	88.1
1988	402.9 (16.4)	18.88	95.5
1989	387.9 (-5.2)	18.69	93.7
1990	428.2 (10.4)	18.50	92.6
1991	576.5 (34.6)	19.09	96.1
1992	858.4 (48.9)	20.79	105.8
1993	1337.6 (55.8)	24.52	123.5
1994	1464.0 (9.5)	24.94	120.2

Source: *ZGTGNJ* (1992: 390; 1994: 361-363;1995: 233, 363-365)
Note: Gross output values are measured at 1978 constant price and figures in parentheses
         are respective annual growth rates.

while this figure adds to 120.2 in 1994. This rapid expansion starts with a
change in policy which allows and encourages the development of non-
agricultural production. The 1983 Document No.1 titled 'Various Questions
Concerning Current Rural Economic Policy' affirms the significance of
commune-brigade run enterprises (CBREs) in the rural economy. The 1984

Document No.2 titled 'Various Questions Concerning Current Economic Policy' further motivates the pooling of resources to develop the TVEs. Under the new policy, not only the local government, but also the individual households are encouraged to develop the TVEs. The change in policy direction is shaped by both supply-side factors (e.g. the pressure of surplus labour) and demand-side factors (e.g. the increasing demand for non-agricultural products due to the rise of per capita income).

Apart from the rapid expansion, the performance of the TVEs is also noteworthy. As shown in Table 18.1, the labour absorption of TVEs helps reduce the surplus labour in rural China. About 25 per cent of the total rural labour force is now engaged in TVEs. Instead of utilising resources from the government to resolve the problem of surplus labour, the growth of TVEs provides a less costly way to alleviate the problem. Viewing from other perspective, Table 18.2 compares the profit rates between TVEs and state-owned industrial enterprises (SOIEs). It is revealed that for most of the year from 1978 to 1994, the pre-tax and after-tax profit rates of the TVEs are higher than that of the SOIEs except for the years from 1986 to 1989. One must note that the profit rates of the SOIEs must be discounted by the subsidies provided by the central government. Table 3 depicts the huge budget subsidies provided for the SOIEs. The figure steps up from 11.7 billion yuan in 1978 to 36.6 billion yuan in 1994. For most of the years, it shares more than 10 per cent of total government revenue. It is especially true from 1982 to 1991. Thus, if the profit rates of the SOIEs recorded in Table 18.2 are discounted by this factor, their performance will be much more lagging behind the TVEs which are operated under the absence of government subsidy.

Table 18.2: Profit Rates of TVEs and SOIEs 1978-1994 (%)

Year	TVE		SOIE	
	Pre-tax	After-tax	Pre-tax	After-tax
1978	39.8	31.8	24.2	15.5
1979	35.4	29.1	24.8	16.1
1980	32.5	26.7	24.8	16.0
1981	29.1	22.3	23.8	15.0
1982	28.0	20.2	23.4	14.4
1983	27.8	18.5	23.2	14.4
1984	24.6	15.2	24.2	14.9
1985	23.7	14.5	23.8	13.2
1986	19.7	10.6	20.7	10.6
1987	17.0	9.0	20.3	10.6
1988	17.9	9.3	20.6	10.4
1989	15.2	7.1	17.2	7.2
1990	13.0	5.9	12.4	3.2
1991	12.7	5.8	11.8	2.9
1992	14.3	4.8	9.7	2.7
1993	19.0	11.6	9.7	3.2
1994	14.8	9.0	9.8	2.8

Source: *ZGTJNJ* (1992: 391, 431; 1993: 436-437; 1994: 366; 1995:
            403-406)

Note: Profit Rate = Pre or After-tax Profit / Fixed Capital +
           Working Capital

Table 18.3: Budget Subsidies to SOEs 1979-1994

Year	Billion Yuan	Share of Total Government Revenue (%)
1979	11.7	10.6
1980	14.1	12.9
1981	12.6	11.6
1982	19.7	17.5
1983	24.0	19.2
1984	21.8	14.5
1985	25.9	13.9
1986	32.5	14.3
1987	37.6	15.9
1988	44.6	17.0
1989	59.9	20.3
1990	57.9	17.5
1991	51.0	14.1
1992	44.5	10.7
1993	41.1	8.1
1994	36.6	7.0

Source: *ZGTJNJ* (1992: 215, 218; 1993: 215; 1994: 215, 218); Rana and Hamid (1996: 136-7)

Weitzman and Xu (1994) compares the growth rates of output (Y), capital (K), labour (L) and total factor productivity (TFP) of the SOIEs and TVEs from 1979 to 1991. It is clear that the growth rates associated with the TVEs are much higher than that of the SOIEs. It is particularly evident for the growth of TFP. The TFP of the TVEs grows three times faster than that of the SOIEs. Similar results found by Jefferson, Rawski and Zheng (1992) are shown in Table 18.5. Though the estimate of the TFP is not the core of this chapter, all these results reflect that the TVEs have achieve a considerable level of technological progress when comparing with the SOIE and the collective industries in the urban areas.

Table 18.4: Comparison of Growth and Efficiency in the SOIE and TVEs
1979-1991

	National Industry	SOIEs				TVEs			
	Y	Y	K	L	TFP	Y	K	L	TFP
Growth Rate	13.3	8.4	7.8	3.0	4.0	25.3	16.5	11.9	12.0

Source: Weitzman and Xu (1994: 128)

Table 18.5: Estimated Total Factor Productivity Growth in Chinese Industry
(%)

	1980-84	1984-88	1988-92
State Sector	1.8	3.0	2.5
Collective Sector	3.4	5.9	4.9
Urban Township-Village	7.3	6.6	6.9

Source: Jefferson, Rawski and Zheng [1992, quoted from Jefferson and Rawski (1994: 56)]

It is illustrated that no matter in terms of output growth, employment creation, profit rate and growth of TFP, the TVEs have accomplished a good performance record. Under a collective ownership with a unclear delineation of property rights, the success of TVEs seems to pose a paradox for the standard property rights theory.

3. THE STANDARD PROPERTY RIGHTS THEORY AND THE PARADOX RAISED

Though the property rights paradigm is quite diverse in content, some core concepts and propositions can be outlined:[1]

(1) Property rights can at least consist of three categories of exclusive rights: *control rights* which refer to the exclusive rights to use and manipulate the resources; *income rights* refer to the exclusive rights to derive income from the resources; and *transfer rights* refer to the exclusive rights to alienate the resources.

(2) Exclusive rights held by individuals are referred as *private ownership*. Such rights held by the state is termed as *state ownership*. These rights can also be grasped by a community which represents a *communal ownership*. If no agent or organisation has exclusive rights on the resources, it is said to be a *common ownership*.

(3) Due to the existence of positive transaction costs, no property rights are fully specified. However, it is generally agreed that a more well-defined property rights structure with clear residual

---

1   Some major literature on the property rights theory include Alchian and Demsets (1972); Demsets (1967); Furubotn and Pejovich (1974); Cheung (1982). A good survey of the property rights theory can be found in Eggertsson (1990).

claimant can more effectively curb the problem of shirking, free-ride and other opportunistic behaviour. By means of which, the enterprise or system can perform more efficiently.

(4) In the context of transitional economics, it further implies that the pre-condition to reform the formerly centrally planned economies (CPEs) successfully is to transform the state and communal ownership into a private ownership. These move can stimulate the production incentives of the workers and enhance the performance of the enterprises.

Turning to the ownership structure of the TVEs in China, they can be broadly divided into four categories: township-run enterprises (TREs); village-run enterprises (VREs); joint households enterprises (JHEs) and privately owned enterprises (POEs). The first two categories are owned collectively by township (formerly communes) and village (formerly brigades). The JHEs are owned by the households who pool their resources together for production. The POEs are enterprises owned by individuals.

Before 1984, rural enterprises were mainly owned and run by the commune and brigade (commune-brigade run enterprises, CBREs). After the dismantling of commune and brigade in rural China, the CBREs were renamed as TVEs. However, the concept of TVEs has a wider coverage than the CBREs. As discussed above, the TVEs include the enterprises run by the local government (TREs and VREs) and those run by the households and individuals (JHEs and POEs). Table 18.6 shows that the TREs and VREs occupy the major share of gross output value (GOV) of the TVEs. Though the shares of the JHEs and POEs is increasing, the TREs and VREs' share is still more than 60 per cent in 1994. This reflected that a majority of output by the TVEs are produced under government-run enterprises. A number of authors do agree that the TVEs are operated under a communal ownership.[2] The *de facto* owners of the JHEs and POEs is the local community. The ill-defined

---

[2]   See Song (1990); Weitzman and Xu (1994); Chang and Wang (1994).

property rights structure should theoretically lead to ineffective operation and poor performance of the enterprises. However, as illustrated above, the performance of the TVEs is far from unsatisfactory. This seems to pose a paradox to the standard property theory. Weitzman and Xu (1994) tried to resolve this paradox by incorporating a moral parameter in the standard property rights theory. They point out that the property rights theory needs not to be culture free. It is argued that a "cooperate culture" emerges from the rural collective enterprises. This culture can reduce the problems of monitoring and shirking to reach a cooperative outcome. However, as the authors put their theory in a relatively speculative way, whether this theory is able to explain the behaviour of TVEs is subject to further verifications. Further, if this "cooperative culture" really exists, why could such culture not lead to a cooperative outcome in the collectives before the reform. In the following section, instead of verifying Weitzman and Xu's argument, we try to use a principal-agent framework and a regional property rights approach to resolve the seemingly paradox arising from the TVEs.

Table 18.6:Composition of GOV of the TVEs by Ownership 1984-94 (%)

Year	TREs & VREs	JHEs & POEs
1984	85.7	14.3
1985	75.1	24.9
1986	71.1	28.9
1987	67.9	32.1
1988	67.2	32.8
1989	64.7	35.3
1990	64.2	35.8
1991	66.4	33.5
1992	67.3	32.7
1993	64.5	35.4
1994	67.7	32.3

Source: *ZGTJNJ* (1995: 365)

4. PROPERTY RIGHTS STRUCTURE OF THE TVEs AND THE PARADOX RESOLVED

In this section, it is demonstrated that the relationship among the Centre (central government), local government and the TVEs can be viewed from a multiple principal-agent framework. With this framework, a regional property approach is applied to explain why the TVEs with a loosely defined property rights structure can still perform well.[3]

A Multiple Principal-Agent Framework

Between the Centre (principal) and the local government (agent), the primary objective of the Centre is to maintain a stable flow of fiscal revenue from the localities and to reduce the subsidies to local government. To ensure this objective is fulfilled, the secondary objective is to facilitate the economic growth and development in the localities. To guarantee the local government to achieve the objectives, the fiscal contract system requires the local government to submit a portion of local fiscal revenue and shoulder the responsibility for financing the local government. In return, the local government is entitled a financial autonomy after fulfilling the Centre's requirement. Further, more autonomy on economic policy is allowed for township and village governments (TVGs).

Another level of principal-agent relationship is found between the TVG (principal) and the TVEs (agent). The primary objectives for the TVGs are (1) to fulfil the fiscal requirement of the Centre; (2) to derive enough revenue to finance the TVG; (3) to alleviate the problem of surplus labour; and (4) to enhance the welfare of the community. The major source of providing revenue for the TVGs comes from the TVEs' profit. Therefore, whether the

---

[3] An application of principal-agent framework and regional property approach in China's state-owned enterprise can be found in Granick (1990).

TVG can derive adequate funding to fulfil its targets depends very much on the performance of the TVEs. The performance of the TVEs, in turn, relies on another principal-agent relationship: that is the TVE manager (principal) and the TVE workers (agents). The manager on the one hand has to fulfil the targets set by the TVG and on the other hand to maximise his own welfare through the position he holds in the enterprise. For the TVE workers, the principal target is to enhance their benefit within the enterprises and to raise the communal welfare.

With such a multiple principal-agents relations, the agent will maximise his objective function subject to the target set by the principal, which can be expressed as: max Ua Up where Ua and Up are the objective functions of the agent and principal respectively. Under this relationship, the problem of asymmetric information exists as the principal does not possess full information of the agents' behaviour. Shirking and other opportunistic behaviour may arise.[4] The degree of such behaviour depends on (1) whether the reward and property rights structure designed by the principal provide enough incentive for the agents; and (2) whether the principal and the agents have conflicting objective functions[5]. If the property rights structure is conducive to higher work incentives and the objective functions are less conflicting, the disincentive problem will be less severe.

A Regional Property Rights Analysis

The above section has described the principal-agents relations among the Centre, the TVG, the TVEs, the TVE managers and the workers. Here, we try to examine the TVEs' behaviour from a regional property rights perspective. Under a regional property rights structure, exclusive rights are not assigned to an individual, but to a locality or community. The regional property rights are less well-defined than the private property rights. However, in the following

---

4   For a classical discussion on agency costs, see Jensen and Meckling (1976).
5   Conflicting objective functions are referred as fulfillment of one objective is at the expenses of the others.

analysis, it is argued that though under a principal-agent hierarchy with regional property rights, the TVEs can still perform well for the reasons that (1) the property rights structure of the TVEs is able to enhance the residual benefit and control rights of the contracting parties involved; and (2) it can fulfil the multiple objectives of the principal and agents.

As mentioned before, the *de facto* owner of the TVE is the local community which acts on behalf by the TVGs. So the TVG has influence on the major business decisions and on the issue of hire and fire of the enterprise manager[6]. However, the appointed manager has a high degree of autonomy in daily operation of the enterprise. As the market of inputs and outputs facing the TVEs are under free market operation and no direct subsidy by the Centre and the TVG, the TVEs have shouldered their own responsibilities of profit and losses. So the TVEs face a much harder budget constraint than their state counterparts.

In terms of benefit distribution, the TVEs are required to pay tax to the Centre as well as the management fees to the TVG. Table 18.7 shows that the Centre has derived substantial revenue from the TVEs through taxation which increased from 2.2 billion yuan in 1978 to 64.0 billion yuan in 1992. More importantly, it is noted that the retained profit, which is a direct measure of the residual benefit, of the TVEs also demonstrated a rapid increase from 8.8 to 111.6 billion yuan in 1992. The positive growth rate for retained profit is recorded and the growth is spectacular except 1989 and 1990.

For the retained profit, Table 18.8 shows that a major share is used for reinvestment and production expansion of the TVEs. This reinvestment carries its significance at least in two ways. First, it maintains the operation and the profit making activities of the TVEs, which is essential for the

---

6   Song (1990) pointed out that more than 80% of enterprise managers are appointed by the
      TVG.

Table 18.7: Government Tax and Retained Profit of TVEs 1978-1992

Year	Pre-tax Profit (billion yuan)	Government Tax	Retained Profit	Growth Rate of Retained Profit
1978	11.0	2.2	8.8	
1980	14.4	2.6	11.8	24.2
1985	42.5	13.7	28.7	28.5*
1986	50.8	17.7	33.2	15.3
1987	64.5	22.2	42.3	27.7
1988	89.2	31.0	58.2	37.3
1989	96.8	36.5	60.3	3.7
1990	101.2	39.2	62.1	2.8
1991	118.8	45.5	73.4	18.2
1992	175.3	64.0	111.6	52.1

Sources: *ZGXZQYNJ* (1978-1987: 569); *XZQYTJZL* (1989: 2-3; 1992: 1)
Note: 1985 figure is the annual average growth rate for 1980 to 1985.

survival of the enterprises. Second, production expansion can maintain the labour absorption capacity of the enterprises. It avoids intensifying the problem of surplus labour.

Other residual profit will be paid in the form of fees to the TVG. These fees are primarily used for subsidising agricultural production and enhancing the communal welfare. Though the time series data provided in Table 18.8 is limited, it reveals that almost 30 per cent of retained profit was diverted to subsidise agriculture in 1978. Such share has been decreasing in the 1990s, but still up to 9.4 per cent in 1992. Other uses include the expenditure on communal welfare, rural education and other township development. Actually, the Centre does require the TVG to be responsible for these expenditures. This helps reduce the financial burden of the Centre on the localities.

Table 18.8: Distribution of Retained Profit for Major Uses (%)

Year	Reinvest-ment	Agricultural Subsidies	Communal Welfare	Rural Education	Township Develop-ment
1978	35.1	29.9	4.5	n.a.	n.a.
1980	39.7	19.2	5.7	n.a.	n.a.
1990	20.6	12.5	3.8	2.4	0.8
1991	22.2	11.8	4.0	2.5	0.8
1992	25.1	9.4	4.0	2.9	0.9

Source: *XZQYTJZL* (1992: 1)
Note: n.a. = not available

After a brief look at the benefit distribution of the TVEs profit, it is logical to raise the question: who is the residual claimant of the benefit? The answer is best put by Weitzman and Xu (1994: 132-3): "... none of the residents or the executive owner have the exclusive rights of the ownership associated with the traditional property rights theory....There is no residual claimant in the traditional sense." However, it is observed that various principals and agents involved, to a certain extent, benefit from the emergence and operation of the TVEs. The Centre is able to derive revenue from the enterprises and at the same time reduce its financial burden on the localities. The TVGs on the one hand fulfil the fiscal requirement of the higher level government, but also obtain funds through the collection of fees paid by the TVEs to finance the daily operation of the government bodies and to enhance the welfare of the community. Though there is no systematic study on the benefit derived from the TVEs by the TVG officials, it is evident that the material well being of the officials has been raised in recent years. For the workers engaged in the TVEs, their benefits are directly linked with the wage and bonus received. Table 18.9 depicts the average annual wage of the TVE workers, which exhibits a steady growth. Finally, as the *de facto* owner of the TVEs, citizens of the localities benefit from a better employment opportunity and the enhancement of communal welfare.

Table 18.9: Average Annual Wage of TVE Workers 1978-1994 (yuan)

Year	Annual Wage	Growth Rate
1978	306.6	
1980	398.2	29.8
1985	676.4	14.0
1986	737.8	9.1
1987	835.7	13.2
1988	1009.3	20.7
1989	1126.3	11.6
1990	1216.1	8.0
1991	1254.1	3.1
1992	1636.3	30.5
1993	2380.5*	45.5
1994	2892.3*	21.5

Source: See Table 18.7.
Note: 1993 and 1994 figures are derived from *XZQYCWTJHB* (1994: 6). The figures cover only the TREs and VREs, but not the JHEs and POEs. So these two figures are not strictly comparable with each others.

Several conclusions can be drawn from the above analysis:

1. If a regional property right structure is patterned and institutionalised, enhancement of residual benefit and control rights can still stimulate the work and investment incentives of local agents (i.e. the TVGs, the TVEs and their managers and workers)[7].

2. Under a principal-agent hierarchy, less conflicting objective functions can lead to a more cooperative outcome. As reflected above, the various objective functions (such as revenue raising, profit seeking, employment creation and etc.) of the Centre, TVGs, TVEs and the workers are not conflicting in nature. This reduces the inclination to opportunistic behaviour.

3. Though the formal rules do not specify clearly the share of benefit received by every principal and agent (e.g. the proportion of retained profit used for workers' bonus or managers' fringe benefit), under a repeated game played among the Centre, TVGs and the TVEs, informal rules are developed to constraint the behaviour of the parties involved. The principal is assumed to have the right to design the rules (i.e. the institutions) to reach its objectives, but if such rules hamper the benefits and incentives of the agents, it will cause the agent to respond strategically to protect their benefit. This may finally endanger the cooperative game played between the principal and agents.[8] If this scenario is logically valid, it can be
applied to the case of rural China. The Centre has the rights to design and manipulate the rules and the macroeconomic policy.

---

7   Wu and Zhang (1995: 51-68) make a good discussion on the Centre and local relationship in China using a regional property rights perspective.

8   An application of game theory to cooperation can be found in Miller (1992: 182-198). A more extensive study of game theory of cooperation can be referred to Axerlrod (1984).

However, any change in rules and policies by the Centre is incremental rather than radical. This is a logical move to avoid hampering the incentives of the TVGs and TVEs. On the other hand, to prevent the Centre from modifying rules to reduce the benefits of the localities, the TVG and the TVEs have to meet the requirement set by the Centre. This cooperative equilibrium can be described as case of Nash equilibrium[9].

5. CONCLUDING REMARK

Some authors pose the paradox that TVEs in China are operated under a communal ownership, but their performance is comparable to their private counterparts. This seems to contradict the standard property rights theory. This chapter seeks to resolve the paradox by analysing the regional property rights structure of the TVEs in the context of a multiple principal-agent hierarchy. It is revealed that the agents are less inclined to opportunistic behaviour and perform relatively well mainly because:

(1) the residual benefits and control rights of the retained profits are assigned to the agents of the locality. Though such rights are not assigned to a individual, agents involved have received increasing benefit in the past years;

(2) the principal and agents have less conflicting objective functions;

(3) the repeated games played between the principals and agents maintain a cooperative equilibrium; and

(4) the fiscal requirement, market competition and the absence of government subsidy facing the TVEs further press the TVEs to be efficient.

---

9   A Nash equilibrium defines as a situation no player in the game can further benefit on the condition that they maintain their original strategy. See Tirole (1988: 206).

These conclusions not only resolve the paradox posed above, but also sheds some light on the reform plan of the transitional economies such as China, Vietnam and the Eastern European countries. The "shock therapy" advocates suggest a rapid and fundamental transformation from a socialist (collective) system to a market (private property) system while the gradualists propound a relatively slow and partial reform agenda. The "shock therapy" advocates argue that gradual and partial reform will only continue to bring in distorted signals to the market and the defective elements will remain. Clearly delineated private property rights, instead of communal ownership, are pre-conditions to promote incentive and performance. However, this chapter demonstrates that gradualism and a certain degree of communal ownership in rural China do not conduce to poor performance. This conclusion should provide second thoughts for the "shock therapy" advocates.

REFERENCES

Alchian, A. A. and Demsetz, H. (1972) Production, Information Costs, and Economic Organization, *American Economic Review*, 62(5): 777-795.

Axelrod, R. (1984) *The Evolution of Cooperation*, Basic Books, New York.

Bureau of Township-Village Enterprise, *Xiangzhen Qiye Tongji Ziliao* (*XZQYTJZL*, Statistical Data of Township-Village Enterprises), various issues.

Bureau of Township-Village Enterprise, *Xiangzhen Qiye Caiwu Tongji Huibian 1994* (*XZQYCMTJHB*, Collection of Financial Statistical Data of Township-Village Enterprise).

Byrd, W. A., and Lin, Qingsong Eds.(1990) *China's Rural Industry: Structure, Development and Reform*, Oxford University Press, New York.

Chang Chun and Wang Yijiang (1994) The Nature of the Township-Village Enterprise, *Journal of Comparative Economics,* 19(3): 434-452.

Cheung, S.N.S. (1982) *Will China go "Capitalist"?*, Hobart Paper 94, Institute of Economic Affairs, London.

Demsetz, H. (1967) Towards a Theory of Property Rights, *American Economic Review*, 57(2): 347-359.

Furubotn, E.G. and Pejovich, S. (1974) Introduction: the New Property Rights Structure. pp. 1-9 in: Furubotn, E.G. and Pejovich, S. (eds.), *The Economics of Property Rights*, Ballinger, Cambridge.

Eggertsson, T. (1990) *Economic Behavior and Institutions*, Cambridge University Press, Cambridge.

Granick, D. (1990) *Chinese State Enterprises: A Regional Property Rights Analysis*, University of Chicago Press, Chicago.

Grossman, S. J. and Hart, O. D. (1986) The Costs and Benefits of Ownership: A Theory of Vertical and Lateral Integration, *Journal of Political Economy,* 94(4): 691-719.

Ho, P.S. Samuel (1994) *Rural China in Transition, Non-agricultural Development in Rural Jiangsu,* Clarendon Press, Oxford.

Jefferson, G. H. and Rawski, T. G. (1994) Enterprise Reform in Chinese Industry, *Journal of Economic Perspective*, 8(2): 47-70.

Jefferson, G. H., Rawski, T. G., and Zheng, Yuxin (1992) Growth, Efficiency, and Convergence in China's State and Collective Industry, *Economic Development and Cultural Change,* 40(2): 239-266.

Jensen, M.C. and Meckling, W. H. (1976) Theory of the Firm: Managerial Behaviour, Agency Costs and Ownership Structure, *Journal of Financial Economics*, 3(4): 305-360.

Kung, J. K. (1995) Equal Entitlement versus Tenure Security under a Regime of Collective Property Rights: Peasants' Preference for Institutions in Post-reform Chinese Agriculture, *Journal of Comparative Economics,* 21(1): 82-111.

Matthews, R.O.C. (1986) The Economics of Institutions and the sources of Growth, *Economic Journal* 96: 903-918.

Miller, G. (1992) *Managerial Dilemmas: the Political Economy of Hierarchy*, Cambridge University Press, Cambridge.

Nee, Victor (1992) Organization Dynamics of Market Transition: Hybrid Forms, Property Rights, and Mixed Economy in China, *Administrative Science Quarterly,* 37: 1-27.

North, Douglass C. (1990) *Institutions, Institutional Change and Economic Performance.* Cambridge University Press, Cambridge.

Pitt, Mark M., and Putterman, Louis (1992) Employment and Wages in township, Village, and other Rural Enterprises, *Mimeo,* Brown University.

Putterman, Louis (1993) Ownership and the Nature of the Firm, *Journal of Comparative Economics,* 17(2): 243-263.

Rana, P.B. and Hamid N. eds. (1996) *From Centrally Planned to Market Economies: The Asian Approach,* Vol. 2, Oxford University Press, Hong Kong.

Song, Lina (1990) Convergence: A Comparison of Township-Run Firms and Local State Enterprises, in WW. Byrd and Q. Lin, Eds., *China's Rural Industry: Structure, Development and Reform,* Oxford University Press, New York.

State Statistical Bureau *Zhongguo Tongji Nianjian* (ZGTJNJ, Statistical Yearbook of China), various issues.

Svejnar, Jan (1990) Productive Efficiency and Employment, in WW. Byrd and Q. Lin, Eds., *China's Rural Industry: Structure, Development and Reform,* Oxford University Press, New York.

Tirole, J. (1988) *The Theory Of Industrial Organization,* MIT Press, Mass.

Weitzman, Martin, and Xu, Chenggang (1994) Chinese Township - Village Enterprises as Vaguely Defined Cooperatives, *Journal of Comparative Economics,* 18(2): 121-145.

Williamson, Oliver (1985) *The Economic Institutions of Capitalism,* Free Press, New York.

Wu, G.G. and Zhang, Y.N. (1995) *Lun zhongyang difang guangxi (A Discussion on Central-Regional Relationship),* Oxford University Press, Hong Kong.

Zhongguo Xiangzhen Qiye Nianjian (ZGXZCYNJ, Yearbook of China's Township-Village Enterprise), Nonye chubanxue (Agricultural Press), various issues.

INDEX